Beyond the Heroic "I"

UNCONSCIOUS PLAGIARISM.
A Case of "Mimicry" in Natural History recently observed in
the London streets.

"Unconscious Plagiarism," *Punch*, **January 1909.**

Beyond the Heroic "I"

Reading Lawrence, Hemingway, and "Masculinity"

Stephen P. Clifford

Lewisburg
Bucknell University Press
London: Associated University Presses

Associated University Presses
440 Forsgate Drive
Cranbury, NJ 08512

Associated University Presses
16 Barter Street
London WC1A 2AH, England

Associated University Presses
P.O. Box 338, Port Credit
Mississauga, Ontario
Canada L5G 4L8

The paper used in this publication meets the requirements
of the American National Standard for Permanence of Paper
for Printed Library Materials Z39.48-1984.

Library of Congress Cataloging-in-Publication Data

Clifford, Stephen P., 1962–
    Beyond the heroic "I" : reading Lawrence, Hemingway, and
"masculinity" / Stephen P. Clifford.
        p.   cm.
    Includes bibliographical references and index.
    ISBN 0-8387-5357-4 (alk. paper)
    1. Lawrence, D. H. (David Herbert), 1885–1930—Characters—Men.
2. Hemingway, Ernest, 1899–1961—Characters—Heroes. 3. Masculinity
in literature. 4. Heroes in literature. 5. Narration (Rhetoric)
6. Self in literature. 7. Men in literature. I. Title.
PR6023.A93Z62145   1999
823′.912—dc21
                                                                98-13066
                                                                CIP

PRINTED IN THE UNITED STATES OF AMERICA

Contents

Acknowledgments

THIS book has come about through the conversations many people have graciously shared with me. At the University of Washington, where this project began as a dissertation and has since metamorphosed significantly, I received invaluable assistance and criticism from Sydney Janet Kaplan, Jack Brenner, Donna Gerstenberger, and Malcolm Griffith. Fr. Stephen C. Rowan, dean of the College of Liberal Arts at Seattle University and former chair of the English department, provided a foundation for much of my teaching and scholarship, and he continues to be both a valuable colleague and mentor. And at St. Joseph's College of Maine, my most immediate academic community, Sr. Phyllis Doyle and Dr. Edward Rielly, chairs of the English department, and Sr. Mary Ellen Murphy, the Vice President of Academic Affairs, continue to offer welcome support for my endeavors. Most importantly, perhaps, my students at Seattle University, The College of St. Catherine, and St. Joseph's College have continued to challenge readings of Lawrence and Hemingway and have engaged me in exciting conversations about gender, culture, and literature—conversations that I hope have enriched them as much as they have me.

My editors and readers at Bucknell University Press and the press's director, Mills F. Edgerton Jr., have insightfully guided my revision, as has Julien Yoseloff of the Associated University Presses, for which I am indebted. Professor Peter Balbert, chair of the English department at Trinity University in San Antonio, Texas, provided advice and direction that caused me to rethink various arguments, to strengthen others, and to add still new analyses; the end result is a much stronger study. I would also like to thank the organizers of the 11th Annual Gender Studies Symposium, held at Lewis and Clark College in April 1992, where I had the opportunity to present some of my initial readings of *Women in Love,* as well as the *Northwest Conference for British Studies,* where I have presented my readings of narrative theory and authorial fictions. Susan F. Beegel and the editorial readers of *The Hemingway Review* have offered insight into my readings of Hemingway, and I am grateful for the journal's permission to reprint here a version of my essay on Hemingway's *In Our Time* which it originally published. Joseph Urgo, book review editor for *College Literature,* has generously allowed me to test my reading as a reviewer.

In addition, Bill Crean's insights into gender and the academy have been invaluable in our many long conversations, from which I have always emerged with dramatically new and valuable perspectives previously unavailable to me. I wish also to sincerely thank Paul and Sally Clifford and Gene and Rosemary Hasseler, who have continually supported me through the sometimes long years of graduate and postgraduate study. Finally, Terri Hasseler's sensitive and demanding readings of the manuscript in its various manifestations have challenged me, as have her insights into the subtleties of gender and theory that have sometimes escaped me, and her confident belief in my work has made her an endless source of critical and personal inspiration.

*   *   *

Excerpts from chapter 4 originally appeared as "Hemingway's Fragmentary Novel: Readers Writing the Hero in *In Our Time*," published in *The Hemingway Review,* Spring 1994 (13:2). Copyright © 1994 The Ernest Hemingway Foundation. Reprinted by permission.

The following material is reprinted with permission of Scribner, a Division of Simon & Schuster:

From "On Writing." Excerpted from THE NICK ADAMS STORIES by Ernest Hemingway. Copyright © 1972 by The Ernest Hemingway Foundation.

From ERNEST HEMINGWAY: SELECTED LETTERS, 1917–1961, edited by Carlos Baker. Copyright © by The Ernest Hemingway Foundation, Inc.

From Philip Young's Introduction to THE NICK ADAMS STORIES by Ernest Hemingway. Introduction Copyright © 1972 by Charles Scribner's Sons.

From A FAREWELL TO ARMS by Ernest Hemingway. Copyright 1929 by Charles Scribner's Sons. Copyright renewed © 1957 by Ernest Hemingway.

From THE SUN ALSO RISES by Ernest Hemingway. Copyright 1926 by Charles Scribner's Sons. Copyright renewed © 1954 by Ernest Hemingway.

Beyond the Heroic "I"

1

Noli Me Tangere: Dodging the Heroic "I" in the Narratives of Lawrence and Hemingway

WHEN I was eleven years old, grocery stores still gave out S & H Green Stamps, which my mother usually discarded in a junk drawer in the corner of the kitchen. Caught up as I was then with the Robin Hood stories (I even went to a grade-school costume party at Halloween dressed as Errol Flynn, my costume consisting of a slim moustache drawn on with eyeliner and a tinfoil sword—no one knew who I was, even after I explained it to them), I saved up the Green Stamps to buy a bow-and-arrow set, complete with pointed, metal-tipped arrows—the real thing. My father helped set up the small paper target in the back yard, taping it to a cardboard box set against the stone wall that separated the neighboring hay field from our property. I practiced with the bow for several afternoons, usually missing the target and either losing the arrows in the deep grass of the field— which meant that they would be crushed by the threshing machine used to gather the hay—or sending them splintering against the stone wall, hopelessly broken and sending me to the local Kmart sporting goods department to replenish my supply.

I became bored with trying to hit the target long before I got any better at it. There didn't seem to be much point to it, especially because I spent most of my time shagging arrows in the deep grass. I thought of stalking small animals with it once or twice, and actually spotted a grouse in the rusty fall leaves in a nearby wood. But I didn't shoot at it, and I never bothered hunting for other targets. The whole Robin Hood mystique faded pretty quickly once I realized I would never hit the bull's-eye, never mind split an arrow in the bull's-eye in two. Instead, I developed a strange game for myself that, had my parents found out about it, surely would have meant the confiscation of my bow.

This game involved evading my own arrows, making myself both weapon and target. I would stand firmly poised in a spot in the backyard, feet apart, arms above my head, the yellow bow describing

13

the arc of the sky. I would draw the arrow back until the feathered tip tickled my right ear, and release the bowstring, sending the arrow straight into the air above my head. Having marked the spot I had been standing on with a faded Frisbee or an old rag, I ran to one side or another, watching the flight of the shaft as it moved upward, reached its apogee, and turned menacingly back to the earth. Occasionally it landed near the spot where I had been standing when I first shot it upward, and frequently the wind made predicting its course much more difficult, sometimes landing it on the roof of the house, other times bringing the arrow closer to my escape than I had intended.

This childhood game is an important metaphor for my own reading of the fiction of D. H. Lawrence and Ernest Hemingway. As a metaphor, it reflects Jane Tompkins's definition of theory as "analysis that is not an end in itself but pressure brought to bear on a situation."[1] Although my childish arrows thankfully never penetrated their target—an end in itself, a sort of Prufrockian Truth "pinned and wriggling on the wall" (or the ground, as it were)—they certainly brought pressure to bear on a situation, causing me to evaluate my own place as both subject/catalyst of the arrow's flight and its potential object/target. Similarly, this study is a result of my own bringing pressure to bear on the value I have placed on the fiction of two modernist writers whose very names conjure up for many readers the worst of masculinity, misogyny, and patriarchal authority. However, the reputation shared by these modernists may have less to do with the fiction itself and more to do with the readers who have defined the predominant ways of reading novels such as *Women in Love* and *The Sun Also Rises*. One of my goals in this study is to reconsider the significant limitations often placed, however subtly or unintentionally, upon the fiction of Lawrence and Hemingway by critical readers—the archers of my opening metaphor—during the last fifty or sixty years. There has been and still is an overriding tendency to read Lawrence's and Hemingway's fiction through the authority of biography and to install the "real" Lawrence or the "actual" Hemingway as the heroes of their fictional works, masquerading as Rupert Birkin or as Jake Barnes.

Consider, for instance, a very recent example of biographically based criticism in Nancy R. Comley and Robert Scholes's *Hemingway's Genders: Rereading the Hemingway Text*. The very first line of their preface reads like a disclaimer: "We believe that Ernest Hemingway remains an interesting writer because it is possible to read him in more than one way." Simply needing to make such a statement about a literary *corpus* illustrates the condition of Hemingway in the

American literary canon. "To all who have read him in one way, as an embodiment of monolithic masculinity—and to all those who have resisted him on those grounds—we ask simply that you try reading him our way."[2] However, notice what has happened here— Comley and Scholes want us to read *him,* that is, *Hemingway*-as- text, their way, *not* to reconsider the *fiction-as-text* in light of current cultural or gender theory. Ultimately, Comley and Scholes want first to recoup Hemingway as a conflicted man in the arena of gender and second to illustrate the ways that gender conflicts faced by the biographical figure are evident in his fiction. To do this, they rational- ize a study of "the Hemingway Text" as "a cultural matrix that we share with Hemingway, as this matrix appears when we imagine Ernest Hemingway at the center of it."[3] As an authoritative and per- haps heroic center, the search for Hemingway becomes a clearly Oedipal quest in the hands of Comley and Scholes, despite frequent attempts to identify themselves against such a focus, as when they claim, almost defensively, "We are not interested in reducing Hem- ingway to some Oedipal formula that would obscure the unique features of his own way of organizing sexual materials in his life and work. But the life and work themselves—the Hemingway Text— present us with certain patterns that are too insistent to ignore."[4] Interestingly, even the title of this work ascribes gender and gender roles to Hemingway in a kind of sly nod toward authorial intent, or at least control.

Thankfully, Comley and Scholes have acknowledged that their re- construction of Hemingway is "imagined,"[5] that is, a construct, but that doesn't dissuade them from their project which, on the one hand, recoups the author-as-center even as, on the other hand, it attempts to bring to analysis the cultural narratives that influence Hemingway's fiction and that would, one might think, decenter the author. Largely because of such biographical reconstructions by criti- cal readers, the fiction of Lawrence and Hemingway has been identi- fied by many as masculine in its subject matter and as misogynistic in its approach—whether reading Rupert Birkin's overbearing at- tempts to control Ursula in *Women in Love* or Jake Barnes's preoccu- pation with bullfights and Brett Ashley in *The Sun Also Rises.* Indeed, Carol Siegel has noted that, although Lawrence is "one of the most frequently mentioned male authors in feminist criticism," women readers continue to have significant problems in approaching his work.[6] She writes, in *Lawrence among the Women,*

> *The* feminist question about Lawrence was whether his work belonged
> to the dominant and misogynous literary tradition, which attempts to

silence actual women in favor of a male-defined feminine, or whether
Lawrence could be considered part of the ongoing revolt of the marginalized, through which women's voices intrude into the dominant
discourse.[7]

For Siegel and other readers, the distinction is not always clear in
either Lawrence's fiction or in critical readings of him. However,
approaching the fiction of these two modernists is less a problem
of reading autobiographical narratives written by men who have been
identified as misogynists and more a problem of reorienting *readers*
to the perspectives and positionalities available when the heroic,
masculine narrative is put aside. "We should look as skeptically at
feminist descriptions of Lawrence that reduce him to a symbolic
Other," Siegel states early in her study, "as we do at patriarchal reduc-
tions of women writers."[8] Because Hemingway and Lawrence have
been perceived as so oppressively "masculine" and biographically
bound, avoiding rather reductive readings of their fiction is often
difficult. But the target is not nearly as finished or as stable as we
have been told.

The Production of the Heroic "I"

In an interview in *Writer's N.W.* magazine, novelist Marilynne Robinson indicates our inherent need to construct what might be called
heroic narratives, that is, narratives that are essentially incomplete,
if not faulty, because they recognize only one subject position as
valuable. She claims,

> We reduce things to one narrative characteristically. Narrative charges
> things with value. It's probably difficult or impossible for human beings
> to think in other terms than those, but if you're going to do history you
> have to realize that narrative does rearrange information spontaneously.
> You have to understand that and understand the possibility of other narra-
> tives. There's no way to solve the complexity of understanding as a prob-
> lem. But if you acknowledge the complexity of evidence then you've
> lengthened your chains.[9]

In the desire to find a way into the world of a novel, readers often
rely on the construction of a hero, a single subjective experience
that would appear to be more valuable than others in the text. Like
David Copperfield in his deliberations at the very beginning of his
own novel—"Whether I shall turn out to be the hero of my own life,
or whether that station will be held by anybody else, these pages

must show"—readers frequently want to know whose experience will provide the most validity, the most value in the reception and understanding of the text, and as such a common readerly habit is to cling to this need for a hero at the center of a narrative, whether that hero is the main protagonist of the novel, a biographical authority, or even the reader himself as he posits a critical response to the fiction. Reconsidering narrative subjectivity, however, allows the reader to turn his gaze away from the singular hero and toward those habits which control the construction of heroic narratives.

My readings beyond the "heroic I" in the narrative rely largely on the narrative theories proposed by Teresa de Lauretis in *Alice Doesn't* and *The Technologies of Gender.* In the construction of hierarchical value structures in narratives, readers engender narratives as well. The heroic quest narrative, which might serve as a kind of formalist deep structure in the ways texts are commonly approached—following a valuable subject through beginning, middle, and end of his quest, complete with the kind of rising tension and climax that defines male sexuality—is the traditional form of what de Lauretis refers to as the "Oedipal" or mythic narrative. The oedipal narrative favors a singularly dominant point of view and a pattern of structural development that allows the elitist perspective of the hero at the center of the text to retain its supremacy over other possible perspectives. In "Desire in Narrative," she suggests that, in examining any narrative, readers must also take into account the desire of the multiplicity of individuals within that narrative and how that desire shapes (or attempts to shape) the narrative. Traditionally, however, narratives have been read in a singular way: offering an expository introduction, a series of events or complications that lead to climax, resolution, and ultimate closure, whether satisfactory or unsatisfactory, for the central hero.[10]

Certainly, desire and narrative subjectivity have had little to do with augmenting this formula. de Lauretis turns to what she sees as Robert Scholes' reduction of this narrative movement to sexual terms to emphasize the dominance such an approach to the narrative has had in prose fiction; he writes, in *Fabulation and Metafiction:* "The archetype of all fiction is the sexual act. . . . For what connects fiction—and music—with sex is the fundamental orgastic rhythm of tumescence and detumescence, of tension and resolution, of intensification to the point of climax and consummation."[11] Scholes is of course recognizing a single narrative possibility, that which conforms to a *masculine* sexual paradigm, and as such it reflects the kind of structure that Joseph Campbell referred to as "monomyth," borrowing the term from Joyce—the archetypal journey of the hero through a series of obstacles that brings him to climax and resolution of the quest. But Scholes cannot be faulted for his masculine metaphor here, even though de Lauretis and other theorists might like to place such blame. Instead, his paradigm of the orgasmic masculine narrative reflects not a personal bias but what Margaret Jackson refers to as a broader cultural "primacy of the penis." If the process of reaching sexual orgasm is to serve as the metaphor for the construction of the narrative, as Scholes hoped it would in his theory, then the cultural model of sexuality has served him well. "Male sexuality has been universalized," Jackson writes, "and now serves as the model of *human* sexuality." Indeed, Jackson quotes Masters and Johnson to illustrate just how fully the primacy of the penis has become embedded into our cultural definitions of sex. According to Masters and Johnson, "The functional role of the penis is that of providing an organic means for physiologic and psychologic increment and release of both male and female sexual tension."[12] This is Scholes's metaphor for the construction of narratives, and the limitations of this masculine bias are not only Scholes's, as Jackson's study indicates, but the culture's, as well.

With this cultural shortsightedness in mind, then, it is easy to see how the subjective perspectives traditionally attended to in the narrative by the critical reader have been those of masculine figures engaging in these typically masculine narrative "quests," making the reading of "deep structures" within narratives so compelling to formalist critics. De Lauretis writes, "In this mythical-textual mechanics, then, the hero must be male, regardless of the gender of the text-image, because the obstacle, whatever its personification, is morphologically female" (*Alice Doesn't*, 118–19). Other positionalities, those which offer perspectives that refuse to accept such "Oedipal logic" (*Alice Doesn't*, 125), naturally become obstacles for the heroic and "masculine" text to overcome. Virginia Woolf illustrates her attempt to move beyond the ubiquitous hero while reading a new novel by "Mr. A"; in *A Room of One's Own*, she writes,

> But after reading a chapter or two a shadow seemed to lie across the page. It was a straight dark bar, a shadow shaped something like the letter "I." One began dodging this way and that to catch a glimpse of the landscape behind it. Whether that was indeed a tree or a woman walking I was not quite sure. Back one was always hailed to the letter "I." One began to be tired of "I."[13]

This is the heroic "I," the hero of the Oedipal narrative—a presence who may be constructed as the "main" masculine character or guiding force of the novel, and who may also be resurrected by readers as the pseudobiographical "spirit" of the author/authority as legendary artist-hero. The obstacles behind that fictional or pseudo-biographical heroic "I" are those aspects of the narrative which de Lauretis suggests might be seen as morphologically "feminine." She claims that "to say that narrative is the production of Oedipus is to say that each reader—male or female—is constrained and defined within two positions of a sexual difference thus conceived: male-hero-human, on the side of the subject; and female-obstacle-boundary-space, on the other" (*Alice Doesn't*, 121). The narrative that denies such phallocentric rigidity engages in a process of recognizing the ways in which individual desire obstructs a singularly dominant perspective and the ways in which it asserts its own perspective while denying authoritative climax and ultimate closure of any single approach to the text.

The metaphor from my childhood experience with which I began this chapter threatens to remain trapped in a classically masculine narrative—a (morphologically) masculine arrow/phallus that is aimed intrusively at the (morphologically) feminine target. The appeal of archery was for me an extension of the heroic and masculine narrative prescribed by the Robin Hood tales, whether those created around Errol Flynn, Disney animation, or, much later, and long after I had lost my childhood bow, Kevin Costner. However, what the Robin Hood narrative failed to tell me in its limited perspective was that it *was* limited and that that narrative was not necessarily the only one available. As I found that I couldn't accomplish what I now know are feats of Hollywood staging and film editing rather than of heroism or archery, other narrative possibilities and perspectives became available. As a metaphor for the narrative that denies the phallocentric, the dangerous, childish game—shooting arrows into the air above my head, and hoping I could avoid getting hit—not only made available the masculine/phallic perspective of the hero/archer/arrow but also that of the target. Indeed, the desire of another narrative perspective beyond that of the heroic, Oedipal narrative reveals what is an essential contradiction to the heroic perspective: in this case that the hero's target refuses to behave as or even to be defined as target.

As I found in the prescriptive nature of the Robin Hood narrative, the very act of reading may become the trap that places the critic in the inherent role of hero, as Susan Winnett argues in her essay, "Coming Unstrung: Women, Men, Narrative, and Principles of Pleasure." She claims that "the same analytic paradigms that give us professional access to texts have already determined the terms in which we accede to, comply with, or resist the coercions of a cultural program for pleasure that is not interested in—and whose interests may be threatened by—the difference of women's pleasure."[14] While I cannot speak for women's pleasure, the pleasure of the text—a pleasure that is so often defined by the overcoming of obstacles placed in the critical reader's way—seems to have become an almost irrevocable part of critically responding to or "re-vising" the text. The traditionally Oedipal approach to the narrative favors just such a singularly dominant point of view and a pattern of development which allows that elitist perspective to retain its supremacy over other possible perspectives. "The very work of narrativity," de Lauretis writes, "is the engagement of the subject in certain positionalities of meaning and desire" (*Alice Doesn't*, 106). The hero of the narrative follows a quest that remains a phallocentric progression through narrative time, which ends inevitably in climax and closure, quite satisfying masculine desire. Other avenues of subjectivity and desire remain unexplored within such an essentialistic narrative reading, ignored by the "versionless version" of a given story, as Barbara Herrnstein Smith calls the deep structure Seymour Chatman seeks in the various revisions of the Cinderella tale.[15] The problem with such a nearsighted approach is echoed in Alice Jardine's complaint as she asks, "Do theories of narrative structure in the male realm always have to be modeled upon traditional male desire: beginning, middle, end? What about problems of enunciation, voice, and silence?"[16] Other positionalities, those offering perspectives which refuse to accept such closure, become obstacles to the dominant perspective of the masculine text.

Within the academic discourse community, there are certain standards of reading and criticism that have remained relatively immobile, despite the significant changes in the critical landscape during the past twenty years. Virginia Woolf recognized this immobility in her reflections on the closed academy in *A Room of One's Own*, in which she writes, "I thought of the organ booming in the chapel and of the shut doors of the library; and I thought how unpleasant it is to be locked out; and I thought how it is worse perhaps to be locked in."[17] Our ways of reading and responding to texts as critics are primarily phallocentric and phallogocentric—limited to the sanctioned methods and language of the most influential of critics. Compounding this problem further, Elaine Showalter has recognized the disingenuousness of those males who profess to practice feminist critical theory and yet who continue to keep the canonical male writers at the center of their literary universes. In her essay, "Critical Cross-Dressing: Male Feminists and the Woman of the Year," she writes, "the patriarchal literary canon has a centripetal force and a social power that pulls discussion toward its center. . . . Reviewing the first wave of male feminist criticism, one notes that it nearly all "happens" to be about texts signed by men: Rabelais, Richardson, Hemingway, Lawrence."[18] It would appear that in her gynocritical approach, Showalter has already exposed me as a fraud, caught as I apparently am in the centripetal force of the literary canon, by isolating the two male writers whose narratives I have proposed to study. However, my interest in Lawrence and Hemingway is not an attempt to affirm their status in a traditional modernist canon, but to suggest that it is not only the canon which is in need of revision, but also the ways we read even those figures who have inhabited the canonical center. It is what Teresa de Lauretis indicates must be "a rereading of the sacred texts against the passionate urging of a different question, a different practice, a different desire" (*Alice Doesn't*, 107). Before that different desire can be considered, however, the dominant practices of reading narratives in the relatively brief (but often regarded as definitive) history of critical response to Lawrence's and Hemingway's fiction must be reconsidered. Toril Moi explains, "The main theoretical task for male feminists, then, is to develop an analysis of their own position, and a strategy for how their awareness of their difficult and contradictory position in relation to feminism can be made explicit in discourse and practice."[19] That analysis of "their own position," which Moi outlines, is the metaphoric arrow I turn upon the ways in which Lawrence and Hemingway have been read and might be reread. To examine Lawrence and Hemingway and the readerly claims for their masculinity or against their misogyny is finally to examine the ways the masculine narrative has been constructed by readers who have attempted to install a dominant hero, whether in the novels themselves or in the critical narratives created around biographical and similarly Oedipal heroic centers.

Lawrence, Hemingway, and Auto-Oedipal Adoration

Early in Milan Kundera's novel, *Immortality*, a radio announcer plugs a new book for his listeners. "In a singsong that imitates the fading melody, he announces the publication of a new biography of Ernest Hemingway, the one hundred and twenty-seventh, yet this time a truly significant one because it discloses that throughout his entire life Hemingway never spoke one single word of truth."[20] I don't know if, as of 1990 when the novel was first published in its author's native Czech, this was an accurate count of the available biographies of Hemingway; it actually seems a rather small number considering the number of scholars, friends, acquaintances, friends of acquaintances, and live-bait salesmen who have written biographical or semibiographical books about his life. In any case, Kundera constructs the problem of authority early in his novel, the disparate attempts to isolate definitive reality from mere fiction, even incorporating himself as a character in his fiction. To explore this problem, he relies on the near mania surrounding the desire of readers and critics to read Hemingway-the-man in an authoritative way.

Curiously, critics have spent a great deal of ink and energy in exhuming artifacts of the biographical author in the fiction of both Lawrence and Hemingway. Identity in reading the fiction all too frequently becomes a search for the author's identity; details of the life of the authority behind the fiction seem to be more important for the readers of these modernist writers than for those scholars of other modernists, or even of other writers of any literary period. Carl Eby has recently written of the problem of discovering biographical identity in reading Hemingway, "Hemingway used the raw material of his life to forge fiction only to use that fiction to reinterpret and fictionalize his life (a process which bedeviled him and continues to bedevil all but the most careful of his critics)."[21] Thus, even when critical readers *think* that they have discovered artifacts of the "actual" Hemingway, they have often only unearthed a new layer of fiction. But in their continued digging, Lawrence critics traditionally focus on his relationship to his mother, his attachments to Jessie Chambers and Louie Burrows and other women, and to his marriage to Frieda von Richthofen; Hemingway's readers have clung to his antagonism toward his mother, to his failed marriages and the fourth marriage to Mary Welsh, and to his obsession with the "manly" pursuits such as hunting, boxing, and bullfighting which informed his public persona. In an article for the *Arizona Quarterly*, Peter L. Hays even combines the two tendencies, examining father/son relationships in Hemingway's life and fiction, and entitling his essay "Hemingway, Nick Adams, and David Bourne: Sons and Writers." He is, of course, making a direct reference to the mother/son relationships that haunt readings of Lawrence's fiction, especially in *Sons and Lovers*. Following his examination of similarities between fictional and biographical events in the marriages of Dr. Henry Adams and Dr. Clarence (Ed) Hemingway, Hays concludes of their sons, the fictional Nick *and* the authorial Ernest, "It is no wonder that Nick rejects John's well-meaning advice to marry. It is also no wonder that Hemingway saw masculine authority in guns and insisted on dominating in each of his four marriages."[22] To look merely for Lawrence and Hemingway in the fiction is to engage in the construction of our own heroic, Oedipal narratives—which become, if the metaphor of male sexuality has been the most common approach to representing emplotment in the narrative, autoerotic readings of narratives—and to reduce the act of reading to a phallocentric and self-obsessed pursuit. The autoerotic or auto-Oedipal narrative obsession is a reliance on finding a quantity or paradigm which is already a known quantity and which offers little opportunity for creative discovery—what Lawrence referred to as "sex in the head." It may be pleasant temporarily, and may even be exciting, but it offers little chance of further understanding the textual or the readerly narratives. This is especially true for the critical search for autobiographical artifacts in fiction, artifacts that will somehow construct for the reader an authoritative "reality" which is both definitive and conclusive. Millicent Bell reduces the Hemingway text, and concurrently all fiction, to autobiography when she paradoxically claims, "Autobiographic novels are, of course, fictions, constructs of the imagination, even when they seem to incorporate authenticating bits and pieces of personal history. But all fiction is autobiography, no matter how remote from the author's experience the tale seems to be; he leaves his mark, expresses his being, his life in *any* tale." Her latter assertion is a dangerous one for critical reading, because it ultimately prescribes the conscription to authorial and authoritative narratives, the events of the life dominating the reception of the work of art. Although she argues against the tradition of simplistic readings of Hemingway's *A Farewell to Arms* as overt autobiography in her essay, "Pseudoautobiography and Personal Metaphor," Bell claims that although events of the novel may not correspond one-for-one to the events of Hemingway's World War I experience, they do reveal "fetishes of autobiography, trophies of the personal, chief of these the famous wounding at Fossalta, which Hemingway often recalled."[23] Perhaps Bell's point might be better expressed by Seán O'Faoláin in *The Vanishing Hero* when he writes, "Every novelist reveals his sympathies by his obsessions."[24] But readers must ask themselves, what purpose do these fetishes of autobiography serve in a reception of the text and of the multiple perspectives it asserts?

While the connections between fiction and biography are interesting and have produced some important critical biographies, including John Worthen's 1991 entry in the new Cambridge biography of D. H. Lawrence and Kenneth Lynn's 1987 *Hemingway*, many readers seem unable to move beyond this tendency to read for the "actual," historical, or autobiographical Lawrence or Hemingway in finding meaning in their fiction. For instance, Sheila MacLeod exhibits a common assumption that *Women in Love*'s Birkin is a transparent front for Lawrence himself. She believes that *"Women in Love* reads like the novel in which Lawrence tried to work through the problem of his own homosexuality, while never quite admitting it, never quite coming to terms with it."[25] For MacLeod, Birkin's failure to fulfill both a physical and spiritual relationship with Gerald is Lawrence's failure to accept, or even understand, his own homosexual urgings. "I also think he is being evasive," she continues, speaking of Lawrence. "He does not want us to know too much about Birkin's family, especially his relationship with his mother, because then both he and we should have to confront the problem of Birkin's homosexuality head on. The underlying assumption is that the reader will not be in sympathy with Birkin's plight."[26] The fiction becomes no more than an archaeological artifact, with which we can reconstruct Lawrence's life and possibly homosexual conflicts, without taking into consideration what is happening to the construction of gender and identity in the character named Rupert Birkin and in his relationships with Gerald Crich, Ursula Brangwen, and Hermione Roddice.

Similarly, Peter Balbert's *D. H. Lawrence and the Phallic Imagination* attempts a defense of Lawrence as a male author who has been attacked by feminist and proto-feminist critics, turning his attention to what he claims are the ideological misreadings performed by Kate Millett, Carolyn Heilbrun, and Hillary Simpson. In exploring the prescriptive nature of what he calls "Lawrence's sexual dialectic" in *Sons and Lovers*, Balbert concludes that *"Sons and Lovers* must speak to us of biographical secrets. It reveals how Lawrence-Paul promises to make love at least well enough to write his novel, as he learns to abandon those counterfeit passions which nullify the force of his phallic imagination."[27] Lawrence is ultimately the subject of his own fiction in such a biographical reading, and the events of the novel serve merely as a Rorschachian inkblot for the state of the author's psyche. Later, in his chapter on Ursula's role as corrective influence in *Women in Love*, Balbert writes, "There is no persuasive sense in any of Lawrence's correspondence, or in the reliable reports of his contemporaries, that this 'inevitable friction' he mentions in his letter and analyzes in the Hardy essay was not fully relevant to his marriage with Frieda."[28] This conclusion may well be biographically "true," but as I encounter such passages in texts that purport to extend readings of the fiction, I wonder why it is necessary to revert to the essentially prescriptive narrative of biography and where are the readings of Paul or Birkin in the contexts of their literary and social narratives? Why reduce the text to the status of biographical and authorial artifact?

Of course, biographically bound readings, a version of the cult of celebrity so dominant in U.S. culture at this end of the twentieth century, can lead to some strange assertions. Critic after critic, spurred on it would seem by Mark Spilka's writing about the novel, cannot resist turning to Lawrence's impotence and his overtly sexual novel (and with this observation I have, ironically, included it in my study as well; is *this* evidence of the primacy and power of the biographical/Oedipal narrative?). This line of reasoning leads Spilka, in his essay, "Lawrence versus Peeperkorn on Abdication," to bemoan the loss of Lawrence as a kind of sexual mentor to his readers. After concluding that "by the end of 1926, when he began writing *Lady Chatterley's Lover*, Lawrence was wholly impotent," Spilka remarks, "It seems to me, if not a critical embarrassment, at least a critical perplex, or better still, a critically embarrassing perplex, that *Lady Chatterley's Lover* was written by an impotent man."[29] As a reader of the essay, and of Lawrence, I found myself wondering, How does he come to this critical place? By presuming our collective disappointment upon learning that a novel about sexuality and the passional connection—a novel that sometimes seems more sex manual than fiction, as Michael Bell notes[30]—should have been written by an impotent man. "In a sense," Spilka writes, "we have all trusted Lawrence as much as, if not more than, his prophetic tale. . . . But now that others have spoken for us, now that the bald truth is public knowledge, our grounds for trusting him must be reassessed."[31] Thus, so the critical conclusion goes, we subjective and experienced readers cannot trust the text of the novel, because we cannot find authority for its validity in the life of the author at the time of its composition.

As Kundera suggests in *Immortality,* the construction of authorial-bound narratives is no less evident in the fiction of Ernest Hemingway, and it has been especially prevalent in the foundational criticism of writers such as Carlos Baker and Philip Young. Long the premiere critic of Hemingway's fiction, and still considered by some as his "definitive" biographer, Carlos Baker's focus on the Hemingway Hero illustrates the difficulty readers have in moving beyond the biographical. This hero image becomes archetypal for Baker, several fictional figures bearing a singular set of traits, behaviors, and qualities that tend not to distinguish one character from any other of Hemingway's creations. On the role of hero as pragmatist as it is defined in *Death in the Afternoon,* Baker wrote,

> The heroes Hemingway chooses, Goya on canvas and Maera on the bloody sand, are *aficionados* of the actual, believing in what they empiri-

cally know, facing the facts of life, one of which is the fact of death, in full consciousness of the inter-relations and psychological interdependence of the two. The same sturdy quality of belief runs like a thick red line through the whole gallery of Hemingway heroes, and evidently through the consciousness of the artist to whom they owe their origin.[32]

Such a sweeping generalization, moving from the complete body of fiction to the biography of the Hemingway persona, calls into question the necessity of reading very much of his fiction at all. Apparently, the writer is unable to move beyond a stock character, an archetypal figure who remains essentially the same despite minor changes in external details such as names and situations. Indeed, although Frederick Crews refers to Baker as Hemingway's "former idolater,"[33] other readers have been similarly adoring of the modernist writer, including Robert Penn Warren who wrote of *A Farewell to Arms,*

> It crowned the success story of the American boy from the Middle West, who had hunted and fished, played football in high school, been a newspaper reporter, gone to war and been wounded and decorated, wandered exotic lands as a foreign correspondent, lived the free life of the Latin Quarter of Paris, and, at the age of thirty, written a best seller—athlete, sportsman, correspondent, soldier, adventurer, and author.[34]

This analysis is clearly not about the novel at all, but a romantic portrait of the author who ultimately provides a more attractive focus for Penn Warren's attention than does *A Farewell to Arms.*

Philip Young is only slightly more subtle in his attraction to the biographical figure. In his study of Hemingway's fiction, *Ernest Hemingway: A Reconsideration,* Young identifies Nick Adams as a thinly veiled Hemingway and as the prototypical Hemingway hero. "The real hero," Young writes, "is the protagonist who was up in Michigan and was wounded while fighting as an American in the Italian army, who lived and wrote fiction in Paris; he is the generic Nick Adams."[35] Young's professed subject here is the fictional character of the stories, but his analysis which points to a kind of narrative deep structure—all proper parts fitting a single story—seems to center the foundations for the character in the life of the author. Indeed, this becomes clearer as he continues in the preface to Scribners' 1972 collection of Hemingway's Nick Adams stories into a single volume, claiming that "the events of Nick's life make up a meaningful narrative in which a memorable character grows from child to adolescent to soldier, veteran, writer, and parent—a sequence closely paralleling the events of Hemingway's own life." Of course, this is not really a very uncommon line of development for any individual who lives during wartime, and yet Young insists upon reductively identifying the fictional character with the "real" writer. He goes on to explain the rationale for collecting and chronologically arranging all of the stories that feature Nick Adams as an essentially biographical act.

> In this arrangement Nick Adams, who for a long time was not widely recognized as a consistent character at all, emerges clearly as the first in a long line of Hemingway's fictional selves. Later versions, from Jake Barnes and Frederic Henry to Richard Cantwell and Thomas Hudson, were all to have behind them part of Nick's history and, correspondingly, part of Hemingway's.[36]

For Young, like the Lawrence of Spilka, Balbert, and MacLeod, the writer's life is the essential stuff of fiction. To be able to identify certain characters, usually the main protagonists, as stand-ins for the author is to be able to define and authoritatively delineate the value of the work of fiction itself.

Recently, during an introduction to literature class, we spent two class periods on the short story, "The Short Happy Life of Francis Macomber." Although it was the only Hemingway story we read during the ten-week quarter, we spent about half of the first day trying to work through students' responses to the popular authorial persona. "Wasn't he a real womanizer?" "Didn't he drink like a fish?" and "Didn't he commit suicide?" were the primary concerns of the largely freshman students, concerns that had not surfaced earlier in the quarter and would not reappear again. My freshman students wanted finally to share Young's belief about the power of the persona behind the fiction: "Last and most important is the fact that these pieces throw new light on the work and personality of one of our foremost writers and genuinely increase our understanding of him"[37]—not our understanding of the fiction, or of our roles as readers, but of the ultimate responsibility of an authority. This, for my freshman readers, leads to a singular conclusion and a crutch that many refuse to discard: that the only way to read a text is to read, if not for authorial intent, then certainly voyeuristically, for an author's accidental exposure of himself. Frederick Crews claims that the recent availability of Hemingway's manuscripts and uncollected work at the Kennedy Library in Boston, and elsewhere, has actually hampered critical approaches to Hemingway. He writes,

> In large measure, what has been restored to us is Hemingway the celebrity—the figure that he himself, the supreme self-publicist of modern letters, created in the thirties and shrewdly marketed through articles

and interviews depicting a life of action, courage, and connoisseurship. It says something about our own shallow era that so many of us are happy to revert to that trivial conception of our most influential novelist.[38]

This is a pessimistic, if somewhat accurate, reckoning of the responses to Hemingway's fiction as an artifact of his life. That is not to say that there is no exciting new scholarship available; certainly in recent years, Mark Spilka's study of gender and androgyny and Susan F. Beegel's editorial direction of *The Hemingway Review* have been two highlights of Hemingway scholarship, just as Carol Siegel and Linda Ruth Williams have produced indispensable studies of Lawrence.[39] But as Miriam B. Mandel suggests in *Reading Hemingway,* echoing my students' preconceptions, so many readers "are so unused to looking for the intellectual furniture in this particular artist's mind that even when we stumble across it, we miss it."[40] Of course, we miss this intellectual furniture because reading Hemingway's fiction has long been reduced to a kind of functional minimalist approach to literary analysis-as-interior decoration, to extend Mandel's metaphor: reading for Codes, reading for Oedipus, reading for the biographical narrative.

In their introduction to the first volume of the Cambridge biography of Lawrence, David Ellis, Mark Kinkead-Weekes, and John Worthen write, "Our culture does often appear bound by the idea of a personal core or centre, an 'essential self,' out of which character grows in a process of development."[41] This is indeed the critical narrative Spilka and MacLeod, Baker and Young, and many other readers of Lawrence and Hemingway ascribe to, a narrative that demands the construction of an autobiographical presence as hero of the text, thinly veiled behind a character whose Oedipal quest we must focus upon. "Pseudo-biographical" approaches assert Lawrence's and Hemingway's lives as the texts that must be interpellated from their fiction, a process that dates back to Middleton Murray's early reflections on Lawrence in *Son of Woman* and Wyndham Lewis's judgment of Hemingway as "The Dumb Ox." Such readers supplant an authorial figure, the man named David Herbert Lawrence, the man who had an "abnormally close" relationship with his mother, as the biographical teaser in the Penguin 1989 paperback edition of *Women in Love* promises, as the hero of the fiction—whether to debase, upbraid, or glorify him for his life and work. In Bernard Malamud's 1979 novel, *Dubin's Lives,* William Dubin attempts precisely this technique in writing his biography of Lawrence. Dubin is a harried biographer who finds his attempts to write the life of another inextricably entwined in his attempts to live his own life, and the process of biography becomes a self-reflective process of autobiography, as Dubin's thoughts reveal:

> You assimilated another man's experience and tried to arrange it into "thoughtful centrality"—Samuel Johnson's expression. In order to do that honestly and well, you had to anchor yourself in a place of perspective; you had as a strategy to imagine you were the one you were writing about, even though it meant laying illusion on illusion: pretense that he, Dubin, who knew himself passing well, knew, or might know, the life of D. H. Lawrence: who seemed not to have stepped beyond his mythic mask.

Malamud's fictional biographer, or the critical reader, is finally unable to move beyond himself in attempting to recoup the life of the authority. "Which is to say that all biography is ultimately fiction," as Dubin concludes. "What does that tell you about the nature of life, and does one really want to know?"[42] Patricia Waugh seems to agree that the biographical approach to fiction tells us less about the work of fiction and more about our readerly desires. In *Metafiction*, she observes, "We tend to read fiction as if it were history."[43] Reading becomes a search for causality, an act of moral-making in which we can see what has happened when certain real people behave in certain ways. In his essay on Lawrence, Lessing, and "the battle of the sexes," Spilka betrays just such a desire when he writes, "What attracts men as well as women to Doris Lessing's fiction these days, we might conclude, is what attracted them to Lawrence's: namely, an autobiographical intensity by which images of the author's self are put on the line and exploited with an honesty so self-searching and unsparing as to anticipate most of our critical objections to those images."[44] The danger in this kind of approach is clear to Ellis, Kinkead-Weekes, and Worthen: "Of all the dangers biographers have to fear, the so-called 'genetic fallacy'—explanation in terms of origins—should be less in evidence here. We have learned to distrust hindsight, because reading the later man back into the earlier always implies determinism."[45] I find it extremely interesting that biographers are unwilling to create such dangerous fictions as moralistic/deterministic narratives, yet readers of the fiction are often quite willing to erect these narratives for themselves. What's more, such reading for the representative of the heroic author is not as easy as it would appear, as Alison Light suggests of Lawrence's role in *Sons in Lovers* in her article, "Feminism and the Literary Critic":

> My objections . . . point to my recognition that if Lawrence *is* Paul, he is also Paul's mother and girlfriends, and if, as Millett does, we take their

part, we haven't somehow escaped Lawrence but exposed the way in which novels, as constructs of the imagination, might be attempts at "ungendering" and, however unsuccessful, at dispersing or even transgressing the gendered experience of an author and its usual restraints.[46]

Light raises an important question: If we are going to read for Lawrence-as-authority, where do we place him? Is it as simple as reading the figure who looks or sounds or acts the most like Lawrence as Lawrence? This seems to be Ken Russell's plan in casting a bearded Alan Bates as Birkin in his 1969 film adaptation of *Women in Love;* Bates's Birkin is an obvious visual representation of Lawrence in the film. Clearly, MacLeod isn't alone in seeing Lawrence's reflection in Birkin. Of course we *can* point to Birkin as representative of Lawrence; there are several occasions in which the fictional character seems to mouth the author's nonfictional writing. However, Linda Ruth Williams asks the all-important question, "On what terms do we challenge this, in order to see Lawrence in his degraded women as well as in his men, enjoying those feminine traits he also reviles?"[47] If Birkin is a fictional construct created out of autobiographical experience by D. H. Lawrence, then so are Ursula, Gudrun, Gerald, and, for that matter, all the characters and situations described within the pages of the novel *Women in Love*. As Birkin has been described as Lawrence's mouthpiece,[48] a reader so inclined to find the author in the text might also hear him in Ursula. One instance of this impression is especially striking as she contemplates the daisies Birkin has tossed into the water, spinning in their Dervish dance. She tells him, "You know that a daisy is a company of florets, a concourse, become individual. Don't the botanists put it highest in the line of development? I believe they do."[49] Ursula has her own theories of individuality and identity, and here she instructs Birkin. The essayistic Lawrence turns to red poppies rather than daisies in the "Study of Thomas Hardy," but his message is quite similar:

> But in my poppy, where at the summit the two streams which till now have run deviously, scattered down many ways, at length flow concentrated together, and the pure male stream meets the pure female stream in a heave and an overflowing: there, there is the flower indeed.[50]

Similarly, if I wished to trace Lawrence back to his fictional characters, Gudrun might also illustrate the writer, especially in her theories of art and representation. Of the relatedness of her life and her art, she agrees with Loerke: "The two things are quite and permanently apart, they have nothing to do with one another. *I* and my art, they have *nothing* to do with each other. My art stands in another world,

I am in this world" (526). Interestingly, this echoes Lawrence's admonition to the reader of *Fantasia of the Unconscious:* "But remember, dear, reader, please, that there is not the slightest need for you to believe me, or even read me. Remember, it's just your own affair. Don't implicate me."[51] Of course, Loerke confuses the matter in the novel by admitting that the figure of the woman on the horse in his carving is representative of a student he frequently abused—and here, were we so biographically inclined, we might turn to records of Lawrence's abuse of Frieda. But this kind of search for the authority could develop in several seemingly legitimate directions, all of which ultimately erect Lawrence as hero, as biographical center of his texts, and all of which ignore the desire of each individual represented within the narrative. Linda Ruth Williams writes, "It is easy to slip into unthinking psychobiography with Lawrence's work because he is such a polemicist, writing from a central 'I' subject position despite the glaring contradictions of that 'I', and despite its own famous protestation, 'Never trust the artist, trust the tale.'"[52] The pleas made by Gudrun in the novel and by Lawrence in *Fantasia* are not merely early manifestations of New Critical approaches to literature and art, but are attempts to suggest critical narratives other than the heroic narrative which reconstructs the author-as-hero of the text.

The Death of the Heroic "I" and the Birth of Multiple Subjectivities

Hemingway echoes Lawrence's desire not to be implicated in his fiction in a letter to F. Scott Fitzgerald dated 24 December 1925. He writes, in his typically informal shorthand, "Review of In Our Type [*sic*] from Chicago Post says all of it obviously not fiction but simply descriptive of passages in life of new Chicago author. God what a life I must have led."[53] The playful surprise here betrays a realization that not only is *he* writing fiction, but his readers seem to be creating their own fictions as well, with the "real Hemingway" as their subject. Manipulating our understandings of the seemingly impermeable boundaries between fiction and reality, Milan Kundera expands upon this authorial reticence by creating a presumably fictional account of Hemingway's friendship and conversations with the German romanticist Goethe in the afterlife. In Kundera's novel, *Immortality*, we find Hemingway sharing Goethe's resigned inability to control the narrative of his own life.

"You know, Johann," said Hemingway, "they keep bringing up accusations against me, too. Instead of reading my books, they're writing books about me. They say that I didn't love my wives. That I didn't pay enough attention to my son. That I punched a critic on the nose. That I lied. That I wasn't sincere. That I was conceited. That I was macho. That I claimed I had received two hundred and thirty war wounds whereas actually it was only two hundred and ten. That I abused myself. That I disobeyed my mother."

Goethe's response to Hemingway's complaint is his revelation of the utter inability to control the narrative of his own life: "That's immortality. . . . Immortality means eternal trial."[54] The real horror for this fictional Hemingway is not in his suicide, but in the creative activity that begins following his suicide and in his inability to take his immortality along with his life. Upon killing himself, he sees the writing and revising of himself take place before his corpse.

I was lying dead on the deck and I saw my four wives squatting around me, writing down everything they knew, and standing behind them was my son and he was scribbling too, and that old dame Gertrude Stein was there writing away and all my friends were there blabbing out all the indiscretions and slanders they had ever heard about me, and behind them a hundred journalists with microphones jostled one another and an army of university professors all over America was busy classifying, analyzing, and shoveling everything into articles and books.[55]

Everyone is scribbling out their own account, their own understandings of Hemingway which, in the book *Immortality* whose subtitle on the cover of my edition is "A Novel," is precisely what Kundera is doing as he writes/narrates his novel. And finally it must be what I am doing as I attempt to move beyond Hemingway's life as a phallocentric narrative in his fiction. And although the fictional Hemingway's references to his wives and son and Gertrude Stein in the passage above are certainly autobiographical, no one would take this novel as a legitimate artifact of Hemingway's life or experience—even if Kundera admitted to some sort of Yeatsian intercourse with the spirit world. This portrait of Hemingway is clearly fiction, and yet in many ways it is no more fictive than much of the exhumation of the Hemingway persona which purports to offer authoritative, critical readings of the fiction.

When Roland Barthes defines the constructedness of authorial figures in the narrative by separating "reality" from the "paper beings" of the text in "Introduction to the Structural Analysis of Narratives," he asserts a death of the Author as the controlling or central, recoverable hero of the text. Barthes claims that, from a structuralist perspective, "the (material) author of a narrative is in no way to be confused with the narrator of that narrative" because *"who speaks* (in the narrative) is not *who writes* (in real life) and *who writes* is not *who is*."[56] In this way, he holds, attempts to recoup an authorial persona behind the narrative are bound to fail, because the authority of "reality," the real life of the author, itself becomes constructed through the language of the text. "Decipherment" and "disentanglement" are the terms he calls upon in "The Death of the Author,"[57] decipherment being the search for the "right answer" or The Truth of the text hidden in the text, most often hidden in the life of the author/authority. Disentanglement is the process of, as Reina Lewis describes it, "untangling the web of structures that form the text without assigning a 'secret' or 'ultimate' meaning."[58] Barthes also calls for "anti-theological activity" in the act of reading, the eradication of the controlling figure of an Author-God constructed by the reader, whether by assumption (assuming that the acts of the novel are biographical artifacts) or through biographical research, who presides as the ultimate center (and Oedipal hero) of the text.[59]

Following Barthes, however, many critics have blanched at the notion of the death of the author. Comley and Scholes claim that it is Hemingway who remains at the center of the "Hemingway Text," that collection of canonical and noncanonical works which comprise the aesthetic yield of the writer-as-creative source. They write, in *Hemingway's Genders,* "Nietzsche kept wondering when people would get around to noticing that God was dead. Proponents of 'The Death of the Author' seem to be experiencing a similar problem. We believe that the concept of an 'author' is necessary for literary interpretation." They then differentiate between a "strong concept" of the author—that is, the concept of authorial intent—and a "weak concept," which leads them to the assertion that "we have only textual records of what he said, did, wrote, and so on. . . . By putting Hemingway at the center, we mean that we will privilege his time and place over ours, that we will accept the best factual evidence of a biographical and bibliographical sort as decisive, and that, in short we will make our imagined Hemingway as realistic or 'true' as we can."[60] Thus, Comley and Scholes claim to eschew authorial intent as a fiction, even as they construct a figure presumed to loom behind the corpus of Hemingway's literary production, a figure who remains "decisive" and "necessary for literary interpretation." Frederic Crews argues more directly against the death of the author in *The Critics Bear It Away,* expressing concern for a readerly irresponsibility that might accompany such a "death." "Methodologically, the key feature of poststructuralist criticism is its downgrading of what Michel Foucault belittled as 'the author function.' Once writers have been discounted as the primary shapers of their works, critics are free to 'liberate signifiers from the signified'—that is, to make a text mean anything or nothing according to whim."[61] With the death of the Author comes critical anarchy, as Crews sees it; but Crews, unlike Comley and Scholes, refuses to settle for "outright hero worship of the sort that transforms an Ernest Hemingway or a John Updike from a spiteful, ethically confused, yet often compelling writer into an icon of pure masculinity or matchless sophistication."[62] A happy medium somewhere between idolatry and the study of an author's aesthetic influences and sources is what Crews calls for in a reevaluation of the place of the author in literary study.

The notion of the death of the Author has been a problem for feminist critics as well, and Nancy K. Miller notes the seeming complementarity of feminism and such authorial effacement. In "Changing the Subject: Authorship, Writing and the Reader," she writes, "to the extent that the Author, in this discourse, stands as a kind of shorthand for a whole series of beliefs about the function of the work of art as (paternally authorized) monument in our culture, feminist criticism, in its own negotiations with mainstream hegemonies, should have found a supporting (if not supportive) argument in the language of its claims. It is, after all, the Author, canonized, anthologized, and institutionalized, who excludes the less-known works of women and minority writers from the canon, and who by his authority justifies the exclusion." Indeed, Miller admits that literary feminism has benefited from this poststructuralist approach as it has removed the burden of patriarchal control over the canon or the text. However, she also problematizes this notion of the death of the Author, especially as it comes all-too conveniently with the burgeoning awareness in the patriarchal academy of women's literary production and its role in the canon. After centuries of Author worship, that is to say, the culturally bound worship of males as the primary producers of "valuable" and literary texts, the death of the *female* Author becomes suspect. "The critical potential of such an alliance [between feminist criticism and proponents of the death of the Author], however, has by now proved to be extremely vulnerable. The removal of the Author has not so much made room for a revision of the concept of authorship as it has, through a variety of rhetorical moves, repressed and inhibited discussion of any writing identity in favor of the (new) monolith of anonymous textuality, or 'transcendent anonymity,' in Michel Foucault's phrase."[63] In feminist criticism, then, the author plays a significantly different role, not as monolithic or heroic Author but as a locus of the creation of identity and of the concommitant conflicts and constructions that attend the assertion of that identity. As for Crews, Miller recognizes that what we have come to know as "the death of the Author" is dangerous as an absolutist or universalized principle of critical activity.

Miller concludes in her essay that "the postmodernist decision that the Author is dead, and subjective agency along with him, does not necessarily work for women and prematurely forecloses the question of identity for them."[64] Although she writes of the question of identity as it is foreclosed for women writers, this is an important problem for readers of Lawrence and Hemingway as well; after all, their respective identities as "masculine" writers have been used both to idolize and to upbraid and dismiss their contributions. Thus, although the death of the Author is desirable in a critical endeavor whose goal is to dodge the oedipal narrative to encounter various subjective perspectives in the narrative, those locations of subjectivity which inform readings of the text must be recouped. Paradoxically, one location of subjectivity must be the writer/author himself. Reina Lewis writes of agency and the multiple positions of meaning in the text in *Gendering Orientalism:*

> The liberation of meaning from author to reader offered by Barthes does not have to exclude the social. Whilst the reader as a positionality in relation to, or even formed by, each text may be a neutral space, the agents who occupy it bring with them a subjectivity (there must be a subject of sorts to perform the reading) that is formed in and through its experience of the social—a realm demarcated by differences of race, class and gender. If meaning lies in reading rather than in the text, then any text has a multiplicity of possible meanings that will be produced by each individual reader according to the subjective baggage they bring to the site of reading."[65]

The reader, according to Lewis, supplies much of the social "baggage" that informs readings of the text, whether or not the reader's ideological base acknowledges what she refers to as "the traditional humanist reverence for the author." Of the *authorial* subject that also brings this baggage to the composition of the text, Lewis believes that "It should be reconsidered, not to restore the theme of an originating subject, but to seize its functions, its intervention in discourse, and its system of dependencies."[66] Thus, as my opening metaphor suggests, the critical endeavor of reading must be to consider subjectivity and its accompanying sociocultural baggage from various locations and perspectives, archer, arrow, bow, and target, neither to discard outright any single perspective nor to accept the primacy of a single heroic narrative.

I should note here that there seems to be a desire among some
critical readers of Lawrence to limit the ways and perspectives from
which we may legitimately speak about Lawrence's work. Some proponents of a "right" way of addressing the fiction go so far as to
attempt to silence certain modes and ideological approaches. This
desire seems mainly rooted in disapproval with certain culturally
bound techniques of reading, especially feminist theory, which fail
to erect a Lawrence who may be defined as "valuable" or "desirable."
On critical ideology, Kingsley Widmer in *Defiant Desire: Some Dialectical Legacies of D. H. Lawrence,* asserts of the practice of close
reading as it serves the analytical process, "I am not going to much
demonstrate what used to be called 'close readings' of the selected
texts (really rather remedial work, whether done in symbolistic, psychological, archetypal, or semiotic manner)."[67] Close reading of the
text is dismissed outright, it seems, as below the station of serious
critics, whatever their method. But this is a rather brief and ultimately
minor complaint from Widmer; more surprising examples of foreclo-
sure on the critical process come from readers such as Mark Spilka,
Peter Balbert, and Michael Bell.

In his Introduction to *Renewing the Normative D. H. Lawrence: A
Personal Progress,* "Terrors and Affinities, Deaths and Renewals,"
Spilka dismisses what he identifies as certain undesirable critical
practices. "My contention is, as already indicated, that [Lawrence]
has also been misappropriated and, more recently, diminished and
dismissed; and beyond that, and I think more seriously, he has been
exposed along with other major writers to a wider and possibly dead-
lier context of competing cultural codes."[68] His attempt to "renew"
attitudes and approaches to Lawrence is at least in part, according
to Spilka, because certain readers are taking advantage of the writer
and threaten "his" very well-being. Who has manhandled and misappropriated Lawrence in such a way? We learn three pages later, and
I quote him at length:

> [Lawrence's] normative claims are not simply being opposed, as by femi-
> nist counterclaims: they are being reduced to codes and stereotypes,
> counters in a cultural game in which he is seen chiefly as a destructive
> and damaging player upon innocent sensibilities.
> . . .
> In one sense, then, the wheel has come full circle. What might be called
> the early bourgeois objections to Lawrence's work, based largely upon
> ignorance, prejudice, and fear, have been replaced by current ideological
> demonstrations of his own bourgeois and sexist prejudices, based on
> informed and radically skeptical theories about cultural politics. . . . The
> problem is, at least for me, how to sort out the valid from the invalid

suasions of his work, for with many current semiotic and deconstructive critics, and quite possibly most, there are no longer any valid moral or aesthetic functions for literary "texts." It is here that my own progress from moral formalism through critical pluralism into the engaged confrontations of these collected essays, but above all into my own cultural speculations, seems to me more suited to Lawrence's present needs than other current approaches.[69]

Thus, the culprits—as they so often seem to be for readers such as Spilka—are those who bring their "cultural politics" into the realm of literary study: feminist, gender, and cultural critics, as well as semioticians and deconstructionists. And not only do these ideological approaches misread Lawrence, but they apparently mirror the very bourgeois sensibilities that caused Lawrence's novels to be banned as pornographic to begin with. Thus, critical readers, to extend this argument further, practice a kind of censorship when they engage in analyses of the literary text in ways that are bound up in ideological approaches that fail to understand the moral purpose of his novels and short stories.

In a telling example of biographical criticism in the final line of the above passage, Spilka presumes to know better what "Lawrence" needs—despite the hardly forgettable fact that *Lawrence* has been dead for nearly seventy years, and presumably needs little, if anything, now—than do other disingenuous practitioners of "theories about cultural politics" who are not interested in polishing the biographical idol that has been constructed and that remains the center of Lawrentian readings for some critics. And, later, in his essay, "Lawrence versus Peeperkorn on Abdication," Spilka once again attempts to define an authentic space for critics who are "true Lawrenceans": "According to that critical godfather of *all true Lawrenceans,* Harry Moore, Lawrence's impotence 'dates from that terrible illness in Mexico in 1925, from which Lawrence never recovered'" (italics mine).[70] Not only is this authentic space singularly and unfailingly mapped out by the biographical narrative, to which all of Lawrence's prose and poetry must be causally applied, but the critical godfather of that space must be Lawrence's early biographer, Harry Moore. Although this is an affectionate nod to a fellow and foundational critic, it is a limited critical space, selective in its membership, but Spilka is not alone in employing such an ideological stance.

In his phenomenological approach to Lawrence, Michael Bell is, like Spilka, insistent upon the "normative" claims of Lawrence, complaining of "socialist and feminist readings which have sought to deny the normative claims in Lawrence's vision of English social history and of the sexual relation respectively." Without responding to any critical studies in particular, unlike Peter Balbert who specifically indicates the sources of his critical dismay in his own study, Bell concludes that "even the best of these readings [from socialist and feminist perspectives] suffer, in the context of Lawrence studies, from essentially working out their own concerns on Lawrence without being able to relate their strictures to what it is that makes him positively interesting or important."[71] For his own ideological support, Bell then cites Balbert's sometimes stridently antifeminist study, *D. H. Lawrence and the Phallic Imagination*, without himself citing readings of Lawrence which have failed to portray Lawrence's fiction as "interesting or important." Thus, Bell dismisses outright "even the best of" feminist, cultural, and presumably Marxist readings of Lawrence—without citing any of *these*, either—because these ideological approaches are not *his* ideological approaches (and make no mistake about it, phenomenology is ideologically bound). "Unfortunately," Bell continues, "acquaintance with such thought [as structuralism, poststructuralism and deconstruction] has not so much alerted people to Lawrence's own awareness of language as draw him into their own essentially alien, and misleading, preoccupations. This is not, of course, to say that philosophical parallels are irrelevant to Lawrence. On the contrary, they are very much to the point when they are appropriate."[72] We may conclude, then, that it is Bell and readers who share his ideology who would deem when the more "alien" theoretical approaches to Lawrence are appropriate. And because none are called upon in his text, it would seem as though they are never appropriate.

The problem in dodging the heroic "I" is complex and is not solved in simply eradicating certain subjective positions within the text or without. The death of the Author as a whimsical way for readers to avoid responsibility is certainly not what I advocate as a reader of Lawrence and Hemingway. Writers need not be "discounted as the primary shapers of their works," to borrow Crews's concern; instead, as readers, we must be responsible for moving beyond the Oedipal perspective of the text as hero-centric, biographical artifact and for acknowledging the multiple perspectives that come into play in the shaping of the work of art. Indeed, the writer of *The Rainbow* or of *The Sun Also Rises* remains a vital participant in the critical act of reading beyond the heroic narrative, because the construction of the text takes place in the midst of vital sociocultural influences and aesthetic and representational choices which the writer brings to bear on the worlds of Ursula Brangwen and Brett Ashley. The author becomes mediator between our readerly experience of the narrative and the multiple perspectives of the text, and to limit the text to a singular biographical or theoretical perspective is to restrict the aesthetic and critical possibilities of the text. Instead of "the death of the Author," I propose "the death of the critic-as-heroic I." Once readers are able to move beyond the idolatry of Oedipal constructions of biographically bound narratives in the fiction of Lawrence and Hemingway, we can begin to respond to those antagonistic readers who see only the bombast of self-centered masculine and the degradations of misogyny in their fiction.

Reading the fiction of Lawrence and Hemingway primarily for biographical authority is extremely problematic, then, because it demands that we ascribe to a critical narrative that is monological and definitively Oedipal. Furthermore, this closed way of reading allows us to eradicate our own roles and responsibilities as readers and writers of the text, roles that Malamud's Dubin struggles with in attempting to recoup Lawrence. By focusing on the men named Lawrence or Hemingway and on the events of their lives, or on the conditions of their psyches that led to the creation of works of fiction, I am allowed to ignore my own personal involvement in problems raised by the fiction, including my reactions to the very sociocultural influences and conflicts that are addressed by the text. As a critical reader writing my analyses of *The Rainbow* or *The Sun Also Rises*, I am also writing myself—the writing of the essay (as the reading of the text) is an undeniably autobiographical act grounded in various subjective positions. This is one of the reasons reading (and claiming to value) the fiction of Lawrence and Hemingway is so difficult for me—the writing I do when I read their fiction is often in danger of being informed by the critical and popular definitions of these writers as misogynistic, which also make me guilty by association. Of course, representing myself in my text is never easy, nor are the ways Lawrence represents himself in his texts, as Patricia Waugh illustrates:

> The individual recounting his or her life is a different individual from the one who lived it, in a different world, with a different script. . . . as soon as any of us put ourselves on paper we create fictional characters of ourselves. And as soon as any of us put fictional characters on paper, we write our own autobiographies, the "scripts" of our lives.[73]

As a scriptwriter I am also an autobiographer, writing images of myself and the ways I make meaning when reading Lawrence and Hemingway. However, the Steve Clifford I write is neither preexistent nor prescriptive; the act of reading is a much more active, writerly mode of making meaning, a personal scripting of self in conversation with the text. This is itself an anti-Oedipal way of encountering the text, because the hero is continually obscured, continually changing with new writerly experiences. Imposition of a pseudobiographical authority denies any readerly writing of the text, whether that text is the novel or the reader himself. Bakhtin puts it even more simply and more effectively, if in sexist terms: "In the novel, man is never coincident with himself."[74]

In his foreword to *Women in Love*, an essayistic Lawrence echoes Bakhtin, writing, "This novel pretends only to be a record of the writer's own desires, aspirations, struggles; in a word, a record of the profoundest experiences in the self."[75] This would seem to be a blatantly autobiographical explanation of the novel, a claim made by Lawrence that there is little that is fictional about the novel. The key word here, however, is *pretends;* this novel is pretense, fiction, as is the voice of the foreword. The novel, and Lawrence's "nonfiction" introduction to the novel, fails to resurrect the definitive Lawrence, despite the repeated readerly attempts at locating him as monomythic hero. Ellis, Kinkead-Weekes, and Worthen realize the danger of this attempted recuperation of Lawrence in writing the biography, and acknowledge the fine line between biography and fiction when they explain their approach: "Variety of approach will at least mean variety of style: three different voices to tell Lawrence's story—but at the same time give the lie, by their very difference, to the idea that any single view, however detailed and comprehensive, could ever be 'definitive'; any pattern of interpretation *the* pattern."[76] The three biographers, while working together, have set out to illustrate the different Lawrences that are available, indicating that we need not settle on a biographical hero. Yet many readers of the fiction continue to assume a definitive pattern that underlies the fiction, a versionless version of D. H. Lawrence or Ernest Hemingway which must ultimately deserve our attention.

The readerly admonition in *Fantasia* and Gudrun's denial in *Women in Love*, which I cited earlier, make a significant aesthetic claim which is not merely a version of "art for art's sake" or a revaluation of New Critical isolationism. I do not believe that avoiding reading for the author is an essentially New Critical act, because I don't wish to construct either the text *or* the reader as central hero, the former secreting the truth, available only to the successfully questing reader. Our desire to install such an Oedipal hero who will complete the quest and enact the moral quite often obscures other possibilities for reading and recalls the cry of the speaker of Lawrence's poem, "Noli Me Tangere":

Noli me tangere, touch me not!
O you creatures of mind, don't touch me!
O you with mental fingers, O never put your
    hand on me![77]

Hemingway constructs a similar complaint in his lesser-known poetry. In an untitled poem written in 1926, the year of the publication of *The Sun Also Rises* he writes,

And everything the author knows
He shows and shows and shows and shows
His underclothes
Are more important than the sun.[78]

The sun of the final line may well be a reference to the reception of *The Sun Also Rises,* itself published in 1926 and received by some readers as an "obvious" record of the author's experience in Paris. A later line in the poem reads, "Another author loves his mother,"[79] which Nicholas Gerogiannis assumes in his notes to the poem is a reference to Lawrence's *Sons and Lovers*—which, as Balbert illustrates, is frequently read as a document of Lawrence's relationship with his own mother. Hemingway, like Lawrence, recognizes the problems that arise when the author's underclothes take center stage in his fiction.

As a desire to find an authorial hero at the center of the text and to follow him through an already prescribed Oedipal narrative, the auto-Oedipal is finally an autoerotic act of reading in that it becomes a tendency that allows the reader to produce a predictable and rather limited reaction to the text. In a letter to Bertrand Russell dated 12 February 1915, Lawrence wrote, "The repeating of a known reaction upon myself is sensationalism. . . . The ordinary Englishman of the educated class goes to a woman now to masterbate [*sic*] himself. Because he is not going for discovery or new connection or progression, but only to repeat upon himself a known reaction."[80] Lawrence's metaphor reveals the kind of lack of critical discovery that the autoerotic search for the heroic narrative demands. By turning the masculine arrow away from the hero-centric target, by reorienting ourselves to other locations of desire in the narrative, we may begin to recognize the multiple voices and narrative possibilities in the fiction of Lawrence and Hemingway.

A Note on My Approach

Because I have chosen in this study to address readings of gender and narrative in the fiction of both D. H. Lawrence and Ernest Hemingway, two extraordinarily prolific writers from whom there is ample material for consideration, I have had to make choices that would emphasize some texts at the expense of others. I have, then, decided to focus on novels and short stories that are most often encountered by readers of Lawrence and Hemingway, the "seminal" texts that provide the foundation for many readerly attitudes about these modernists' fiction, and about women and men as they are effectively reflected and/or falsely portrayed, according to readerly temperament and insight.

Also, the texts that I study run along chronologically parallel lines, opening a modernist window which frames the events of World War I, of suffrage, and of the vastly changing social and literary climate in the predominantly English and European locations of the short stories and novels. The time frame of these texts begins in 1915 with Lawrence's publication of *The Rainbow* and continues in the 1920 release of *Women in Love,* considered by many to be his finest novels in technique, in characterization, and in their experimental quality. Hemingway's reputation as a writer of fiction is initiated with his *Three Stories and Ten Poems* (1923), leading to his first short story collection and its multiple revisions, *in our time,* marked by the collection's initial release in 1924 and by its subsequent republications as *In Our Time* in 1925 and 1930. *The Sun Also Rises* (1926) precedes Lawrence's final novel, *Lady Chatterley's Lover* (1928), which is in turn followed shortly afterward by the young American's second novel, *A Farewell to Arms,* in 1929. Although Hemingway never shared the misfortunes of outright censorship that Lawrence's novels, especially his last, were subject to, much of the public reception of his first two novels mirrors that of Lawrence's, including a brief banning in Boston of *A Farewell to Arms.*[81] This chronology is not meant to suggest a kind of literary or ideological complicity between the two writers; rather, the novels and short stories that I have chosen to write about arise from shared sociocultural settings, events, and attitudes which are frequently reflected in the text, just as our own readerly attitudes and experiences manifest sometimes radically divergent readings.

Each chapter focuses on a single narrative or set of narratives, as opposed to developing the chapters along thematic lines, a method that writers such as Carol Siegel and Linda Ruth Williams so successfully demonstrate in their recent readings of Lawrence's fiction. Instead of reading multiple texts along thematic lines in each chapter, I have preferred to consider the ways that the narrative of a single work has been influenced by the construction of gender and the expression of narrative desire within that text and by various critical readers of that text. Of course, many thematic and narrational con-nections are shared between texts like *The Sun Also Rises* and *A Farewell to Arms*, and others reach from one writer to another, as many readers have illustrated through the focus on language and its modern disability in *A Farewell to Arms* and *Lady Chatterley's Lover.* I will endeavor to make these interchapter and intertextual connec-tions between texts and techniques whenever appropriate.

Finally, I have used the Penguin paperback editions of Lawrence's *The Rainbow* (edited by John Worthen, 1989 printing), *Women in Love* (edited by Charles L. Ross, 1989 printing), and *Lady Chatterley's Lover* (edited by Michael Squires, 1994 printing). As for reading Hem-ingway, I have made reference to the standard Charles Scribner's Sons editions of *In Our Time, The Sun Also Rises*, and *A Farewell to Arms*. Bibliographic information on all secondary materials is in-cluded in the endnotes and bibliography.

Part I
Locating Desire in the Narrative:
D. H. Lawrence's Sister Novels

MANNERS AND MODES.
CROSSING THE ROAD–1925.

"Manners and Modes," *Punch,* 1 April 1925.

2

"All women must have a husband": Revising Gender, Marriage, and the Narrative Covenant in D. H. Lawrence's *The Rainbow*

In D. H. Lawrence's short story, "Odour of Chrysanthemums," Elizabeth Bates confronts the dead body of her husband with questions, attempting to define her relationship to the corpse, her own sense of self, her own identity.

> For as she looked at the dead man, her mind, cold and detached, said clearly: "Who am I? What have I been doing? I have been fighting a husband who did not exist. *He* existed all the time. What wrong have I done? What was that I have been living with? There lies the reality, this man."[1]

I am always struck by the quality of Elizabeth's epiphany at this moment. The reality of her life until now has been a deathly, corpse-like existence as mother and wife, with no sense of an identity beyond that of her social roles. She gains the dignity of a proper name only in the second section of the story, when her husband's death is confirmed; in the first segment, Elizabeth is referred to merely as "the mother" or "the woman" or, in the final paragraphs, as "Mrs. Bates." What's more, we are told by the narrator that her mind is "cold and detached"; this sounds like the kind of judgment a prosecuting attorney would use to implicate a suspect in a case of suspicious death for her lack of emotional involvement, and it is supposed to alienate our sympathies for her as she stands beside the grieving mother.

But Elizabeth isn't guilty of any crime, not even of the "crime" of emotional frigidity. Her coldness and detachment are symptomatic not of emotional failure, but of a death that overcomes her as well as her husband. Her seemingly contradictory identification of "a husband who did not exist" and the statement that follows, "*He* existed all the time," suggests her recognition of the deathly power the patriarchal figure of the husband has had over her—she isn't mourning the man who died, because she had no real relationship with this "separate stranger with whom she had been living as one flesh" (300). "*He*" is not the individual man—Walter Bates—but the corpse, the body of the *husband*, her "Master" as Mrs. Rigley refers to him (291). This problem of mastery and domination is clear in the fact that she sees this relationship as a battle: "I have been fighting a husband who did not exist" and in her question, "What wrong have I done?" Elizabeth is hardly the victor, despite her husband's death, but she isn't the perpetrator of some wrongdoing or failure either. Instead, she must transcend this notion of her life as a dualistic battle if she is to really live at all. The individual man, the man who was supposed to be her husband in a truly "passional" marriage, to borrow one of Lawrence's own terms, never existed behind the overpowering facade of the social role he took on as master, and the individual woman that she begins to recognize in her moment of epiphany has been suppressed in the role she was conscripted to play as wife in the traditional, linear social narrative of marriage, an oppositional role she may now move beyond. Her cold, detached state mirrors the state of the dead husband, and because she is no longer "wife," she may now begin to live without the "fear and shame" of death that comes with wifely subjugation (302). She has found a way to escape this linear social narrative—marriage—and may begin to recognize other possibilities for herself.

This seems to me one of the most important moments in Lawrence's fiction, because it dramatically represents the individual's need to evaluate and define, or perhaps reevaluate and redefine, the construction of personal identity. For all of Lawrence's preaching for a "passional" relationship which destroys individual ego and which unites woman and man in a transcendent new identity, he frequently provides moments of breakthrough for his individualized men and women. Michael Bell notes, in *D. H. Lawrence: Language and Being,* that like Blake, "Lawrence similarly distinguished self-interested ego from individual identity understood as a form of belonging or relatedness."[2] This definition of an individual self is often mistakenly identified as a failure in the individual by critical readers who take Lawrence's cue and argue for the primacy of a relationship that transcends self and ego. And although transcendence of self in a committed relationship is indeed crucial in Lawrence's fiction, the possibility of such growth, which moves the *individual* beyond the limitations of social custom and tradition, is manifest only as the individual comes to significant awareness of her own identity. Elizabeth can recognize her conscription to a fixed social narrative, the divisive mastery of "husband" and the submission of "wife," only when the center of that narrative breaks down. Carol Siegel notes in *Lawrence among the Women,* "As a provider of domestic service, or even as a lady who is responsible for overseeing the running of the home, woman in capitalist society cannot renounce subjectivity because she has not been granted it within any of the structural systems that determine her cultural meaning."[3] Thus, women such as Elizabeth must find a way to discover subjectivity, even as the larger modernist project, according to Siegel—and even as Lawrence's philosophy of a transcendent union—seems to renounce subjectivity. Elizabeth is no longer obstacle to the familial hero, in dualistic opposition against him, but is herself center and subject of her own narrative of identity. And she is finally not mother or wife or Mrs. Bates, but Elizabeth (and is even referred to with the endearing nickname "'Lizabeth" from Walter's mother as they prepare the body for burial [301]).

"Odour of Chrysanthemums" offers the kind of destruction of the masculine or heroic quest narrative which is evident in Lawrence's most successful fiction. The central heroes of this body of fiction are individuals who evince the desire and ability to move beyond narrative conscription—whether to a social/cultural narrative or to a temporal/historical structure of causality in the textual narrative. Like "Odour of Chrysanthemums," Lawrence's *The Rainbow* is a novel which radically revises masculine quest narratives on both the textual and the sociocultural levels. In this novel and its "sister" novel, *Women in Love,* Lawrence's "central heroes" are not central at all in the sense of a narrative that posits a hero at the center of the "deep structure" of a text, a Prince Charming who must rescue Sleeping Beauty. Instead, they are in the process of decentering themselves in an attempt to be freed from the kinds of narrative conscription implicit in a formalistic reading of a narrative "deep structure," which is precisely the construct Elizabeth Bates questions upon the death of the familial hero in "Odour of Chrysanthemums."

Unfortunately, many critical readers haven't acknowledged this kind of reevaluation of the ways individual identity is constructed in Lawrence's fiction, and some have rather reductively categorized his fiction as merely phallocentric and misogynist. Although I will agree that there is a great deal of "masculinism" to deal with in the fiction, I don't believe that it adds up to a rather masculine revel for Lawrence, or an assertion of male dominance and feminine worship of the phallus. In her 1975 essay, "Love and Power: A Reconsideration of Sexual Politics in D. H. Lawrence," Lydia Blanchard complains of the problem she faced in reading Lawrence's fiction. "Those of us who admire the fiction of D. H. Lawrence, and particularly those of us who are women, are faced with continuing difficulty in our attempts to separate his work from his reputation."[4] I often find myself sharing this sense of discomfort over Lawrence's reputation for overbearing masculinity, but I'm not sure that this reputation is always a shortcoming of *Lawrence's fiction* so much as it is a condition of our own unfamiliarity with and surprise at the people and relationships he writes about. I like the confusion and discomfort Middleton Murray exhibited when he wrote of Lawrence's fiction: "Somewhere in ourselves we were set against the experiences he wanted us to partake . . . there were realms of experiences, which Lawrence knew, which I had not entered. Even now I cannot pretend that the fearful struggle between Anna Lensky and Will Brangwen in *The Rainbow* is a thing I understand."[5] In a more recent reading of the novel, David Holbrook echoes Middleton Murry's sense of estrangement from the couples in the novel when he writes, "We find ourselves bewildered by long episodes in which characters battle one another, unable to find solutions."[6] These are honest and accurate readerly reactions to Lawrence, and they betray a bewilderment that caused such reviewers as James Douglas to write of *The Rainbow,* simply, "These people are not human beings. They are creatures who are immeasurably lower than the lowest animal in the Zoo" (*Star,* 22 October 1915). After all, it is much easier to consider this the work of a depraved man than to presume you have any connection with his characters or situations in the "real" world, for then the matter becomes personal and demands an evaluation not only of the fiction but of the reader's perspective, as well.

In bringing pressure to bear on the fiction of D. H. Lawrence, I want to consider the problem of masculinity in Lawrence's sister narratives, *The Rainbow* and *Women in Love.* They are sister narratives in the sense that both novels attempt a radical revision of linear heroic narratives on the textual and sociocultural levels; Lawrence's "central heroes" are rarely central at all, but are decentering themselves in an attempt to be freed from the kinds of narrative conscription we see Elizabeth Bates questioning in "Odour of Chrysanthemums." Lawrence is often accused of misogyny in his theories of phallicism, of being too interested in various aspects of masculine domination of the feminine. However, I find the more that I read these novels, the more I find constructs of masculinity that have been set up as straw men, and if we are paying close attention, these constructs tend to deconstruct, and finally to break down, often rather ridiculously. As readers who see the merely sexual and the frequent *attempts* at domination by male characters, we are often mislead into constructing critical narratives of masculinity ourselves, and placing them into the texts as fixed ideological positions to either extol or disparage.

This is an easy trap to fall into in reading Lawrence's fiction, as Middleton Murray admitted. His *Son of Woman* relegates Lawrence's work to the merely phallocentric, and it is perhaps easier for him to read *Women in Love* as misogynistic and degrading when Middleton Murray makes his mind up about the novel. In *Son of Woman*, he identifies Lawrence's "hidden desire" in writing the novel: "To make [the insatiable female] subject again, to re-establish his own manhood—this is the secret purpose of *Women in Love*. . . . He creates a sexual mystery beyond the phallic, wherein he is the lord; and he makes the woman acknowledge the existence of this ultra-phallic realm, and his own lordship in it."[7] Such claims against Lawrence's assertion of masculine power and singularly phallocentric vision are widespread; perhaps the most well-known (and most often cited as ideologically narrow) example is Kate Millett's early feminist study of his work in *Sexual Politics*. And, in opposition to antagonistic readings by Millett, Carolyn Heilbrun, and Hilary Simpson, among others, critics such as Norman Mailer and Peter Balbert have both promoted and defended the masculine phallocentric—or at least the "phallic imagination," which Balbert differentiates as the "metaphor, participant, and metaphysical center of the novel [which] suggests Lawrence's renewing and existential view of love and sex."[8] And although I think Balbert makes an important point when he claims that "phallic preoccupations in Lawrence's fiction do not suggest that he is anti-woman,"[9] he neglects to fully recognize the attempts in the fiction to eradicate phallocentric centers of power—whether those centers are represented by males or females in the fiction— and to replace them with an emphasis on individual desire. Finally, Lawrence himself doesn't make a counterapproach to this reading of his fiction easy, considering the theories of phallicism proposed in *Fantasia of the Unconscious*, as in later novels such as *The Plumed Serpent* and *Lady Chatterley's Lover*, that have had an unfortunate tendency to inform the ways contemporary readers and critics approach the Lawrence canon as a whole.

Although there is certainly evidence to be found that can undeniably prove that his fiction is at times phallocentric and gender biased, it has seemed to me as I read Lawrence, even while reading the problematic fiction and essays, that this notion of his overbearing masculinity and phallicism has sometimes been overstated, even by the essayistic Lawrence himself. What the two novels originally conceived as *The Sisters* do so well together is to illustrate the desire to move beyond simplistic, fixed definitions of individuality based on gender roles and narrative positions (hero vs. Other), and to offer that "mapping of differences" de Lauretis recognizes in the anti-Oedipal narrative. In this chapter, I will explore the ways that *The Rainbow* constructs a historical and linear narrative through the marriages of Tom and Lydia, and Anna and Will Brangwen. This is the narrative that Ursula Brangwen struggles against and finally successfully rejects so that she may assert her own narrative desire, redefining "marriage" as a social construct that would limit her possibilities. Hilary Simpson writes, in *D. H. Lawrence and Feminism, "The Rainbow* is unique among Lawrence's major fictions in its presentation of the historical process—a process which stretches by way of an essentially matrilineal descent from the first Brangwen woman who turns to 'the spoken world beyond,' through to Ursula's complex, isolated and essentially modern struggle for self-definition."[10] Rather than accept an oppositional role in the heroic narrative that marriage represents in the lives of her ancestral models, Ursula moves closer to an understanding of the passional commitment necessary in a truly balanced relationship, a relationship she knows she cannot find with her fiancé, Anton Skrebensky. But discovery of a more ideal and transcendent relationship is not possible in Lawrence's pair of novels until Ursula, like Elizabeth Bates, redefines herself and her own desires as separate from the gender codes and socially conscribed roles assigned to her in the Oedipal narrative.

Desire and Gender: Ancestral and Cultural Voices

From the earliest moments in *The Rainbow,* Lawrence is interested in considering women's desire and the social codes and customs that tend to block that desire. In part I of chapter I, the narrator tells us that "the women were different" at Marsh Farm.[11] Men at the farm—abstractions of men, because Lawrence does not begin to develop character until part II of chapter I—seem satisfied and confident in the directions of their lives: "It was enough for the men, that the earth heaved and opened its furrow to them, that the wind blew to dry the wet wheat, and set the young ears of corn wheeling freshly round about; it was enough that they helped the cow in labour, or ferreted the rats from under the barn, or broke the back of a rabbit with a sharp knock of the hand" (42–43). Lawrence even offers, amid the service of the earth and nature in this passage, a sexual complicity on the part of the earth, which "heaved and opened its furrow to them," a passage that echoes a description only a page earlier, in which men feel "the pulse and body of the soil, that opened to their furrow for the grain" (42). Although the earth opens its furrow in the later passage in an agrarian metaphor for availability in female sexuality, the designatation "*their* furrow" earlier indicates men's full possession of themselves and of the feminine earth. Indeed, men's lives on the farm are replete with allusions to sexuality and domination, as the narrator tells us, "They knew the intercourse between heaven and earth . . . They mounted their horses, and held life between the grip of their knees, they harnessed their horses at the wagon, and, with hand on the bridle-rings, drew the heaving of the horses after their will" (42).[12] Men's control and insight is paramount in these descriptions, and we can recognize early images of *Women in Love*'s Gerald Crich in the domination of the horses after the will of man. And the complicitous earth itself desires these men, clinging "to their feet with a weight that pulled like desire" (42).

But women at the farm are another matter, and Lawrence's narrator balances the paragraph on what men *have* with a passage of equal length, if greater emphasis, on what women want:

> But the woman wanted another form of life than this, something that was not blood-intimacy. Her house faced out from the farm-buildings and fields, looked out to the road and the village with church and Hall and the world beyond. She stood to see the far-off world of cities and governments and the active scope of man, the magic land to her, where secrets were made known and desires fulfilled. She faced outwards to where men moved dominant and creative, having turned their back on the pulsing heat of creation, and with this behind them, were set out to discover what was beyond, to enlarge their own scope and range and freedom; whereas the Brangwen men faced inwards to the teeming life of creation, which poured unresolved into their veins. (43)

Interestingly, Lawrence's abstractions in setting up the lives of men and women move from a pluralistic "men" to the singularity of "woman," a figure who looks out upon what she desires but who has no recourse to fulfill these desires. Only after woman has been made singular does the narrator turn to "man in the world at large" (43), a singular figure who is positioned in a greater landscape, reflecting his greater opportunity for movement and control. Michael Bell claims that this introduction is not an abstract commentary on the social conditions of men and women in general but that it serves to introduce us very specifically to unique situation of the Brangwen family. He quite effectively explains the affect of the historical progress of the novel, writing, "As we know, Lawrence's vision of origins in *The Rainbow* was precisely such a backward projection from the present in that it was the last part to be written of a story which, in its successive revisions, had extended steadily into the past. To explain the experience of his modern heroine he had to extend back through her family, and through a larger social history, to a metaphysical vision."[13] However, when Bell turns from the historical movement of the novel as a whole, a movement embodied by the development of three generations of the Brangwen family, to the less specific introductory section of chapter I, he abandons the import of that "larger social history" to argue for the specificity of this passage in its reference to the Brangwens in particular. Arguing for the "polar nature of Lawrence's thought," Bell concludes, "So, for example, when the narrative records the lives of the early Brangwens as divided into a male absorption in the life of the farm and a female aspiration to a larger world, we recognize that this is not a general definition of men and women, nor even a gendered prediction of the behaviour of the book's major characters. It is the premonitory and ancestral manifestation of a fundamental structure within the Brangwen psyche at large; an energising polarity to be variously expressed in the lives of all the individuals."[14] Bell is correct in arguing that the novel *presents* these men and women as Brangwens; this much is evident in the early paragraphs of the chapter. However, the narrative very consciously shifts from references to the Brangwens and to the specifically referential pronoun "they" and moves toward a portrayal of the psyches of men and women in the abstract. Perhaps these men and women *are* specific to the vaguely mythic and pastoral ancestors of the Brangwen family, from their traditional roles to the more modern questioning of the propriety of those roles; but they are also abstract references to men and women of England, caught up in the greater social constructs that determine the very different realms of movement and opportunities available to men and to women. Reading these men and women only as Brangwens too easily avoids the broader problem of gender identity, rejecting what we know of the difference between the divided realms of masculinity and femininity to claim that this is only true of the polarity of the Brangwen psyche.

Moreover, this movement from the plural "men" to the singular abstraction of woman is an important narrative shift for Lawrence, because the novel will ultimately direct us toward Ursula, the singular, modern woman who will reject the propriety of her ancestral models and of social expectation and who will find a way to "enlarge [her] own scope and range and freedom" (43). Ursula's ability to see this way is clearly undeveloped as yet, because the early narrative focuses on woman's desire to see *as men see,* that is, in a heroic or Oedipal narrative. "[S]he strained her eyes to see what man had done in fighting outwards to knowledge, she strained to hear how he uttered himself in his conquest, her deepest desire hung on the battle that she heard, far off, being waged on the edge of the un-known. She also wanted to know, and to be of the fighting host" (43). Linda Ruth Williams' definition of "Lawrence's modern woman" positions her as a clear descendant of these ancestral and mythic women who seek the vision and knowledge that men possess. In her fascinating 1993 study, *Sex in the Head: Visions of Femininity and Film in D. H. Lawrence,* Williams writes, "Lawrence's modern woman is the epistemophile *par excellence;* she has cathected all of her sexual desire onto the drive to know. Her will to know has possessed and perverted her 'natural' desires, and so she takes more into her conscious system than is good for her. When sex comes into the head, it is matched with an attitude to knowledge and thought which is passionate and (for Lawrence, perversely) sexualised. Sex in the head is twinned with the *desire* to know."[15] Lawrence marks the origins of this modern desire to know with women's earlier unsat-isfied desires which were unavailable because of the social bound-aries in this pastoral setting. Notice in the Lawrence passage, however, the dependence on the Oedipal language of battle and conquest that is relied upon in this desire; men's conquest must also be women's desire for conquest, it is assumed by the narrator, because woman struggles to *see* the outer worlds of men beyond the house. In a sense, woman desires to see through men's eyes, according to this representation of her desire. This oppositional atti-tude, evident in the language of the masculine quest—fighting, con-quest, battle—will provide the greatest of difficulties for Tom and Lydia, who manage, almost accidentally, to supercede the Oedipal opposition of hero and defeated, although Will and Anna will be unable to move beyond these oppositional dynamics. Only Ursula becomes conscious of the problems of the heroic narrative, and her success, and the novel's, comes in her ability to find an alternate narrative that rejects mere confrontation for a kind of transcendence beyond antagonistic conflict. Ursula is the woman who comes to knowledge *without* having to ascribe herself to becoming "of the fighting host," and in doing so, she must also, to play with the title of this study, learn to *see* differently, "beyond the heroic eye" of masculine conflict to other narrative possibilities.

As Ursula and Skrebensky walk back to Yew Cottage from the Marsh in the chapter of *The Rainbow* entitled "First Love," the narra-tive becomes a time machine of sorts, folding back upon itself to suggest a closed and endlessly repeating cycle of events, regressing as well as progressing:

> Hesitating, they continued to walk on, quivering like shadows under the ash-trees of the hill, where her grandfather had walked with his daffodils to make his proposal, and where her mother had gone with her young husband, walking close upon him as Ursula was now walking upon Skrebensky. (345)

As this passage reflects, Lawrence has constructed a rather traditional historical narrative in *The Rainbow,* a narrative that is almost epic in its portrayal of several generations of the Brangwen family. As an aspect of the historical narrative, Ursula's future seems determined by the events of her ancestral past and by the expectations constructed for her as a young woman in an early twentieth-century English middle class family. She, too, is aware, if only vaguely at first, of a sense of entrapment, of a definition of her place that she has no control over. "Ursula was aware of the dark limbs of the trees stretching overhead, clothed with leaves, and of fine ash-leaves tressing the summer night" (345). The ash trees close her in where she stands, keeping her from moving beyond this deterministic path that will undoubtedly end in her marriage to Skrebensky.

Of course, Ursula doesn't marry Skrebensky, and her ability to avoid this seemingly inevitable outcome, especially in a narrative that would demand that she continue the Brangwen story in a traditional manner, is indicative of her desire to break free of a narrative that would conscribe her to a certain outcome. As Teresa de Lauretis claims in her essay, "Desire in Narrative," "All narrative, in its movement forward toward resolution and backward to an initial moment, a paradise lost, is overlaid with what has been called an Oedipal logic—the inner necessity or drive of the drama—its 'sense of ending' inseparable from the memory of loss and the recapturing of time" (*Alice Doesn't*, 125). The Oedipal logic of a masculine quest narrative would commit Ursula to a coherent and monological narrative, demanding that her story mirror those of her ancestors in an endlessly repeating fashion, much like the metaphoric walk she takes with Skrebensky under the ash trees. Indeed, in her essay, "Feminist Fictions and Feminist Theories of Narrative," Margaret Homans explains the gendered nature of narratives that function both on textual and social levels:

> In recent years there has been an unusual consensus, among feminist critics who consider themselves to be doing narrative theory, about the problems posed by conventional sequential narrative for representing

women. Starting from psychoanalytic and/or structuralist premises, virtually all these critics take it as axiomatic that the structure of narrative
itself is gendered and that narrative structure is cognate with social
structure.[16]

But Ursula refuses to be the mere prize at the end of Skrebensky's
heroic quest or to submit to the expectations of a controlling, deterministic narrative—whether a textual narrative or a narrative of social
structure—whose patterns may be traced far back as the biblical
book of Genesis and the Judeo/Christian creation myth. At least implicitly, *The Rainbow* promises narrative progression through a
repetitious linear history, tracing three generations of Brangwen marriages and affirming a covenant of sorts with the reader, a covenant
not unlike that of the biblical story of God's symbolic covenant with
Noah reflected in the novel's title. That readerly covenant is the promise that the narrative will develop along certain guidelines which
reflect either the successful completion of a heroic quest narrative—
typically ending in marriage—or in failure, the wounded hero unable
to complete his quest.

However, Ursula Brangwen is hardly a Fisher King in *The Rainbow,*
and as she successfully subverts this narrative covenant, she manages to deconstruct the traditional heroic quest narrative Lawrence
has carefully constructed in the earlier chapters of the novel. In this
way, Ursula almost metafictively calls attention to the novel as a
formalistic structure within which she refuses to submit to the
"proper" historical climax, whether in the social narrative of marriage
or in the textual climax of the novel itself. By examining her relationship with her suitor, Anton Skrebensky, as it follows the two earlier
marriages in the novel—those of her grandparents, Tom and Lydia
Brangwen, and of her parents, Will and Anna Brangwen—we see
the ways in which a mythic, deterministic narrative—the singularly
definable deep structure of the masculine narrative, the monomythic
quest—may be subverted by Ursula's desire to reinvent her own
narrative. She does this only by discovering what she refers to as
"the earth's new architecture" (548), a discovery that is not unlike
Elizabeth Bates's epiphanic recognition of her own identity and desire. This discovery is only possible once the heroic center of the
masculine narrative has been displaced, and as this happens, Ursula's new architecture becomes a metaphor for the reinvention of
a narrative that refuses to place value on a singularly heroic center.
This metaphor is especially significant for Lawrence who, in drafting
the larger epic novel he hoped would become *The Sisters,* must
himself discover ways of responding to narrative tradition in *The*

Rainbow before he may begin to compose the more fragmentary and experimental narrative of his following novel, *Women in Love.*

The masculine or Oedipal narrative sets Ursula up as both hero and obstacle to the narrative progress; for Ursula to fulfill her "quest," she must accept her role with Skrebensky as it reflects that of her earlier models of femininity, her mother and grandmother. de Lauretis recognizes differentiated gender roles for male or female heroes in the phallocentric narrative as she compares the very different options available for the hero of the narrative, according to his/her gender: "The end of the girl's journey, if successful, will bring her to the place where the boy will find her, such as Sleeping Beauty, awaiting him, Prince Charming. For the boy has been promised, by the social contract he has entered into at his Oedipal phase, that he will find woman waiting at the end of *his* journey" (*Alice Doesn't,* 133). Indeed, only a few lines prior to the narrative description of Ursula's place in history, her role is assigned by the narrator: "Still she waited, in her swoon and her drifting, waited, such as the Sleeping Beauty in the story" (345).[17] In this sense, there are elements of the fable in Ursula's narrative, elements that may look forward to the fabular qualities of *Lady Chatterley's Lover* which many critical readers have identified. If we were tracing the Sleeping Beauty figure in *The Rainbow*, we might turn to Hilary Simpson's analysis of "The Dreaming Woman" in Lawrence's fiction, a figure who shares a dual, if conflicting, heritage: the modern, self-possessed New Woman and the spiritual and earthy Pre-Raphaelite woman, whom Simpson sees most clearly in *Sons and Lovers*'s Miriam.[18] However, Ursula is neither Sleeping Beauty nor the Pre-Raphaelite ideal in *The Rainbow*, and if this novel is in any way fabular, the moral of the story must illustrate the ways in which Ursula makes a break with the Oedipal quest narrative, that is, with the fabular qualities of the Sleeping Beauty narrative to which she is conscripted by gender and by the historical precedents set by her family and her culture.

By the end of the novel, Ursula has no desire to participate in the romance of a Sleeping Beauty fable by marrying Skrebensky. Her defiance and unwillingness to adhere to this tradition contrasts sharply with the desire many characters of the novel—mostly, but not exclusively, male characters—have for retaining this narrative tradition, for continuing in their own Oedipal quests and fulfilling their heroic goals. *The Rainbow* is a novel about marriage—not a surprising claim, considering an earlier draft was titled *The Wedding Ring*[19]—but it is *not* a marriage novel, at least not in the traditional sense, because it is not a novel merely interested in affirming the social tradition upon which marriage rests. Marriage is a condition of domination and conquest in the novel, and the antagonistic destruction of the self in the marriages—Tom and Lydia's, as it begins, Will and Anna's, Winifred and young Tom's, and in the potential marriage Skrebensky courts from Ursula—is quite unlike the positive annihilation of self Ursula and Birkin experience in the following novel. Ursula is the catalyst for the destruction of this narrow concept of marriage as a masculine narrative in *The Rainbow,* a destruction that continues through her in *Women in Love.* Ursula's desire to "break out of it, like a nut from its shell which is an unreality" (545) becomes a break with both the finality of the monologic and phallocentric epic narrative of marriage and with the social narratives that equally demand her to play her part well as the Sleeping Beauty. *Women in Love* is an impossible novel for Lawrence to write—and perhaps an equally impossible novel for us to read—without the context of Ursula's break from these narratives provided in *The Rainbow.*

In his examination of the novel, Peter Balbert claims in *D. H. Lawrence and the Phallic Imagination* that the affirmation of the condition of marriage is itself Lawrence's central theme in the first of these sister novels. He aptly notes that the institution of marriage works "as a theme that Lawrence uses as a form of visionary ligature to integrate the pattern of repetition and to provide the doctrinal insistence so important to him."[20] I like Balbert's description of the novelistic pattern as a "visionary ligature," because the movement through several relationships, all grounded in one way or another in traditional and formal notions of marriage, binds the narrative together; without the affect of the earlier marriages, the later marriages and near-marriages carry less thematic import. However, the thematic focus on marriage does not support the traditional or formal notions of marriage as a social construct; indeed, marriage is itself a faulty institution which Ursula—and we readers—must come to revise through our understanding of the earlier marriages in the novel. Of marriage in the novel, Balbert writes,

> . . . it is Lawrence's emerging faith in marriage, and not feminism, that is the driving force in his composition of *The Rainbow.*
>
> *The Rainbow* is a testament to the conservative impulse in Lawrence that is at the heart of his most apocalyptic doctrines; it reflects a sensibility inclined towards traditional forms of worship, stability, and passion, even though he wishes to transmute and invigorate the forms.

Although this need not be an explicitly feminist novel—despite Lawrence's claims that he would do more for women than suffrage in writing it—I don't quite understand how Balbert can make this claim for Lawrence's conservatism and traditionalism, given the gradual destruction of this conservative impulse throughout the novel, and in the revision of "marriage" to mean something quite different for Birkin and Ursula in *Women in Love*. That conservative impulse is best reflected in part I of chapter I, in the clearly delineated boundaries and experiences to which men and women are conscripted in marriage, and Lawrence's modern woman must find a way to reject this impulse in favor of a state of marriage which will allow for the transcendence of both woman and man to a balance that is beyond individual ego but that allows for individual identity and desire. Balbert continues his argument by indicating that marriage in *The Rainbow* is based on the social and legal tradition binding two people together. "Indeed, [Lawrence's] radical notions of the vital relations between men and women in *The Rainbow* are framed by an affirmation in each Brangwen generation of the legal state that sanctions a marriage."[21] I think Lawrence moves considerably far beyond the *legal* bond of marriage, especially in the later novel, getting there by illustrating the consequences and failures of socially sanctioned institutions, such as marriage, which base themselves on the masculine narrative opposition of hero and obstacle, victory and defeat. In "The Marriage of Opposites in *The Rainbow*," Mark Kinkead-Weekes illustrates the ways that readers attempt to understand the conflicted marital relationships in the novel and of the very real difficulties in achieving a marriage of true minds which become evident in Lawrence's novel. "By learning the 'basic' language of the marriage of opposites, one tries to understand Tom and Lydia, and Anna and Will, and to find ways of grasping the nature of their relationships in *essence*. One has also to understand their *personal histories,* as relationships change and settle, through the passage of time. By then bringing to bear the sweep of *social history* into an increasingly complex definition of personality, one sees how what Lawrence meant by marriage becomes both richer in potential, and more difficult to achieve."[22] Indeed, only one couple of the novel, Tom and Lydia, achieves the rich potential of marriage in this sense, and they discover it by accident, wholly removed from the mere social and legal contract that they know as their formal "marriage."

Rainbows, Marriages, and Narrative Covenants

This Lawrencean revision of the institution of marriage against conservative definitions becomes clearest when we consider the four appearances of rainbows in the novel. None of these points in the text can really be called climactic in the narrative sense of closure or resolution, including the final apparition that concludes the novel. They do, however, offer places in the narrative in which there are moments of revelation, allowing the participants the kinds of epiphanic insight evident in Elizabeth Bates's self-examination in "Odour of Chrysanthemums." In addition, the appearance of the rainbow suggests the possibility for a covenant that transcends the merely formal arrangement of marriage in society, and the meaning of that metaphysical covenant reflects significant moments of transcendence, but not necessarily completion, in the relationships and identities of those who experience it. The first manifestation of the rainbow occurs two years after Tom Brangwen and Lydia Lensky are married, as they finally come together in a spiritual consummation that has had little to do with their marital agreement at all. Tom's inability to enter the "closed circle" of her previous history, represented by the ring she wears from a previous marriage (74), keeps him from being able to form any sense of communion with her. Later, her desire confuses him. "He could not get definitely into touch with her. . . . He suffered very much from the thought of actual marriage, the intimacy and nakedness of marriage. . . . They were so foreign to each other, they were such strangers" (93). Their relationship finally becomes a dual of sorts, a test of wills in which the two are supremely divided:

> Brangwen could not understand. . . . It was too much for him. And there she sat, telling the tales to the open space, not to him, arrogating a curious superiority to him, a distance between them, something strange and foreign and outside his life, talking, rattling, without rhyme or reason, laughing when he was shocked or astounded, condemning nothing, confounding his mind and making the whole world a chaos, without order or stability of any kind. (98)

Lydia may as well be speaking in her native Polish as she talks to Tom. There is no communication here, and more importantly, no communion between Tom and Lydia, despite the legal contract between them. In fact, it is evident that Lydia is merely following tradition; she explains to an angry Anna, who doesn't want Tom in her mother's bed: "But I must have a husband, darling. All women must have a husband" (104). This clearly isn't an expression of her desire, but of the "Oedipal logic" that instructs her position in the social narrative.

On Tom and Lydia's marriage and their attempted communion, John Worthen writes in *D. H. Lawrence and the Idea of the Novel*,

"Fulfilment is not even a matter of being at one with the wheeling universe, but of allowing the impersonal self to be 'small and submissive to the greater ordering.'"[23] Tom learns this only after years of marriage to Lydia, but this is not to say that Tom and Lydia remain unchanged in their formal marriage; indeed, Tom is greatly affected by Lydia, so much so on the evening of his proposal that he begins to wonder whether he can survive the union of marriage to a woman who is so foreign to him. "Such intimacy of embrace, and such utter foreignness of contact! He could not bear to be near her, and know the utter foreignness between them, know how entirely they were strangers to each other" (84). Peter Balbert recognizes her impact on Tom here, looking forward to the transcendent union they accomplish only after the delivery of their child. "The enveloping cosmos presents no merely symbolic correspondence to Tom's unpredictable relations with Lydia and not any pantheistic celebration of inscrutable natural energy. It becomes a felt and *participatory* reflection of what Tom has achieved with his fiancée; in effect, his vitalistic perception of the unknown in her will lead him to his fundamental appreciation of the energy beyond her."[24] Balbert reads this moment as an achievement, rather than as a first step toward a much later communion between Tom and Lydia. That energy that Lydia is in closer proximity to, in Balbert's argument, is what Tom requires from her, despite what he perceives as her foreign nature. Balbert claims through Lawrencean essentialism that women are closer to the transcendent as a result of the "mystery" of their wombs. Citing Lawrence's essay, "The Crown," he writes, "Put simply, Lawrence envisages women as a step closer to the unknown than men, because 'the womb is full of darkness and also flooded with the strange white light of eternity.' Although the lack of a uterus puts the male at an unbridgeable distance behind the female in proximity to the transcendent, his need to perceive that unknown is as urgent as the female's." This unbridgeable distance may well be what Tom feels in defining his separation from Lydia. The problem with this Lawrencean approach, however, is in the utilitarianism of the desire men have for women; because men lack access to the transcendent beyond, lacking as they do what Balbert calls "the stabilizing biology of a womb, that ingrown potential for linking with eternity,"[25] men must turn to women as a mere stage or landscape in their own heroic and Oedipal quests, and thus fail to reach that smallness and submissiveness that Worthen indicates is necessary for fulfillment. Of course, such an approach also demands that these men, recognizing women and their wombs as mere stages, disregard the individual desires that the women in their lives feel, desires that are quite often very different from their own.

If Tom shares this essentialist definition of women that Lawrence proposes and that Balbert seeks to legitimize, then it is no wonder that he cannot find a place of communion with Lydia, even after he has had "access" to her womb, impregnating her. Their separation is perhaps most complete during Lydia's night of labor, when despite Tom's unifying rationale ("Elsewhere, fundamental, he was with his wife in labour, the child was being brought forth out of their one flesh" [111]), Tom remains as distant from communion with Lydia as she does from him. We know of Tom's thoughts during her pregnancy and preceding her labor: "She suffered, but he was out of doors, full in life, and it would be ridiculous, indecent, to pull a long face and to insist on being miserable" (110). Similarly, Lydia cannot find Tom in her solitary experience: "He stood there fair-bearded and alien, looking at her. She knew something of him, of his eyes. But she could not grasp him" (112). Communion and fulfillment have not been available through intercourse and childbirth, apparently, and neither has the conventional state of marriage provided the transcendence of their foreignness to each other.

It is only when Lydia confronts Tom about his brother Alfred's own desire to keep a mistress that they begin to communicate, unexpectedly echoing each other's complaints much to their astonishment:

> "You come to me as if it was for nothing, as if I was nothing there. When Paul came to me, I *was* something to him—a woman, I was. To you I am nothing—it is like cattle—or nothing—"
> "You make me feel as if *I* was nothing," he said.
> They were silent. (131)

This is the moment when Tom and Lydia begin to create a new relationship, a "perpetual wonder of the transfiguration" (133). It *is* a transfiguration for Tom and Lydia, and a significant communion; but it has nothing to do with the social state of marriage the two entered into two years ago. Indeed, we are told that "Their coming together now, after two years of married life, was much more wonderful to them than it had been before. It was the entry into another circle of existence, it was the baptism to another life, it was the complete confirmation" (133). Communion between the two is an accident of the social tradition of marriage, an accident that is possible only when both abandon the conflict that marriage has demanded in its social roles—husband and wife, master and servant. Only then can they realize the other's position and reject the Oedipal narrative of the victor that the tradition of marriage demands. "She waited for him to meet her, not to bow before her and serve her. She wanted his active participation, not his submission" (132). There is no need for the domination and submission that Lydia's explanation to Anna suggests. The new balance clarifies things for Tom: "He did not understand her foreign nature, half German, half Polish, nor her foreign speech. But he knew her, he knew her meaning, without understanding" (133). It is no accident that the rainbow appears as a covenant *beyond* their social agreement; as a covenant, the rainbow is only possible during that meeting of the two individuals in a balance of wills.

But this is a very private, personal change in Tom and Lydia that allows them to communicate for the first time in their married lives. As in the abstract gender roles of the novel's introduction, Tom and Lydia continue to play their public roles and to remain separate in the realm of men or the realm of women. Privately, however, they have moved beyond such barriers into a mutual self-possesion beyond mere ego, and certainly beyond the formalities of the social contract of marriage. "And always the light of the transfiguration burned on in their hearts. He went his way, as before, she went her way, to the rest of the world there seemed no change. But to the two of them, there was the perpetual wonder of the transfiguration" (133). Tom and Lydia's accident of marriage, although revolutionary, remains private and unavailable in their public lives. In contrast, Anna and Will's later marriage will be played out in a much more public realm, but will lack the transfiguration that their predecessors experience, and Ursula's goal in the latter half of the novel will be to find a way to combine the private transcendence of gender and ego and the public expression of these new identities.

Tom and Lydia's transfiguration becomes less possible in the relationship between the adult Anna and Will Brangwen. The second manifestation of the rainbow is seen only by Anna, shortly after the birth of Ursula and her victory over Will. There is no union between the couple in this revelation, as there was for Tom and Lydia, but a division between the two. It seems Anna has learned from her mother's explanation of a woman's duty—that she must have a husband—but she remains adamantly unwilling to submit herself to him. At first, Anna attempts to reject that social narrative conscription of marriage. Confronting Tom and Lydia in bed, she asks:

"*Why* do you sleep with *my* mother? My mother sleeps with me," her voice quivering.

"You come as well, an' sleep with both of us," he coaxed.
"Mother!" she cried, turning, appealing against him.
"But I must have a husband, darling. All women must have a husband."
"And you like to have a father with your mother, don't you?" said Brangwen.
Anna glowered at him. She seemed to cogitate.
"No," she cried fiercely at length, "no, I don't *want.*" (104)

Anna's denial here foreshadows Ursula's desire to avoid the seemingly inevitable conclusion Skrebensky offers later in the novel. But Anna's desire is modified by Will's courtship and by the expectations placed on her to take a husband, despite Tom's fears of losing her. "To whom did she belong, if not to himself?" (157). Anna's development into a self-possessed and powerful woman begins on the night when Tom brings her into the barn and away from her mother, who is in labor. Worthen writes that "The little girl, totally immersed in her grief and loneliness, is shocked and stimulated into the birth of another awareness. . . . Tom brings her (and us with her) to such an awareness of impersonal life going its own way, that it counters her self-absorption."[26] Indeed, what Tom does is revolutionary, considering the separation of gendered lives and realms in the introductory pages of the novel; he introduces her to the realm of men as the narrator in part I describes it, beyond the house and the limitations of women's lives. Tilly objects to Tom's bringing Anna out of the house, and can only exclaim "God-a-mercy!" (117) in her surprise at Tom's success in calming the child. For Anna, "A new being was created in her for the new conditions" (115). She finds peace in the barn, despite her occasional sobs, and falls asleep in Tom's arms. Michael Bell notes of this scene, "Held in Tom's arm the child is in felt connection, through him, with an impersonal life. The effect of this, as with [*Sons and Lovers*'s] Mrs. Morel, is the recovery of her individual, personal poise."[27] This new being, her awakening, and her changing identity is the thematic focus of much of the next two chapters, "Childhood of Anna Lensky" and "Girlhood of Anna Brangwen" (although the latter chapter proves much more important in Anna's development). As Worthen claims that Tom's action "counters her self-absorption," it provides the child with a vital sense of self-possession that will dictate her later relationship with her cousin, and soon-to-be husband, Will.

Will and Anna enter into the social and legal contract of marriage, the second ancestral model of the sacrament in the novel, but Anna remains unwilling to be the submissive wife. Both begin to realize their relationship as a contest of wills, as a dualistic conflict in which there must be a victor. Anna knows this as the relationship develops:

> . . . as time went on, she began to realise more and more that he did not alter, that he was something dark, alien to herself. She had thought him just the bright reflex of herself. As the weeks and months went by she realised that he was a dark opposite to her, that they were opposites, not complements. (210)

Will also recognizes the conflict he is entering into, but this seems to be the essential conflict which marital union demands. As husband, he believes that he is conscripted to play a certain role:

> He knew himself what a fool he was, and was flayed by the knowledge. Yet he went on trying to steer the ship of their dual life. He asserted his position as the captain of the ship. And captain and ship bored her. (214)

Neither sees the kind of transcendent union Tom and Lydia experience as a likely possibility in their marriage, and both assume aggressive positions against the other as the only means of survival in a relationship that threatens potential defeat for each. If the social contract of marriage is necessarily a victor/defeated dichotomy for them, then both act on their desires to be victorious, to eliminate the obstacles to their singular success. This causes each to see the other not as partner, as equal in balance with the other, but as something threatening and hazardous. Anna is horrified by his overbearing will: "Sometimes, when he seemed like the darkness covering and smothering her, she revolted almost in horror, and struck at him. . . . Because she dreaded him and held him in horror, he became wicked, he wanted to destroy. And then the fight between them was cruel" (211). Will's reaction to Anna is similar. She, too, is horrible as an obstacle in his contest: "In his moments of intensest suffering, she seemed to him inconceivable, a *monster,* the principle of cruelty" (229; italics mine). Will's inability to move through Anna, who remains an obstacle to him, threatens to destroy him, and she becomes monstrous to him, inhuman in her willfulness. In "Desire in the Narrative," de Lauretis notes the role of these monstrous obstacles in the heroic narrative. "Medusa and the Sphinx, like the other ancient monsters, have survived inscribed in hero narratives, in someone else's story, not their own; so they are figures or markers of positions—places and topoi—through which the hero and his story move to their destination and to accomplish meaning" (*Alice Doesn't,* 109). Anna refuses to become merely a marker in Will's heroic narrative;

she is herself hero, and she is determined to be victorious in their contest of wills.

After kissing Anna for the first time during their courtship, Will feels this threat Anna offers him as obstacle.

> To his wonder, he had stopped her at the gate as they came home from Ilkeston one night, and had kissed her, blocking her way and kissing her whilst he felt as if some blow were struck at him in the dark. . . .
>
> And the youth went home with the stars in heaven whirling fiercely about the blackness of his head, and his heart fierce, insistent, but fierce as if he felt something baulking him. He wanted to smash through something. (153)

While he kisses her, "blocking her way," she responds by blocking his way, "baulking him." Will recognizes a need to break Anna, to make her submit to him, just as she strikes back. But it is Anna who is "victrix" in this contest of wills, and it is only when Will has been removed as an obstacle that she can begin to sense fulfillment in her role as wife and mother according to her desires. When he leaves, she finds relief in her role as heroic questor: "Everything delighted her, now he was gone, the insulator, the obstruction removed, the world all hers, in connection with her" (209). This is *her* quest, and Anna refuses to submit to Will as hero/patriarch/master. Of course, this also keeps them from any kind of real communion in marriage; while Anna experiences her own vision of the rainbow, it is not a covenant that eradicates their strangeness to each other in the way that it is for Tom and Lydia. Instead, she becomes "a door and a threshold, she herself" (238), a promise in her new childbearing.

Anna's desire both for self-possession and for heroic victory over Will is expressed in her solitary, naked dancing which begins in Will's absence. Celebratory dance, usually performed in a state of undress, is recalled throughout Lawrence's novels, from Anna's dance before the fire, to Gudrun's dance before the cattle at the water's edge, to Connie Chatterley's dancing in the rain. Balbert dismisses Anna's desire as he assigns vindictive and destructive meaning to Anna's dance, reading it as an attack and sympathizing instead with Will. "When Anna understandably becomes alienated by Will's obvious resentment of this 'fulfilment' in her, she punishes him by means of her naked dance." He later refers to it as her "annihilating dance,"[28] which it is only when Will intrudes on her privacy, causing her to flinch and to quickly fasten up her hair, a movement that serves to partially mask, at least symbolically, her previous state. The problem with this critical assertion of Anna's desire to punish

Will is that it ignores her own desire and her motivation to dance, supplanting it with sympathy for the wounded husband. Balbert is correct when he writes that "Will senses that her pre-emptive dance signifies his ritual murder,"[29] but Will's recognition of this dance as murderous and the desire that motivates Anna to dance are not the same. Notice how similar Will's reactions are on seeing her dance to those which Tom felt toward Lydia: "The strangeness, the power of her in her dancing consumed him, he was burned, he could not grasp, he could not understand" (225). Anna is foreign to Will, in much the way that Lydia was removed from Tom; between Will and Anna, however, their relationship manifests itself as a contest for victory, which only one of them may win in an Oedipal narrative. So if Anna's dance is threatening to him, the threat is located in this oppositional dynamic, not in Anna's desire to dance. Note that we are told that "she had to dance in exultation *beyond* him" (225; italics mine); this is Anna's attempt at a kind of transcendence beyond their conflict and in shameless pride of her own beauty. While she is "dancing his non-existence" once Will comes into the room, she is also "dancing herself to the Lord, to exultation" (225). Although Will does feel punished and defeated as he stands before Anna, this is none of Anna's doing; her desires are quite different and apart from those of her husband, and it is this difference and the resultant lack of a shared and empathic vision that is the cause of much of the conflict between them. Consider the dialogue that they engage in on Will's intrusion. Will asks,

> "What are you doing that for?"
> "Go away," she said. "Let me dance by myself."
> "That isn't dancing," he said harshly. "What do you want to do that for?"
> "I don't do it for you," she said. "You go away." (226)

Balbert's claim that Anna is vindictive and that she is *punishing* Will clearly doesn't attend to her express desire; the dance is not about him, at least not directly. In fact, it is Will who punishes Anna, his questions suggesting impropriety and his continued presence finally causing her to dress and to end her celebratory dance. Anna's cry clearly indicates that it is Will who has violated her, not the other way around: "I can do as I like in my bedroom. . . . Why do you interfere with me?" (226)

Although Anna seems in many instances to have been victorious in her ability to keep from submitting to Will as husband—see, for instance, her simple utterance on delivery of Ursula: "Anna Victrix" (234)—she is still described in the terms of the Oedipal narrative, as feminine landscape for some heroic movement to pass through. In this case, the hero is not Will—he must find his victory else-where—but it is the temporal and linear narrative itself, the promise that the narrative will progress in a certain, prescriptive way. "Through her another soul was coming, to stand on her as on the threshold, looking out, shading its eyes for the direction to take" (238).

Anna's character becomes extremely complex in this marital strug-gle. Her character appears to be a proto-feminist of a sort, a wife determined to refuse the social role forced on her, to deny the kind of marriage Elizabeth Bates is trapped in prior to her husband's death. But Anna fails to move beyond the Oedipal narrative, beyond the terms of the heroic struggle in the social agreement, to realize possibilities other than those of conflicting wills. Indeed, in the midst of labor, we are told that "She knew she was winning, winning, she was always winning, with each onset of pain she was nearer to victory" (233). Susan Winnett recognizes the problem of women's participation in the Oedipal narrative in her essay, "Coming Un-strung: Women, Men, Narrative, and Principles of Pleasure," in which she writes,

> In the erotics of oedipal transmission, the woman is always a stage (in both senses of the word) for or in the working out of a problem of paternal interdiction, toward the moment of "significant discharge" when the son frees himself from the nets of paternal restriction and forces a self-creation—however ironized this process may be.[30]

Thus, although Anna seems to become feminine hero, significantly revising the sociocultural definition of the role of the wife in her aggressive assertion of her own primacy in the relationship, she remains trapped in the masculine narrative as an obstacle, the land-scape or stage from which the heroic narrative will progress in the terms of the Oedipal logic and will continue to influence the lives of her descendants, particularly Ursula's. In the "Study of Thomas Hardy," Lawrence complains of the direction early forms of feminism took, and he might be read by some as rather chauvinistic and threat-ened by this desire for independence when he writes, "The woman-suffragists, who are certainly the bravest, and, in the old sense, most heroic party amongst us, even they are content to fight the old battles on the old ground, to fight an old system of self-preservation to obtain a more advanced system of preservation." But Lawrence is complaining less about women's independence and more about their entry into the traditional social systems that he knows are faulty.

Note, too, that Lawrence realizes the antagonistic role of the con-quering hero, the old battle of self-preservation that demands sub-mission from the other. He continues, "Law can only modify the conditions, for better or worse, of that which already exists."[31] This is so because that which already exists under the governance and control of men is already a hopeless failure for Lawrence, and his hope for women's new social roles is a hope for revolution and a break from that "old system," not merely for new players in the same game. Thus, there exists the failure of the state of marriage as we see it between Anna and Will, and as it would be between Skrebensky and Ursula. As long as "the old battle" persists, there can be none of the communion Tom and Lydia accidentally discover when each realizes the other's perspective because the institution has remained the same; only the gender roles in marriage have been exchanged, which is no progress at all for Lawrence. Instead of hero, Anna becomes a stage through which the heroic narrative continues to dominate the idea of marriage.

De Lauretis writes, "The ancient monsters had a sex, as did the gods, in a mythology whose painstakingly rich articulation of sexual difference was to be boiled down to the stark Platonic opposition man/non-man" (*Alice Doesn't*, 109). This is the articulation Tom and Lydia begin their marriage with and that Anna and Will cannot es-cape. But as Anna becomes a monstrous figure—both because she becomes "man" in this paradigm, refusing to submit to the husband, and because Will cannot either defeat or move through her—he must turn to other "non-man" figures to assert his own masculinity. His desire to create a woman in his image is evident in the doll-like Eve he carves in the Genesis wood carving, a figure Anna jeers at, and in his desire for the carvings he finds in a Nottingham shop in a book on Bamberg Cathedral.

> He lingered over the lovely statues of women. A marvellous, finely-wrought universe crystallised out around him as he looked again, at the crowns, the twining hair, the woman-faces. He liked all the better the unintelligible text of the German. He preferred things he could not under-stand with the mind. He loved the undiscovered and the undis-coverable. (205)

These statues are images of the ideal woman for Will. There is no need to understand them—especially because their texts are in a language foreign to him. Because he cannot read the German, a situation much like Tom's early inability to understand Lydia, he can create the "texts" of these women. More importantly, "these were wooden statues, 'Holz'—he believed that meant wood. Wooden statues so shapen to his soul! He was a million times gladdened" (205–6). It is fitting that Will is a wood carver and that these wooden statues are so appealing. They are precisely the kind of women he wants to create, to dominate—and precisely the kind of wife Anna refuses to become.

Will's heroic salvation comes as he does "smash through something" (153), even if it cannot be Anna. He takes his desire for victory elsewhere; because he cannot dominate Anna, he finds a surrogate in the young working-class girl at the Nottingham music hall. And as he leads her away from her girlfriend to a secluded park, with the excitement of his potential fulfillment at hand, there is a critical shift in the tone and presentation of Will's narrative. He considers her by his side, thinking, "She fitted in there very well. It was a real good fit, to walk with her like this" (272). This pair of sentences doesn't sound like Lawrence's usually descriptive prose at all—a "real good fit" is hardly the kind of description the narrator offers elsewhere. Of Lawrence's prose, Worthen writes, "It is one of the great ironies of people's reaction to him that his language has so often been assumed to be careless, repetitive and banal . . . when, in the case of *The Rainbow* at least, it is innovative, experimental and deliberate."[32] Throughout this seduction scene, the style and language of the narrative becomes surprisingly reminiscent of the "tough" and "masculine" prose style Hemingway will become known for. Consider, for instance, the narrative description of Will and Jennie's rest in a secluded area of a park:

> He led her into the Park, where it was almost dark. He noticed a corner between two walls, under a great overhanging bush of ivy.
> "Let us stand here a minute," he said.
> He put down the umbrella and followed her into the corner, retreating out of the rain. He needed no eyes to see. All he wanted was to know through touch. She was like a piece of palpable darkness. He found her in the darkness, put his arms round her and his hands on her. She was silent and inscrutable. But he did not want to know anything about her, he only wanted to discover her. And through her clothing, what absolute beauty he touched. (272–73)

As he plans and engages his domination of Jenny, Will's narrative becomes full of simple, staccato sentences and clauses, not at all the descriptive Lawrencean prose, the complex sentences, the metaphoric passages we are used to. Instead, we are simply told "He liked her—he liked the feel of her—he wanted to know her more closely. . . . He liked best his new self" (273). This simple narrative style, the repetition of "he liked" as the subject and verb of three simple sentences, places Jennie as the initial object of Will's masculine desire.[33] But that object of desire and admiration is finally the image of himself as victorious, not of Jennie as sex-object at all. This narrative shift evinces the very masculine tension Will feels at the ensuing domination of Jennie, and at the promise of his climax and victory. There is no room here for the narrator to expound on a metaphoric description of the dark nook, for instance, or on a process as rhythmic and complex as Will and Anna's bringing the sheaves together so they might lay in the dark. In that instance of a sexual union which draws on their early conflict, we find quite a different description of their activity. "Gradually a low, deep-sounding will in him vibrated to her, tried to set her in accord, tried to bring her gradually to him, to a meeting, till they should be together, till they should meet as the sheaves that swished together" (161). But the location, the activity of the inner self in the narration of Will's affair with Jennie is unimportant, at least to the narrator—this is merely a corner between two walls, with a bush of ivy, with no vibrating wills, no swishing of sheaves, no accord. What is important is the heroic progress and climax through this location, that is, Will's victory in their dual. *Who* she is is unimportant—Will realizes later that "he did not know her name" (276). But, had Will been at all interested in knowing who she was, he would have learned it as we do in the narrative—as the two girlfriends part, the second, Gertie, confirms their plans by calling out, "All right, Jennie" (271). But Will doesn't take notice of this. Instead, she is referred to merely as "his girl" throughout the section, and we have the narrative admission that "About the girl herself, who or what she was, he cared nothing, he was quite unaware that she was anybody. She was just the sensual object of his attention" (272). Here, Scholes's masculine sexual metaphor for the narrative applies; Will is solely concerned with a singular climax, with the rhythmic interplay of the simple sentences.

Will is significantly affected by this seemingly simple rendezvous. Anna seems to realize what has happened to him, remembering her mother and Tom discussing his father's—Alfred's—affair (277). But she is not concerned with this possibility; instead, the likelihood that Will has had an affair comes as a kind of relief for her, because it has allowed Will to find victory as well, without her need to submit to him. Interestingly, their sexuality becomes quite violent and "shameful," as Will momentarily sees it (280), following his affair and separate victory. Balbert reads their sexual intercourse following Will's affair as "a sensual duel of discovery,"[34] but there is no discovery here; Will and Anna each come together to separately enact their own heroic fantasies and to affirm for themselves their own superiority. Indeed, the narrative tells us of their contact now, "This was what their love had become, a sensuality violent and extreme as death. They had no conscious intimacy, no tenderness of love. It was all the lust and the infinite, maddening intoxication of the senses, a passion of death" (280). And in this self-centered passion which separates each from the other, even as they encounter each other sexually, the narrative even offers Will's rape fantasy as he engages in sexual intercourse with Anna following his affair: "She waited for his touch as if he were a marauder who had come in, infinitely unknown and desirable to her. . . . He was another man, revelling over her" (278). This passage is told from Will's perspective, delineating his discoveries as he encounters her as a "perfect stranger" (278), not unlike Jennie. Will's transformation allows him now to displace Anna with a fantasy of her desire for another man, for a marauder who will violently take her—and to whom she will gladly submit. David Holbrook concludes, in *Where D. H. Lawrence Was Wrong about Woman*, "What Will is shown to 'learn' from his adventure is an abandonment of the 'moral position' so he can give himself up not only to lustful impulses, but hostile forms of sexuality from which all the elements of mutual respect are dissociated."[35] Thus, the strangeness that Tom and Lydia seek to overcome remains as the central defining characteristic of Will and Anna's relationship, allowing them both to be identified as victorious heroes on separate, if parallel, Oedipal quests.

This victory of Will's marks a significant transition for him. Now that he, too, is victorious in his Oedipal narrative, he becomes a "new man"; "it set another man in him free" (281). And, now the victorious man, he can become involved in the greater social narrative as well, taking on the boys of Cossethay to teach them wood carving. It is important to note here as well that, only now, after fathering four girls, does Anna give birth to a son. It is surely no accident that the child is his namesake, referred to as Billy; like Anna, Will is also ready to become threshold to the temporal movement of the narrative as masculine, heroic presence. He becomes the Christ-like teacher of young boys, taking on twelve of them—his disciples—and ending his once close relationship with Ursula.

It is too easy to accuse either Will Brangwen (or Lawrence) of misogyny, although there is certainly a significant presence of loathing, of the desire to destroy the feminine Other here. Although Anna's desire for self-preservation and will to victory certainly do revise the predominant identity of wife and mother in the family, she and Will are both trapped in an Oedipal narrative that demands their antagonism. This is a revision that only changes the players in the battle rather than the terms of the narrative itself, and as such, there is no "mapping of differences" in their relationship. In many ways, they are perhaps the most fully divided and separate of any couple in *The Rainbow,* and they become a prototype for the relationship between Gerald Crich and Gudrun Brangwen in *Women in Love,* as well as an example of the state of marriage Ursula and Birkin will reject.

It is Ursula who experiences the third and fourth manifestations of the rainbow as she becomes the promise of the masculine narrative's progress. Ursula and Anton begin their courtship in much the way Tom and Lydia and Anna and Will began, believing in the hierarchy previously constructed by the Oedipal logic of the societal roles. Ursula is the temptress according to this paradigm, challenging his masculinity, sending him "mad, mad with desire, with pain, whose only issue was through possession of her body" (348). For the still-young Ursula, this is the role she is *supposed* to play, according to the tradition of romantic love. "It was a magnificent self-assertion on the part of both of them, he asserted himself before her, he felt himself infinitely male and infinitely irresistible, she asserted herself before him, she knew herself infinitely desirable, and hence infinitely strong" (348). Notice there is nothing said about *her* desire, or whether she finds him equally desirable; she falls quickly into the role of object of desire with no reciprocal expression of her own desires. Although Ursula has realized her failure to measure up to the romantic ideals she holds from reading Tennyson's "Idylls of the King" and other romantic love stories, despairing that "she *must* have fair hair and a white skin" (310), she continues to find the measure of herself and her romantic responsibilities in Anton's ideal.

> Nevertheless, it was begun now, this passion, and must go on, the passion of Ursula to know her own maximum self, limited and so defined against him. She could limit and define herself against him, the male, she could be her maximum self, female, oh female, triumphant for one moment in exquisite assertion against the male, in supreme contradistinction to the male. (349)

This passage certainly does seem to support Millett's complaint about *Women in Love,* that Lawrence's fiction "presents us with the new man arrived in time to give Ursula her comeuppance and demote her back to wifely subjection."[36] This Ursula is still under the influence of the Oedipal narrative, in which she accepts her role as goal for the conquering hero: "The Sons of God who took to wife the daughters of men, these were such as should take her to wife"

(321). Until now, she has been taught to believe in this sort of wifely subjection as the hope of her identity in the Oedipal narratives proposed for love and marriage. But Ursula does not remain fixed on the romantic narrative of wifely subjection, and thus Millett's analysis is shortsighted; Ursula's development and her concommittant rebellion against these socially sanctioned romantic ideals begin quite early in her relationship with Anton.

The first sign of Ursula's desire to break from this narrative in which she must identify herself only through Skrebensky is in her initial identification with the moon, a symbol that remains important for her throughout *The Rainbow* and *Women in Love*. She has no desire to battle against him, as Anna fights Will, even though her dance, like Anna's, becomes a dance of liberation; instead, Ursula feels him "like a loadstone weighed on her, the weight of his presence detained her. She felt the burden of him" (365). But there is another presence in the distance, and Ursula realizes the rising of the full moon, beginning to identify herself with it. "Oh for the coolness and entire liberty and brightness of the moon. Oh for the cold liberty to be herself, to do entirely as she liked" (365). Although it is Skrebensky who points it out to her, this "cold liberty" is reminiscent of the condition we find Elizabeth Bates in—"cold and detached" from the dead man (300), just as Ursula would find herself removed from his inert form. The moon, in Ursula's revision of it as a signifier, becomes an image of her desire for separation, no longer a symbol of romantic union. Margaret Homans writes, "changing traditional narrative, or finding alternatives to it, can have emancipatory effects for women,"[37] and although Homans speaks more directly to the woman writer who manipulates the traditional narrative, this liberation is certainly true for Ursula's social narrative, as well.

Skrebensky has no wish to free her from his desire, however. Like *Women in Love*'s Birkin in the chapter entitled "Moony," he sees Ursula's moon as a watery creature; however, unlike Birkin, this is a creature that Skrebensky wishes to capture.

> But he must weave himself round her, enclose her, enclose her in a net of shadow, of darkness, so she would be like a bright creature gleaming in a net of shadows, caught. Then he would have her, he would enjoy her. How he would enjoy her, when she was caught. (366–67)

Anton wants to trap the moon in what may be a fisherman's net, especially considering the watery metaphors describing the evening, the "strange, ecstatic, rippling on the surface of the dance, but underneath only one great flood heaving slowly backwards to the verge of oblivion" (364). This metaphor of the fishing net may connect Anton to Birkin's contemplation of the moon in the water, but their desires are quite different. Skrebensky is interested in domination here, in securing the prize that awaits him at the conclusion of his heroic narrative, a prize that leads him to marriage. In the later novel, Birkin wants to destroy the image of desire that would cause him to *want* to entrap her watery image in such a net to begin with.

The consummation of their relationship offers no real connection between Skrebensky and Ursula; instead, she discovers the true nature of the Oedipal narrative in which she is merely prize or landscape. His worship of her moony image is manifest in his very self-conscious prayer, beseeching her, "Let me come—let me come" (368). Having been captured, Ursula becomes the climactic resolution of Skrebensky's masculine narrative, the landscape in which his conflict takes place, the monstrous obstacle who is "fierce, corrosive, seething with his destruction" (368), and the prize at its conclusion. Once he has reached this climax, there is only an emptiness remaining. "But there was no core to him: as a distinct male he had no core" (369). The core of his identity is in his physical/sexual desire—the climactic tumescence and detumescence of the masculine narrative that Scholes refers to in *Fabulation and Metafiction*—which has been abated, thanks to Ursula. He has been destroyed by her, and although triumph is supposedly hers, it seems a rather empty victory. With the "dead" Skrebensky beside her, she awakens, asking herself the kinds of questions Elizabeth Bates puts to herself:

> She was overcome with slow horror. Where was she? What was this nothingness she felt? The nothingness was Skrebensky. Was he really there?—who was he? He was silent, he was not there. What had happened? Had she been mad: what horrible thing had possessed her? (368)

That horrible thing was Skrebensky himself and her conscription to the subservience of love and marriage as a romantic ideal. She attempts to affirm these ideals as she asks him, "Isn't it lovely?" (369). But she receives no communication from Anton, no reciprocal sign of love; there is apparently no need for any communion beyond *his* heroic/sexual consummation and climax.

There is, as a result, no communion or consummation for Ursula in the mass celebrated on the following morning. She repeats her question, "Wasn't it lovely?" (371) and receives the same deathly silence from him. As Ursula reads the initial appearance of the rainbow in the Genesis morality tale, in which man and woman are rewarded for following a paternalistic contract with the deity, she begins to reject the notion of this prescribed historicity, of her assigned role in the arc of the rainbow, just as she begins to reject the paternalistic law set down in Genesis, including the image of the masculine deity himself. There is no covenant for her in the biblical command to go forth and multiply. "Ursula was not moved by the history this morning. Multiplying and replenishing the earth bored her" (371). It is important that the *history itself* fails to move her, because this originary tale is a direct antecedent to the linear and historical narrative constructed in *The Rainbow.*

In *Fantasia of the Unconscious,* Lawrence provides a moment of metafictional commentary on his essayistic storytelling: "In the beginning—there never was any beginning, but let it pass. We've got to make a start somehow."[38] This is the kind of realization Ursula is coming to following her "romantic" evening. For Skrebensky, the linearity of history remains of primary significance. As a "brick in the whole social fabric, the nation, the modern humanity" (374), Skrebensky "represented the great, established, extant Idea of life, and as this he was important and beyond question" (375). Of course, that great, established, extant idea has its construction in the Oedipal narrative which extols his role as conquering hero and which positions him in the realm of men, as part I of chapter I indicates. However, Ursula has no desire to be so established, to conform to the masculine narrative dictates of her religion (she even wishes herself a pagan nymph, to jeer at Noah [372]) or of her culture, and she begins to explore ways out through her relationship with Winifred Inger and her position as a schoolteacher.

The lesbian relationship with Winifred Inger seems at first to offer an alternative to the demands of the Oedipal narrative for Ursula. However, I have always been disturbed by Winifred's sudden decision to marry Ursula's Uncle Tom Brangwen; it seemed as though Lawrence backed too easily out of a socially unacceptable situation, attempting to somehow recoup Winifred. Winifred and Ursula's relationship certainly seems to go well at first, and it seems to suggest a legitimate way out of the heroic narrative that is represented, for Ursula, in Skrebensky. Winifred's commentary on men and marriage is important in this respect: "Love is a dead idea to them. They don't come to one and love one, they come to an idea, and they say 'You are my idea,' so they embrace themselves" (390). We certainly see this in Will's desire for the statues in Bamburg Cathedral and in his adulterous, if short-lived, affair with Jennie, and we see it in Skrebensky's desire to capture Ursula, to make her Mrs. Skrebensky. "They are all impotent, they can't *take* a woman. They come to their own idea every time and take that" (390). This is a wonderfully suggestive pair of sentences. Although Winifred's explanation might sound to some like a desire for the kind of rape fantasy Will engages earlier—the violent desire to be physically taken—Winifred understands that men cannot accommodate the idea of a woman as a separate individual with her own desires and perspectives. When they do "take" a woman, as in those earlier fantasies, they take the image of their own desire, and never the woman herself.

However, the problem in this relationship between Ursula and Winifred is not located in its lesbian orientation, but in its hierarchical nature; Winifred remains teacher to Ursula's student. There isn't any real chance for equal footing between the two, at least in part because of Ursula's romantic images of her teacher prior to their weekend away. At one point in the chapter entitled "Shame," Lawrence's narrator is himself caught up in the conservative social values still as he writes, "The fine, unquenchable flame of the younger girl would consent no more to mingle with the *perverted* life of the elder woman" (391; italics mine). But the perversion the narrator speaks of here is not simply Winifred's lesbian orientation or, as Peter Balbert would have it, her perverse attitudes toward sex. In the initial tea and conversation between Ursula and Winifred, "The talk was led, by a kind of spell, to love. Miss Inger was telling Ursula of a friend, how she had died in childbirth, and what she had suffered; then she told of a prostitute, and of some of her experiences with men" (386). Paired with Winifred's later assertions about men's attitudes toward women, which I cited above, the topic of discussion is cautionary; Miss Inger is introducing her young charge to the conflict between women's desire, on the one hand, and trouble that women can get into when men are willing only to act on their own sexual needs. While Hilary Simpson also understands the scene as related to the older teacher's angry discourse against men, writing, "Winifred also initiates Ursula into a different aspect of her female heritage from that of the uninterrupted domesticity and childbearing of her mother," Balbert accuses Simpson of attempting to obscure the perversion of the older woman. "Simpson appears not to realize that Winifred's preoccupations with suffering, dirty sex, and death in childbirth tell more about Winifred's relation to love and sexuality than about normative realities of passion and nurturing affections."[39] Of course, Winifred *is* instructing Ursula in the "normative realities" of sex, realities that Balbert chooses himself to ignore: masculine desire and its less desirable consequences, including prostitution and the danger of childbirth, and Balbert is too quick to assume the narrator's attitude of disapprobation in judging the teacher's motives.

The real problem in the relationship between the two women is located in Winifred's position of power, in her willful demands on Ursula to let her teach the young girl, to train her to become something quite other than herself. Ursula rejects this impulse, and rejects Miss Inger as she does so. In *Modern Heroism,* Roger Sale writes, "But having effectively shown Ursula how mechanized the world of men is, Miss Inger has no alternative but to try to be manlike, dominant, willful."[40] I do think that the teacher has other alternatives, or at least she believes she does in her relationship with Ursula. However, her desire to teach, to train her student blindly places her into a position not unlike Skrebensky's; instead of the loadstone weighing Ursula down, she becomes a "heavy cleaving of moist clay" (391), threatening to dominate Ursula in much the way a male lover would.

If Winifred is to marry, according to Ursula's desire, Tom Brangwen is surely the man for Winifred Inger. Although he, too, is caught up in the social machine, Tom doesn't seem to fit the masculine expectations of the social narrative. The first description of Tom Brangwen Jr. is one of an effeminized male:

> Tom was a rather short, good-looking youth, with crisp black hair and long black eyelashes and soft, dark, possessed eyes. . . . He gave place entirely to the other person, and at the same time kept himself independent. He scarcely existed except through other people. . . .
>
> He had a subtle, quick, critical intelligence, a mind that was like a scale or balance. There was something of a woman in all this. (283)

Not only does Tom appear womanly, but he performs the role of the feminine object in the hero narrative extremely well, giving way and scarcely existing. Earlier in "Shame," Ursula has despaired over this identification of herself: "She gave something to other people, but she was never herself, because she *had* no self" (382). But Tom's character suggests the desirability of submission, especially in his relationship with his brother Fred as "an almost passionate love. Tom watched over Fred with a woman's poignant attention and selfless care" (284). And this description continues as the adult Tom Brangwen is described as "handsome, with his womanish colouring and dark eyes and black close-cut moustache" (354).

If Winifred is going to marry a man and be in closer accord with the social machinery, it would seem that a "feminine" man such as Uncle Tom would be the perfect choice. And yet these descriptions of Tom as a womanly male are belied when we see him walking down the drive to meet Ursula and Winifred, looking "manly, handsome, curiously like any other man of action" (394). It seems a disguise is required when he is engaged in the social fabric; he is not identified as a man of action, but as *curiously like* one. Of course, Winifred must manufacture a similar disguise as "a rather beautiful woman of twenty-eight, a fearless-seeming, clean type of modern girl whose very independence betrays her sorrow" (383). It is important that Wiggiston, the place Winifred and Uncle Tom will live, has "no centre, no artery, no organic formation" (393). The social machine, while still in place in the marriage between Tom and Winifred, has shifted slightly; gender roles have been manipulated, and the artifice of the Oedipal narrative becomes painfully clear to Ursula as she attempts to define her role as an individual.

Ursula clearly recognizes the entrapment she faces should she accept the roles of wife and mother in the social construct of the Oedipal narrative: "Always the shining doorway ahead; and then, on approach, always the shining doorway was a gate into another ugly yard, dirty and active and dead. Always the crest of the hill gleaming ahead under heaven; and then, from the top of the hill only another sordid valley full of amorphous, squalid activity" (487). Her identification of the Oedipal narrative is less idyllic than Gerald's passage through the Alps at the conclusion of *Women in Love,* but is still similar to his aspirations: "Having gained one ridge, he saw the vague shadow of something higher in front. Always higher, always higher" (*Women in Love,* 574). Of course, for both Ursula in the conclusion of *The Rainbow* and for Gerald in *Women in Love,* the pursuit of this quest must result in death. It surely means the death of her individual identity, as she begins to realize it. "Already it was a history. In every phase she was so different. Yet she was always Ursula Brangwen. But what did it mean, Ursula Brangwen?" (487). For Skrebensky, it means that she must assume her role beside him in the social fabric. This is especially evident as he sabotages her attempts at studying for the B.A. examinations. "Secretly he hoped she would fail, so that she would be more glad of him" (511). And when Ursula does indeed fail to pass her exams, Skrebensky comforts her by eliminating her identity as an individual: "All you know, you know, and if you are Mrs. Skrebensky, the B.A. is meaningless" (526).

The Oedipal narrative proves to be an extremely difficult construct to make a break with, as Ursula discovers, and clinging to the romantic ideal is often easier in her reunion with Skrebensky than answering that question, "What did it mean, Ursula Brangwen?" We see this reversion to romantic love on his return: "Thus a tissue of romance was round them. She believed she was a young wife of a titled husband on the eve of departure for India. This, the social fact, was a delicious make-believe" (505). Not only does Ursula seem to resign herself to marriage, knowing the falsity of her relationship to him, but in doing so she is in danger of committing herself to the project of Empire that Anton represents, yet another version of the Oedipal narrative. That tissue of romance begs an unanswered question, Should Ursula indeed marry Anton and join him in India? Could Ursula successfully play the role of Memsahib? This is another social role she seems destined to play should she accept Anton, and it is a role that she is unable to free herself from the romantic ideal the masculine narrative offers, however false, until she acts on her own desire to visit Rouen.

The threat of her transformation comes to Skrebensky when he realizes that "she followed after something that was not him" (507)— that Ursula might act on her own desire. The final evening, spent once again in the moonlight, once again threatens to destroy him, but this time it is no Oedipal resolution, no masculine climax, but his inability to conquer her in her refusal to engage in that contest. It isn't that Ursula challenges Anton, or is somehow stronger than him; she is simply no longer available to him in the limited way he defines their relationship, and he becomes afraid of her. Ursula is finally monstrous to Skrebensky, not in her opposition to him, but in her unavailability. "He never thought of Ursula, not once, he gave her no sign. She was the darkness, the challenge, the horror" (535). Skrebensky marries a surrogate—not unlike Will's need for a surrogate for Anna in his conquest of Jennie—but the desire to write her own narrative takes an enormous toll on Ursula, nearly destroying her in the process.

Roger Sale makes an important distinction about Ursula's character. She is, he writes, "the fulfillment of 'woman becoming individual,'" and not simply a victim of the historical processes of disintegration."[41] She is, in fact, the catalyst for this disintegration, willfully taking part in forsaking the masculine narrative for other possibilities. Ursula is not a victim in her decision to find other ways of living, and she is not caught up in what is simply the modern disintegration of social norms and values. She must be the agent for change in her own life, a change that will not occur, as the progress of the linear, historical narrative suggests, unless she finds a way to make it happen. Of the Oedipal logic built into our concept of history, de Lauretis explains, quoting Hayden White, that

The history proper, in the modern definition, achieves both narrativity and historicality by filling in the gaps left in the annals and by endowing events with a plot structure and an order of meaning. This achievement is possible only when the historian works from an ideological frame of reference, that is to say, when the history is grounded in "the idea of a social system to serve as a fixed reference point by which the flow of ephemeral events can be endowed with specifically moral meaning." (*Alice Doesn't*, 127–28)[42]

The social system that works as such a fixed point of reference in the historical progression of *The Rainbow* is the central sacrament between men and women, the legal contract of marriage that carries with it norms and moral guidelines from which Ursula is desperately attempting to free herself. And to do so not only is to affect individual experience, but to call into question that ideological frame of reference itself. Ursula's ultimate denial of the Oedipal narrative to which marriage demands her conscription is very nearly a metafictive commentary on her own narrative—she must find a way to extricate herself from the inevitability of the Oedipal narrative that her family (and on another level, Lawrence the writer) has constructed according to societal guidelines, and to write her own conclusion, in which nothing of the Oedipal narrative is concluded. The fourth and final appearance of the rainbow occurs in the final lines of the novel, as Ursula recovers from her illness: "She saw in the rainbow the earth's new architecture, the old, brittle corruption of houses and factories swept away, the world built up in a living fabric of Truth, fitting to the over-arching heaven" (548). The covenant is not in the legal, social agreement Tom and Lydia first enter into, or in the Oedipal conflict between Anna and Will, but within Ursula herself, apart from any promise of or need for conscription to marriage as a social institution and a framework for the gender roles as they are played out in the novel's introductory paragraphs. Indeed, she begins to sound an awful lot like Birkin by the end of the novel when she discusses marriage: "Love—love—love—what does it mean—what does it amount to? So much personal gratification. It doesn't lead anywhere" (527).

Reading Narrative Desire: Critical Antagonism and Ursula's Revisionary Success

Many critical readers have had problems with Ursula's newfound independence and identity, especially as it exists outside of, and even in spite of, the sacrament of marriage that forms the narrative pattern of the novel. Of these readerly difficulties, Carol Siegel writes, "Almost as long as there has been literature, men have used it to complain about the dangerous power of woman and to argue that she must be controlled."[43] And Simpson notes that, of Hardy's *Jude the Obscure,* which offers Sue Brideshead as the "literary paradigm" of the New Woman and a figure whom Lawrence writes about in his "Study of Thomas Hardy," reviewers chafed at the "heroine whose chastity sprang not from ignorance or innocence, which a legal husband might rightfully hope to dispel, but from a conscious sense of her own sexual autonomy."[44] This sounds very much like the reaction many contemporary critics have to Ursula, whom they categorize unsympathetically as a failure and as a monstrous impediment to the more likable Skrebensky. Indeed, numerous (and primarily male) readers have concluded that Ursula is both dangerously destructive in her willfulness and a failure in her inability to accomplish marriage. In his landmark study, *The Creation of "Lady Chatterley's Lover,"* Michael Squires cites the "unadmired . . . brutally willful female," a Lawrencean figure that begins with *The Rainbow*'s Ursula, in his estimation. "In *Lady Chatterley* she is Bertha Coutts; but her origins go back to Ursula Brangwen. In *The Rainbow,* despite the fine fervor of her quest, Ursula brandishes a destructive power that annihilates her lover Skrebensky." Gavriel Ben-Ephraim similarly notes that, "As early as *The Rainbow* Lawrence shows the fearfully destructive side of female assertion," indicating "the harpylike power" of Ursula as she "annihilates" Skrebensky who is, he claims, "circumscribed and dissolved in the circle of Ursula's stronger ego." How is Ursula more destructive, and therefore less desirable, than Skrebensky in his desire to possess Ursula in marriage, to trap her in his net? As I read these analyses, I find myself wondering why Squires and Ben-Ephraim would identify Ursula's desire for self-sufficiency and for a movement beyond traditional social roles as a shortcoming rather than as her success.[45]

But they are not alone: Kingsley Widmer in *Defiant Desire: Some Dialectical Legacies of D. H. Lawrence* echoes Ben-Ephraim's analysis of Ursula, claiming that "she becomes a predatory 'harpy' (of Lawrence's legion of such), insatiable and out to destroy maleness." Poor Skrebensky is the victim for these critics, who, like Peter Balbert, have adopted a masculine/heroic critical stance and thus recognize the monstrous Ursula ("harpylike") as both threat and moralistic lesson. Balbert decides that Ursula is finally degraded and dangerous. "The history of Ursula's long affair with Skrebensky, which concludes with the antiprothalamic trappings of a miscarriage, an emasculated male, and a sick female, stands as Lawrence's warning of the pathology in a love that does not produce a joint singling out." Thus, Balbert hints at a moralistic warning against women such as Ursula, the "sick female" who has not only emasculated her potential husband but who has miscarried the result of what could have been a productive marriage. As his analysis continues, Balbert focuses his sympathies on Skrebensky as modern victim. "So she indulges in a form of competitive sex with him that is both necessarily *at his expense* and necessary for her own growth into the woman who marries Rupert Birkin, a man who will demand that otherness be achieved through polarity or 'star-equilibrium'" (italics mine). Skrebensky is not a victim in this relationship; instead, he must come to terms with Ursula's desire and, failing to do so, can only define Ursula in much the way that Balbert and other critical readers define her: "She was the darknesss, the challenge, the horror" (535).[46]

A related assumption about the state of Ursula's health and identity in the novel's concluding chapter is evident in Balbert's claim for her miscarriage in the aforementioned passage. Among other critics who read Ursula's brief "pregnancy," and her sudden return to a state of childlessness, as evidence of a miscarriage, Kingsley Widmer mistakes Ursula's confrontation with the horses as a manifestation of her fantasies and points to the end results of this fantasy as her miscarriage, alluding, perhaps, to a sense of blame we should assign Ursula. He writes, "In the conclusion, the pregnant Ursula, after a semifantasy scene in a field with threatening horses (apparently metaphors for the masculinity which she wantingly fears—the later more sophisticated heroine of *St. Mawr* will choose the horse in a kind of transcendendal bestiality), becomes ill and miscarries."[47] Note Widmer's problems in reading Ursula's desire in this passage. Not only does he completely misunderstand her desire ("wantingly fears"?) but he assumes the actuality of the pregnancy and the fantasy of the horses, rather that addressing these elements the other way around. Ursula's fantasy of pregnancy (actually more like a nightmare) is a manifestation of her guilt, given her transgression against social codes that would position her as Anton's good wife. The pregnancy is a fantasy/nightmare revealing her dual anxieties: On the one hand, she fears entrapment within the society's strictures and with Anton in marriage, but on the other hand, she is anxious about this dangerous choice against marriage. Worthen writes, "The more modern the history recounted by *The Rainbow*, the more it brought to a head the problem of being an individual in a society, inescapably in and of that society."[48] This problem is indeed intensified for Ursula in the ultimate chapter of the novel, and her self-doubt and anxiety regarding her rejection of Skrebensky cause her to temporarily reconstruct a version of that "tissue of romance" which she habitually turns to as a safe, if unsatisfactory, means of identification.

The threat of pregnancy comes, after all, rather suddenly in the introductory paragraphs of the final chapter of the novel, a chapter that shares the novel's title and thus intensifies its overarching thematic emphasis. Ursula must respond both to her family's reaction to her break with Skrebensky ("They looked blank and angry" [536]) and with her own anxiety over the dangerous state of her independence, which may seem like isolation now that Anton is gone.

> Suddenly a shock ran through her, so violent that she thought she was struck down. Was she with child? She had been so stricken under the pain of herself and of him, this had never occurred to her. Now like a flame it took hold of her limbs and body. Was she with child? (536)

Despite many readers' assumption that she *is indeed* pregnant, nothing in her physical condition or in the narrative confirms her fears. Yet Ursula can use this concern for her own condition to reconstruct that earlier romanticized self with Skrebensky, fantasizing as she does so about the security such an identity would offer. Of course, such an identity would also require her to renounce her independence and self-possession, and while she claims "she was glad in her flesh that she was with child" (536), she is being disingenuous; this would be an easy out for her. Ursula's fantastic pregnancy is an attempt to alleviate the pressure of the social conflict that begins with her family but that has greater implications for the role of women in the greater social arena; after all, if she were indeed pregnant, the condemnation of an illegitimate pregnancy would surely mirror the denunciation of her as an independent, unmarried, and "arrogant" young woman. Her own self-recriminations certainly tell us a great deal about her knowledge of the attitudes she might provoke in those around her: "Her mother was right, profoundly right, and she herself had been false, trashy, conceited" (537). The key word is "trashy" as it emphasizes her improper and immoral behavior, as judged by social standards for women like her, both in her actual disengagement from Skrebensky and in her fantasy of an illegitimate pregnancy. Thus, she attempts to construct, in her recriminations, a more traditional feminine identity which also demands that she be rescued by Skrebensky, the father of her fantasy-child: "Who was she to be wanting some fantastic fulfilment in her life? Was it not enough that she had her man, her children, her place of shelter under the sun? Was it not enough for her, as it had been enough for her mother? She would marry and love her husband and fill her place simply. That was the ideal" (537).

And with that dream of pregnancy she attempts to eradicate the desire to see, to know that which men know, the desire of "woman" to "be of the fighting host" (43). In her new identity, Ursula adopts a facade of humility, which she understands as antithetical to conceit and arrogance (or empowerment). But even humility is tinged with her deeper knowledge that such a role would be a mistake. "A great mood of humility came over her, and in this humility a bondaged sort of peace" (537). That *bondage* offers a security that she pretends is "peace," and it leads her to write her letter of submission to Skrebensky, continuing the romantic fantasy from which he might emerge, a renewed Prince Charming to her more secure Sleeping Beauty. "It is your child, and for that reason I must revere it and submit my body entirely to its welfare" (537). But even as she attempts to resign herself to a fantasy of maternal and spousal bliss with Skrebensky, she recognizes her inner rebellion at that prospect: "a gathering restiveness, a tumult impending within her. She tried to run away from it" (538).

The point at which readers often decide that Ursula has quite literally suffered a miscarriage comes in her recovery following her ordeal with the horses. In her delirium, Ursula's conflict between the security of the romantic identity of wife and mother, and the self-possessed and independent individual that she desires to be in seeing and knowing her world, finds resolution as she finally gets him, like a fever, out of her system. "Throughout her illness, distorted into vague forms, persisted the question of herself and Skrebensky, like a gnawing ache that was still superficial, and did not touch her isolated, impregnable core of reality. But the corrosion of him burned in her till it burned itself out" (544). As a corrosive element, Skrebensky—and the social codes that would have accompanied a traditional marriage to him—might threaten to destroy Ursula's sense of self, but she eliminates that element and arises more confident in her identity apart from him. The line that readers most often turn to in ascribing miscarriage, and their moral disapprobation, to Ursula simply reads, "There would be no child: she was glad. If there had been a child, it would have made little difference, however. She would have kept the child and herself, she would not have gone to Skrebensky. Anton belonged to the past" (546). This is not a rationalization of an actual miscarriage but a declaration of Ursula's renewed strength and self-possession, her willingness to acknowledge her own desires in the face of any familial or social condemnation. Siegel's claims that "Every Lawrence heroine, even those who fail miserably, forcefully determines the course of her life through her own choices" certainly applies to Ursula's success at achieving independence at the end of the novel's titular chapter, and it is an identity that is *not* at the expense of a victimized suitor or aborted child.[49] The source of Ursula's success is finally evident in her confrontation with the horses.

In the events that lead from her confrontation with the horses, Ursula's rejection of the social narrative that demands that she marry, bear children, and serve her husband (or, conversely, gain antagonistic domination over him, as we see in Anna and Will's marriage) is a rejection of the socially bound ancestral history offered in *The Rainbow* itself. Worthen writes of Lawrence's accomplishment in *The Rainbow*, "That sense of the beyond, of the unknown, is the realm of experience on which Lawrence is concentrating; for the first time in his career he is concerned to express a sense of people's lives which is not mainly dependent on their past."[50] Ursula may herself move beyond the models of her ancestral past, dismissing her temporary fantasy of maternity and marital bliss. Of the use of the narrative in psychoanalysis, de Lauretis writes, "A case history is really a metahistory, a metadiscursive operation in which the 'analysand' (this is the emphasis of the neologism, and why it is preferred to 'patient') has had equal opportunity to participate" (*Alice Doesn't*, 130). Ursula demands this opportunity to be engaged in the construction of her own identity, of her own narrative, without the social conscription to Oedipal logic. Indeed, Ursula's rejection of the Genesis history she reads in church, her denial of the paternalistic narratives of religion and culture, and her ability to escape the powerful horses by taking an unexpected route out of the field, indicate her willingness to abandon the antagonistic Oedipal narrative altogether. Because she cannot outrun the horses—and because she has no means of controlling them in the way that Gerald will master his horse in *Women in Love* (a mastery that Ursula violently rejects in that novel)—she finds an escape in a narrative direction that completely avoids the need for domination or submission.

This conflict avoidance is not a weakness or failure in Ursula. Notice the determination of her actions that contradict her former trancelike state of inaction:

Then, suddenly, in a flame of agony, she darted, seized the rugged knots of the oak-tree and began to climb. Her body was weak but her hands were as hard as steel. She knew she was strong. She struggled in a great effort till she hung on the bough. She knew the horses were aware. She gained her foot-hold on the bough. The horses were loosening their knot, stirring, trying to realise. She was working her way round to the other side of the tree. As they started to canter towards her, she fell in a heap on the other side of the hedge. (542)

Ursula becomes the active principle of the scene as the repetitive quality of the subject-verb pairings indicate: "she darted," "She knew," "She struggled," "she hung," "She knew," "She gained," "She was working," "she fell." No longer is Ursula herded by the "massive body of the horse-group" (542); instead, in her recourse to another narrative possibility, she leaves the narrative of conflict and conquest behind, causing the horses to come apart as they futilely attempt to understand their inability to overpower her and finally becoming "almost pathetic" in their lack of comprehension (542). Ursula's escape from the horses becomes a metaphor for what Homans calls an "extra-narrative space" which might "make possible the impossible representation of women's desire, at least in a narrative that equates linear progress with masculine desire and a woman's love with stasis."[51] Indeed, not only does her movement upward, around the tree and over the hedge, mark an avenue that the masculine horses cannot comprehend, but Ursula's movement begins to address her anxiety about the social conflict that she fears will arise in her rejection of Skrebensky, and in her fears of pregnancy. In outwitting the horses, she has found a way to acknowledge her own desires and to do so without being "of the fighting host" of men (43); she has changed the terms of knowledge and vision in the world.

Of this scene, Mark Kinkead-Weekes explains, "Like all Lawrence's best scenes, the real significance [of the scene] lies not in symbol but in process, in what happens. If we ask, not merely, 'what are the horses?' but 'what happens to Ursula?', we see her confronting the challenge, *and failing to meet it.*" Although Kinkead-Weekes is absolutely correct about the kind of questioning we must engage in as readers, especially as readers who are sensitive to multiple locations of desire in the text, his conclusion is faulty. Ursula fails in a *confrontation* with the horses, this is true; she is not a *victor* in the way that Gerald successfully battles against the will of his horse in the well-known scene in *Women in Love.* But her success—and I believe that it is an unqualified success—is in finding an alternative narrative path which takes her away from a confrontation that she did not desire in the first place. Kinkead-Weekes continues his reading of the scene,

As she and the horses pass and re-pass she is forced to know them. As they work themselves up for a climactic confrontation she will have, this time, to go through in full awareness. And she cannot do it. She is terrified. Her limbs turn to water. She climbs a tree and collapses on the other side of the hedge. Instead of going through [what Kinkead-Weekes calls a "bursting the barrier of the Other"], she lapses into the element of water alone, becomes unconscious, inert, unchanging, unchangeable, like a stone at the bottom of a stream. This is her "Flood." She fails, and failing, she nearly dies literally, as well as inwardly.[52]

I disagree with Kinkead-Weekes's conclusions, because Ursula quite actively succeeds in changing the terms of the conflict, just as she has succeeded in changing the terms of the historical narrative on which the novel is built. This is the power of *The Rainbow:* Despite the models for "proper" behavior and for "proper" socially con- scripted narratives of marriage and family that form the foundation of her ancestry, Ursula is able to revise the narrative according to her own desires. Is there a kind of death in her renunciation of the romantic figure who would be rescued by Skrebensky? Yes, and through this metaphoric death and confident revision of herself, she eludes the barriers of social and historical narratives to become an independent and powerful woman, the woman who will instruct the proselytizing Birkin in marriage in *Women in Love.* Worthen more accurately recognizes Ursula's self-determination in the event when he writes, "The question of whether she actually meets flesh-and- blood horses, or whether the whole experience is visionary, is irrele- vant. Whether the horses are real or not, her experience at this junc- ture makes them matter internally, emotionally, psychologically, psychically. It is she who makes the significance of the encounter, out of the way in which it serves to challenge her decision."[53]

Ursula's ability to find this route might liken her to Dora's rejection of the analytic narrative in the Freudian case history. Of Dora's action, de Lauretis claims, "By breaking off analysis, 'Dora' refused to join in the telling of her life history. . . . 'Dora' questioned the analyst's account and denied it narrative closure, turning what should have been her case history into a doubtful, unreliable chronicle" (*Alice Doesn't,* 131). In many ways, this decision to reject a narrative re- flects Ursula's rejection of the identities she has been unwillingly assigned.

I have no father nor mother nor lover, I have no allocated place in the world of things, I do not belong to Beldover nor to Nottingham nor to England nor to this world, they none of them exist, I am trammelled and entangled in them, but they are all unreal. I must break out of it, like a nut from its shell which is an unreality. (545)

Ursula's desire is to avoid the dictates of the masculine narrative in which she must either be beaten into submission by husband/hero, or in which she must herself be victor and herself maintain the Oedipal narrative. It is a promise she makes to herself finally, a covenant of sorts that signals new possibilities, a promise of a way out of ancestral narrative. This is where readers who cite marriage as the ultimate thematic focus and goal of the novel find themselves assuming Ursula's failure, because, in her revisionary attitudes toward the social tradition of marriage, she doesn't achieve a successful marriage herself. Worthen writes, "Each generation's search and fulfilment is that of its marriage—except for the last, where Ursula does not reach the relationship which enables her to come to her fulfilment or her sense of self."[54] Although Ursula does not reach a transcendent relationship, she *does* attain a sense of self that moves beyond the limitations of the abstract woman of part I of chapter I. Ursula's decision to reject a life with Skrebensky is a very public move toward selfhood which keeps her from being circumscribed by house and hearth, by marriage, and by the limitation of woman's vision in the social tradition that marriage has demanded. Ursula can now see a new way toward fulfillment that is not dependent on stale gender roles, and this new vision will lead her to a relationship with Rupert Birkin that is based on an integration and balance of selves, a relationship unlike any that Brangwen women have previously had available.

This is not to say that *The Rainbow* merely provides Ursula with a new quest toward marriage. Peter Balbert claims that "A willingness to see the Ursula on the last page as complete and emblematic tends to serve the fashionable interests of sexual politics,"[55] a comment furthering his polemic against feminist theory. Reading Ursula as complete may well be wishful, because she continues to develop throughout *Women in Love;* however, reading Ursula's desire for independence from a prescribed narrative is not merely fashionable, and in this sense Balbert is mistaken when he argues against feminist readings of Ursula's "opposition to middle-class values of marriage and fecund motherhood."[56] He finally concludes only that Ursula has one choice in her life: "There is a more crucial reason for anticipating the next novel," he writes. "The history of the composition of *The Rainbow* and *Women in Love* supports the view that the end of *The Rainbow* is really the beginning of Ursula's search for the right husband."[57] Not only does Balbert ignore Ursula's narrative progress in *The Rainbow,* but he disregards Ursula herself as she defines marriage in her conversation with Gudrun on the very first page of *Women in Love:* "More likely to be the end of experience" (53).

Ultimately, Balbert would put Ursula in her place and cause her to accept the conservative tradition of marriage and her wifely duties that she spends the whole novel rebelling against. He is much more accurate when he realizes that the former novel's conclusion is "an announcement of Ursula's realization of the kind of marriage she needs";[58] not that marriage is inevitable for her, or that she would dominate a marriage by creating a man, but that in a true marriage, "The man would come out of Eternity *to which she herself belonged*" (*The Rainbow*, 547; italics mine).

Anaïs Nin's understanding of Lawrence's fiction as a "system of mobility" is especially effective, and she explains this system in relation to his treatment of interpersonal relationships. She writes, "It is this struggle for balance which is at the basis of Lawrence's descriptions of love and hate, destruction and creation, between men and women. He was aware of the see-saw rhythm in relationships."[59] Notice that she doesn't see this rhythm as the "tumescence and detumescence" of Scholes' masculine sexual paradigm, but as an attempt at balance, a balance that must implicate both individuals, whose fulfillment comes not in climax but in a continual dialogic, or perhaps passional, movement. If there is a center of balance, it is not phallocentric in her metaphor, not a dualistic struggle for domination and climax, but a continually shifting center whose locale depends on the relationship the two in marriage hold.

In the final chapter of *The Rainbow*, Ursula recognizes the limited perspective of a humanity that chooses to ignore the possibilities in the darkness around them. "Yea, and no man dared even throw a firebrand into the darkness. For if he did he was jeered to death by the others, who cried, 'Fool, anti-social knave, why would you disturb us with bogeys? There is no darkness' (488). This is how Lawrence's project continues in *Women in Love:* to explore the possibility for balance rather than conflict and to disturb the assumptions made by the oedipal narrative about gender and relationships, about problems of desire and control in the narrative. Although Lawrence's narrative remains relatively linear, the social narrative he takes as the subject of *The Rainbow* breaks down through Ursula; this leads him to be able to deconstruct the structural narrative in *Women in Love*, which becomes episodic and self-reflexive. While Gudrun and Gerald enact the traditional heroic narrative in an antagonistic battle that demands either the submission of will or the death of one of them, Ursula and Birkin's relationship manages to move beyond the heroic narrative, largely the result of Ursula's persistence and desire for other narrative possibilities.

Lawrence so often seems misogynistic for so many readers of *The Rainbow* and *Women in Love* because he constructs a model of misogyny, the social and textual masculine narratives that assert what de Lauretis calls "the crime of Oedipus . . . the destruction of differences" (*Alice Doesn't*, 120). What so many readers neglect to recognize in these novels, however, is that Lawrence is constructing these models as straw men. Siegel emphasizes "the importance Lawrence gave the representation of women's dissenting and contradicting voices," voices that tend to respond in sometimes discordant terms to the very dictates set up the the narrative itself.[60] Ursula's ability to recognize and move beyond the masculine narrative is initiated in *The Rainbow* and is fulfilled in *Women in Love,* in which the narrative becomes more fully dialogic. These are fully intertextual novels, perhaps sister narratives, to borrow Lawrence's original title for the novels, and Ursula's movement away from Skrebensky and her subsequent relationship with Birkin means little without her struggle agaisnt the dictatorial social narrative from which she must first free herself in *The Rainbow.*

3

Getting Rid of "the exclusiveness of married love": Questioning Constructs of Masculinity in *Women in Love*

Iɴ the conclusion to *Women in Love,* Ursula steadfastly demands that "You can't have two kinds of love." She is directly referring to Birkin's desire for attaining fulfilling and complete relationships with both men and women, or more precisely, with both Gerald and herself. "You can't have it, because it's wrong, impossible" (583). Birkin's response is one of denial, "I don't believe that," giving him the last word in both the conversation and in the novel. Critics who have written vehemently against the kind of phallocentrism they find in Lawrence's novels, and particularly in *Women in Love,* might see this conclusion as yet another instance of Birkin's attempts at a very masculine mastery over Ursula. Her perspective cannot be correct in this reading of Birkin, because she must succumb to his domination, remaining "a star in its orbit" (213). By allowing the dominant male to have the final say, according to this argument, Lawrence has propagated his own assertion of the man's right and will to power.

Sheila MacLeod explains the conclusion as evidence of Birkin's indecision: "Birkin is torn between loving men and loving women or, rather, between loving Gerald and loving Ursula."[1] I also see this indecision in Birkin, but I don't see it as a preferential choice to be made between Gerald and Ursula, or between male and female. Clearly, Birkin wants relationships with *both;* he doesn't feel he should have to conform to a social system that demands that he love a single woman and be considered "heterosexual"—that is, "normal"—or that he love a single man and be labeled "homosexual," the kind of socially defined deviance an early reviewer of the novel is repulsed by:

> In real life we should not be troubled with Mr. Lawrence's characters—
> they would be safely under lock and key. For instance, there is the idiot

who undresses and wallows in wet grass, delighting to have his back scratched with thistles and his skin lacerated with fir-cones. Doctors have a name for this sort of thing.[2]

MacLeod goes on to explain that "Birkin is not being entirely honest with Ursula. The novel ends on his disbelief, but it is Ursula who speaks with the voice of common sense."[3] But "common sense" is precisely what Birkin is reacting against; Birkin's desire is to reject the need for a social narrative that demands such exclusivity. However, Ursula's rejection of this express desire to have it both ways is not simply her rejection of Birkin's homosocial, or even homosexual, tendencies; instead, Ursula also alludes in her dissent to her earlier instruction of the Birkin who would have his love in conflicting ways. On the one hand, Birkin is the proselytizing advocate of social rebellion in his desire to be freed from the restrictions of social expectations, including those which govern the sexual and marital relations between men and women. But even as he preaches, he behaves hypocritically by adopting a pose of male domination, identifying himself, perhaps unknowingly, as a traditionally masculine member of the society he would seek to repudiate. This is the paradoxical duality that Birkin struggles with in *Women in Love* and that Ursula must instruct him against if they are to transcend the limitations of social narratives for a more passional and spiritual marriage.

A significant problem for Birkin—and, by extension, for the other inhabitants of the novel—is in his attempt to transcend the boundaries of the socially prescribed Oedipal narrative that would define him as "masculine." Escaping this definition of gender and identity is especially difficult for Birkin, as it is for readers of Birkin, because he is representative of that group of people who are supposed to *benefit* from the social narratives of domination and submission, that is, men. There are prescribed expectations for the masculine hero and the feminine stage, expectations that support the continuity of the societal narrative through marriage, the sacrament that opens the novel. He protests to Gerald, who doesn't admittedly share in this belief, "You've got to get rid of the *exclusiveness* of married love. And you've got to admit the unadmitted love of man for man" (440). Birkin's desire to transcend the "common sense" of traditional forms of love and marriage is more importantly, and more subtly, a struggle for his own identity as it has been defined through the Oedipal logic of gender; his protestations against love and marriage are as much protestations against the construction of gender and identity demanded by an Oedipal logic. But, as Queen Gertrude might say of him, Birkin protests too much. Even as he claims to be searching for avenues other than those of the heroic, masculine quest—the social narrative that Anton Skrebensky follows so well in *The Rainbow* and that Gerald Crich becomes a model for in *Women in Love*— Birkin practices the masculinity of overweening reason over sexual/ sensual and emotional experience, especially as the latter are defined by the conventions of romance and marriage. John Worthen quite accurately writes of the contradictory nature of Lawrence's novel when he writes of Lawrence, "What he felt he had understood in the spring of 1916 was his own social role, for ever outside the conventional ideology of society—and yet strangely attached to that society, still."[4] Although I do not want to suggest that Worthen's biographical Lawrence and the fictional Birkin are necessarily related, as many readers have, this is the kind of paradoxical relationship to society that the novel reveals in Birkin's simultaneous rejection of the social narrative and in his behavior, which would place him very securely in a position of masculinity.

This questioning of his identity, of the problem of maleness and masculinity, is much more indirect in this novel, however; if there is a professed thematic center in *Women in Love,* it might not seem to be the construction of masculinity. Ursula Brangwen and Elizabeth Bates are inspired to question femininity, feminine submission, and their roles in the Oedipal narrative, at least in part because of their condition as women—the group of people whose subservience has been expected in the social system they are each caught in. Indeed, if its title is any indication, the subject of this novel is presumably the relationships that develop for Ursula and Gudrun Brangwen. And, instead of a revaluation of self and masculine identity, we are often left with an impression of Birkin's desire for what seems like male supremacy and phallicism.

A significant reason for this feeling lies in our readings of Rupert Birkin and his tendency for "the Salvator Mundi touch," as Ursula complains of it (189). What is conspicuously absent in the title of the novel itself are the men the Brangwen women have these relationships with: Why isn't this novel entitled *Women and Men in Love?* After all, this is a remarkably well-balanced novel, and critics have effectively illustrated its dialogic nature.[5] Although the first chapter begins with Ursula and Gudrun discussing love and marriage, for example, it ends quite symmetrically with Gerald and Birkin on their way to Shortlands to discuss the same subject in the second chapter—women and men discussing the problems with modern conceptions of love and marriage. But the title of the novel is remarkably one-sided, as is Lawrence's professed goal in writing *The Sisters:* to illustrate and affirm "woman becoming individual." Worthen asks a series of questions that illustrate the problematic assumptions of the title: "It isn't *Men in Love*—though it might have been: but are they in love? What are the women in love with—themselves? *Does* Gudrun love Gerald? Does Ursula not love Birkin 'too much' (as he insists)?"[6] If *Women in Love* is Lawrence's attempt to throw the firebrand into the darkness, to expose possibilities other than those prescribed by the Oedipal narrative, then it would seem that an evaluation of the roles males play, within the narrative that seems to favor masculine experience, would be of significant importance.

Where in the novel, one might ask in continuing Worthen's process of questioning the text, does Lawrence explore men's roles, men as beings individuated in the face of historical/social/cultural relationships and expectations? Is Birkin Ursula's counterpart in this way, attempting to break out of the nutshell? Is this why so many readers believe he is merely a Lawrentian mask? The seeming absence of men in the novel's title, and the phallocentrism that has become a given for many readers of Lawrence, recalls for me the essential Freudian attempt to define women by asking the question: What do women want? In "Femininity," Freud explains, "Throughout history people have knocked their heads against the riddle of the nature of femininity. . . . Nor will *you* have escaped worrying over this problem—those of you who are men; to those of you who are women this will not apply—you yourselves are the problem."[7] Of course, the "people" knocking their heads are men in this Freudian dilemma, looking for a way to define and thus objectify women. It is interesting to note the Oedipal narrative at work in this passage—the masculine hero/critic/psychoanalyst fighting against an obstacle, a wall of inscrutable femininity to be knocked down for heroic victory. Teresa de Lauretis rephrases and redefines the Freudian question: "What is femininity for men?" (*Alice Doesn't*, 111), whereas Carol Siegel, in turn, reads the questions more particularly, writing, "In literary terms, the question Lawrence puts to the sphinx is not What do women want? but What do I mean in her language?"[8] In reading *Women in Love*, what is conspicuously left out is often conspicuously the subject at hand—masculine desire masked by an image of the feminine as the purported subject.

In her first chapter of *Speculum of the Other Woman*, Luce Irigaray responds to this masculine dilemma as it was posed by the Freudian need to define and objectify woman:

> So it would be a case of you men speaking among yourselves about woman, who cannot be involved in hearing or producing a discourse that concerns the *riddle*, the logogriph she represents for you. The

enigma that *is* woman will therefore constitute the *target,* the *object,* the *stake,* of a masculine discourse, of a debate among men, which would not consult her, would not concern her. Which, ultimately, she is not supposed to know anything about.[9]

I'm reminded of Birkin in this passage and of Ursula's impatient responses to his theories of transcendent relationships. "Oh it makes me so cross, this assumption of male superiority! And it is such a lie! One wouldn't mind if there were any justification for it" (213). Irigaray constructs the basic tenets of the Oedipal narrative here, illustrating how ridiculous the assumptions of masculine knowledge are.[10] The Freudian question is echoed throughout the novel by the male characters, primarily by Gerald and Loerke. In the Alps, Gerald asks Birkin, "What *do* women want, at bottom?" (522). Birkin's response is one of confusion and confessed ignorance. Shrugging his shoulders, he tries: "Some satisfaction in basic repulsion, it seems to me. They seem to creep down some ghastly tunnel of darkness, and will never be satisfied till they've come to the end" (522). But this is less a definition of women's desire than a nearly verbatim repetition of Ursula's description of *him* during their earlier excurse as a "foul, deathly thing . . . you want *yourself,* and dirt and death" (389). And Birkin admits his inability to answer, again shrugging his shoulders in bewilderment. And later, Loerke's narrative echoes his male counterparts in the novel: "What was it, after all, that a woman wanted? Was it mere social effect, fulfillment of ambition in the social world, in the community of mankind? Was it even a union in love and goodness? Did she want 'goodness'?" (549). Both Loerke and Gerald, men who share more distinct similarities than differences in the novel, want definitive answers to their questions. Women—and for these two men, mainly Gudrun—don't seem to adhere to the image men have of them. Loerke has tried to settle the matter by shaping an image of his assistant in bronze, naked and humiliated. Gerald would like his definition "at bottom" to reveal a woman like the Pussum. When Birkin describes the women of London Bohemia as "girls who are living their own lives, as they say," Gerald's eager interpretation is merely, "All loose?" (111). Of course, when he is with Pussum, she is not the center of his desire. Instead, we find him "acutely and delightfully conscious of himself, of his own attractiveness. He felt full of strength, able to give off a sort of electric power" (117). Woman becomes a reflection of the power and prowess of Man, if she is fulfilling her feminine duties, it would seem. And with the Pussum, Gerald can at least plan to easily pay her for services rendered once he wishes to move on to other prospects.

In this chapter, I want to explore the problem of masculinity as it is revealed in the men in love in the novel. More specifically, I want to consider definitions of masculinity as they are evident in two seemingly contradictory figures. On the one hand, Birkin is the man of reason, forever rational and embattled as he confronts his baser urges and desires that threaten to undermine his reason. Gerald, on the other hand, is the man of action who ascribes to his urges for conquest and victory in all realms, from his role as the "Industrial Magnate" to his relationship with Gudrun. While Birkin battles his sexual desire for Ursula, Gerald actively seeks out Gudrun, sneaking into the Brangwen house in the night. Thus, Birkin might at first seem "unmasculine," or at least moving beyond the traditional definitions of masculinity that a heroic man of action might embody. However, both operate under the Oedipal logic of masculine identity that posits the male as the active principle in a heterosexual relationship and that asserts control through reason and logic over emotion. "*Women in Love* is a very carefully constructed experimental novel," Worthen writes, "designed to elicit paradox rather than fall helplessly into it."[11] Perhaps the greatest paradox of the novel centers around Birkin's professed desire to extricate himself from the masculine and heroic narrative even as he upholds that narrative through his definition of himself as rational and through his use of very masculine tropes to express a supposedly unconventional philosophy. By considering Birkin's dilemma as the man of reason, by comparing it with Gerald's role as the man of action, and by analyzing their mutual relationship, we may come to understand both the tenacity of the Oedipal masculine narrative and the ways in which other narrative desire, especially Ursula's, becomes necessary in an attempt to achieve a passional and transcendent relationship between men and women.

The Man of Reason

In Lawrence's prologue to *Women in Love,* Birkin's desire is divided in a way that is quite different from the division he feels in the novel's conclusion:

> This was the most insufferable bondage, the most tormenting affliction, that he could not save himself from these extreme reactions, the vibration between two poles, one of which was Hermione, the centre of social virtue, the other of which was a prostitute, anti-social, almost criminal.[12]

In the abandoned foreword, we see Birkin caught between desire for the virgin and the whore—Hermione or an unnamed prostitute.

Importantly, Hermione's virginity is based upon her Oedipal role as a "center of social virtue," the upholder of moral codes that guide gender and class proprieties, while the ambiguous prostitute is without identity beyond her service to masculine sexual desire. This dilemma is transferred to Gerald in the final draft of the novel, however, and, perhaps more importantly, to Julius Halliday. Birkin describes Halliday to Gerald as insane in his oppositional desire: "He wants a pure lily, another girl, with a baby face, on the one hand, and on the other, he *must* have the Pussum, just to defile himself with her. . . . It's the old story—action and reaction, with nothing in between" (152).[13] The masculine attempt to define "what women want" or the roles they play as women in love often becomes a much more accurate portrait of what men want and how men identify themselves and women within the Oedipal narrative. But masculine desire isn't necessarily male desire. Or, to put it differently, conscription to an Oedipal social narrative and to becoming a center of social virtue is a demand made upon males as it is upon females, and it is this conscription that Birkin claims to reject—which is why he is no longer interested in a virgin/whore dichotomy as the representative object of his desire in the completed novel.

In exploring the social construction of masculinity, it is helpful to return to the "Sleeping Beauty" narrative that I discussed in the previous chapter on *The Rainbow,* a construct Kate Millett mistakenly identifies as the dominant theme in *Women in Love.* In *Sexual Politics,* she writes,

> Ursula is presented as an incomplete creature, half-asleep in the tedium of her spinster schoolmistress life. Birkin will awaken her according to a Lawrentian convention whereby the male gives birth to the female . . . yet nothing materializes, and she becomes more and more her husband's creature, accepting his instruction. . . . What she does become is a nonentity, utterly incorporated into Birkin.[14]

Given my reading of Ursula in the previous chapter, I hardly think that she is presented as either incomplete or half-asleep; indeed, as I will illustrate later in this chapter, it is Ursula who must call Birkin on his empty claims for transcendence and on his very masculine expectations. But Millett's reading, which has become for many readers of Lawrence easily dismissable because of her ideological assumptions, serves as an important model of ways that readers may be mislead by the novel's philosophical spokesman. The awakening that Millett refers to above is an important reference to the kind of mythical/heroic narrative de Lauretis recognizes, through the work of Vladimir Propp and Jurij M. Lotman,[15] which places the woman as dormant prize awaiting reclamation by the victorious male. As I illustrated in the previous chapter, de Lauretis outlines just such a mythic narrative journey in which the feminine subject becomes goal or object for the masculine questor, Sleeping Beauty to her Prince Charming. Through this social contract, the female becomes both a victim to be rescued and a prize to be won. Is it any wonder, then, given Birkin's continual preaching, that Millett might recognize in Birkin the characteristics of the dominant masculine hero and, as a result, make the mistake of assuming that Ursula plays the corresponding role of victim/prize? However, it is important to recognize that, by virtue of this same social contract, the male is promised fulfillment and climax with the tacit assumption that *this is a condition that every young man should—and perhaps must—adhere to.* It assumes desire for domination of the feminine prize and instructs the male in his social milieu to ascribe to this condition as fundamentally "right." Gerald obviously has no problem with this contract, and accepts it wholeheartedly in his pursuit of Gudrun. The trouble with Birkin is that he questions this social contract, refusing merely to accept a prize at the end of a heroic contest. His thoughts about a future with Hermione recognize both the attraction of tradition and the repulsive quality of settling oneself into a predetermined social role. "He was thinking how lovely, how sure, how formed, how final all the things of the past were—the lovely accomplished past. . . . And then, what a snare and a delusion, this beauty of static things— what a horrible, dead prison Breadalby really was, what an intolerable confinement, the peace!" (154). For Birkin, the only remedy to such a confinement is in the creation of a new topos, a new narrative location beyond Breadalby which will allow for a relationship unencumbered by social dictates: "If only one might create the future after one's own heart" (154). His desire is for something quite different from Breadalby and marriage—for a relationship of balance with Ursula. And his desire extends beyond a merely dualistic balance, but for a relationship with Gerald as well, which oversteps the boundaries of the social contract significantly.

Of course, it has been argued by readers like Millett that Birkin's heart's desire is for domination, for supremacy over a woman-as-object, quite like Gerald and Loerke. Robert Kiely acknowledges, "The wish for harmony appears to be confused with the will to dominate" in the novel. David Holbrook sees it as something more than domination: "The love Birkin feels for Ursula is full of death," he writes, and the drowning that they witness at Willey Water "stands itself for the deathly effects of 'horrible merging.'" Citing another kind of dominance, Mark Spilka has concluded that Birkin is the hero of the novel, coming to much the same conclusion that Millett does in assigning him a dominant role, even if they place differing emphasis on the quality of Birkin's character. Spilka writes, in "Lawrence's Quarrel with Tenderness," "In this novel there are again two women, spiritual and sensual, in the hero's life. Hermione Roddice is the spiritual vampire, the upper-class intellectual who resembles Miriam Leivers in hyperconscious intimacy. Ursula Brangwen is sensual and emotional, like Clara Dawes, an uprooted independent woman with romantic predilections. The hero, Rupert Birkin, is articulate and insightful, like Paul Morel, but more messianic, and more consciously concerned with selfhood."[16] What is interesting to note in Spilka's analysis is his reversion to an oppositional dichotomy that Birkin is torn between, much like the virgin/whore dichotomy Lawrence abandoned in exploring Birkin's character. The character may easily be mistaken for the novel's central hero, given his outspoken proselytizing and seeming domination of the moral center, but Birkin, as Ursula so often likes to point out, is a hypocrite. And Peter Balbert effectively notices that, although Birkin stands as a kind of destructive principle in the novel, Ursula emerges as the Lawrencean figure who achieves a transformation unavailable to other denizens of the midlands. But the destructive and dominating quality of marriage-as-a-social construct is precisely what Birkin claims to react against, as we learn in the early lines of chapter 16, "Man to Man": "The old way of love seemed a dreadful bondage, a sort of conscription" (269). Birkin desires to confine neither himself nor Ursula to the traditional and hierarchical relationship that the institution of marriage demands, and his desire for what may seem a rather confining *Blutbruderschaft* with Gerald is a response to the social dictates that refuse to openly recognize such relationships between men. Meanwhile, his relationship with Hermione manifests only a kind of repetitive conflict, the kind of repetitive conflict Gerald and Loerke ascribe to in their relations with women, and Birkin wants something more than conflict:

> How known it all was, like a game with the figures set out, the same figures, the Queen of chess, the knights, the pawns, the same now as they were hundreds of years ago, the same figures moving round in one of the innumerable permutations that make up the game. But the game is known, its going on is like a madness, it is so exhausted. (156)

If Hermione had her way, Birkin would play the king of chess to her queen and fulfill his role as dutiful patriarch. He should be the heroic male, willing to dominate and impose his will upon a submissive wife, as Hermione seems to suggest when she advises Ursula: "You should have a man like the old heroes—you need to stand behind him as he goes into battle, you need to *see* his strength, and to *hear* his shout. . . . You need a man physically strong, and virile in his will, *not* a sensitive man" (376). Of course, Ursula has been through this kind of relationship already, with Skrebensky in *The Rainbow*. And Birkin is not a hero, not a *Man*, as Hermione observes on several occasions. At the classroom, she jeers at him "as if he were a neuter" (93), and during their stay at Breadalby he is not a man, but a changer: "He is not a man, he is treacherous, not one of us" (149). Gerald's narrative confirms this impression that Birkin is by no means manly or heroic. "Birkin was delightful, a wonderful spirit, but after all, not to be taken seriously, not quite to be counted as a man among men" (272). Indeed, it is Gerald who appears to be the masculine hero of the novel and who continually attempts to live up to the heroic role Hermione asserts as proper and fitting—a role that ends for him in "heroic" death in the Alps.

Hermione poses a problem for Birkin; like Gerald's desire for the Pussum or Loerke's desire for the figure of the young Godiva, Hermione evinces a desire for an Oedipal relationship in which she will be reflected as the female hero in her lover's image. She is described as "a man's woman, it was the manly world that held her" (63) in the first chapter of the novel. As female hero, she is comfortable with the metaphors of conflict Gerald uses, as when she discovers Ursula at the mill and assumes the role of hunter trapping a fox: "And now we've run you to earth" (196). The hunter is a frequent figure in Lawrence's novel, although it is rarely connected with a female figure; the constellation Orion (the hunter) dominates the night sky in the Alps (500), while Gerald frequently compares himself to a hunter, for whom "The world was really a wilderness where one hunted and swam and rode" (294). He is also a hunter in the latter chapters of the novel, holding the professor's daughters in his power like a "palpitating bird" (504). While this figure is very much tied up in the leisure life of the aristocracy, it is also closely related to the image of the gamekeeper, which will become central to the identity of Mellors's character in *Lady Chatterley's Lover*.

However, in addition to the masculine hunter imagery, we also learn that Hermione is not an invincible hero: "She always felt vulnerable, vulnerable, there was always a secret chink in her armour" (63). Although Gudrun is ready to accept her conflict with Gerald and is determined to be victorious over him, Hermione's victory is more subtle. Like Gerald, she clings to notions of propriety, and her desire is to play her role of wife within the social conscription of the aristocracy. As such, that chink in her armor is her femininity, the role she must play to the heroic masculine figure. But this is hardly a submissive role for Hermione, because her most significant goal is to shape her mate in her image. Birkin accuses Hermione of manipulating objects of her desire in the way she manipulates the furnishings of his rooms at the mill. Of her desire for knowledge, he tells her, "You want to observe your own animal functions, to get a mental thrill out of them . . . you want the lie that will match the rest of your furniture" (91). Finally, he accuses her, like Gerald and Loerke, of desiring only an image of herself: "What you want is pornography—looking at yourself in mirrors, watching your naked animal actions in mirrors, so that you can have it all in your consciousness, make it all mental" (92). This is what "love" represents to Birkin, at least in the social understanding of love, courtship, and marriage: a predictable, repetitive connection without any real communion in or annihilation of the self with the Other. Thus, Birkin explains his desire to move beyond the physical, to eliminate the danger of desire and the visual image that Ursula represents to him. As Ursula asks him if he considers her "good-looking," he retorts, "Don't you see that it's not a question of visual appreciation in the least? . . . I don't *want* to see you. I've seen plenty of women, I'm sick and weary of seeing them. I want a woman I don't see" (210). If he cannot admire her objectively, he believes that he will fail to see the reflected image of his own masculine desire. Birkin is well aware of traditional relationships between men and women that depend on singular centers of desire and domination, and his outburst against Hermione's pornographic desire to see herself in her lover is a rejection of that masculine, Oedipal narrative in his own relationships. It is an evaluation of common understandings of love and marriage that is quite similar to Winnifred Inger's complaints in *The Rainbow:* "Love is a dead idea to [men]. They don't come to one and love one, they come to an idea, and they say 'You are my idea,' so they embrace themselves" (*The Rainbow*, 390). The trouble with love, for Birkin, especially as it is represented by Hermione, is its self-reflective nature; the lover sees only himself and his own desire reflected in the object of love, and Birkin claims to want a love that transcends the egocentric self, which breaks through the mirrors and discovers a closer bond to the Other.

But the manipulation of the Other to create a reflection of one's self may well be evident in Birkin, despite his protestations, as he attempts to mold Ursula into a reflection of his own rational image. Gudrun complains that "He can't hear what anybody else has to say—he simply cannot hear. His own voice is so loud" (341). And Ursula regularly accuses him of wanting only a disciple, a follower who will submit to his will like a satellite in orbit around a star. But throughout his frequent "Hamlet-like excoriations," as Avrom Fleishman calls them, Birkin believes that he is using his superior reason to attempt to break away from traditional forms of the Oedipal hero narrative in love and marriage.[17] In his essay, "Reason, desire and male sexuality," Victor J. Seidler traces the cultural development of *reason and rationality* as qualities that set the masculine apart from the feminine, allowing masculinity a cultural value that is not shared by the feminine. Men, Seidler writes, "have learned to appropriate rationality as if it were an exclusively male quality denied to others, especially women."[18] This would seem to be Birkin's attitude in his preaching to Ursula, advocating not a dual release of will but expressly demanding that *Ursula* drop her "assertive *will*," her "frightened apprehensive self-insistence" (327) so that he might bring wisdom to her. "Knowledge," Seidler writes, "has become increasingly viewed as a commodity which can be accumulated and stored. It becomes a means of self-assertion within a competitive society in which men have constantly to prove their worth in relation to others."[19] Birkin cannot seem to relinquish the "Salvator Mundi touch," his self-conscious display of his superior knowledge, as he advocates a revision of the social constructs of marriage and identity. He is continually preaching, as nearly everyone in the novel complains, and his instruction is usually aimed at Ursula. In "Mino" he tells her, 'What I want is a strange conjunction with you,' he said quietly;—not meeting and mingling;—you are quite right;—but an equilibrium, a pure balance of two single beings;—as the stars balance each other'" (210). Ursula takes this to be evidence of his desire for her to play satellite to his star, but it is not merely her mistaken interpretation that leads her to this conclusion. For Seidler, "The masculine resolution of the Oedipus complex leaves men with a sense of reason as an independent faculty and source of morality which has lost connection with its emotional origins. They are constantly working out the correct thing to do, often out of touch with the emotional realities of their relationships."[20] Birkin seems to want to be the hero of his own philosophical, and as such masculine, narrative, even while he claims to want an annihilation of both his egocentric self and of his conscription to a masculine social narrative. As such, he frequently fails to realize the extent of his separation from Ursula, who reads very different meaning in his behavior.

Ursula is stunned, for example, upon discovering Birkin's assault on an image—the reflection of the moon in the water—recognizing it at first as an expression of hatred. But he merely explains, "I wanted to see if I could make it be quite gone off the pond" (325). Birkin wants to destroy the reflection of the moon in the water because, as a visual image for him to appreciate, it promises to become an image reflecting only his own desire, which would cause him to want to keep her, to dominate her. Ursula is quite familiar with the pornographic gaze of desire and possession, and not only through Miss Inger's instruction; she and Gudrun are made subject to it following the incident at the railroad crossing with Gerald and the Arab mare. As they walk home, two miners express their identification of the sisters as objects of their desire, especially attracted to Gudrun's colorful stockings.

> "What price that, eh? She'll do, won't she?"
> "Which?" asked the young man, eagerly, with a laugh.
> "Her with the red stockings. What d' you say?—I'd give my week's wages for five minutes;—what!—just for five minutes." (173)

Ursula's complete silence during this exchange is at least partly a refusal to recognize their attempted appropriation of Gudrun and her, but it is also indicative of a narrative that illustrates the sisters' absence from the men's desire. Gudrun antagonistically loathes them, but otherwise this passage is not about Ursula and her—their perspective is not accounted for in the narrative here, as it is elsewhere, because this scene is about the masculine desire for the availability of the selfless, mirrorlike female. Like Gerald's need to pay off the Pussum, the miners want a convenient outlet for sex that will reflect only their own desire, and which they can conveniently dispose of, even if it means forfeiting a week's wages, without risk of giving "Your missis . . . summat to say to you," as the younger man warns his partner (173). Linda Ruth Williams reads this passage through Angela Carter's essay, "Lorenzo as Closet Queen," as evidence of a kind of literary cross-dressing, an opportunity for the novelist to "try on" women's clothes and, presumably, their identities. "When Gudrun and Ursula parade in front of the miners in Chapter 1 of *Women in Love,* it is *Lawrence's* exhibitionism which is indulged, but the girls who have to endure the ridicule of the mob." Williams indulges in some critically suspect biographical readings here; after all, the passage is not about the women, who are sexually objectified, but about the masculine desire which would appropriate these visually available figures. And Ursula and Gudrun are hardly "parading" here; they have no desire to be so villified by the miners whose stares and comments they must endure. Williams's otherwise excellent readings of masculine beauty as the subject of the gaze in the novel threaten to break down here in their seeming attempt to reveal Lawrence's own "gender-bending"; until, that is, she illustrates her primary concern: that the women in colorful dress, made to stand before the ogling miners, are indeed reflective of masculine desire. "Lawrence is *so* good at female impersonation that he *has* to be a man: only a man can conceive the image of perfect femininity so immaculately."[21] How do Gudrun and Ursula represent perfect femininity? By serving as female spectacle available to the miners' lecherous gazes, despite the contradictory desire of Ursula and Gudrun simply to be left alone.

Birkin understands that sexual desire for Ursula as a physically attractive woman promises the danger of falling into the same expectations that the miners have for the Brangwen sisters. Her image is dangerous, he believes, because it threatens to incite in him irrational behavior, that is, sexual/physical desire. In throwing stones at the moon's reflection "Like a madness" (324), Birkin is attempting an eradication of himself, of his own willful desire for the Other as reflective object of himself, and thus his stoning of the moon's reflection isn't an act of hatred, but of desperation and of confusion. It is no accident that the moon served as a metaphoric image of Ursula in *The Rainbow,* an image that Skrebensky wished to entrap in a net and to control. In the logic of masculinity, to eradicate an image of Ursula is to remain in control of his reason. Seidler claims, "It is women, defined as sexual creatures by Rousseau, who have subsequently been seen as constantly tempting men away from the path of reason and morality. It is as if women are to be blamed for reminding men of their sexuality."[22] And the last thing that Birkin wants to be reminded of is his sexuality, as he tells Ursula and us: "I hate ecstacy, Dionysic or any other. It's like going round in a squirrel cage" (328).

This scene in "Moony" helps to explain Birkin's odd reaction in "Water-Party" during the passionate lovemaking between Ursula and him following Diana Crich's death. There is a real conflict taking place within him here as we learn that, "In spite of his otherness, the old blood beat up in him" (255). He seems to be rejecting any form of physical passion with her, while at the same time experiencing a very real sexual desire for her and for his own climax:

> "Not this, not this," he whimpered to himself, as the first perfect mood of softness and sleep-loveliness ebbed back away from the rushing of passion that came up his limbs and over his face as she drew him. And soon he was a perfect hard flame of passionate desire for her. Yet in the

small core of the flame was an unyielding anguish of another thing. But this also was lost; he only wanted her, with an extreme desire that seemed inevitable as death, beyond question. (255–56)

His rejection of physical passion is related to his rejection of the visual image of his desire; in desire, Birkin recognizes only his limited self and his egocentric experience of sexual pleasure. The small, anguished thing that is lost is his rational distance which he believes he must maintain against "baser" desires. Implicit for him in this union are the traditional forms of conquest and domination; despite her passionate response to him, notice that, like the scene of the miners' desire, there is no mention of Ursula's perspective during their lovemaking. The following paragraphs are completely about Birkin: "Then, satisfied and shattered, fulfilled and destroyed, he went home away from her, drifting vaguely through the darkness, lapsed into the old fire of burning passion" (256). This isn't merely Lawrence's inability to describe the woman's experience of sexuality, but a necessarily limited focus on Birkin's perspective. What Birkin fears in a sexual relationship with her is his phallocentric desire and a lack of any spiritual union with her. But what he also fears is a loss of control of *himself*, of his ability to remain logical and to find a rational path to passion. Seidler notes that sex has been identified as irresponsible behavior, because "sexuality is supposedly beyond the control of reason" for men who define themselves as the defenders of reason.[23] The narrative exclusion of Ursula in this passage, and in the miners' scene, illustrates the reality of a monological phallocentrism in masculine desire, and in a way, Birkin fears are twofold. First, he fears sexual contact because he believes that Ursula will become for him simply an agent of his desire, as she does in this scene and as the miners would hope for, only an agent of his physical climax. As such, they will fail to attain the transcendent relationship he claims to desire. Second, however, he fears losing control of his rationality and thus of his masculine responsibility to keep control over the feminine influence of emotion and the physical. Without reason, Birkin's argument might go, there can be no transcendence of the social coding that would conscribe them to play specific roles in a heterosexual relationship. "The body is to be feared," Seidler writes, "because it threatens to disturb and upset the kind of control so closely identified with masculinity."[24] Of course, Birkin's desire to retain a tight rein on his masculine reason will *also* prevent him from achieving a transcendent relationship with Ursula, because he is so in need of controlling the conditions of their relationship. Thus, because of Birkin's contradictory behaviors and his faulty belief that his reason will help him to escape the prescribed masculine role that he is supposed to play in sex and marriage, he is in a no-win situation; transcendence with Ursula is unattainable, because he is never *with* Ursula.

In "Moony," Ursula accuses him of finally wanting to possess her as an object, a disciple, to confirm his genius: "You want me to be your thing, never to criticise you or to have anything to say for myself. You want me to be a mere *thing* for you!" (327). Although he denies this, he proves this lasting desire for her as object of his love (or theory) by deciding, in the same chapter and quite on his own, that she must marry him. This impulse for the heroic victory of his egocentric theories, which profess a kind of selflessness, is what makes Birkin so exasperating and so ridiculous, as Ursula notes when she hears him rant about Cybele and Syria Dea (323). Anais Nin wrote of him, "[Lawrence] has created his Birkin . . . who carries the burden of Lawrence's earnestness, of his almost (to Ursula) ridiculous exaltations. And all the while Lawrence has also created the characters who *answer Birkin,* who state the other side of the case, who make him ridiculous, and who put him in the wrong."[25] In a more contemporary analysis, Carol Siegel echoes Nin by isolating those dialogic characters as the female characters of the fiction. "Lawrence's fiction does not present us with a female representation of nature lying helpless in the grasp of a hermeneutics of male supremacy, but, instead, with female characters who, as Kermode points out, consistently undercut the doctrinal pronouncements of both the author and his fictional spokesmen."[26] The single individual whose responses Birkin most depends on is Ursula, and it is she who supplies this balance, making their relationship quite different from the conflictual relationship between Gudrun and Gerald. Although there is certainly a kind of conflict between Ursula and Birkin, it is finally not a conflict that demands victory of one agent or the other; it is instead a dialogue that allows Birkin to begin to move beyond the masculine narratives of domination and submission to find that "strange conjunction" with Ursula.

Without Ursula's balance, without her equal response to him and his theories, Birkin does threaten to remain a rather domineering Oedipal hero, the hero of his own theories of spirituality and marriage. He manages to reject this role in his relationship to Hermione. As she attempts to strike at him with the lapis lazuli a third time, his response is, "No you don't, Hermione . . . I don't let you" (164). Rather than strike back at her, or cry in pain, or even curse her, he simply refuses to enter the conflict, to play the game of domination and submission or to be the obstacle that she must smash, and he walks out. With Ursula, however, he cannot seem to make this transition away from the masculine narrative so easily. Ursula responds to this failure in his endless instruction, often revealing to him just how ridiculous he is and always demanding that he recognize other possibilities, other approaches to the spiritual union he desires. "You are just egocentric," she insightfully concludes. "—You never have any enthusiasm, you never come out with any spark towards me. You want yourself, really, and your own affairs. And you want me just to be there, to serve you" (326).

Avrom Fleishman claims that Birkin's character depends on his dialogic relationship with Ursula—that never do we find him soliloquizing merely for our silent benefit as a readerly captive audience. "So thoroughly dialogical is the way of life depicted in the novel— quite apart from the dialogical method of that depiction—that Birkin seems to be able to explore his own ideas only by expounding them to others."[27] In a passage that Fleishman considers expressly dialogic, the dynamics of the relationship between Ursula and Birkin become clear. Birkin moralizes as he instructs her with,

> "I want you not to care about yourself, just to be there and not to care about yourself, not to insist—be glad and sure and indifferent."
>
> "Who insists?" she mocked. "Who is it that keeps on insisting? It isn't *me*."
>
> "I know." he said. "While ever either of us insists to the other, we are all wrong." (328)

Fleishman ends the passage here, indicating the dialogism in their use of language itself—each are speaking in the same terms, dramatically represented in the repetition of the word "insist." But the language and the ideas take on different meanings for their users; notice that Ursula mocks Birkin, manipulating his words and meanings, even as those words allow the couple to participate in a dialogue which informs them both. The sentence following Birkin's epigrammatic final statement above is important, however; he continues, "But there we are, the accord doesn't come" (328). Birkin claims that he has reached an understanding, through Ursula's refutation of his instruction, that his insistence is itself debilitating to the relationship. But he ends up by continuing to insist that an accord be produced, that some climactic event will reveal suddenly and surely the end of his quest for a perfectly spiritual union with her. Ultimately, even as Birkin descries the Oedipal narrative of conflict and climax, it is this concept of climax that he clings to. Earlier, Gerald criticizes Birkin for his desire to be "right": "Damn you, Rupert, you want all the aphorisms your own way." Birkin denies this, saying, "No, I want them out of the way, and you're always shoving them in" (81). But this masculine insistence upon Birkin's superior reason and presumably advanced use of language continues to come between Ursula and him. There is a double standard here: Birkin is still struggling with his own insistence on being "right" and supremely rational, on reaching a goal in which his philosophy will reach successful heroic completion, even as he insists that Ursula relinquish such willfulness. It is Ursula who must reveal to him this continual insistence and his inability to liberate himself from a rather traditional, masculine way of thinking.

Birkin has continual difficulty not only with his need to assert his "superior" masculine reason over the traditional social concepts of love and marriage, but with another social "institution," language itself. This is quite a significant shortcoming in his desire to find a state of marriage in which an individual sense of self is destroyed and replaced with nonhierarchical and metalinguistic—or supralinguistic—unity of thought and purpose. In "Mino," he reveals his essentialistic ideal to Ursula: "'There is,' he said, in a voice of pure abstraction, 'a final me which is stark and impersonal and beyond responsibility. So there is a final you. And it is there I would want to meet you—not in the emotional, loving plane—but there beyond, *where there is no speech and no terms of agreement*" (208–9; italics mine). Birkin illustrates his tenacious masculinity in this express desire not only for avoiding the empty institution of marriage, as he might define it, but for eliminating emotion, as well, to reach a place beyond language. In a culture that values masculine reason, Seidler writes, "Emotions and feelings are likewise denied as genuine sources of knowledge within the culture. Rather, they are associated predominantly with weakness and femininity, and so as antithetical to the 'strengths' with which boys learn their sense of masculine identity."[28] Birkin claims, at least, to value a transcendence that would eliminate both feminine emotion and masculine reason, but there is something disingenuous in his desire. To reach this plane of being beyond the emotional, however, Birkin must necessarily rely upon language to communicate himself to Ursula. And it is because of his frequently faulty use of language, and especially of metaphor, that he so often fails to truly communicate his desires to her, or to fully understand them himself.

That Birkin frequently relies upon unfortunate and inappropriate metaphors in describing his ideal topos and his ideal relationship illustrates his entrapment within a masculine narrative of reason over emotion. The two most obvious faulty metaphors are the satellite in orbit about a star, which Birkin claims Ursula has misunderstood (213), and the suggestion that "woman is the same as horses: two wills act in opposition inside her. With one will, she wants to subject herself utterly. With the other she wants to bolt, and pitch her rider to perdition" (202). This is a problematic metaphor because we have already seen the way that the masculine rider would deal with a horse that wants to bolt in Gerald's mastery of the mare. As a result of these and other metaphors Birkin attempts, Ursula can only recognize through their failure Birkin's seemingly perverse desire: "You! You truth-lover! You purity-monger! It *stinks*, your truth and your purity. It stinks of the offal you feed on, you scavenger dog, you eater of corpses. . . . What you are is a foul, deathly thing" (389). She reacts not so much to his vaunted idealism here, perhaps, but to the images he presents which are still so tied up in the social and narrative hierarchies that he claims to be breaking away from. Birkin certainly seems to desire nothing more than the old, dead ideals of masculine domination and feminine submission because he is still caught up in his desire to teach Ursula and in his need to be the hero of his own theorizing.

Language is at the center of the problem of a "pure" relationship for both Birkin and Ursula, a situation they both seem to recognize. Seidler writes, "For men, language often seems universal and objective, as if it were always a matter of following an impersonal set of reasons." Indeed, Birkin seems to think that language is itself impersonal and unemotional, supremely logical (and thus masculine). Birkin's desire to break away from the kind of social convention Gerald so adamantly adheres to demands at the same time that he do so within that social and linguistic sphere—that Birkin's often feeble attempts to explain to Ursula his desire to break free from conventional "love" and marriage relies upon his use of quite conventional tropes. Citing Carol Gilligan's *In a Different Voice*, Seidler notes the potential for gaps between male illocutionary acts and female perlocutionary response: "Men, confident in the superiority of the impersonal modes of argument they have inherited, become deaf to the different terms in which women often conceive issues."[29] Such gaps are referred to by Timothy Gould, in his essay, "The Unhappy Performative," as "illocutionary suspense" or "perlocutionary delay." Citing the work of J. L. Austin, Gould explains, "a kind of gap opens up between the possibility of uptake (which is necessary for the happiness of the illocutionary utterance) and the successful achievement of the desired perlocutionary effect."[30] Thus, Birkin's express illocutionary act of instructing Ursula reveals his perlocutionary desire ostensibly to cause her to find a kind of spiritual, ego-less transcendence with him. However, his instruction also exhibits a desire to cause her to realize her lack of awareness (and perhaps her debt to him?) and to be awakened by his reason. This is evident as he tells her, "I want you to drop your assertive *will,* your frightened self-insistence, that is what I want. I want you to trust yourself so implicitly, that you can let yourself go" (327). However, in the gap between his utterance and her response, Ursula clearly does not model either the explicit or the implicit perlocutionary affects that Birkin desires, and she responds instead in mockery and contempt: "Let myself go! . . . *I* can let myself go, easily enough. It is you who can't let yourself go, it is you who hang on to yourself as if it were your only treasure. *You—you* are the Sunday School teacher. *You—* you preacher!" (328).

Ursula is well aware that language, as they attempt to use it, is fraught with imprecision. "She knew, as well as he knew, that words themselves do not convey meaning, that they are but a gesture we make, a dumb show like any other" (254). In like fashion, Birkin also recognizes both the limited nature of language and the inability to move beyond individuality to a place of real intimacy without it. He admits to his own frustration with conventional tropes early in the novel, caught in his reliance upon the traditional and patriarchal creation myth in the book of Genesis. "'The eternal apple,' he replied in exasperation, hating his own metaphors" (90). For Michael Bell, "In *Women in Love* the language theme focuses the constant recognition of a possible mismatch between emotional experience and mental conception whereby an all-important experience may be somehow conceivable yet out of reach. Or, more subtly, the experience perhaps lies to hand but is not conceivable."[31] Birkin realizes the simultaneous need for language and its inherent limitations which might both promise experience and limit the full expression of that experience.

> There was always confusion in speech. Yet it must be spoken. Whichever way one moved, if one were to move forwards, one must break a way through. And to know, to give utterance, was to break a way through the walls of the prison as the infant in labour strives through the walls of the womb. (254–55)

This process of moving forward, of moving through the womb of language, suggests the creative endeavor Birkin desperately desires in his conception of love as a complete union of self and other. But it is finally not an individualistic process, as the birthing metaphor would suggest. It is a process that must finally be enacted through a language which itself denies fixity of meaning and purpose in a living dialogue, a "mapping of differences" in de Lauretis' terms. Notice the problematic metaphor that Birkin calls upon in this passage. Even as he seems to predict Jameson's definition of the prison house of language, Birkin's metaphor changes shape to become the imprisonment of the womb which exists as an Oedipal barrier, through which the fetal hero must emerge successfully if linguistic meaning may be made. Of course, once we posit the concept of a "fetal hero," the metaphor falls apart, and language becomes imprecise. In his essay, "Discourse in the Novel," Bakhtin describes the contradictory process of reaching dialogue in and beyond language as the centripetal and centrifugal forces of language. They are those forces which simultaneously attempt to fix language and meaning, and to deny authoritative meaning and systematization, allowing him to indicate that "no living word relates to its object in a singular way."[32] Although Bakhtin's metaphor arises out of physics and de Lauretis' originates in biology and sociocultural gender representations, both seem to illustrate the creativity inherent in the process of language as a "living" thing which cannot be pinned down by Birkin's masculine metaphors.

This creativity is for de Lauretis the anti-Oedipal ability to recognize various subjective perspectives, perspectives that Birkin has difficulty acknowledging from his limited masculine, rational, and exclusive perspective. It may well correspond to Birkin's notion of the essential inequality of human nature: "One man isn't any better than another, not because they are equal, but because they are intrinsically *other*, that there is no term of comparison. The minute you begin to compare, one man is seen to be far better than another, all the inequality you can imagine, is there by nature" (161). It is not through a masculine paradigm of domination and subordination, of right and wrong or victor/defeated, that the individual truly develops, but through the ability to recognize new perspectives as different and yet necessary to the evaluation of one's own. This is why the events of "Excurse" provide such a significant turning point for Birkin. It is in this chapter that he can finally recognize his own desire for a kind of mastery through reason, even as he professes to abhor this hierarchical relationship. He is "born out of the cramp of a womb" (393) in this chapter—not through some heroic effort or insistence of his own, but through Ursula's ability to help him realize his essentially static and deathly adherence to the masculine narrative, his unwillingness to abandon it just as he was unwilling to completely break with Hermione.

The Man of Action

Gerald, unlike Birkin, fully and openly acknowledges the propriety of the masculine, heroic narrative of gender, love, and marriage. He admits his own sense of a patriarchal kind of propriety, of a "right" way of doing things, early in the novel. "If you're doing a thing, do it properly, and if you're not going to do it properly, leave it alone" (81). This is why he is so plagued by his inability to give the Pussum a gift of money—the relationship, a commercial rather than romantic relationship, in Gerald's view, hasn't been terminated properly and she might still have expectations of him, especially in her state of pregnancy, that would make further demands upon him which he has no desire to fulfill. Doing things properly involves one's ability to sustain an image of one's self as successful and autonomous, to recognize a singular center of desire and volition within his own narrative.

Lawrence's brief return to the conventions of the historical narrative occur in chapter XVII, "The Industrial Magnate," and it is fitting that this chapter presents a narrative about Gerald's history and development as "Deus ex Machina," the god in the social machine of the colliery (301). The machine is Gerald's metaphor for the Oedipal narrative, and as he takes over the workings and improvements of the colliery from his sick father, he erects himself as the very center of the workings of the machine. His life is about control over others. Gerald's reply to Birkin's question in an earlier chapter, "What has your life been, so far?" is neither offhanded nor casual, but a statement of his life's philosophy: "Oh—finding out things for myself—and getting experiences and making things *go*" (108). He is the ultimate agent of action and desire in his own narrative, and there is little room for diverse perspectives or other positionalities of desire in his quest.

Indeed, Gerald is clearly identified as a sort of epic hero in this chapter: "The days of Homer were his ideal, when a man was chief of an army of heroes, or spent his years in wonderful Odyssey" (294). He is not merely heroic, but chief of an army of heroes, the singularly dominant force in his own life and in the lives of those around him. His greatest fear, as he admits to the Pussum, is of being bound, unable to act upon his own desires, unable to surpass an ultimate obstacle—which is why his impending marriage to Gudrun later in the novel becomes a form of doom for him, a kind of unheroic submission. Of the machine and his role as center, he rationalizes, "was not the history of mankind just the history of the conquest of the one by the other?" (302). Gerald continually strives for this role of conquering hero, and when the colliery begins to run smoothly under his hand—when this part of his quest seems to have been successfully completed—he finds himself at a loss. "But now he had succeeded—he had finally succeeded. And once or twice lately, when he was alone in the evening and had nothing to do, he had suddenly stood up in terror, not knowing what he was" (306). With no quest to pursue, Gerald seems to lose his sense of identity, and I am reminded of the kind of restive need for asserting his identity as a conquering hero that we see in Tennyson's poem about an aged Ulysses.

> It little profits that an idle king,
> By this still hearth, among these barren crags,
> Matched with an aged wife, I mete and dole
> Unequal laws unto a savage race,
> That hoard, and sleep, and feed, and know not me.
>
> (1–5)

Earlier there is a more direct reference to Tennyson as Birkin accuses Hermione, "It's all that Lady of Shalott business. . . . You've got that mirror, your own fixed will, your immortal understanding, your own tight conscious world, and there is nothing beyond it. There, in the mirror, you must have everything" (91). These images of the hero bent on his or her own reflections link Gerald and Hermione in interesting ways, as I will illustrate shortly. But Gerald's goal is for ultimate domination in his "separate element," as we find in his swimming exhibition before Ursula and Gudrun. The fact that he "loved his own vigorous, thrusting motion" in the cold water (97) isn't surprising; like Scholes's metaphor for narrative progression, he is determined to recognize a singular means of movement and completion, with himself at the center of his heroic development through various supportive landscapes and obstructions. And that possession demands subjugation of those landscapes and obstacles, not for merely utilitarian purposes, as his leadership over the colliery might suggest, but to propagate that image of himself as heroic victor. We learn, in "The Industrial Magnate," that "it was his will to subjugate Matter to his own ends. The subjugation itself was the point, the fight was the be-all, the fruits of victory were mere results. . . . The profit was merely the condition of victory, but the victory itself lay in the feat achieved" (296). As the Brangwen sisters watch him swim, the feat achieved is his performance, which does not go unnoticed. Linda Ruth Williams reads this scene, and others in Lawrence's

fiction that reveal men as spectacles for the female gaze, as "facilitat-
[ing] the staging of a series of images of male beauty."[33] She notes
that women's experience is "the dominant framing device" in *Women
in Love,* allowing us and them to examine men—and especially the
masculine behavior of the men who are set up to be viewed—as
objects of desire.[34] "Lawrence also sets up a paradigm for the understanding of sexual difference as a dynamic of display and *mis*recognition, exhibitionism, voyeurism, and *mis-seeing,* which is present
in all sexual situations throughout his work. . . . For Lawrence—
known so well as the writer of heterosexuality *par excellence*—masculinity finally stands alone, the spectacle to end all spectacles,
blindingly beautiful."[35] Thus, within only a few pages, we have Gerald
constructed as a spectacle, before which Gudrun and Ursula are
placed. But Gerald is no mere object as spectacle; indeed, he remains a kind of essentialized figure of masculinity in his "possession
of a world to himself" (97). The cold water that buoys Gerald up
supports his movement through it as a submissive landscape of
sorts, and, as spectacle of the female gaze, he remains heroic, "im-
mune and perfect" in his separation from them (97). Williams cites
"the image of women as seers, visual subjects rather than objects,
whose power and fatal flaw is their scopophillic thirst" in Lawrence's
fiction. As women in the narrative transform men into objects of
desire, they affirm men's own desirable images of themselves *as*
desirable, even as these female viewers provide a safe medium
through which men may examine other men. "Most importantly,"
Williams writes, "women's eyes function as the legitimate (read heterosexual) lens through which men can be viewed and enjoyed."[36]
Thus, although the act of seeing may on one level seem to reveal
the desires of women in love, it also serves to make safe the examination of men's bodies and of masculinity, an examination that is obscured by the pretense of watching women.

It is fitting that Gudrun complains of Gerald's freedom when she
and Ursula discover him swimming, complaining also of her restrictions as a woman. "God, what it is to be a man!" is her exclamation;
she continues, explaining to a surprised Ursula who doesn't share
her opinion, that as a man "You haven't the *thousand* obstacles a
woman has in front of her" (98). Later, as Gerald explains to an
outraged Ursula, obstacles that refuse his mastery, such as the Arab
mare before the railroad crossing, must be either tamed or eliminated. "I consider that mare is there for my use. Not because I bought
her, but because that is the natural order. It is more natural for a
man to take a horse and use it as he likes, than for him to go down
on his knees to it, begging it to do as it wishes, and to fulfill its own

marvellous nature" (200). There are only two possibilities in his view: domination or submission. As masculine hero, Gerald refuses the possibility that he might be dominated. When Birkin calls upon the masculine metaphor of women as horses, we have already been offered the masculine definition of this simile: dominate or submit, and submission is, in the masculine view, unnatural. But while Ursula refuses this philosophy, Gudrun seems to share Gerald's view of life as an Oedipal narrative, pitting a heroic figure against lesser beings to be dominated. She certainly complements him, as he realizes upon walking her home in the evening from Shortlands. With Gudrun, the relationship from the first is oppositional—its basis seems to exist in conflict. "He seemed to balance her perfectly in opposition to himself, in their dual motion of walking. So, suddenly, he was liberated and perfect, strong, heroic" (412). This isn't a unifying kind of balance but almost a negation—Gerald is liberated, but Gudrun remains merely a reinforcement of his heroic standing in his perspective. Later, following Diana Crich's death, she becomes both goal or prize to be gotten and landscape upon which his conquest can be acted out. "There was Gudrun—she would be safe in her home. But he could get at her—he would get at her" (424).

Gerald does get at her, stealing into the Brangwen house in the dark and successfully attaining her room at the top of the stairs. There he finds consummation and redemption:

> Into her he poured all his pent-up darkness and corrosive death, and he was whole again. It was wonderful, marvellous, it was a miracle. This was the ever-recurrent miracle of his life, at the knowledge of which he was lost in an ecstacy of relief and wonder. And she, subject, received him as a vessel filled with his bitter potion of death. She had no power at this crisis to resist. The terrible frictional violence of death filled her. (430)

This is the miracle of Gerald's life; his sexual victory, the fulfillment of his desire, has erased the defeat he faced at the water party with his sister's death. But Gudrun, the mere vessel, is quite pained by it all, as we see in her tormented waiting for the clock to strike five o'clock and dawn. "There was nothing to do but to lie still and endure" (432) for Gudrun, hardly a statement of any miraculous effect of this incident on her experience and certainly indicative of her very different desire, which Gerald cannot recognize. The "terrible frictional violence" is once again Gerald's act of desire, his limited experience of consummation and climax which leaves him walking away from the Brangwen home at dawn "in a grateful self-sufficiency" with little thought for Gudrun or her experience (436).

But masculine victory is not a foregone conclusion for Gerald in his relationship with Gudrun, as he discovers at the water party. As hero, the first of Gerald's defeats is from Gudrun, as she strikes the first blow, and promises to strike the last against him. She is an obstacle he has not conquered at the water party, as he has been able to conquer the mare; the next defeat will come at the lake, with Diana Crich's death, and while his conquest may seem complete in his nocturnal invasion, his final defeat will await him in the Alps. Gudrun is herself quite willing to engage him in conflict, to attempt a heroic victory of her own. It is Gudrun who, in her introductory discussion of marriage with Ursula, claims that marriage is itself impossible. "The man makes it impossible" (55), she claims, at least in part because of his desire for a wife's submission and the end of her experience. For Gudrun, who refuses to accept this role, any intimate relationship between a man and her must exist in conflict, as Linda Ruth Williams suggests when she claims, "Gudrun's cold power is not developed alone—it cannot exist except in a relation of dominance."[37] As Gudrun carries Gerald away in the canoe, rowing because his hand is injured, we find her "subtly gratified that she should have power over them both. He gave himself, in a strange, electric submission" (243). This is a submission that Gerald clearly feels is not proper to a masculine code of behavior, and he returns to action at the first chance he is allowed, diving into the water to attempt a rescue of Diana and the young doctor. And once again, Gerald becomes a kind of spectacle in the water, an element from which he will now emerge not as a hero but as a failure, unable to complete the rescue. When Gudrun comments on the distance Gerald has noted between them, both literally in the canoe and more figuratively in their developing relationship, she speaks in error: "Yet we cannot very well change, whilst we are on the water" (244). But they do change. Compare Gudrun's initial, envious, and admiring reaction to Gerald-as-spectacle in his first waterborne appearance with her vision of him as he arises from the water without his drowned sister or her husband:

> Gudrun again watched Gerald climb out of the water, but this time slowly, heavily, with the blind clambering motions of an amphibious beast, clumsy. Again the moon shone with faint luminosity on his white wet figure, on the stooping back and the rounded loins. But it looked defeated now, his body, it clambered and fell with slow clumsiness. He was breathing hoarsely too, like an animal that is suffering. He sat slack and motionless in the boat, his head blunt and blind like a seal's, his whole

appearance inhuman, unknowing. Gudrun shuddered as she mechanically followed his boat. (250)

Her estimation of Gerald as a powerful masculine figure has indeed changed quite radically from her earlier appreciation of his swimming figure or of his domination of the mare, in which she was "spellbound" by him, "glistening and obstinate" in his control of the mare (169). "In terms of the whole voyeuristic economy at work here," Williams writes of Gudrun's earlier act of watching Gerald on the mare, "it does at least serve to make Gerald into the visual object she needs him to be. Dispassionate it may be, but Gudrun's visual sexuality must above all make her man into a spectacle of masculinity before she can lose herself to the sight of him."[38] According to Williams, Gudrun's power comes from her ability to reduce Gerald into an almost cinematic image of desire, noting that in the two key scenes of Gerald's prowess—the initial swim and the breaking of the mare—we readers depend on Gudrun's perspective for our own experience of Gerald. But Williams does not also note the point at which Gudrun's desire is radically altered as she witnesses his failure at Willey Water. There is no losing of herself in her image of Gerald in the above passage, because this image is no longer masculine and powerful or enviable to the competitive Gudrun. Gerald's now pitiful image in Gudrun's perspective predicts his struggles with the masculine identity that he constructs for himself, and his "Once anything goes wrong, it can never be put right again—not with us" (251) proves to be prophetic in his increasing conflict with and against Gudrun.

Men in Love: The Trouble with Sexual Identity

For Gerald, the physically vigorous and visually appealing man of action, the hold on masculinity is actually more transitory and less secure than is Birkin's masculinity as the man of reason. While both men continue to assert their masculine narratives, countered and instructed by the women in their lives, they arrive at a kind of stalemate in their homosocial relationship with each other. Birkin's desire to "have it both ways" remains unfulfilled in *Women in Love* and thus denies climactic conclusion of either his desire to break away from the socially imposed codes of behavior between men, and between men and women, denying also any conclusivity in novel regarding the nature of male-male relationships. In fact, rather than answer questions regarding the place of homosexuality or of an expanded homosociality in the culture, Birkin's relationship with Gerald is confusing because it seems full of double standards. Earlier I suggested that Birkin attempts to reject a physical relationship with Ursula to avoid the traditional hierarchical conflict he expects from love and marriage; masculine reason is superior, in Birkin's mind, to the temptations of feminine physicality. But with Gerald, he is eager to find excuses for their physical contact, including wrestling in the nude. And his desire to form a *Blutbruderschaft* with Gerald would seem to disregard his contempt for the formal bonds love and marriage imply.

An early dialogue between the two men sheds some light on their relationship and Birkin's seemingly contradictory desires. Gerald asks him, "You don't believe in having any standard of behaviour at all, do you?" To which Birkin's reply is, "Standard—no. I hate standards. But they're necessary for the common ruck" (81). This is an important moment between the two men because it indicates Birkin's desire to eradicate not only the social standards that would bring men and women together, including marriage, but also those conscripted behaviors which would drive men apart from each other. Relationships between males do demand certain standards in that social contract promised the young man, among which is a social mandate against overt expressions of love or intimacy. In Hemingway's fiction, for example, the aficionado is the primary symbol of this secretive masculine intimacy, and we get an effective portrayal of the relationship between aficionados in *The Sun Also Rises* as Jake Barnes describes Montoya.

> He smiled again. He always smiled as though bull-fighting were a very special secret between the two of us; a rather shocking but really very deep secret that we knew about. He always smiled as though there were something lewd about the secret to outsiders, but that it was something that we understood. It would not do to expose it to people who would not understand.[39]

There is little need for an expression of intimacy between men, and physical expressions are limited to those which will seem most insignificant and least effusive—and even these are not quite acceptable, as Jake notes of Montoya: "He put his hand on my shoulder again embarrassedly" (*The Sun Also Rises*, 131).

This is the social construct of gendered behavior that the males in *Women in Love*, and more specifically in early twentieth-century England, are supposed to adhere to. In the abandoned foreword to the novel, the exaggerated desire of Birkin, Gerald, and William

Hosken to mask their intimacy after their skiing trip in the Alps is evident. "Outwardly they would have none of it. Outwardly they only stiffened themselves away from it. They took leave from each other even more coldly and casually than is usual." The "it" that they avoid is the expression of affection for each other in their shared experience. "They knew they loved each other, that each would die for the other," but social codes for masculine behavior outlaw such expressions of intimacy.[40] This attitude of indifference is essentially the way that Gerald and Birkin behave toward each other, at least in the early chapters of the novel. As they discuss marriage and Birkin's need for fulfillment, for instance, we have the following dialogue between the two:

> "But whom will you marry?"
> "A woman," said Birkin.
> "Good," said Gerald. (155)

Gerald's sarcasm betrays a sort of worry that Birkin might overstep those social boundaries of decency and masculinity and admit to feelings of closeness for Gerald, or worse, to homosexual desires. Birkin does not admit either here, and there is a continual concern in the early chapters of the novel that such an admission would be at the very least indecorous. Their relationship is described as friendly but decidedly platonic in "Shortlands":

> There was a pause of strange enmity between the two men, that was very near to love. It was always the same between them; always their talk brought them into a deadly nearness of contact, a strange, perilous intimacy which was either hate or love, or both. . . . They intended to keep their relationship a casual free and easy friendship, they were not going to be so unmanly and unnatural as to allow any heart-burning between them. They had not the faintest belief in deep relationship between men and men, and their disbelief prevented any development of their powerful but suppressed friendliness. (83)

These are men who, like the aficionado, will admit to nothing "unmanly" or "unnatural" in their relationship with each other. They are friends, but they are wary of any crossing of boundaries of behavior that would cast their masculinity in doubt. And yet we have a rather contradictory description of their relationship shortly afterward in which there is indeed desire between the two men, turning the negative "heart-burning" into an attractive "heart straining":

> There was a silence between them, and a strange tension of hostility. They always kept a gap, a distance between them, they wanted always

to be free each of the other. Yet there was a curious heart straining towards each other. (155)

No longer is there any value judgment regarding their feelings for each other as "natural" or "manly"; instead, the narrative becomes more open, more willing to explore possibilities that have been taboo. The narrative itself seems to conspire to reveal antisocial, antimasculine attitudes that the two men harbor as it looks forward to their developing relationship and the events of "Gladiatorial."

How is it that, as the novel progresses, Birkin enters willingly into a physical relationship with Gerald, when he attempts to reject such a relationship with Ursula? The easy answer would be to simply label him as homosexual. Certainly he expresses much more overt homosexual desire in the abandoned prologue to *Women in Love:* "All the time, he recognized that, although he was always drawn to women, feeling more at home with a woman than with a man, yet it was for men that he felt the hot, flushing, roused attraction which a man is supposed to feel for the other sex."[41] But even in this passage, Birkin's dilemma is *not* whether to love women or men; his real difficulty is with what he "is supposed to feel" in his antagonism toward a construction of gender relationships that demands he be concretely identified and behave in certain acceptably masculine ways. Maria DiBattista writes of the prologue, in *"Women in Love:* D. H. Lawrence's Judgement Book," "the state of the male soul, the sexual torments of Rupert Birkin, was symptomatic of modern disease."[42] But these are not necessarily sexual torments, as George Donaldson writes in "'Men in Love'? D. H. Lawrence, Rupert Birkin and Gerald Crich." "Readers who have sought to escape what is unsatisfactorily indefinite, by supposing a homosexual implication, have some excuse for their conduct, even though there is no clear justification for it."[43] We cannot pin down the behavior or desires of Birkin precisely because *he* cannot define them for himself; his much valued reason does not help him to define himself with Gerald as he might define himself with Ursula because he is left only with socially defined identities in a kind of binary opposition: heterosexuality or homosexuality. Even in his relationship with Gerald, Birkin is seeking to evaluate his own identity and to call the construction of masculinity and social norms of behavior into question, and his unfulfilled desire to "have it both ways" may be as close as he comes to an understanding of yet another means of identification, bisexuality.

In coming to an understanding of Birkin's dilemma, consider the following description of his wrestling match with Gerald as it compares with the passage describing Birkin and Ursula's lovemaking following the water-party, a passage that I cited earlier and in which he struggles against a phallocentric physical desire for her:

> He seemed to penetrate into Gerald's more solid, more diffuse bulk, to interfuse his body through the body of the other, as if to bring it subtly into subjection, always seizing with some rapid necromantic foreknowledge every motion of the other flesh, converting and counteracting it, playing upon the limbs and trunk of Gerald like some hard wind. It was as if Birkin's whole physical intelligence interpenetrated into Gerald's body, as if his fine, sublimated energy entered into the flesh of the fuller man, like some potency, casting a fine net, a prison, through the muscles into the very depths of Gerald's being. (349)

Isn't this the sort of physical passion that Birkin wants to move beyond in his relationship with Ursula? Why does he enter into it so eagerly, and in terms of subjection and entrapment? In his budding physical desire for Ursula, we hear only despair: "'Not this, not this,' he whimpered to himself" (255). The physical expression of affection between men is beyond the terms of the social contract and thus taboo, although it becomes the central value in relationships between men and women, as the Sleeping Beauty tale illustrates in the prince's kiss. To break with the narrative dictates guiding male-male interaction, it seems that men must move beyond the spiritual and unspoken bonds of male friendship and become physical with each other. Sport—wrestling, here—becomes one way, and perhaps the easiest way, to enter into that expression of love between men and still remain within what can be rationalized in the homosocial relationship as an intimate but "safe" endeavor. For when physical intimacy between men is allowed in a culture such as that of early twentieth-century England, it is so only within the specific guidelines of contest or combat. In other words, there must be an acknowledged and socially sanctioned set of rules for physical contact, as in Hemingway's definition of the aficionado's touch. The wrestling match provides just those rules which legitimize their touch and allow contact, although their unnecessary nudity calls that legitimation into question.

Notice that there is no real climax or victory in this relationship; at best, we have "a sharp gasp of breath, or a sound like a sigh" now and then (349). Shouldn't there be a more significant climax here if Scholes's masculine sexual metaphor of tumescence and detumescence may be applied to a very male situation? But neither of the two is willing to accept the role of victor:

> "I could have thrown you—using violence," panted Gerald. "But you beat me right enough."

"Yes," said Birkin, hardening his throat and producing the words in the tension there, "you're much stronger than I—you could beat me—easily." (350)

This is not so much a contest in terms of the Oedipal narrative, but a much more significant balance that is discovered between these physically different men. Birkin is able to challenge Gerald despite the physical frailty of his body, which is emphasized throughout the novel, and he is only able to do so because neither man is interested in dominating the other. Ironically, domination of the other is what most competitive sporting contests, including wrestling, value. Birkin finally explains his desire for a complete relationship with Gerald in this way: "We are mentally, spiritually intimate, therefore we should be more or less physically intimate too—it is more whole" (351). This physical relationship is not so much a double standard for Birkin, I think, but an attempt to move beyond the linear social narrative that prohibits men from physical intimacy. "Life has all kinds of things," Birkin tells Gerald. "There isn't only one road" (355). Importantly, George Donaldson comments on the wrestling match, "It could be argued that the scene is implicitly sexual, or that the feelings of one or other or both men are, but even that is not incontrovertible."[44] The lack of climax, whether sexual or competitive, denies any conclusive definition of the relationship between the men, and thus the narrative itself echoes Birkin's conclusions regarding the multiplicity of identities and experiences.

Following their wrestling match, Gerald is more open to Birkin than at any other moment or to any other person—including Gudrun—in the novel. He tells Birkin, "I don't believe I've ever felt as much *love* for a woman, as I have for you—not *love*" (354). Earlier, Gerald does confess, perhaps in a sort of delirium, in what he might pass off as a moment of weakness following the death of his sister, his feelings for Birkin: "You mean a lot to me, Rupert, more than you know" (257). But this honesty doesn't last, and later he denies this love. He is by and large not ready to openly admit a bond, a complete connection to Birkin, and this becomes especially evident when his friend suggests they enter into a *Blutbruderschaft* together. Gerald excuses himself from the embarrassing commitment, saying only, "We'll leave it till I understand it better" (278). An interesting turnabout has happened in the narrative; Gerald has become a version of the man of reason, insisting to apply logic and the need to understand to their relationship, while Birkin becomes a version of the man of action, albeit an anti-Oedipal action that eliminates the need for social restriction on their homosocial behavior. They switch roles, cross-dressing in a sense, not between genders, as Williams and Angela Carter have suggested is the underlying theme of *Women in Love,* but between modes of masculinity. Gerald tells Birkin, "Surely there can never be anything as strong between man and man as sex love is between man and woman. Nature doesn't provide the basis" (44), and he seems to have repressed, or at least forgotten, his earlier admissions. Again, he denies his feelings in his silence, when Ursula asks him about Birkin's happiness: "He was very quiet, as if it were something not to be talked about by him" (460). Like a good aficionado, Gerald recognizes that there are certain things a man does not give expression to. Interestingly, only in their mutual relationship can Birkin and Gerald move beyond the masculinity of social narratives of gender. But Gerald's stubbornness will leave him dead in the Alps by the novel's conclusion, having reached a specific, if undesirable, climax in his masculine contest with Gudrun, while Birkin's ability to eschew the masculine in his relationship with Gerald promises to facilitate his transcendent union with Ursula.

This leaves Birkin, at the novel's conclusion, disgusted by the sheer masculinity of the dead stallion he remembers, a figure he associates with Gerald's inability to question and to revise his own identity and masculinity. Birkin's final desire to have it both ways is a desire to break with that gendered social contract, that Oedipal narrative which demands conscription to certain standards of behavior for successful passage through the heroic quest. But Birkin finally isn't interested in such resolution. Roger Sale writes, "The will to dominate in Lawrence is not so much homosexuality as it is an evasion of the ideal heterosexuality," and that definition I think may be extended to include an evasion of any ideal imposed by a prescribed social contract.[45] Birkin's need to express his relationship with Gerald is evidence of the lack of exclusivity of that star-equilibrium he and Ursula will enter into by the end of "Excurse." Birkin's final words in the novel, "I don't believe that" (583), refuse to bring closure either to his process of questioning the construction of his own identity or to the novel's narrative itself.

Women in Love: Beyond the Heroic

Only the women of *Women in Love* are able to draw masculinity successfully into question and to reveal it—whether as an aspect of gendered behavior or as a heroic narrative progression—as necessarily limited and essentially destructive. Lawrence's Ursula and Gudrun perform centrally dialogic roles in the novel by addressing masculinity in ways that the men in love may not. Carol Siegel extends this role of women to one of textual skepticism. She writes, "To a certain extent, Lawrence conceived of woman's body as textual, as we can see in his conflation of femaleness and the literary when he assigns the oppositional voice of the tale to female characters. Female presence in his fiction deconstructs the discourse of the teller."[46] In this view, Ursula does not simply *counter* Birkin as an equally destructive and willful hero of the narrative; instead, her role as protagonist serves to expose the masculine narrative of reason that Birkin constructs. Similarly, Gudrun counters Gerald's man of action by taking the very role upon herself as a textually reflexive response to her partner's narrative demands as a masculine hero. But the roles that are played by Lawrence's female protagonists are not simply oppositional to maleness or masculinity in a binary or dualistic pattern. Michael Bell writes of the danger of falling into simplistic and allegorical readings in an examination of these relationships, noting "it is always important not to slip into seeing it as the story of the 'good' Lawrencean couple contrasted with the destructive 'modern' couple. The book is rather a Dostoevskeyan psychomachia in which the major figures are potentialities of each other."[47] Ursula and Gudrun become textually skeptical or textually reflexive by actively addressing the masculine behaviors and assumptions of Birkin and Gerald and, in doing so, cause us to address the anti-Oedipal nature of the narrative of *Women in Love* itself. Although Birkin and Gerald would be the tellers of their tales of their relationships with the women, Ursula and Gudrun cause the tellers to acknowledge other narrative possibilities and perspectives, refusing meanwhile to accept the discourse of the masculine tellers as either complete or desirable. Although Gudrun reflects Gerald's narrative by becoming herself a masculine hero, forcing their narrative to a tragic and undesirable conclusion, Ursula confronts Birkin's rational heroism with skepticism, finally rejecting it and its symbols outright and refusing to define their relationship as progressing toward a specific narrative place or conclusion. The latter couple's relative success is a result of Ursula's ability to deconstruct the heroic and masculine narrative that would find a definite conclusion for the hero; she seeks instead to be "no place" *with* Birkin and to be without the culmination of the heroic quest in a place of domination or submission, victory or death.

As a textually reflexive figure, Gudrun seems to support Gerald's heroic ideal when she claims that, "To marry, one must have a free lance, or nothing, a comrade-in-arms, a Glucksritter" (464). Gudrun desires a fellow adventurer with whom she can find conquest. Of course, Gerald refuses to be a comrade-in-arms, a fellow hero, but the chief of heroes, the leader of the quest. She later creates an image of her romantic fantasy as a reaction against the possibility that she might be forever alone, that she might never find that comrade-in-arms. A preferable solution would be a romantic image of marriage:

> She suddenly conjured up a rosy room, with herself in a beautiful gown, and a handsome man in evening dress who held her in his arms in the firelight, and kissed her. This picture she entitled "Home." (466)

She begins to realize the horror of this romantic image, and of the heroic ideal, as she sees Gerald as "a Napoleon of peace, or a Bismarck—and she the woman behind him" (511). Once again, this is her realization of the futility of marriage; it is the man who will make things impossible, in Gudrun's estimation, the man who will require of her the end of experience. Rather than end the relationship altogether and abandon Gerald in the Alps by leaving with Birkin and Ursula, or even by herself, however, Gudrun embraces conflict and challenges Gerald to a contest of wills. The opening line of the novel's penultimate chapter indicates her desire to challenge Gerald's overbearing need for masculine domination and to accept the role of victor for herself: "When Ursula and Birkin were gone, Gudrun felt herself free in her contest with Gerald" (538). Like him, she finally sees only two possibilities: domination or submission, victory or defeat. "The deep resolve formed in her, to combat him. One of them must triumph over the other" (506).

This contest involves the artist Herr Loerke, to whom Gudrun begins to be attracted. However, Loerke is hardly a change from what Gerald represents, but promises merely to replace him as another male who will demand Gudrun's submission. This is perhaps most evident in the figure he has created of the naked girl astride the horse. When Gudrun asks him if he slapped her, his reply sounds remarkably similar to Gerald's explanation of his power over the Arab mare. Of beating the girl, Loerke explains, "Yes, I did [beat her] . . . harder than I have ever beat anything in my life. I had to, I had to— it was the only way I got the work done" (528). The only way Gerald can train his mare to conform to his will is to force it to endure the passing train, to beat it into submission: "She must learn to stand— what use is she to me in this country, if she shies and goes off every time an engine whistles?" (200). Loerke's young Godiva is a figure of submission and humiliation, and a visual object that is representative not of the student's beauty, but is reflective of his own power, his own identity. Ursula is disturbed by the horse's unrealistic and brutal appearance, just as she is repulsed by Gerald's treatment of his mare, and only she is able to identify the sculpture's true subject: "I know it is a picture of himself, really" (525). Despite Gudrun's and Loerke's claims that art and reality have no bearing on each other, Ursula recognizes his desire in the figure that has refused to consider the desire of the young Godiva.

In their discussions about art, Loerke also claims that "art should *interpret* industry, as art once interpreted religion" (518). This belief would seem to suggest Gudrun's desire for empowerment over Gerald, who is the representative of the industrial machine. However, Loerke's desire for power and control, although in many ways more insidious than Gerald's brutality, is finally not much different from it, as we soon discover in the narrative:

> The greatest power is the one that is subtle and adjusts itself, not one which blindly attacks. . . . He, Loerke, could penetrate into depths far out of Gerald's knowledge. . . . But he, Loerke, could he not penetrate into the inner darkness, find the spirit of the woman in its inner recess, and wrestle with it there, the central serpent that is coiled at the core of life. (549)

Loerke's desire to wrestle a central serpent is indicative of this desire for power, for embracing the phallic representation of the Oedipal narrative in a conflict in which his desire must be the motivating force of the heroic quest.

Interestingly, Peter Balbert sees this "eternal triangle," as Gudrun refers to her conflict with Gerald and Loerke, as evidence of what he determines as her "manipulative use of Gerald and her decadent partnership with Loerke."[48] But her role in the conflict seems no more manipulative than Gerald's role, especially given his near-sighted intrusion into her home as a means of satisfying his own desire and his growing fantasy with her death as the ultimate form of victory. Because there are only two possibilities for Gerald—domination or submission—then his victory can be complete only when the threat of his domination, his doom in marriage, is eradicated. His desire for a final victory is ignorant of the result; her death becomes only an accident of the victorious consummation of his desire. This becomes more evident as Gerald becomes more driven by the challenge she has leveled at him. He imagines,

> what a perfect voluptuous consummation it would be to strangle her, to strangle every spark of life out of her, till she lay completely inert, soft, relaxed forever, a soft heap lying dead between his hands, utterly dead.

Then he would have had her finally and forever; there would be such a perfect voluptuous finality. (560)

What he would have, finally and forever, is his perfect woman: relaxed, soft, perfectly voluptuous, and, most of all, compliant. Similarly, Loerke's demand for submission from his women and his borderline pedophilia (of the childish Godiva in the figure, he explains "I don't like them any bigger, any older. Then they are beautiful, at sixteen, seventeen, eighteen—after that, they are no use to me" [529]) seem to suggest the real decadence. Some of Loerke's final comments in the novel are in his ironic expostulation, "Vive le heros, vive—" (572), broken off by Gerald's blow to his head. Gerald is the self-styled defender of the heroic, of the normative values of masculine power and moral righteousness, and, as such, his best response to Loerke is one that smashes through the obstacle to his masculine ideal.

It is strange that Hermione and Gerald are never attracted to each other, given their persistent attempts to uphold the social ideals of masculine and feminine propriety. They share significant similarities in the novel, at one point even sharing the same wounds. Hermione crushes the fingers of her hand as she strikes Birkin with the lapis lazuli, and Birkin experiences the horrific realization that she is left-handed. By itself, there is little that is horrific in this realization. Oddly, however, Gerald shows up at the water party some time later with a wounded left hand, bandaged, with the off-handed explanation that the fingers were crushed in machinery. This is a surprising coincidence and suggests for me a significant relatedness between the two, at least on the level of their service to the machine, to the manifestations of the Oedipal narrative to which they ascribe. But then again, perhaps it is not strange at all that Hermione and Gerald are not attracted to each other. Each is looking to mold their prospective spouses into images of themselves, and neither would be willing to succumb to such manipulation. When Birkin becomes a threat to Hermione's desire to play the role of heroic spouse and aristocratic matriarch, Hermione assumes the role of hero more aggressively, determined to eradicate any obstacle—including Birkin—that would impede her.

And then she realised that his presence was the wall, his presence was destroying her. Unless she could break out, she must die most fearfully, walled up in horror. And he was the wall. She must break down the wall. She must break him down before her, the awful obstruction of him who obstructed her life to the last. It must be done, or she must perish most horribly. (162)

These are the terms of the Oedipal narrative that Hermione operates within, at least in part because she has learned them so well as a guardian of social propriety. Although she is quite willing to take on a social role as wife, her strength comes in her refusal to submit to another's revision of her expectations. She is determined to play the game correctly, and because Birkin is continually trying to revise and manipulate her understandings of love and marriage, he becomes an obstacle to her quest for proper social roles. Compare her delight at striking at Birkin with the lapis lazuli with the delight Gerald feels upon his realization that Gudrun must die. Of Hermione, as she prepares to strike Birkin, we learn, "What delight, what delight in strength, what delirium of pleasure! She was going to have her consummation of voluptuous ecstacy at last! It was coming!" (163). This is a very sexual desire and delight, looking forward to a very masculine narrative and sexual climax ("It was coming!"), which is also evident in Gerald's arousal as he considers the direction his relationship with Gudrun must take:

> "In the end," he said to himself with real voluptuous promise, "when it reaches that point, I shall do away with her." And he trembled delicately in every limb, in anticipation, as he trembled in his most violent accesses of passionate approach to her, trembling with too much desire. (545)

Murder becomes a form of sexual fantasy for Gerald and Hermione, and the destruction of their obstacles becomes a consummation of their heroic quests, quests that were in jeopardy of defeat. This is especially true for Gerald, because, in his relationship with Gudrun, "Marriage was like a doom to him," and at the same time "He was ready to condemn himself in marriage" (440). The irony of these murderous fantasies is, of course, his own demise as he attempts to reach "always higher, always higher" toward an increasingly distant climax in the Alps, peak after peak rising and unattainable (574). Gerald even perceives his own murder when the figure of the half-buried Christ looms over him, identified finally as the *Lord* Jesus, a seemingly more powerful hero and a phallic image rising from the snow and threatening the final blow against the masculine hero. Of Gerald, Worthen accurately writes, "his physical death is a spiritual tragedy."[49] But Gerald's death, both spiritual and physical, is much more ignominious than murder, because, awaiting a murderous blow that never comes, he finally falls down, incapable of climbing any further, and dies.

It is fitting that, upon seeing Gerald's frozen body, Birkin remembers "a dead stallion he had seen: a dead mass of maleness, repugnant" (582). Gerald serves as a primary representative of the masculine, heroic narrative and of its limitations. At an interesting point in the narrative of "Snowed Up," a single paragraph links Loerke's narrative thoughts on power, desire, and the penetration of Gudrun's inner darkness—and his version of the Freudian question, What do women want?—with Gerald's role in his relationship to Gudrun, beginning with a statement of a similar act of penetration: "Gerald had penetrated all the outer places of Gudrun's soul." Between these divided paragraphs, which illustrate Gerald and Loerke's desire for power in the penetration of the feminine, is the definition of the masculine desire for conquest in the Oedipal narrative. We see this desire manifest in the conflict between Gerald and Gudrun, from which we may extrapolate the relationship between Loerke and Gudrun in her decision to follow him to Dresden. The paragraph that separates those of Loerke and Gerald states,

> But between two particular people, any two people on earth, the range of pure sensational experience is limited. The climax of sensual reaction, once reached in any direction, is reached finally, there is no going on. There is only repetition possible, or the going apart of the two protagonists, or the subjugating of the one will to the other, or death. (550)

According to the dictates of the Oedipal narrative, especially as it is manifest in the social roles of domination and submission demanded of love and marriage, Gerald's death is almost a foregone conclusion. Williams agrees, noting what she defines as Gudrun's desire for domination, especially as it is expressed in her visualization of Gerald. "As Birkin says early in the book, 'It takes two people to make a murder: a murderer and a murderee,' and so Gerald slips into his role as submissive to Gudrun's dominant. Any negotiation in between about these roles must always be read as sexual experiment or playing with loaded dice, for Gudrun *has* to win."[50] In the paradigm of victor/defeated, someone must face defeat, and in this case, he loses his conflict. Gudrun will not do any better with Loerke in Dresden; instead, the relationship is likely to play itself out again in similar fashion unless she is able to revise her understanding of conflict and gender roles in relationships and leave Loerke behind.

Although Gudrun's oppositional voice, to borrow Carol Siegel's description of women in Lawrence's novel, contradicts the masculine narrative by adopting it and by defeating Gerald, she remains rather trapped in the narrative of heroic conflict, as her relationship with Loerke suggests. Ursula, however, is able to voice an equally defiant opposition while at the same time making a break with this kind of narrative conscription. In fact, Ursula's ability to find narrative perspectives beyond those which call for domination and submission is manifest much earlier than is Birkin's. Following their lovemaking in "Water-Party," in the scene that I cited earlier illustrating Birkin's helpless and ineffectual reason in the face of sexual desire, Ursula realizes herself at an end even as Birkin is aware only of his own desire. Unlike Birkin, who "only wanted her, with an extreme desire that *seemed inevitable as death,* beyond question" (256; italics mine), Ursula recognizes herself more dangerously at the brink of a kind of death. "Unless something happens . . . I shall die. I am at the end of my line of life" (260). Ursula realizes the significance of Birkin's affect on her, not because she has been awakened like a Sleeping Beauty by her masculine savior, but because she has discovered her very active role in the relationship, a role that means the death of her previous understandings of identity and marriage. "Unless I set my will, unless I absolve myself from the rhythm of life, fix myself and remain static, cut off from living, absolved within my own will. But better die than live mechanically a life that is a repetition of repetitions" (261–62). Death, or the revision of one's perspectives, is not merely submission to another way of seeing. It is a very active and willful process that Ursula instigates within herself, moving beyond the narrative boundaries of her life and experience and recognizing previously unknown possibilities. She and Birkin must both take on active roles in finding that spiritual union, that topos in which all antagonistic selfism is eliminated. But those active roles are not the traditional roles of husband and wife, victor and vanquished; Ursula comprehends the need to move beyond the mechanical repetition of marriage that Gerald and Loerke, and finally Gudrun by antagonistically adopting their masculine approaches, believe in. This is why Ursula becomes so frustrated with Birkin—it is not admiration or romantic love she feels for Birkin in "Sunday Evening," but hatred, because he continually urges her to a selflessness which she already understands and which he is so unwilling to accept for himself.

In his chapter on *Women in Love,* Peter Balbert quite effectively illustrates the trouble with common misreadings of Ursula's role in the novel, especially as early feminist critics such as Millett read Ursula only through the distorting lense of Birkin's perspective. "Such a common misreading by feminists of Ursula's role is surprising given their frequent calls for woman's active sexual partnership in marriage; for such *is* the status that a persistent Ursula both encourages and achieves with her headstrong and often contradictory husband." Like Carol Siegel, Balbert reads the Ursula of *Women in Love* as a character who provides a crucial and contradictory voice to the overt philosophizing of the seemingly central character and dominant voice, Birkin. Balbert notes that Ursula "is used skilfully by Lawrence to fashion a sustained and effective critique of Birkin's most cherished theories; indeed, she holds to an unembroidered view of human conduct, natural energy, and sexual response which is at least as legitimate as the celebrated dialectics about star-equilibrium, corruption, and isolate polarity proposed by Birkin."[51] Compare this conclusion to Siegel's later feminist reading of the insight which Ursula gains in her relationship with the pontificating male: "The end result of Birkin's continual battle with Ursula's sentimental pretensions and feminine posturing is her discovery of an incisive female voice that repeatedly and authoritatively undercuts his pronouncements."[52] Balbert's identification of the problematic readings of Ursula in early feminist analyses of the novel looks forward to later feminist studies which acknowledge the character's transformational role in the narrative. Indeed, Balbert seems himself to have significantly changed his mind about Ursula, considering his readings of her failure in *The Rainbow,* when he writes, "There is no suggestion here by Lawrence of vindictiveness in the Brangwen who was born to the proud optimism of the rainbow vision."[53] Ursula is empowered in her ability to experience a kind of death that rejects the inactivity of the traditionally feminine role of wife or disciple (to Birkin as teacher) and simultaneously to avoid the antagonism that the masculine narrative of domination employs. Indeed, she defines Birkin's own antagonism at the end of "Water-Party" as a continued threat to her own well-being, clearly aware of the hypocrisy of his theories of transcendence: "It was as if he were a beam of essential enmity, a beam of light that did not only destroy her, but denied her altogether, revoked her whole world. She saw him as a clear stroke of uttermost contradiction, a strange gem-like being whose existence defined her own non-existence" (268). Ursula reads the masculine narrative of domination and submission quite effectively in Birkin, well aware of her absence both in his sexual desire in "Water-Party" and in his masculine rationality. And as she comes to a realization of her position in his narrative and in the relationship, Ursula must either remain nonexistent or cause Birkin to *see* her and to recognize her desire in his own limited perspective.

Only after Ursula throws the rings at Birkin's feet and reveals him for the hypocrite that he is can he begin to understand ways to move beyond this need for heroism, beyond the need for successful completion of his theories in her submission to them and for the dominance of masculine reason. Now, in "Excurse," we find Birkin "tired and weak. Yet also he was relieved. He gave up his old position" (391). He is no longer interested in dominating her with his theories of spiritual union and selflessness; only now is Birkin able to experience selflessness in another's revelation of herself. Ursula now also understands the need to move beyond the limitations of phallocentric language and visual desire of the Other that Birkin has been trying to express to her. To reach Birkin, we find that "She would have to touch him. To speak, to see, was nothing" (402). Although this touch is indeed the physicality Birkin is afraid of earlier, it is much more than a kind of phallocentric physical desire. The narrative in "Excurse" is much more balanced, more even-handed, in its portrayal of both Birkin's and Ursula's experience because they have reached a point in which both recognize the relationship as a process of balance. We are given a simple statement of their new sense of communion: "She had her desire fulfilled, he had his desire fulfilled" (403). Neither has been dominated or subjected; both have discovered new perspectives, new positionalities from which they may revise their own understandings of each other. In "Lawrence's Quarrel with Tenderness," Spilka reads the change in Birkin as a kind of submission or defeat by a more dominant Ursula. He writes of Birkin, "His views are modified, ultimately, to allow for 'the yoke and leash of love,' which he accepts in the chapter called 'Excurse,' where Ursula accepts the primacy of selfhood. But it is love as a bond, a binding yoke, which Birkin acknowledges, and his stress on impersonal desire prevails."[54] I disagree with Spilka's reading here, because in this analysis of love as a bond, the couple remain divided. Ursula's throwing aside of the rings and her confrontation with Birkin are meant to move them *beyond* love as a bond, which is all Birkin can see; by the end of the chapter, they have both discovered something new. Gudrun and Gerald, on the other hand, do regard love as a bond, and thus bound, one must destroy the other for a kind of Oedipal victory.

Instead, the balance that Ursula and Birkin discover is the living creativity, or the re-creativity, which becomes important to Birkin's desire for freedom from the kind of narrative, marital conscription Hermione represents. And it is only with Ursula that the limitations of self and language finally begin to be transcended, as well. We can see this in Birkin's realization of the suspension of self, of the first person singular pronoun, "I":

Even when he said, whispering with truth, "I love you, I love you," it was not the real truth. It was something beyond love, such a gladness at having surpassed oneself, of having transcended the old existence. How could he say "I" when he was something new and unknown, not himself at all? This I, this old formula of the age, was a dead letter.

In the new, superfine bliss, a peace superseding knowledge, there was no I and you, there was only the third, unrealised wonder, the wonder of existing not as oneself, but in a consummation of my being and of her being in a new one, a new, paradisal unit regained from the duality. (459)

There is no desire for masculine ascendancy or domination here— no desire for the heroic "I"—but for complete and total self-effacement in the process of discovering new positionalities and possibilities, of discovering, as nearly as possible, that Other's per-spective. In such a process of creativity, of the kind of intimacy that Birkin pursues, conventional, masculine narratives, including those which would limit the individual to certain sociocultural gender roles and narratives, are surpassed. This transcendence is exemplary of the narrative desire Birkin exhibits in *Women in Love* in his attempts to move beyond the old, conscripted sort of love.

The ideal topos that I mentioned earlier, that plane of meaning which moves beyond linguistic referentiality and which Birkin is so adamantly seeking, is finally not a fixed goal or final conclusion for Birkin and Ursula at all. Gerald and Gudrun are continually at-tempting to find "centers" in their relationship, ideal locales for their relationship/conflict to be played out, leading them finally to the Alps. "This was the center, the knot, the navel of the world," we are told of the Alps, "where the earth belonged to the skies, pure, unapproachable, impassable" (492). They seem to believe that their conflict can reach a happy conclusion if only they can make it to the right place, to a certain successful goal. Of course, the Alps become an important center for Gerald and Gudrun, providing a locale for their final conflict, their conclusive battle against each other.

For Ursula and Birkin, however, such centers or landscapes would finally be indicative of an Oedipal narrative in which they must pass through various landscapes to a single, final goal, a prescribed para-disal promise that comes with victory over an obstacle. In that prom-ise would lie the necessity of domination, if not of one over the other, then of obstacles that impede their path toward a transcendent utopia. However, their star equilibrium doesn't require they reach some conclusive goal, some definite place that may only be reached by smashing through obstacles, but only that they remain in a kind of unified balance, *dis*placed. Following their most significant under-standing of each other, during their aimless excurse through the countryside, Birkin suddenly wants to abandon all centers. "I should like to go with you—nowhere," he says. "It would be rather wandering just to nowhere. That's the place to get to—nowhere. One wants to wander away from the world's somewheres, into our own nowhere" (398). Their desire is now simply to "wander off" (398). He believes, now working it out for himself rather than instructing her, "It isn't really a locality. . . . It's a perfected relation between you and me" (398). John Worthen claims that the novel itself creates this "nowhere" as a response to the society in which the novel exists and upon which it comments. "*Women in Love,* like all novels, is in a continually shifting relationship with the society of its production; it dramatises that society, it may even reflect it, but it also creates its own world; in this case, an insistently other world."[55] The three rings that Birkin gives Ursula symbolize for both of them the desire to move beyond a single Oedipal narrative which would be traditionally defined in the society of the novel's production through the single wedding ring for couples like Gerald and Gudrun. In the image of multiple rings are multiple possibilities for their lives together, none of them quite fitting comfortably as Ursula tries them on, and all able to be discarded should other possibilities arise.

In his study of the novel as dialogic, David Lodge claims that "*Women in Love,* too, is a kind of philosophical adventure story whose chief characters are questing, with religious fervour, for some new, ultimately satisfying way of life, at a moment of crisis for civilization."[56] If the novel may indeed be considered a quest of some sort, it is an anti-Oedipal quest that constructs and at the same time deconstructs the singular vantage of the heroic, masculine perspective. As it constructs the masculine narrative of the hero in Birkin, Gerald, and Loerke, and even in Gudrun, it also offers perspectives through which Ursula and Birkin may question the construction of masculinity and identity. Hilary Simpson writes of the misleading sense of single-mindedness of the novel's philosophical and domineering voices, voices that sometimes obscure other perspectives. "Even in, say, *Women in Love* (written largely during the war), the notion of male supremacy is only one of a whole range of controversial subjects discussed, often in a spirit of intellectual play, by the central characters. Ultimately, the reader of *Women in Love* feels that Lawrence has no one axe to grind; in a complex presentation of possibilities and potentialities we are not forced to take sides."[57] This is true because *Women in Love* provides the grounds for a mapping of narrative, social and gendered differences, the potential for a breaking out of the nutshell that Ursula begins in *The Rainbow.* The revision of the narrative of marriage becomes a desire for recreativity of both the self and other, for what Anaïs Nin called a process of mobility in the novel: *The becoming always seething and fluctuating.*"[58] It is finally the point much of Lawrence's fiction and essays attempt, as he suggests in *Fantasia of the Unconscious.*

> In one direction, all life works up to the one supreme moment of coition. Let us all admit it, sincerely.
>
> But we are not confined to one direction only, or to one exclusive consummation.[59]

Part II
Re-vision and the Heroic Narrative: Perspectives in Hemingway's Early Fiction

Diehard (stroking his beard). "MY DEAR GIRL. IT'S OUR ONLY CHANCE LEFT. AS SOON AS YOU CAN IMITATE THIS WE'RE DONE."

Diehard golfer, *Punch*, 11 February 1925.

4

"She liked it . . . she wanted it . . . she had to have it . . .": Desire and the Narrative Gaps of *In Our Time*

In a review of a young Ernest Hemingway's first collection of short prose, *In Our Time,* D. H. Lawrence recognized the contradictory nature of a book whose generic definition seemed difficult to establish. "*In Our Time* calls itself a book of stories, but it isn't that," he wrote. "It is a series of sketches from a man's life, and makes a fragmentary novel." There are several very interesting things happening in Lawrence's review, not the least of which is this temptation to define the collection as a novel, however unorthodox, however experimental or fragmentary the text might be as an extended narrative. Lawrence's review exhibits many of the difficulties readers have had with the text, especially considering its unusually dynamic nature and the changes it has undergone since its initial publication in 1924 as *in our time.* For instance, in the two-sentence passage I quoted above, Lawrence wants to expand the generic definitions of the novel to include a book that doesn't seem to cohere as a complete narrative at all—the argument has been made by other readers that these are individual short stories, some published elsewhere, collected in a single text, and not a novel as such. At the same time, however, Lawrence also wants to *affirm* a narrative center in this fragmentary text, even while suggesting that the text remains incomplete, by claiming that the collection is finally from the experience of a single individual. Whether that individual is Hemingway or Nick Adams is unclear in the passage above, but Lawrence does go on to focus on Nick Adams's role in the text as a unifying force. "It is a short book: and it does not pretend to be about one man. But it is. It is as much as we need to know of the man's life."[1] That one man would seem to be Nick Adams, who is the only character, aside from a brief mention of Krebs of "A Soldier's Home," that Lawrence believes is worthy of mention.

That Lawrence should recognize the fragmentary nature of the text and at the same time attempt to construct a narrative around Nick Adams that is not fragmentary at all, but as cohesive as that of any traditional novel, illustrates the problems this text poses for readers. Lawrence writes that, as a novelist, the Hemingway of *In Our Time* doesn't settle for the security of a traditional novelistic narrative that might focus on a single protagonist—a story about some *one* or some *thing*. "He keeps on making flights, but he has no illusion about landing anywhere. He knows it will be nowhere every time."[2] And yet as a reader/reviewer of the text, Lawrence paradoxically attempts to find security for himself, to land somewhere safe, by isolating Nick Adams as the central perspective of the text, however fragmentary he claims it is, together. In many ways what Lawrence is doing, as many readers have done since, is to create a linear, Oedipal narrative, complete with heroic center, which will install a sense of focus or perspective that he otherwise has difficulty finding in the text. He has created a place, a landscape, in which he is comfortable landing his understanding of Hemingway's fiction. To successfully locate the hero in the text in this way is for many readers the culmination of their own critical quests—the puzzle of the narrative has been figured out and made to fit a standard paradigm. For readers of Hemingway, this paradigm offers a sense of a masquerading narrative authority in Hemingway's fiction, an authoritative presence these readers have come to know as the "Hemingway Hero."

The promotion of the Hemingway Hero may well be the most unfortunate development in Hemingway criticism. It has authoritatively informed readings of his fiction in such a way as to reduce it for many readers to a series of codes set for the American pioneer and sportsman—and to provide a sense that Hemingway has more in common with reading *Field and Stream* than with reading "literature." In his seminal 1966 study, Philip Young describes the restrictive guidelines the Hemingway hero must measure up to: "This is the Hemingway 'code'—a 'grace under pressure.' It is made of the controls of honor and courage which in a life of tension and pain make a man a man and distinguish him from the people who follow random impulses, let down their hair, and are generally messy, perhaps cowardly, and without inviolable rules for how to live holding tight."[3] Consider the antagonistic conflict Young has constructed in this definition of the code hero: on the one hand, we have the Hemingway hero, held up as a Platonic (or, to use Nietzsche's term, Apollonian) ideal of manly perfection. Its dialectical opposite appears to be the individual who betrays a rather chaotic, Dionysian sensibility by acting upon the desires of "random impulses." Again, we encounter a dualistic opposition between stoic masculinity and control, and a subjectivity that values individual desire and the mutability of the narrative—the masculine, Oedipal hero and the obstacles that threaten to impede his progress.

In the mythology of the Oedipal hero, as Teresa de Lauretis points out, Young's messy, cowardly, undisciplined individuals were manifest as monsters, as the Sphinx obstructing Oedipus's journey. As such, those figures who do not survive as heroes must exist only to serve a central perspective that is not their own. Young's analysis of Hemingway's code hero finds its basis in the Oedipal narrative that demands that a single perspective, a single source of narrative desire, prevail over other, less useful, perhaps less "manly," positionalities in the text. De Lauretis develops her thoughts on the role of the monster in the Oedipal narrative by indicating the ways individuals in the narrative are assigned gendered roles. Returning momentarily to a crucial passage from "Desire in the Narrative," which I used to illustrate the relationship between Will and Anna Brangwen in chapter 2, de Lauretis outlines the way difference is delineated in the narrative: "The ancient monsters had a sex, as did the gods, in a mythology whose painstakingly rich articulation of sexual difference was to be boiled down to the stark Platonic opposition man/non-man" (*Alice Doesn't*, 109). This is an important opposition, because it is precisely the kind of paradigm of self and other that Young and other readers of Hemingway's fiction have constructed, relying upon it as a sort of readerly template which might be placed with ease over any of the author's texts for immediate access to the "correct" way of reading the text. Joseph DeFalco follows Young's lead, and in doing so confirms de Lauretis's observations, as he delineates the role of the hero engaged in his definitively masculine endeavor:

> Here men face the ultimate test, or some symbolic reflection of that test, by trying to rise above the contingencies of life. . . . In Hemingway's treatment of the ideals a man may hold, he forces consideration of the efficacy of the commitment to an ideal in a world where values have been prostituted to other gods, chiefly Mammon and unfaith. The man who commits himself to these false ideals is personified by Hemingway as *"No-man."* (Italics mine.)[4]

The Hemingway Hero exists, ideally, in a world of independent heroes, generally men: men without women, men without "no-men" or "non-men" in DeFalco's and de Lauretis's lexicon. To be anything other than masculine—either in one's socially ascribed gendered attributes (qualities that "make a man a man") or in the role of the central hero of the narrative—is to be finally monstrous, undesirable, disposable in the progress of the narrative's central perspective. To continue to refer to the protagonists of Hemingway's short stories and novels as manifestations of this Hemingway Hero is to align those characters with the unchanging, fixed form of the epic hero. As Bakhtin defines it, the world of the epic refuses the kind of heteroglossia implicit in the novel as a genre—it is a completely closed entity. In "Epic and Novel," he writes, "Tradition isolates the world of the epic from personal experience, from any new insights, from any personal initiative in understanding and interpreting, from new points of view and evaluations. The epic world is an utterly finished thing . . . it is impossible to change, to rethink, to reevaluate anything in it."[5] If to read Hemingway is to read for the code hero, as Young sees it, then reading *In Our Time* or *The Sun Also Rises* is merely a process of locating a previously defined perspective through which we can expect nothing new, much like the tradition of the epic hero that Bakhtin delineates. It is no wonder that a colleague, looking down his nose at my choice of texts for this study, could proclaim that he had "moved beyond Hemingway." In the introduction to her collection of critical essays, *Hemingway's Neglected Short Fiction*, Susan Beegel acknowledges that "such ideas have been a Procrustean bed for Hemingway's fiction in the hands of less adept critics who have striven to cut all of his stories to fit this model or discarded them in frustration when they refused to fit."[6] Thus, even while readers such as D. H. Lawrence recognize the fragmentary nature of a novelistic text that lands nowhere, inhabits no single topos, it is easier to cling to an epic heroic Nick Adams and to discard mention of other less central individuals who also inhabit the text.

However, despite Young's insistence that the Hemingway hero is just such a closed figure, a reader willing to look beyond the heroic "I" may realize that much of Hemingway's fiction actually tends to deny this monological reading. Of course, as a Platonic ideal, the masculine Hemingway hero is an unachievable quantity, and to strive for such a goal is to attempt to obscure the uncontrollably messy and even cowardly aspects of one's life—to eliminate the possibility that the individual himself is more monster than hero, more messy than "manly," more impotent than powerful. If we consider Lawrence's designation of *In Our Time* as a *fragmentary* novel, emphasizing the text's refusal to conform to such a heroic narrative despite the attempts of readers to impose one on it through the convenient appearances of Nick Adams, then we must acknowledge that this definition of a concrete and definable Hemingway hero is itself a fiction constructed by critical readers searching for a single authoritative perspective in the text. Read as a fragmentary novel, the chapters both seem to attempt unification of the individual stories and at the same time promote discord through the violence of their imagery and their refusal to hold to a single thematic positionality. Through this ever-present sense of dissonance, *In Our Time* actually proposes that Hemingway's "heroes" are about *obstruction*—they are not merely frustrated men, and women, valiantly facing impossible barriers, heroes who attempt in their own ways to complete a monomythic quest cycle, but are *themselves* barriers and obstructions to the definition of the epic masculine hero who is at the center of the phallocentric narrative. *In Our Time* bears this up despite the attempt to erect an individual—Nick Adams *or* Ernest Hemingway—as the central hero of the text.

Writing Nick Adams as the Oedipal Hero

Although many readers of *In Our Time* consider it a collection of related but separate short stories, some have followed Lawrence's lead and read it both as a novel and as a narrative whose central consciousness is Nick Adams. Indeed, Nick Adams plays a significant role in seven of the sixteen short stories, and he can be identified by name in one of the sixteen chapter vignettes. Joseph M. Flora echoes the common assumption that, although all the stories are not directly about Nick, they all do serve him indirectly. He writes, "Many of the *In Our Time* stories are about Nick Adams, and those that are not make suggestions about his life and help the reader to understand Nick better."[7] Robert M. Slabey takes this way of reading the text a step further and constructs an outline based on the thematic divisions he reads in the text of Nick Adams's life. In his essay, "The Structure of *In Our Time*," he writes, "In broad outline, with occasional counterpoint, the fifteen stories trace chronological events in the life of one man, Nick Adams. The list below indicates a four-part pattern:

        A. Nick Adams: The Young Man
             I.   "Indian Camp"
             II.   "The Doctor and the Doctor's Wife"
             III. "The End of Something"
             IV. "The Three-Day Blow"
             V.   "The Battler"
        B. The Effects of War
             VI. "A Very Short Story"

Slabey defends his analysis of Nick as the central protagonist of *In Our Time* by indicating the implications the non–Nick stories have on similar problems that Nick must be facing. For example, he explains "Mr. and Mrs. Elliot" and "Cat in the Rain," neither of which include Nick Adams, by indicating that they serve only to prepare us for the hero's progress in "Cross-Country Snow." "The marital troubles of Mr. and Mrs. Elliot and of the couple in 'Cat in the Rain' parallel the breakup of Nick's marriage. Because he is 'sick' and prefers the life of a sportsman, Nick's marriage fails."[9] Because Nick Adams seems to be the single individual who appears over and over again in the text, readers commonly look to him as the authoritative, Oedipal center. Similarly, in "The Short Stories after *In Our Time:* A Profile," Colin E. Nicholson writes, "The essential—and impressive—cohesion of the stories collected in *In Our Time* rests overwhelmingly upon the way Hemingway directs the emerging overall consciousness of Nick Adams as protagonist." And Philip Young claims that Adams was indeed the central protagonist and the prototypical Hemingway hero, and that all of the stories in *In Our Time* should be read with Nick in mind. "The real hero," Young writes in *Ernest Hemingway: A Reconsideration,* "is the protagonist who was up in Michigan and was wounded while fighting as an American in the Italian army, who lived and wrote fiction in Paris; he is the generic Nick Adams. All the proper parts fit this single story; the hero is— with each successive appearance—the sum of what has happened to him."[10]

More recently, Debra A. Moddelmog has claimed that the collection is actually a novel of sorts which has been written by Nick Adams himself. In her 1988 essay, "The Unifying Consciousness of a Divided Conscience: Nick Adams as Author of *In Our Time,*" Moddelmog argues that Nick is himself the author of the collection, which becomes a *kunstlerroman* of sorts, a portrait of the artist as a war-ravaged hero. "In approaching the stories of *In Our Time* as if Nick were their author, we discover that it will, indeed, be easier to trace through them Nick's recent psychological history than his actual history."[11] Thus, Nick has himself created both the presumably auto-biographical stories as well as those in which he is not clearly attend-ant. She bases her reading on a nine-page conclusion that Hemingway originally wrote for "Big Two-Hearted River," a passage that he deleted from the final version of the story. In this conclusion, reprinted in Scribners's 1972 collection *The Nick Adams Stories* as "On Writing," Nick has finished fishing the swamp and begins to think about the previous stories that he has written. "Nick in the stories was never himself. He made him up. Of course he'd never seen an Indian woman having a baby. That was what made it good. Nobody knew that. He'd seen a woman have a baby on the road to Karagatch and tried to help her. That was the way it was."[12]

Although this portrait of Nick as the central consciousness of the collection unifies *In Our Time,* especially as it directly refers to events from the first two stories of the collection ("On the Quai at Smyrna" and "Indian Camp"), it also severely limits the collection to a mascu-line reading of the singularly dominant hero's quest. Both Young and Moddelmog read chapter 6—the only vignette in which Nick is identified and in which he lies wounded, making a "separate peace" for himself and Rinaldi (63)—as the climax both of Nick's narrative and of the collection itself. Moddelmog reverts to psychoanalytic theory to explain Nick's involvement in the non–Nick stories that follow chapter 6, including those which have come to be known as the "marriage group" ("Mr. and Mrs. Elliot," "Cat in the Rain," and "Out of Season"). "In a classic psychoanalytic paradox," she writes, "the closer the matter is to Nick the writer, the further away Nick the character is likely to be. The non–Nick stories can thus hold the key to Nick's innermost secrets and fears."[13] Thus, in this reading, even those stories which don't include him are ultimately about him as the hero of the novel.

Young is not nearly so enterprising as either Moddelmog or Slabey prove to be in incorporating these problematic stories into their read-ings. Because "all the proper parts fit this single story" of Nick as central protagonist, Young must do something with what must be the improper parts—those stories which don't fit his heroic narrative. He finally chooses to disregard the stories that are not directly about Nick, because they obstruct his reading of *In Our Time* as a narrative about Nick Adams. "So the unrelated sketches and the stories not about Nick are to be more or less put aside for the moment in order that an obscure but meaningful pattern may emerge."[14] Once Young identifies that meaningful pattern, he neglects to really incorporate the nine non–Nick stories into the pattern. This is an interesting choice of action, because these nine stories do indeed attempt to obstruct a singular, closed version of a dominant hero. Young's and Moddelmog's readings of the hero's narrative journey are Oedipal in nature, choosing to ignore or to obscure those elements and positionalities that obstruct their masculine narrative conclusions. Moddelmog finally believes that, as a novel, *In Our Time* is not fragmentary at all. Contradicting Lawrence's evaluation of it, she writes, "It is a complete work, unified by the consciousness of Nick Adams as he attempts to come to terms through his fiction with his involvement in World War I and, more recently, with the problems of marriage and his fear of fatherhood."[15] Not only is Nick Adams the hero of a mythic landscape which he must move through, avoiding the obstacles that might impede his progress, but he is also the authorial creator of the landscape itself, without whom everyone and everything in the text would cease even to exist.

Reading *In Our Time* as either a bildungsroman or as an autobiographical portrait of Nick Adams as a young man demands that we construct an Oedipal narrative out of the fragmentation of Hemingway's text and that in doing so we install certain values in that narrative. Thus, Nick Adams becomes the most valuable figure and the Oedipal hero; other individuals, because they do not seem to be recoverable as the centers of a single, coherent narrative, may be devalued and finally even disregarded. This hardly seems to be the *In Our Time* that continually interrupts itself with violent and almost carnivalesque chapter vignettes, with individuals who make cameo appearances and then disappear like the cat in the rain, or with those characters at the edges of the narrative who appear, fade, and suggestively reenter the text in various manifestations—the woman giving birth in the back of the wagon, the disgraced bullfighter, the terrified Sam Cardinella. Reversing Laura Mulvey's claim that "Sadism demands a story," Teresa de Lauretis indicates the tendency readers have in forcing such a phallocentric narrative from a text like *In Our Time.* "Story demands sadism, depends on making something happen, forcing a change in another person, a battle of will and strength, victory/defeat, all occurring in a linear time with a beginning and an end" (*Alice Doesn't,* 132–33).[16] Because it might be argued that nothing happens in *In Our Time* if, as a fragmentary novel, it doesn't move from beginning to middle to climactic end, then the tendency for readers is to supply that movement. Joseph

DeFalco does it when he ascribes the essence of the narrative to what Joseph Campbell illustrates as the paradigm of the hero quest in *The Hero with a Thousand Faces*. DeFalco writes, "It cannot be dogmatically stated that all heroes in fiction will follow the precise and stereotyped pattern of the heroic journey down to the last detail, but most follow some aspect of at least one of the categories described by Campbell."[17] The desire to construct a narrative that will mirror readerly expectations, the prefabricated Hemingway hero, allows the reader to grasp at straws, to create a historical and heroic presence out of the merest hint of the masculine narrative.

Robert Scholes acknowledges the habitual nature of this way of reading in his essay, "Reading Like a Man." "We do read as if . . . in reading a text we control its fecund excesses of potential meaning by postulating a historical personage whose intentions, however confused or schizoid, provide the grounds for that recuperative activity we call 'reading.'"[18] When this historical personage is absent, we tend to construct a hero to fill the role, to compose an alternate text in the act of reading for an Oedipal narrative. This desire to create a fixed, accessible narrative around a single individual's experience is carried to almost absurd extremes with Charles Scribners' Sons' 1972 single volume collection of stories featuring Nick Adams. *The Nick Adams Stories* collects sixteen previously collected Nick Adams stories, excising them from *In Our Time*, *Men without Women*, and other collections that feature stories not exclusively about Nick, and combining them with eight previously unpublished and for the most part unfinished works, including pieces of stories such as the "On Writing" section which was discarded from the final version of "Big Two-Hearted River."

In his introduction to the collection, Philip Young argues that such a text is absolutely necessary if we are to make any sense out of Hemingway's fiction. "Until now," he writes, "the stories involving Nick have always appeared so many to a book, in jumbled sequence. As a result the coherence of his adventures has been obscured, and their impact fragmented." Of course, Young is presuming that it is necessary to revise the stories so that they will have more impact upon readers dependent on finding the hero in the text. Rather than consider the implications such fragmentation has for a novelistic *In Our Time* and for these stories in their originary texts, Young would rather rewrite them to fit his own interpretive agenda. He continues in the introduction to *The Nick Adams Stories*, "Arranged in chronological sequence, the events of Nick's life make up *a meaningful narrative* in which a memorable character grows from child to adolescent to soldier, veteran, writer, and parent—a sequence closely

paralleling the events of Hemingway's own life" (italics mine).[19] According to Young, it is only possible to find meaning in the narrative
if we have first rewritten it to locate the Hemingway Hero in his
orderly and Oedipal quest. Thus, Nick has been distinguished from
the stories that "follow random impulses, let down their hair, and
are generally messy, perhaps cowardly, and without inviolable rules
for how to live holding tight," to borrow Young's definition of antiheroic individuals, which I cited earlier, and to apply it to those
stories in *In Our Time* which obstruct a masculine heroic narrative.
Because it is Nick's history that is being sought by readers, so the
reasoning must go, we can only assist them (and Hemingway, who
obscured Nick either intentionally or accidentally) by writing the
character's definitive biography.

de Lauretis explains the ways such a process of reading creates
its own fictions by promoting a coherent historical center at the
expense of those pieces which don't fit and despite any pieces missing from the puzzle. She writes, "The history proper, in the modern
definition, achieves both narrativity and historicality by filling in the
gaps left in the annals and by endowing events with a plot structure
and an order of meaning" (*Alice Doesn't*, 127–28). Consider how
closely Young's equivocation in justifying the publication of *The Nick
Adams Stories* mirrors de Lauretis's analysis of the construction of
a historical/Oedipal narrative:

> If the decision to publish them at all is questioned, justification is avail-
> able. For one thing, the plan for rearranging the Nick Adams stories
> coherently benefits from *material that fills substantial gaps in the narra-
> tive.* Further, all this new fiction relates in one way or another to events
> in the author's life . . . these pieces throw new light on the work and
> personality of one of our foremost writers and genuinely increase our
> understanding of him. (Italics mine.)[20]

Readers who wish to recoup Nick Adams and to create a fully developed historical personage must indeed practice abandoning that textual material which doesn't prove useful and filling in the narrative
gaps through a process of rewriting, or writing over, the text. This is
the single greatest difficulty readers have in approaching *In Our
Time:* to recognize the diverse positionalities in the narrative that
actually refuse the kind of chronologically complete story of a single
life which is so temptingly offered in the appearances of Nick Adams.

Indeed, the conventions that might be expected in a realistic novel,
or for that matter in such prescriptive approaches as Aristotelian
definitions of tragedy, are absent in this text. James M. Cox writes in
"*In Our Time:* The Essential Hemingway," "The true relation between

chapters and stories is one of radical temporal and spatial discontinuity, a discontinuity that makes readers seek all the more to breach
the gap between stories and chapters with attributive connections."
Were each story in the text about a completely different set of characters, with different names, different backgrounds, different experiences, it might be easier to pass *In Our Time* off as a collection
of short stories its author simply wanted to get in print—a sort of
"Hemingway's Greatest Hits" prior to the release of his first novel.
And yet, because individuals, especially Nick Adams, seem to reappear in the text, there is a desire to engage in such reading as that
which allows us to write within the empty spaces, to fill in the gaps
of his biography. Cox continues, "The gaps in reality are the nothing,
the nada, that we instinctively can't stand, and so we seek the old
order of cause and effect sequence. But pursuit of the old order
leads to interpretations that try to find the cause of the madness and
dislocation either in the chapters on the war or, conversely, in the
traumatic experiences Nick has seen, if not suffered, in his early
life."[21] To fill the gaps, as Cox suggests, it is necessary to find causal
connections between discordant parts—to create connections that
explain the relationship between Nick Adams as Oedipal hero and
those individuals and events which seemingly have little, if anything,
in common with him. Constructing such a causal narrative is an
inherently faulty project because to do so is to assume that *In Our
Time* adheres to a narrative of a sort proposed by the Aristotelian
unities of time, place, and action, unities that seem to be absent in
the relationship of chapter vignette to story, character to narrative
progression.

   To commit oneself to an act of reading that devalues certain narrative desires in favor of a centrally dominant perspective is to engage
in constructing a definitive history—a masculine, Oedipal narrative—upon an otherwise indefinite, fragmentary text such as *In Our
Time*. Quoting Hayden White's essay, "The Value of Narrativity in the
Representation of Reality," de Lauretis outlines the process one must
go through to create the narrative as a definitive history: "This
achievement is possible only when the historian works from an ideological frame of reference, that is to say, when the history is grounded
in 'the idea of a social system to serve as a fixed reference point by
which the flow of ephemeral events can be endowed with specifically
moral meaning'" (*Alice Doesn't*, 128).[22] In many ways, the construction of the Oedipal, masculine narrative is all about making moral
meaning; Nick Adams becomes the phallocentric hero of the text at
least in part to allow us to find ways to make the proper parts fit a
whole, to install a kind of propriety in the narrative. However, when

I read some of the stories that readers have attempted to make proper and moral by constructing such a historical narrative, I find that things fall apart; as Yeats suggested, the narrative center does not hold, because the social systems used to make moral meaning tend to be transparently artificial.

This is quite often the case in reading *In Our Time;* moralizing about Nick Adams's role in the stories, or about the experiences and assumptions applied to central characters, is very often a matter of constructing a narrative based upon a larger socially based Oedipal narrative which demands that certain conventions of love and sex, gender and marriage hold true, despite the contradictory implications evident if we examine other locations of narrative subjectivity and desire in the stories. I find this especially evident in reading three of Hemingway's early stories. Two of these stories are in a sense causally related—the first, "Up in Michigan," was rejected by its publisher as obscene and replaced by a new Nick Adams story, "The Battler." Both stories offer difficulties for readers who might like to apply certain moral meaning, certain centrally defined social narratives, as does the middle story in what has been called the marriage cycle of the text, "Cat in the Rain." These are representative stories, one influencing my reading from outside of the text, the others from within narratives constructed around Nick Adams's development or from those defined by the marriage thematic they seem to share. Their relationships to the other stories and to the chapter vignettes in the text illustrate the ways the text denies a single narrative hero and promotes dissonant and conflictual perspectives which, as multiple obstructions to a central narrative, finally provide a kind of narrative cohesion themselves.

When Narrative Obscures Desire: Recovering Multiple Perspectives in the "Fragmentary Novel"

One of the unusual attributes of *In Our Time* is its changing, almost intertextual, nature. Its 1924 predecessor, *in our time,* was made up exclusively of what became the chapter vignettes of the 1925 version, *In Our Time.* The stories were added to the vignettes, and two of those short chapters from the first volume became individual "stories" in themselves—"A Very Short Story" and "The Revolutionist." The first story of the text as it stands now, "On the Quai at Smyrna," wasn't added until 1930, five years after the collection's original publication. Perhaps even more significant, however, are the changes demanded by publisher Horace Liveright prior to the publication of the 1925 version of *In Our Time*. To explore the anti-Oedipal narratives available in *In Our Time*, it is useful not only to take a look at what was included in the published text, but also at a single story that didn't make the final cut, a story significant in its ability to model the larger text's tendency toward moving against the socially conscribed Oedipal narratives readers often bring to it. Like Moddelmog, I also find value in reading *In Our Time* through a text that was exorcised from the final version of the collection. However, unlike the deleted pages of "Big Two-Hearted River," Hemingway did find some use for the short story "Up in Michigan." It's first appearance was in *Three Stories and Ten Poems*, printed along with "My Old Man" and "Out of Season."[23] Hemingway originally included "Up in Michigan" in *In Our Time*, but he was barred by publisher Horace Liveright from keeping it in the collection—which fulfilled Gertrude Stein's prediction that it would never be published because of its sexual subject. Liveright demanded that it be removed and that "obscene" passages be edited from "Mr. and Mrs. Elliot." Hemingway assented, as Carlos Baker writes, and finally replaced it with "The Battler."[24]

If, as de Lauretis indicates, "the very work of narrativity is the engagement of the subject in certain positionalities of meaning and desire" (*Alice Doesn't*, 106), then the exclusion of this story becomes an important element of the text as a model of the desire for the propriety and morality of the masculine narrative that demands certain narrative perspectives to keep silent. Readers of "Up in Michigan" tend to follow Carlos Baker's example in restricting his reference to "Up in Michigan" as simply "the seduction story,"[25] but it is concerned with something much more significant than mere seduction or adolescent initiation, I think. The story opens with Jim Gilmore's arrival in Horton's Bay and with our introduction to Liz Coates, who has "good legs and always wore clean gingham aprons."[26] We soon learn that Liz is attracted to Jim:

> Liz liked Jim very much. She liked it the way he walked over from the shop and often went to the kitchen door to watch for him to start down the road. She liked it about his mustache. She liked it about how white his teeth were when he smiled. She liked it very much that he didn't look like a blacksmith. She liked it how much D. J. Smith and Mrs. Smith liked Jim. One day she found that she liked it the way the hair was black on his arms and how white they were above the tanned line when he washed up in the washbasin outside the house. Liking that made her feel funny. (81)

The passage displays the simple and periodic sentences that Hemingway's style became known for. The simple sentence "She liked it" is repeated six times, while the past tense form of the verb "to like" is used at least once in each of the eight sentences—twice in the sentence in which she transfers the liking of Jim to the Smiths. The lulling rhythm of the repetition is useful is setting up another kind of rhythm, as Jim brings Liz to a nearby dock and has sexual intercourse with her. Alice Hall Petry explains this repetitious quality by assigning the expressions to Liz Coates. She writes, in "Coming of Age in Horton's Bay: Hemingway's 'Up in Michigan,'"

> Hemingway elaborates the qualities which [Liz] finds so intriguing, often using the nongrammatical syntax associated with "puppy love": "She liked it about his mustache." Further, as Sheldon Norman Grebstein points out, the repetition of "She liked" conveys the obsessive nature of her passion, while at the same time suggesting the noncommittal quality of her interest: she "liked" aspects of him, but there is no indication at this stage that she feels her interest would, should, or even could develop into anything more than a rather distant infatuation.[27]

Although there is certainly a youthful quality about Liz Coates, which makes her appear adolescent and a victim of what Petry calls "puppy love," I think there are some dangerous and common assumptions revealed here about the narrative and its representations of individual desire. One problem is the assumption that Liz is either obsessive or really passionate, sexually, about Jim; after all, it is not she who chooses the words to express her thoughts in this way, but the narrator who offers us what we presume is a straightforward representation of her thoughts and emotions. Can we be sure that this is indeed her obsession? And can we be sure it is indeed sexually oriented? After all, Liz seems to be caught up in romantic dreams of him that are not at least overtly sexual: "She didn't want to go to bed yet because she knew Jim would be coming out and she wanted to see him as he went out so she could take the way he looked up to bed with her" (84). Her passion is for Jim to gallantly sweep her off her feet; the fantasy she will take up to bed with her is not one of sexual intercourse on a cold dock, but of romantic love. Her "He's come to me finally. He's really come" (84) is not sexually obsessive, but the response of a young woman who dreams her prince has arrived to reveal his devotion to her. Unfortunately, Liz has bought into the Sleeping Beauty myth that demands that she wait demurely and be rescued by her Prince Charming—which is hardly what Jim turns out to be. Another problem presented in Petry's reading is that this approach implies that the story as told by the narrator is revealed in strictly chronological order. In fact, I believe the narrator knows the story already, and thus this narrator—perhaps a version of Jim Gilmore himself—can manipulate our reception of the story through his use of repetitious phrases such as "She liked it."

The description of Liz's psyche as she is engaged in sexual intercourse for the first time seems rather forced and artificial. "The boards were hard. Jim had her dress up and was trying to do something to her. She was frightened but she wanted it. She had to have it but it frightened her" (85). The narrative claim that "she wanted it" and "she had to have it" seems hardly from Liz's perspective, because it is sandwiched between Liz's repeated "You mustn't do it, Jim. You mustn't" (85). Joseph DeFalco summarizes these climactic events by simply writing, "In 'Up in Michigan' the central character is a young girl who is introduced to the sexual act. . . . After they have made love, her lover falls asleep in a drunken stupor." And Mark Royden Winchell follows suit by writing, "At one level 'Up in Michigan' is a fairly conventional loss-of-innocence tale. . . . At the end of a stroll on the beach, a seduction occurs." Similarly, Petry describes Jim Gilmore's character as "essentially hedonistic" which "begins to emerge under the influence of alcohol."[28] But I have to wonder if these events constitute mere hedonism, seduction, or even if they really address the condition of lovemaking DeFalco refers to, because none of these terms seem to represent Liz's understanding of the situation. Compare the content of Jim's and Liz's dialogue during intercourse, a dialogue that doesn't seem to suggest mutual lovemaking or seduction at all:

> "You mustn't do it, Jim. You mustn't."
> "I got to. I'm going to. You know we got to."
> "No we haven't, Jim. We ain't got to. Oh, it isn't right. Oh, it's so big and it hurts so. You can't. Oh, Jim. Jim. Oh." (85)

However often I read this passage, I can't bring myself to believe that Liz is passionate here, that she is being coy, and that, as the narrator would have us believe, she liked it. In fact, as Jim acts upon his passion, Liz seems to show a very different kind of affection: "She was very frightened and didn't know how he was going to go about things but she snuggled close to him" (85). "Snuggling" does not describe the sexual desire in Liz that is assumed by both Jim and the narrative speaker. As I read "Up in Michigan," I hear a very masculine voice attempting to convince his reader—and himself—that Liz's desires are tied up in being *forced* to engage in sexual intercourse—which is neither seduction nor hedonism, but rape—

by Jim. Lisa Tyler breaks a long readerly silence about the sexuality of this story as she effectively defines the sexual behavior between Jim and Liz as "date rape" in "Ernest Hemingway's Date Rape Story: Sexual Trauma in 'Up in Michigan.'"[29] Indeed, throughout the story we learn of her attraction to him, an attraction that has led her to the dock in the middle of the night. "Liz hadn't known just what would happen when Jim got back but she was sure it would be something" (83); she clearly doesn't fully comprehend the kind of climax Jim has in mind, even as he begins to engage in intercourse. We see Liz's utter inexperience, her lack of knowledge about sexual intercourse. "Jim had her dress up and was trying to do something to her" (85)—she lacks even the vocabulary to be able to describe what that something is, as she exhibits earlier on the same page: She "didn't know how he was going to go about things." In the masculine narrative, as both Jim and the narrator understand it, this something she had in mind must necessarily be the phallic, sexual climax Jim experiences on the dock.

In a letter to John Dos Passos, dated 22 April 1925, Hemingway indicates his thoughts on "Up in Michigan" and on Liveright's rejection of it within the larger text of *In Our Time:*

> They made me take out the Up in Michigan story because the girl got yenced and I sent 'em a swell new Nick story about a busted down pug and a coon called The Battler. . . .
> This Battler story is a hell of a swell story and better than Up in Mich altho I always liked Up in Mich altho some did not. I suppose if it was called Way Out in Iowa, Mencken would have published it if the fucking would have been changed to a community corn roast.[30]

There is a great deal here that makes me want to be offended with this speaker—the seemingly misogynistic reference to Liz Coates, the ethnic slur against "The Battler"'s Bugs, the braggadocio of his tone. But the use of his slang, euphemistic term for intercourse early in the passage ("the girl got yenced") seems very different from his willingness to a more straightforward use the term "fucking" later on. Notice the quality of the act Hemingway describes to Dos Passos—that it is Liz who is getting "yenced" without any apparent desire or willing involvement in the act. She would appear to be a passive player in his description of an act that would seem to be something other than the sexual act as Hemingway later represents it when speaking in more general terms of sexuality/obscenity in fiction.

"Up in Michigan" is very much a story in which individual desire is obscured by the more dominant, masculine narrative. Liz Coates becomes the object of this narrative, but her subject positionality has no bearing for the narrator of the piece, who expects her desire to mirror his own. Of the feminine object in cinematic narrative, de Lauretis writes, "The woman is framed by the look of the camera as icon, or object of the gaze: an image made to be looked at by the spectator, whose look is relayed by the look of the male character(s)" (*Alice Doesn't*, 139). At a remove from this cinematic gaze is the representation offered by the individual whose narrative gaze we depend on in reading this text—the unnamed narrator, who provides for us the narrative framework of the scene. Liz's story is being told by a very masculine narrator, who tries to convince both himself and the reader that this introduction to this form of sexual intercourse is enjoyable for her. Notice that the value judgment in the initial description of Liz is a judgment made by the narrator who is appraising her sexuality: She had "good legs." Following this description of Liz, the narrator's lulling repetition of "she liked it" betrays his own desire for Liz to find enjoyment from the masculine sexual penetration, in part to obscure her protests and to extend his own desire. Students reading this story in my undergraduate literature classes frequently comment that the "she liked it" paragraph reminds them of the argument made by the defense in many rape trials; if the accuser "liked it," wanted it, or asked for it, then presumably the defendant is no rapist and no crime has been committed. In "Desire in the Narrative," de Lauretis explains that "identification is itself a movement, a subject-process, a relation: the identification (of oneself) with something other (than oneself)" (*Alice Doesn't*, 141). The movement of the narrative of "Up in Michigan," a story whose title betrays the invasive quality of the masculine narrative itself, is itself a process of identification with the masculine narrative. We are offered a narrator who closely identifies himself with Jim Gilmore, as we must identify him, in his similarly phallic expression of desire as singularly defined and limited to one form of pleasure—the pleasure of masculine narrative climax.

Consider what is perhaps a more graphic example of this masculine desire evidenced by the speaker of the text. As Liz waits by the fire to see Jim go upstairs, Jim unexpectedly begins to pay her some attention, and the narrator describes the scene in this way:

> She was thinking about him hard and then Jim came out. His eyes were shining and his hair was a little rumpled. Liz looked down at her book. Jim came over back of her chair and stood there and she could feel him breathing and then he put his arms around her. Her breasts felt plump and firm and the nipples were erect under his hands. Liz was

terribly frightened, no one had ever touched her, but she thought, "He's
come to me finally. He's really come." (84)

This is an interesting paragraph in its construction and what it reveals
of the narrative speaker's desire. We begin the description with what
might be a rather ambiguous description of Liz: "She was thinking
about him hard." Is this simply Liz concentrating her thoughts on
Jim? Or is this Liz thinking about Jim *hard,* that is, of Jim's erection
and his physical hardness? The ambiguous syntax of the initial sentence might support either reading. Certainly the narrator uses the
word "erect" later in the passage, also in reference to Liz and hardly
a coincidence. And as the paragraph develops, there is building
sexual tension, from Jim's entry, to the foreplay he engages in with
Liz, and to a narrative climax which resolves the paragraph: "He's
come to me finally. He's really come." Although this isn't a sexual
climax for Liz, it is a climax of her romantic dreams of Jim. However,
I think it does clearly mirror the masculine sexual desire shared by
Jim and the narrator, both pursuing a kind of narrative climax that
assumes, and at the same time negates, an understanding of Liz's
desires.

Susan Swartzlander recognizes a similar narrative technique in
James Joyce's collection of short stories, *Dubliners,* in which supposedly objective third-person narratives begin to align themselves with
the attitudes of the characters they portray. In her essay, "Uncle
Charles in Michigan," she claims that, "Like Joyce, Hemingway used
a narrative voice that adopts not just the idiomatic phrases, but also
the speech rhythms, syntax, and attitudes representative of the characters in 'Up in Michigan.'"[31] This is accomplished, she continues,
through what Hugh Kenner referred to as "The Uncle Charles Principle" in Joyce's text, by "the integration of subjective and objective
elements of a narrative [which] is Hemingway's way of depicting a
scene which reverberates with emotion."[32] And in these scenes from
"Up in Michigan," there would seem to be significant identification
by the narrator at work here—not so much with Liz, however, but
with Jim Gilmore. Thus, if this is a story about rape, it is a rape
perpetrated both by Jim Gilmore and by the narrator as Liz's narrative
desires are obscured and devalued. Since Lisa Tyler has aptly defined
Liz's experience as "date rape" and has claimed that Hemingway's
portrayal of "real" women's experience illustrates the striking similarities between "women's psychological experience of rape" and
"men's experience of combat,"[33] what we must now understand
about the story is that *we readers are implicated* in the attitudes that

allow the rape to happen as long as we accept the narrative argument that "she liked it."

Although Hemingway later defended the story as "rather sad than dirty," according to Carlos Baker,[34] Gertrude Stein's predictions regarding the obscenity of this story were accurate, not because of the description of the sex act that occurs (in which Liz's response consists of phrases like "it's so big and it hurts so" [85]), but because the story portrays an essentially pornographic consciousness, the desire Krebs recognizes in those who only want to hear one kind of war story:

> Even his lies were not sensational at the pool room. His acquaintances, who had heard detailed accounts of German women found chained to machine guns in the Argonne forest and who could not comprehend, or were barred by their patriotism from any interest in, any German machine gunners who were not chained, were not thrilled by his stories.[35]

"Up in Michigan" offers a masculine narrative that attempts to masquerade as a narrative of female desire; although it makes a pretense of recognizing various individual desires, including Liz's, it actually obscures these in favor of a single representation of desire, climax, and closure—that of the heroic quest narrative. Petry writes of this disparity that "The primary sources of the story's excellence are Hemingway's sympathetic etching of Liz, the gentle, ingenuous kitchen maid whose sexual initiation he so graphically records, and his powerful depiction of the glaring disparity between male and female attitudes toward love and sex."[36] This narrative insists that the phallus is the exclusive location of pleasure, a narrative that is obstructed only by Liz's cries of protest throughout the rape. Recognizing it as such reveals the almost ridiculous artificiality of the heroic Oedipal narrative's attempt to obscure other, significant positionalities in the text, and to begin to realize the very different implications of the narrative if we acknowledge those protests against a singular interpretation. At the same time, however, we are faced with the fact that other narrative desire has indeed been silenced, quite successfully, in Liveright's refusal to allow the story to be published in *In Our Time.*

In a letter dated 31 March 1925, Hemingway wrote to Horace Liveright, "You are eliminating the second story—Up In Michigan. The next three stories move up one place each and this new story— The Battler—takes the place at present occupied by—The Three Day Blow."[37] This suggests that "Up in Michigan" had it made the final cut, would have followed the first story, "Indian Camp," and preceded

"The Doctor and the Doctor's Wife" in its placement in *In Our Time*. Had it not been for Liveright, "Up in Michigan" would have divided two of the Nick Adams stories which place him in the milieu of his family life up in Michigan. A story of rape and deception would have divided stories in which Nick watches his father perform a Caesarian section with a pocketknife and catgut leaders, and in which the pregnant woman's husband commits a gruesome act of suicide, and a story in which the relationship between Nick's parents—one a doctor, one an unhealthy Christian Scientist—reveal their essential incompatibility in marriage. And, as Harbour Winn recognizes in "Hemingway's *In Our Time*: 'Pretty Good Unity,'" the climactic scene of "Up in Michigan" takes place along the area of Lake Superior—the town of Horton's Bay—as the events in "The End of Something," in which Nick Adams orchestrates his breakup with his fiancée, Marjorie, clearly a premeditated plan as we see in Bill's later arrival upon the scene.[38]

Marjorie, like Liz Coates, values the ideals of romantic love, believing the old and now deserted mill "seems more like a castle" (32). But Marjorie won't behave like a proper Sleeping Beauty: "I've taught you everything," Nick complains to her, even after demeaning her with the accusation, "You know everything." But it would seem this isn't enough for Nick, because "It isn't fun any more" (34), perhaps because he has little more he can teach her. Marjorie has taken control, as we see Nick sitting on the beach holding the fishing rod, Marjorie actively in control of the boat and the placement of the bait as they prepare to fish, and again as she leaves him, refusing his assistance. The main difference between Marjorie and Liz is in Marjorie's ability to retain her romantic image: "She was afloat in the boat on the water with the moonlight on it" (35). But there is no such romance left for Liz, nor is there any remaining for Nick as Bill finds him lying face down on the beach. These romantic images of love and marriage, and of the desirability of the paternalistic narrative of power and control, rapidly deconstruct themselves in images of women carrying their dead babies about or giving birth in the back of wagons (in which it "rained all through the evacuation" as the final line of chapter II reads, dispelling the notion of a clean getaway in a wartime escape and of the security of a construct such as "family," as it rains during the evacuation of the child from its mother). These romantic images also deconstruct themselves in the tales of opposition, soldiers ignominiously shot down like ducks in a carnival game, or in the image of the cabinet minister—a national leader—who will not stand and face death before the firing squad heroically. "When they fired the first volley he was sitting down in the water with his head on his knees" (51). The minister, a symbol of political power, meets death in a fetal position.

Hemingway's replacement for "Up in Michigan" continues to develop narrative imagery which denies any adherence to such Oedipal structures as the honor of the code hero or the security of the traditional family. "The Battler" has been described as Nick Adams's initiation into the depravity and corruption possible in men, from the deceit of the brakeman who knocks him off the train, to the grotesque figure of Ad Francis and his blackjack-wielding traveling companion, Bugs. It is a crucial story for those readers who believe chapter VI— which follows "The Battler"—is the climax of Nick's quest narrative, in which "He had been hit in the spine" (63), an injury not unlike the damage Bugs must perform upon Ad to keep him under control, striking him as he does at the base of the neck. But this is less a story about Nick Adams, I think, and more an examination of the quality of existence of two individuals who have been driven out of the social narrative in which they don't belong. Ad Francis, while esteemed as a prize fighter, has been driven over the edge—perhaps by being hit in the head too many times—but more importantly by the press, which claimed that he and his wife were actually brother and sister, causing her finally to leave him. "Of course they wasn't brother and sister no more than a rabbit" (61), Bugs reassures Nick, but the damage has already been done to Ad's psyche, and it is all Bugs can do to keep an eye on the ex-prizefighter and to keep him under control.

There is something wrong for many readers in the image of these men traveling together; Bugs's ability to shift from subservience to domination, from servant to master, causes many to question his motives for staying in a relationship with Ad Francis. Philip Young thinly veils this suspicion and characteristically claims that there can be only one conclusion for these men to continue traveling together:

> This story is also, however, among the most suggestive of Hemingway's; there is more that is sinister and unpleasant about this gentle, large, courteous and thoughtful blackjacking colored man than may at first meet the eye, and it can only have one very probable interpretation. . . . Although Nick understands no more than that something is very wrong here, the reader may get the never-stated but potently suggested notion that it is not only Ad who is queer.[39]

In his use of the word "queer," Young is referring to the narrative description of Ad Francis as Nick encounters him: "His nose was sunken, his eyes were slits, he had queer-shaped lips. Nick did not perceive all this at once, he only saw the man's face was queerly

formed and mutilated" (55). The word that is used much more frequently in the story is "crazy"—occurring eight times in the text, as
opposed to versions of the word "queer" which appear twice, only
in the sentences quoted above.[40] But Young's use of "queer" rather
than "crazy" indicates his suggestion that the relationship between
Ad and Bugs is predicated on more than just their mental instabil-
ity—what Young sees potently suggested in the story is reflected in
the common slang use of the term "queer" for homosexuality. Indeed,
other readers also cling to this notion in examining the relationship
between these men. For instance, George Monteiro writes, in "'This
Is My Pal Bugs': Ernest Hemingway's 'The Battler,'" that Bugs's comment to Nick that Ad's good-looking wife could have been his twin
makes his gender preference questionable: "Besides revealing affection and personal feeling, perhaps, these observations suggest that
there exists a strong physical attraction between the two partners in
this home-making couple." As homemakers, these men deviate from
the proper image of what it is to be a homemaker, causing Monteiro
to ask, "Bugs simply sees Ad differently and more attractively. Is it
going too far to say that he sees him with a lover's eyes?"[41]

More forthright in his claim that this is a homosexual relationship
is Joseph DeFalco's analysis of the story. He explains it, being sure
to place Nick at the center of the hero narrative, by writing, "Nick's
first introduction into a world where promises are not kept forms
the early coincidence of his involvement in the central drama by the
fireside of a punchdrunk ex-fighter and an apparently homosexual
Negro."[42] Why DeFalco reads Bugs as "apparently homosexual" is
never answered; he never offers any assistance to his reader which
might allow us to discover the process of reasoning he uses to make
this conclusion. However, his insistence upon installing two narrative paradigms—the Campbellian hero quest and the social narrative
of the traditional family unit—into the text indicates the ways DeFalco
reaches this untenable conclusion. He explains,

> In a symbolic frame of reference, as the sick hero Francis is also the
> ogre figure with whom Nick must do battle on the threshold of maturity.
> In this sense he is symbolic of the father-authority who is both the helpful
> guide and the dangerous presence guarding the entrance into the
> unknown.

Of course, if Ad Francis plays the role of ogre/father in the quest
paradigm, then someone must play the Oedipal role of helpmate/
mother—and the only other individual left for DeFalco to fit into this
part is Bugs. And because Bugs does do the shopping and the cook-

ing, following DeFalco's assumptions, he must be a rather feminine counterpart to the manly fighter. He continues,

> the Negro here is the cook and soother, the hermaphroditic figure who resembles the mother. . . . The fact that he is dark, however, signals the danger inherent in the nature of such a figure. His apparent homosexuality gives further credence to his changeling nature and points to the dangers of the personage who indulges in activities which are *contra naturam*.[43]

Again, there are references to apparent homosexuality, which De-Falco constructs from the fact that Bugs adopts a feminine gender role in the relationship, falling back upon the homophobic stereotype, which suggests that homosexuality means a kind of perverted and misplaced desire for femininity. Again, he never explains his conclusion that Bugs is hermaphroditic, other than in his reference that he does what might be commonly called "women's work." His analysis of the story must finally conclude that both men doing women's work and homosexuality are against the laws of nature and that to accept either role is to become deformed and dangerous to what is "natural" or "normal."

The problem with these readings is not that the suggestion of homosexuality is in itself misplaced or somehow wrong or improper. It is the decision that *this* relationship is representative of homosexuality which poses difficulties. If this is a gay couple, as these and other readers suggest without any real evidence beyond what Eve Kosofsky Sedgwick refers to as the homosocial relationship that exists between men in her study, *Between Men: English Literature and Male Homosocial Desire,* then the representation of homosexuality is presented as occurring in men, and occasionally women, who are deformed and rather monstrous—"sinister and unpleasant" in Young's description. Indeed, there is a great deal of homophobia practiced by readers of Hemingway who assume such figures are ultimately deviants, perverse distortions of a more proper sociocultural narrative.

More significantly, however, is the recurrent suggestion that the locus of evidence for this repulsive homosexuality is Bugs. Consider the qualification DeFalco makes in the passage I quoted above. "The fact that he is dark, however, signals the danger inherent in the nature of such a figure." Not only are Bugs's motives questionable because he seems motherly, but also as a result of his ethnicity; a Black man shouldn't be going around blackjacking white men, or so the implicit argument goes. Surely, had Bugs remained a faithful manservant, a

Rochester or an Uncle Tom bowing and shuffling to "Mr. Adams" and "Mr. Adolph Francis," as he calls them, many of these critical concerns for his deviant and homosexual nature wouldn't have arisen. In the larger social narrative these readers apply to the text, that subservience would have been proper. And of course, Bugs's ethnicity puts other motives into question as well, as Monteiro's comments might suggest: Are Bugs's admiring descriptions of Ad's ex-wife proper coming from a Black man? Or do they also follow from the stereotype of the Black man as somehow monstrous in his sexuality by nature?

Few readers of this story have taken these problems surrounding Bugs' character into consideration, but in her study of American literature, *Playing in the Dark: Whiteness and the Literary Imagination,* Toni Morrison confronts this problematic perception of ethnicity and its role in American literature. She writes, "Race has become metaphorical—a way of referring to and disguising forces, events, classes, and expressions of social decay and economic division far more threatening to the body politic than biological 'race' ever was."[44] It is significant that Bugs is the "dark" center of the story, because his presence as servant and destroyer of Ad Francis demands a troublesome need to reevaluate roles within the moral mechanics of the social narrative. Rather than reevaluate those roles, however, the tendency has been to reassign metaphoric figures with other attributes, other monstrous identities. Morrison argues of the role of African-Americans in American literature, "Just as entertainers, through or by association with blackface, could render permissible topics that otherwise would have been taboo, so American writers were able to employ an imagined Africanist persona to articulate and imaginatively act out the forbidden in American culture."[45] The racist fiction of the Black man is evident in the narrative's descriptions of Bugs throughout—he is most often identified as "the negro" by the narrator, who describes his final instructions to Nick as said "all . . . in a low, smooth, polite nigger voice" (62). These references are surely reminiscent of Hemingway's offensive reference to Bugs as a "coon" in the letter to John Dos Passos I mentioned earlier, and if we want to recoup the biographical author as racist— the typically narrow-minded, white American writer Morrison mentions and upbraids in her study—this is certainly a place we might start. However, looking at the representations in the text itself, without positing an autobiographical hero, we see that the forbidden at work here is based on that image of Bugs's blackjacking Ad, and it translates in a kind of code for many readers to another forbidden topic, one that is less racially suspect: homosexuality. The imagined

Africanist persona becomes an imagined figure of degradation and deviance in readers' responses to it.

Why is Bugs with Ad? How is it that he can get away with doing such damage to a once-respected white man? In part, these questions can be answered through Bugs's explanation of their situation to Nick. Consider the way Ad and Bugs met: "I met him in jail," Bugs tells Nick, "He was busting people all the time after she went away and they put him in jail. I was in for cuttin' a man" (61). Later on, we find that Bugs has sought out Ad after his release from prison; he describes the relationship by telling Nick, "I like to be with him and I like seeing the country and I don't have to commit no larceny to do it. I like living like a gentleman" (61). Although I would hardly call their living situation gentlemanly, Bugs's point here is important. Traveling alone, a Black man in the early years of the twentieth century, Bugs admits he has had difficulty retaining his independence, and perhaps even staying alive. His desire not to have to commit larceny as a way of living certainly suggests that he travels with Ad Francis not only out of friendship, but for safety's sake as well. With Ad he can retain his dignity. Although he must pretend to be servile in his reference to "Mr. Adams" and "Mr. Adolph Francis," and in his service as cook and supplier (the image is indeed reminiscent of the blackface stereotypic routines of early entertainment that Morrison describes), he is finally in control of the situation and of his own destiny in a way that, striking out on his own in that society, he cannot be. They stick to the woods, away from people, because were Bugs to be seen striking a white man, even a crazy white man, in such a fashion, it would surely translate into a prison term and very possibly into a lynching.

Toni Morrison identifies the nearly ubiquitous presence of mother/nurse figures in Hemingway's fiction and recognizes that many of these individuals appear as further manifestations of characters like Bugs. Although these figures appear to be subservient to the hero at the central of the Oedipal narrative, however, they offer a significant means of obstruction and denial of this singular perspective. She writes,

> No matter if they are loyal or resistant nurses, nourishing *and* bashing the master's body, these black men articulate the narrator's doom and gainsay the protagonist-narrator's construction of himself. They modify his self-image; they violate the nurse's primary function of providing balm. In short, they disturb, in subtle and forceful ways, the narrator's construction of reality.[46]

In terms of the masculine narrative, these figures obstruct the hero's progress toward a goal of heroic individuation; they refuse to be merely servants or landscapes assisting in the masculine hero's progress. In his unlikely role in the story, Bugs serves to deny both Ad's violence and Nick's security as the center of the narrative's progress. Because Bugs reveals his desire to deny his role as a mere servant by "tapping" Ad, Nick must be sent away; he has witnessed a taboo act, and Bugs is not willing to strike Ad again—which has threatening implications for Nick should he remain. When Nick leaves the campfire and walks down the railroad tracks toward Mancelona, I find myself wondering more about the continuing scene in the woods than I do about Nick's progression toward the town. Indeed, both Nick and the narrator of the story also find themselves looking backward in this way, as the final lines of the text reveal: "Looking back from the mounting grade before the track curved into the hills he could see the firelight in the clearing" (62). "The Battler" is so successful in its attempts to fragment the Oedipal narrative that even that figure who readers settle on as the central hero has been turned away from the quest, the linear movement that might be characterized by the railroad tracks, to look backward at the woods and the individuals enclosed within them.

Following "The Battler," chapter VI is the final appearance of Nick Adams until "Cross-Country Snow," seven stories and six chapters later and his penultimate appearance in the text. Separating these stories are chapter vignettes that highlight the convenience of religion, the effects of racism (note that chapter VIII begins like an ethnic joke: "At two o'clock in the morning two Hungarians got into a cigar store"; it is a joke that ends with their deaths and the punchline, "I can tell wops a mile off" [79]), and images of bullfighting that are hardly heroic. Similarly, we are given stories that have little to do with the Nick Adams who is recoverable in earlier sections of the text—a failed revolutionary, an engagement that ends in faithlessness and venereal disease, and a marriage of convenience that fails to meet expectations for the Elliots. To assume that these episodes are either about Nick or written by Nick is to construct a narrative that denies other possible narrative perspectives. Indeed, it would seem that, following "The Battler," the narrative follows significantly diverse directions, refusing to keep to the railroad tracks even as it leaves Nick staring "straight ahead brilliantly" in a state of shock (chapter VI, 63). It returns occasionally to a character named Nick Adams, but the repetition of the name doesn't necessarily demand that this is the same person following a singularly linear narrative. The Nick Adams in "Indian Camp" is not the Nick Adams of "Big

Two-Hearted River" at all, if only because of the obvious reason that he has matured, a conclusion James M. Cox also supports: "The Nick who appears in the Nick stories is thus not any more a continuation than he is a repetition of a name in a different unit."[47]

If we depend on the repetition of this character's name to construct a singular heroic narrative, then I wonder if we might do the same for other individuals whose common names are repeated throughout *In Our Time*. Is the Uncle George of "Indian Camp" the same insensitive and domineering George of "Cat in the Rain," the husband of the unnamed American wife? If he is, it would radically revise any notion that these events chronologically parallel Nick's own marriage. Or is the George of "Cat in the Rain" the same George that Nick goes skiing with in "Cross-Country Snows"? And how are these Georges related to George Gardner, the crooked jockey riding Kzar in "My Old Man"? Neither of the former Georges are identified as jockeys, yet Nick is never identified as having the marital problems encountered by the Elliots or by the American couples in "Cat in the Rain" and "Out of Season." Similarly, I am not convinced that Krebs's sister, Helen, is necessarily a different person from Nick's wife, who, as we find in "Cross-Country Snows," is also named Helen. Although the causal relationships are not as evident for these Georges and Helens as they seem to be for the early Nick stories, their connections seem no less artificial to me than the presumption that the non–Nick stories are indeed ultimately concerned with Nick Adams's heroic progression.

Assigning a story such as "Cat in the Rain" significance only as a measure of Nick's broader experience actually commits the same act of suppression a character such as the American wife is attempting to free herself from. While the Italians "came from a long way off to look up at the war monument" (91)—a phallocentric activity not unlike the tendency to go to great lengths to gaze up at the figure of Nick Adams in the narrative—the focus of the American wife's desire is elsewhere. The first line of the second paragraph in the story would seem to suggest that the preceding narrative perspective had been hers, looking out upon the ocean, the garden, and the war monument. "The American wife stood at the window looking out" (91). However, she is concerned with something quite different.

> Outside right under their window a cat was crouched under one of the dripping green tables. The cat was trying to make herself so compact that she would not be dripped on. (91)

The concern for linearity in the opening narrative description of the phallic monument and the shoreline ("The sea broke in a long line in the rain and slipped back down the beach to come up and break again in a long line in the rain" [91]) is broken when the narrative shifts.

Unfortunately, that subject—the cat under the table—has disappeared by the time she gets outside to look for it. The American wife has a strong impression of this cat as something she wanted to rescue, but the maid with the umbrella is unable to help her to recover it. Later, after the failed expedition to rescue the cat, she turns from the window to the mirror. "She went over and sat in front of the mirror of the dressing table looking at herself with the hand glass. She studied her profile, first one side and then the other. Then she studied the back of her head and neck" (93). The woman's scrutiny moves alternately in the story from the square outside the window to her mirror and back again to the window, presumably to look for the cat. But, since we are told "It was getting dark" (93) and "It was quite dark now" (94), it is very likely that her absorption in the window is a manifestation of her scrutiny of her own reflection in the mirror. If it is light enough in the room for George to read, she will very likely be able to see her own reflection in the window, studying neither the monument nor the garden nor the ocean beyond, but herself. Thus, when she sees the cat, she sees it through her own reflection, and both are consequently gone by the time she reaches the square.

If this is indeed what she has been doing—examining herself in the glass—her complaints to her husband are not merely capricious. "I get so tired of looking like a boy" (93), she tells him. George's response is one of arousal and, for the first time in the story, interest, but it is an interest that doesn't acknowledge *her* desire: "You look pretty darn nice" (93). She has been assigned an identity that arouses George but that she has no control over. Similarly, she is referred to primarily as "The American wife" in a narrative that identifies her only as an extension of her husband, who receives the benefit of a given name. And when she isn't recognized as a wife by the narrator, she becomes only "the American girl," a diminutive kind of recognition that offers her scant individual identity. This failure to recognize her on the part of the narrator is not surprising, however, since the narrative has also failed to really see what she is looking at as she stands before the window.

Despite this imposed identity, she seems determined to actualize her desires, both in her attempt to rescue the kitty and in her refusal to acknowledge George's desire before she acknowledges her own:

> "I want to pull my hair back tight and smooth and make a big knot at the back that I can feel," she said. "I want to have a kitty to sit on my

lap and purr when I stroke her. . . . And I want to eat at a table with my own silver and I want candles. And I want it to be spring and I want to brush my hair out in front of a mirror and I want a kitty and I want some new clothes." (93–94)

But George is no longer aroused, and he is not interested in her desires: "Oh, shut up and get something to read" (94). The only individual who seems to be interested in the American wife's desires is the hotel-keeper, who sends the maid out with an umbrella to keep her dry. His reference to her necessarily follows that of the narrator, calling her only "Signora," but offering her the respect she doesn't seem to get from her husband.

> As the American girl passed the office, the padrone bowed from his desk. Something felt very small and tight inside the girl. The padrone made her feel very small and at the same time really important. She had a momentary feeling of being of supreme importance. (93)

There is more feeling for the padrone than is expressed for George, which is not surprising considering the immobility he exhibits from his perch on the bed. It is no wonder that she feels important with the padrone, who, unlike George, is charged with the paternal duty of seeing to the needs of his customers. Because she cannot find her cat, he finally sends the maid to the room with a gift: "a big tortoise-shell cat pressed tight against her and swung down against her body" (94). However, his offering is ineffectual as an attempt to placate her desires; it cannot be the same cat she saw, if only because of her need to rescue the cat herself. Delivered by the hotel-keeper, this cat is rather meaningless.

In critical approaches to "Cat in the Rain," there have been two questions at the center of debate. In his essay, "The Poor Kitty and the Padrone and the Tortoise-shell Cat in 'Cat in the Rain,'" Warren Bennett examines the questions that readers have been unable to solve: "whether there is one cat or two cats in the story, and . . . whether the wife *wants* to have a baby or whether she is already pregnant."[48] Citing separate arguments proposed by John V. Hagopian and David Lodge, Bennett concludes, "In regard to the question of pregnancy, Hagopian's interpretation that the wife 'wants' to be pregnant is more valid than Lodge's counterinterpretation that the wife *is* pregnant."[49] While Lodge, according to Bennett, believes her desire for a cat is a "whimsical craving" that might be associated with someone who is pregnant, Bennett believes that if she were pregnant, her descriptions of her physical state would be much different—she would not feel small and tight, but would actually be getting larger.

Why is it necessary to assume she even *wants* to be pregnant? Is that the stereotypical goal of femininity for readers of this story? And if it is pregnancy that the American wife really desires behind the silver and candles and cats, then she certainly has the opportunity to act upon this desire as George becomes aroused. Instead, however, she doesn't respond to his obvious arousal and continues to try and get him to understand her need to redefine herself. Perhaps like Liz Coates, Nick's fiancée, Marjorie, and Nick himself in "The End of Something," this wife is revealing the disappointing destruction of her image of the romantic love that is supposed to be shared between a husband and wife, especially as they tour the Mediterranean together. As an image that controls a popular conception of love and marriage, it continually seems to self-destruct, especially for the women who realize what it means to be caught in a paternalistic, phallocentric narrative which demands that they play a submissive role to a hero/husband. The disappearing cat, perhaps a distant relative of Alice's Cheshire cat, is indicative of the perverse narrative of romantic love that constructs moral meaning by imposing certain identity, and the American wife's understanding that her own ability to assert her desires within this narrative is becoming remote.

As the wife tries to explain what she is doing out in the rain, the maid only laughs at the idea of the wife seeing a cat in this weather. What is finally so amusing about a cat in the rain for the maid is their utter incompatibility—cats don't like water, they don't belong in the rain, and when they are wet they tend to look rather ridiculous. But the maid and George fail to understand that the disappearing cat is, for the wife, a sign of the failure of the social ideal of love and marriage, and a reflection of her own fading identity as an extension of her husband's desires. It is no coincidence that, as George refuses to allow his wife to have long hair and to act upon her own desires, so we find a *torero* having his pigtail, the paramount identifier of his profession, cut off by an angry crowd in the following chapter vignette.

The Polyphonic Narrative as "Prose Kinema"

Returning again to the effect the excised story has upon the text as a whole, "Up in Michigan" is vital to a reading of *In Our Time* that takes into consideration the multiple perspectives that have been either neglected or forsworn by readers interested in making moral meaning under a restrictive narrative paradigm. The patterns and deceptions constructed by the narrator in "Up in Michigan" are also available elsewhere in the larger text, recalling the conditions of otherwise unrelated stories. In his essay, "You Can Say That Again: Some Encounters with Repetition in *In Our Time*," Don Summerhayes indicates that other passages in the fragmentary novel mirror the "She likes it" repetition constructed in the narrative of "Up in Michigan." For instance, in "The Battler," we find Bugs telling Nick about his own relationship with Ad Francis:

> Right away I liked him and when I got out I looked him up. He likes to think I'm crazy and I don't mind. I like to be with him and I like seeing the country and I don't have to commit no larceny to do it. I like living like a gentleman. (61)

Similarly, in "Soldier's Home," it is Krebs who the narrator describes in his pleasure at looking at the young women of the town:

> Nothing was changed in the town except that the young girls had grown up. . . . He liked to look at them from the front porch as they walked on the other side of the street. He liked to watch them walking under the shade of the trees. He liked the round Dutch collars above their sweaters. He liked their silk stockings and flat shoes. He liked their bobbed hair and the way they walked. (71)

And again in "Cat in the Rain," we find the narrator describing the wife as she leaves the hotel to find the cat she has seen in the rain. Of the hotel-keeper, we find that

> The wife liked him. She liked the deadly serious way he received any complaints. She liked his dignity. She liked the way he wanted to serve her. She liked the way he felt about being a hotel-keeper. She liked his old, heavy face and big hands.
> Liking him she opened the door and looked out. (92)

In many ways, these echo special effects originally installed in "Up in Michigan," and they recall the story as a locus of narrative desire even as it has been excised from the text. Of Krebs's experience, Summerhayes writes, "Words do not correspond (exactly) to experience, but in fact distort it, and lead to the 'lies' or 'complications' he is trying to escape from." As distortions of experience, this repetitious language attempts to assert authority even as it acknowledges the fragility of such a construct—while in each case an assertion is made about individual desire, in at least three of these situations this desire is represented through narrators who are not fully able (or even willing) to comprehend the desires of these individuals. Bugs's liking Ad and their lives together also hides many things, especially the forbidden details of his condition as a Black man in control of his white counterpart. Summerhayes continues, "The sequences of repetition suggest a kind of stream-of-consciousness, or at least a mimicry of vague but compulsive sensations that persistently back off from analytic 'thinking.'"[50]

This repetition promotes a kind of cognitive dissonance in the narrative, bringing stories and situations and individuals together which cognitively don't belong together, certainly not in the way we think of a novelistic narrative. It doesn't create a single narrative perspective—neither Liz nor Jim, Nick nor Bugs, Krebs nor the American wife can be identified as *the* Oedipal hero at the center of the text—but constructs a polyphonic narrative in which various diverse voices all share similar expressions in a narrative mapping of differences. It may be argued that I have conveniently eliminated from my study several of the available voices in the stories and chapter vignettes, as I have suggested that others have done in promoting an Oedipal narrative of Nick Adams as hero. At least part of the problem is the nature of this project—as a single chapter of a larger work, I cannot begin to do justice to all of the stories and perspectives in *In Our Time*—that would be a book-length study in itself. But it is also true that to attempt to be all-inclusive would be to attempt construction of another kind of Oedipal narrative, in which every narrative possibility has been exhausted and accounted for, and which, in a fragmentary, dynamic novel, is quite impossible.

Alice Jardine asks of the traditional impulse toward constructing the heroic, Oedipal narrative, "Do theories of narrative structure in the male realm always have to be modeled upon traditional male desire: beginning , middle, end? What about problems of enunciation, voice, and silence?"[51] These are the very problems *In Our Time* confronts us with if we accept Lawrence's premise that it is actually a fragmentary novel. If "Up in Michigan" proposes the artificiality of the masculine narrative, *In Our Time* demonstrates a refusal to adhere to a single history, to accept a central narrative as either dominant or correct in its imposed morality. To claim that Nick Adams's is the central consciousness of the collection is to ignore the individuals who recognize that "You couldn't get the women to give up their dead babies" ("On the Quai at Smyrna," 11) or that "It isn't any fun to be a poor kitty out in the rain" ("Cat in the Rain," 93). Like "Up in Michigan," *In Our Time* demonstrates the artificiality of limited narrative perspectives, taking for its theme the chaotic nature of narratives as they become subject to violently shifting perspectives and events without narrative climax. Narrative perspective can continually change in this experimental novel, because the protean nature of the shifting chapter perspectives allows for various narratives, whether related or not, to interact between the pages of a single text. Of the effect these chapters have on the text, James M. Cox writes, "Chapters, the conventional unit of the novel, appearing here as visually complete vignettes become a visual atrophy of the novelistic form, but atrophy in the form of violent compression."[52] They come together as that fragmentary novel Lawrence recognized, and finally propose the kind of novelistic heteroglossia Bakhtin proposes in "Epic and Novel": "Reality as we have it in the novel is only one of many possible realities; it is not inevitable, not arbitrary, it bears within itself other possibilities."[53]

All proper parts do not fit a single story, as Young suggested of *In Our Time;* they break apart and refuse to be viewed from a single perspective. The reference made in the title of the collection is an important one, taken from the Book of Common Prayer: "Give peace in our time, O Lord."[54] This is the peace Nick looks for in "Big Two-Hearted River," and the narrative stability Moddelmog and Young propose, but the statement which the collection makes is that in a chaotic world this kind of convenient stability is unavailable. No matter how hard he tries, the individual in Hemingway's fiction is less likely to be able to affirm the "controls of honor and courage which . . . make a man a man," and actually does find himself "without inviolable rules for how to live."[55] Except for chapter 6, the other vignettes do not focus on Nick Adams but on individuals who face only disgrace in the brutal situations they are caught in. It is significant that there is no climax in any of these chapters, nor is there a sense of climax in their progression throughout the novel. We do return to stories about Nick Adams, but, although his is a recurring perspective in the collection, it is by no means the only one, or necessarily the most valuable. Instead, we are given a kind of "prose kinema," to borrow a metaphor from the second canto of Pound's *Hugh Selwyn Mauberley;* the chapters are not merely vignettes or miniatures, as Baker calls them, but are images that contribute to an effect similar to montage in cinema. It is an effect the dying Maera understands; at the conclusion of chapter XIV, we find that "everything commenced to run faster and faster as when they speed up a cinematograph film. Then he was dead" (131). Death of the hero comes when the mechanics of the traditional masculine narrative break down and refuse to work according to expectations of both the phallocentric hero and reader. We are subject to rapidly moving images that deny narrative closure and through which we may begin to perceive the collection as a series of images and perspectives that begin to inform our own attempts to collect and fix a protean narrative such as *In Our Time*.

5

"We could have had such a damned good time together [if only you had a penis]": Critical Phallocentrism and *The Sun Also Rises*

Now you can see. I looked as though I were trying to get to be the hero of this story. But that was all wrong. Gerald Cohn is the hero. When I bring myself in it is only to clear up something. Or maybe Duff is the hero. Or Niño de la Palma. But He never really had a chance to be the hero. Or maybe there is not any hero at all. Maybe a story is better without any hero.

In this passage from chapter 5 of the notebook draft of *The Sun Also Rises*, the narrator who is in the process of becoming Jake Barnes indicates the problems he is having in telling his story, as Frederic Joseph Svoboda illustrates in *Hemingway & "The Sun Also Rises."*[1] Much is as yet unfinished in this draft; Harold Loeb has become Gerald Cohn, who will become Robert Cohn, while Duff and Niño de la Palma have yet to transform into Brett Ashley and Pedro Romero. What the narrator seems to be intent on keeping "unfinished" in his story, however, is the heroic center demanded by the traditional Oedipal conventions of the novel. Svoboda notes, "A clear and admirable hero is the backbone of formulaic fiction," which is precisely what readers have traditionally made of Hemingway's fiction, as I have indicated in my previous chapter on Nick Adams and *In Our Time*.[2] There is a tradition in reading the novel as an epic and linear narrative, a tradition that has demanded that we read Jake Barnes as the central hero who must learn how to live by exhibiting what is now a tired cliché in Hemingway studies, a "grace under pressure." In such a formula, since she cannot be the hero, Brett Ashley vacil-

175

lates between being a wicked witch, a hopeless nymphomaniac frustrated in her inability to have the man she really wants, and her role as the prize at the end of Jake's quest.

In the often analyzed conclusion of *The Sun Also Rises,* we see a prime example of what many readers believe is an exhibition of this formulaic heroic conflict, and we also find a potentially misogynistic situation similar to that which closes Lawrence's *Women in Love.* Brett has once again returned to Jake, if only between her disastrous affair with Romero and her return to Mike Campbell. As she and Jake drive through Madrid and past the policeman with the conspicuously rising baton, she considers the potential they have missed in their relationship: "Oh, Jake . . . we could have had such a damned good time together." Jake's pragmatic response, "Yes. . . . Isn't it pretty to think so?" (247), gives him the last word in the novel he has written, dismissing her romantic imagination while rather stoically bearing his bad luck. Mark Spilka writes in his early essay, "The Death of Love in *The Sun Also Rises,*" "'Pretty' is a romantic word which means here 'foolish to consider what could *never* have happened,' and not 'what can't happen now.'" And while Spilka qualifies the chance for love, for their having a damned good time together, noting that "Even without his wound, [Jake] would still be unmanly," he also narrows the most significant obstacle in Brett's concluding wistfulness to biology and desire: "If he hadn't been wounded, if he had somehow survived the war with his manhood intact, then he and Brett would have become true lovers."[3] Readers have been tempted to supply what for many is the obviously missing part of Brett's thought, the most significant reason for Jake's pragmatism: "We could have had such a damned good time together . . . if only you had a penis." Such an unspoken conclusion emphasizes what many see as her phallocentric desire for a relationship with a "good," fully functioning man.

As the predominant and traditional way of reading Hemingway's fiction, this search for the central, formulaic hero has caused many readers, especially women readers who are offended by what seems to be Hemingway's inherent misogyny, to devalue his work in the canon of American literature. Wilma Garcia sums up many readers attitudes about Hemingway's fiction by noting, "Aspersions have been cast by literary critics and critical feminists at his one-dimensional heroines and bitch women, and a frequent description of Hemingway is that he is a man's writer with whose work female readers have little in common." Mimi Reisel Gladstein defines the offense readers take at his "shallow or superficial portrayal" of women as a result of "Hemingway's narrow concept of masculinity, the subject of much critical derision. The Hemingway hero attempts to drink well, shoot well, throw the straight and true punch, prove his proficiency and potency in intercourse, and when his time comes, die heroically." Similarly, in her recent study of American literature, Toni Morrison sees very few choices for women in such misogynist literature—they are portrayed as either submissive nurses or as "the women who abandon or have difficulty sustaining their nursing abilities; women who destroy the silent sufferer, hurt him instead of nurturing him."[4] These are the responses of many individuals who are taught traditional, one-sided approaches to Hemingway's usually male "heroes" in classrooms and in scholarly articles, and who echo the summary dismissal of one of my students of Hemingway as merely "a man writing for men."

This is an unfortunate conclusion, because I believe that the myth of Hemingway's misogyny, at least in his fiction, is itself a construct created by his readers, and this misogyny is quite often reflective not of *The Sun Also Rises,* for instance, but of the critical readers themselves. Robert Scholes writes, "To justify teaching Hemingway we must make his sexual bias a part of our study, rather than pretend that the matter is inartistic and therefore extracurricular."[5] Many readers of Hemingway ascribe to this belief that to expose Hemingway is to expose absolute meaning in his fiction. For instance, in the chapter of his *Hemingway . . . The Writer's Art of Self-Defense* entitled "Roles and the Masculine Writer," Jackson J. Benson writes, "Hemingway was vitally concerned with re-establishing what he felt were the proper roles of man and woman in their relationship to each other." Those "proper" roles are, of course, the traditional roles men and women have been conscribed to via a sociocultural Oedipal narrative—like the Sleeping Beauty story mentioned earlier—and Benson illustrates them by contrasting what he calls the "feminine" tradition in literature, as opposed to the "masculine" tendencies of Hemingway. "[T]he feminine tradition in literature (in conjunction with those other cultural forces we term *feminism*) tends to confuse the roles of one sex with the other, so that the man is the weaker sex and the woman the stronger, the woman the leader and the man the dependent." Propriety has been confused, social roles have been violated, and therefore this feminine tradition must be overcome by the masculinism of Hemingway's fiction, at least according to Benson. This makes it easy to see why Benson finally reads *The Sun Also Rises* as "the story of a male who becomes a man even though his male equipment does not work, and a female who never becomes a woman even though she is blessed with the best equipment available."[6] For Benson, an individual's biological "equipment"—and the way that individual uses or misuses it—determines his or her proper and inviolable sociosexual roles.

But is this really *Hemingway's* sexual bias, as Scholes calls it? I have to wonder what Scholes means by "his sexual bias," and just how we decide that it is indeed Hemingway's sexual bias we are reading in the fiction. It also seems as though there is less of Hemingway in Benson's conclusion than there is of Benson. Andrew Hook makes a valuable point for those readers dissatisfied with Hemingway's apparent misogyny when he writes that "man and artist are no substitute for each other; and dislike of the one should not mean rejection of both. It is always possible that the fiction may survive the myth."[7] Unfortunately, *The Sun Also Rises* has not survived the myth for many readers, primarily because reading the novel has traditionally meant reading from the limited perspective of the critical Oedipal narrative that has been constructed during the past forty or so years. In fact, Hemingway's reputation for misogyny and for his phallocentric focus on masculinity may be more a result of the assumptions that critical readers have made about social norms and fictional constructs than from elements inherent in the fiction itself.

Of the passage from an early draft of the novel that I quoted above, Svoboda explains, "What Hemingway has suggested is, of course, that maybe a story is better if it moves away from conventional expectations of what elements it should contain."[8] This is a move that readers of Hemingway's novel have largely been unable to make, a condition that is most evident in critical representations of Brett Ashley and Jake Barnes in *The Sun Also Rises.* There are several almost incontrovertible conventions readers of Hemingway cling to, as Sibbie O'Sullivan so effectively illustrates: "The cliche runs like this: Jake, unmanned in the war, is not only physically but spiritually impotent and allows himself to be debased by Brett, that 'non-woman,' that 'purely destructive force.'"[9] To begin to reevaluate Hemingway's fiction is to attempt an approach to the novel from a perspective other than that of the phallocentric narrative which has dominated ways of reading this novel. One way to do this is to reexamine the relationship between the two characters who have served for so long as representatives of ideal masculinity and debased femininity. Brett Ashley must not be limited to being read as the perverted nymphomaniac who represents the degradation at the core of the novel, especially because there is clear evidence in the text that suggests quite the contrary. Similarly, Jake Barnes may not be the honestly heroic, suffering aficionado as he is often construed. Their roles and relationships are much more complex once they are released from the constraints of the phallocentric critical tradition in Hemingway scholarship, and the narrative becomes much more dialogic and experimental once these readerly paradigms are removed. I believe that Hemingway's fiction does indeed problematize the formulaic devices of the Oedipal narrative, as the passage from the draft of the novel suggests, and that the novel is finally both more sensitive to the intricacies of gender roles and relationships and more willing to make a break with the Oedipal narratives of social propriety than most critics will allow.

Critical Readers Engendering the Narrative

Before exploring the ways in which the novel draws the Oedipal narrative into question, I want to survey some of the predominant and foundational approaches to *The Sun Also Rises,* the critical Oedipal narrative that has been constructed in traditional readings of Hemingway's text, and the attitudes these approaches betray. How critical readers have handled the fiction of "a man writing for men" is as significant as Hemingway's own construction of masculinity in the novel itself. As I indicated earlier, Jake remains a hero and a representative of the plight of the Lost Generation, while Brett is finally defined by many readers as promiscuous, as a nymphomaniac, as an evil and devouring bitch, and finally as fragmented, weak, and incomplete in her desire for what she cannot have—normative heterosexual sex with Jake Barnes. Because she cannot serve as goal at the conclusion of the Oedipal hero's quest—as a Sleeping Beauty who refuses such passivity, she is an unlikely prize for a Prince Charming without a sword—then she must be inherently evil and destructive, and antagonistic to the hero's progression. Critics such as Joseph DeFalco illustrate the role of the code hero as a definitively masculine endeavor, while constructing an antiheroic opposition. Recalling DeFalco's definition of the code hero that I quoted in the previous chapter, he writes:

> Here men face the ultimate test, or some symbolic reflection of that test, by trying to rise above the contingencies of life. . . . In Hemingway's treatment of the ideals a man may hold, he forces consideration of the efficacy of the commitment to an ideal in a world where values have been prostituted to other gods, chiefly Mammon and unfaith. The man who commits himself to these false ideals is personified by Hemingway as "No-man."[10]

Brett, as "No-man," is a negative force threatening the sanity and sanctity of the code hero in this reading, who cannot rise above the contingencies of life with such a temptress pursuing him. Similarly, Leo Gurko promotes Jake as the hidden hero of the novel, comparing him with the more classical hero, Pedro Romero.

> Yet this unlikely man, with his discouraging handicap and sterile milieu, is the other hero of the novel—perhaps even the greater, ultimate hero. Burdened by a handicap that would crush most men, he bears it stoically. He never tries to sentimentalize it or pretend it does not exist . . . he has accepted it and gone on functioning as best he can.
>   If one aspect of heroism is to perform great deeds, like Romero, another—perhaps the more impressive—is to surmount severe difficulties through a constant exercise of self-disciplining willpower.[11]

This of course echoes Jake's own code, which he defines as he lies in bed in the dark. "Perhaps as you went along you did learn something. I did not care what it was all about. All I wanted to know was how to live in it." It is a code that he himself claims may in the future "seem just as silly as all the other fine philosophies I've had" (148). And while Jake is the code hero for Gurko, Spilka reads him as a kind of medium between the spiritually separate Romero and the failed chivalric hero, Robert Cohn: "In the Code Hero, the Romantic Hero has finally met his match. As the clash between them shows, there is a difference between physical and moral victory, between chivalric stubbornness and real self-respect." In Spilka's analysis, Jake falls somewhere between the two heroes, an "unhappy medium" possessing neither the physical power of Cohn nor the self-respect and spirit of Romero, and as such he represents a kind of degraded and empty modern hero.[12]

If Jake is the hero who constantly exhibits "self-disciplining willpower" in the novel, as Gurko argues, or the hero who struggles between the poles of the masculine heroic, as Spilka claims, then for most readers Brett Ashley is the individual with the least ability to control herself. Carlos Baker divides the main characters of the novel into two opposing camps: the moral and the immoral. He has defined those camps in this way: "The moral norm of the book is a healthy and almost boyish innocence of spirit, and it is carried by Jake Barnes, Bill Gorton, and Pedro Romero. Against this norm, in the central antithesis of the novel, is ranged the sick abnormal 'vanity' of the Ashley-Campbell-Cohn triangle."[13] To be healthy and boyish is to be virtuous, while anything that doesn't fit within those boundaries is sick and abnormal. Unfortunately, although Brett is introduced as looking boyishly healthy ("She wore a slipover jersey sweater and a tweed skirt, and her hair was brushed back like a boy's. . . . She was built with curves like the hull of a racing yacht, and you missed none of it with that wool jersey" [22]), to be female *and* boyish is out of the question—that would be neither proper nor normal.

But because so many men find the "sick" and "abnormal" Brett Ashley so stimulating, so irresistible, she must be so depraved as to be other than mere mortal. Brett is frequently referred to as a Circe figure by readers, a reference made by Robert Cohn and reported by Mike Campbell in the novel, and Wolfgang E. H. Rudat believes she can be bested only by a Ulysses with a phallic sword bigger than her equally phallic sorceress' wand.[14] Leslie Fiedler suggests that there is a strange attraction to her as a destructive force, like the attraction of men helpless before Circe, which defines her as unwomanly and ultimately as inhuman. He writes, "No man embraces her without being in some sense castrated, except for Jake Barnes, who is unmanned to begin with; no man approaches her without *wanting* to be castrated, except for Romero who thinks naively that she is— or can easily become—a woman."[15] Because Brett does not fully conform to the expectations of these men, fictional characters and critics alike, she is, as Joseph DeFalco suggested earlier, not woman, not even human, but monstrous, "No-man."

As Baker's virtuous hero, Jake does not fall victim to Brett's spells. Baker begins to define her problem as psychological by noting, "As if Brett's own neurosis were somehow communicable, her semivoluntary victims writhe and snarl."[16] Jake does not writhe and snarl like other men, however; he has the clarity of mind to see Brett for what she really is. "Whenever Jake takes a long objective view of Lady Ashley, however, he is too honest not to see her for what she objectively is, an alcoholic nymphomaniac."[17] Baker never explains the grounds for making such an analysis of her psychological state— suffering from nymphomania—which is strange because we would expect a more responsible use of very specific medical terminology. What is stranger, however, is the number of critics who echo this analysis and who have decided that Brett is at the very least promiscuous, and probably suffers from nymphomania.[18] Benson concurs in Baker's analysis, noting that Brett is no run-of-the-mill *femme fatale.* He writes, "Brett assumes a male role in appearance, dress, and manner, and at the same time behaves like a nymphomaniac (confusing?)."[19] He finally decides that her psychological problems are more numerous, but not less serious, than this nymphomania and gender confusion. "Even to the layman, her initial appearance and entrance must suggest more descriptive terms from abnormal psychology than any one person really deserves: *narcissism, sadism, and transvestism* are enough for a good beginning."[20] Again, Benson assumes that we, too, have recognized Brett's entry into the novel, wearing a man's felt hat, as the sign of full-blown transvestism, or that she is any more sadistic or narcissistic than the rest of the expatriates. Actually, Robert Cohn also accuses Brett of sadism, at least in part because she is able to watch the events of the bullfight without turning her eyes—which, as he and Jake believe, a typical (proper?) woman would not be able to do.

> "He said Brett was a sadist," Mike said. "Brett's not a sadist. She's just a lovely, healthy wench."
> "Are you a sadist, Brett?" I asked.
> "Hope not." (166)

Brett's denial is off-handed, attempting to quiet Mike's belligerence (which might itself be considered sadistic) and to ignore the accusation being leveled at her. A sadistic Brett would have spurred Mike's torment of Robert on rather than attempt to quiet him down.

There is no legitimate, professionally informed psychological analysis as this medical jargon is carelessly thrown about; instead, we have an ongoing case of sanctioned name-calling, statements that would be considered libelous were we not dealing in fiction. The only responsible use of the term "nymphomania" is in Roger Whitlow's essay, "Bitches and Other Simplistic Assumptions," in which he at least offers definitions of nymphomania, but doesn't convincingly apply them to Brett's actions or her character. He quotes two psychological texts to interpret the terminology:

> The most significant symptom of Brett's pursuit of self-destruction is her nymphomania. Two of the basic interpretations of nymphomania are 1. that it is merely the open expression of the "natural" female sexual appetite of insatiation which, because of centuries of social restrictions (produced by male sexual limitations), is suppressed in most women; and 2.—the more commonly held of the two—that it represents a woman's attempt to overcome social or sexual self-doubt, by demonstrating, through one sexual experience after another, that she is, in fact, attractive, desirable, wanted.[21]

Thus, Whitlow leaves his reader with two choices: that Brett is quite normal, and that all women are by nature insatiable nymphomaniacs, or that she is insecure and is a retiring wall-flower behind the mask of the dominatrice. These deliberations over the state of her psyche recall that Freudian definition of femininity in which he attempts to define the "riddle of femininity" for men, and in which he tells women "this will not apply [to you]—you are yourselves the problem."[22] Certainly Brett is herself the problem for readers who want her to conform to the passive role she should play beside the Oedipal hero. Once again, Benson locates her as "at the center of all of the trouble . . . the woman who refuses to accept her role as a woman. The only valid internal ideal held by the group in Pamplona is that of the aficionado held only by Jake, which Jake betrays by being seduced through his false sentimentalization of Brett."[23] Benson's use of the phrase "by being seduced" implies that Jake is finally not responsible for his betrayal and that he has not been able to control himself when confronted by the bitch goddess/nymphomaniac/improper Brett.

Interestingly, two women readers of the novel come to quite different conclusions. Linda Wagner-Martin writes, in "Women in Hemingway's Early Fiction," that "the women have already reached that plateau of semi-stoic self awareness which Hemingway's men have, usually, yet to attain," responding effectively to claims of insecurity and nymphomania. In a different vein, Sibbie O'Sullivan recognizes the bias inherent in focusing on Brett's "problem": "Clearly, it is the double standard and nothing else that permits the critics, both male and female, to criticize Brett for sleeping with Cohn and Romero while not criticizing Cohn and Romero for the same act."[24] Indeed, nymphomania is a strange charge to level at Brett Ashley; while Mike does tell Jake, "Brett's had affairs with men before" (143) and that she gives him their letters to read, he is not the most reliable source of information, especially after his first outburst against Cohn. And we are never given absolute proof that she has slept with anyone during the course of the novel—because that would confirm Jake Barnes as a voyeur, since he is the novel's first-person narrator and must in some way witness the events of his story. Instead, Jake admits his penchant for *imagining* the events which take place in others' bedrooms: "I have a rotten habit of picturing the bedroom scenes of my friends" (13).

But assuming that Brett's reaction to Romero does indeed reveal a sexual desire for him; and assuming that Mike Campbell is ever sober enough to participate sexually, or to remember that he did; and even assuming that the affair with Robert Cohn in San Sebastian was indeed sexual, we are left with at most three instances of Brett's sexual activity. She has been married twice and has had some kind of relationship with Jake Barnes. This may be judged promiscuous (depending on one's standards of morality and promiscuity), but it surely doesn't sound like the insatiable appetite of a nymphomaniac as outlined by Whitlow. O'Sullivan explains the rationale for such a degrading but unfounded portrait of the female protagonist: "Such critical abuse is understandable when we realize that Brett is considered part of that long American tradition of the dark-haired bad woman. She must be termed 'promiscuous' and a 'nymphomaniac' if her sexual behavior is to be explained at all. The mainspring of such a tradition is that 'nice girls don't do it.'"[25] What O'Sullivan suggests, a point I will return to in evaluating the relationship between Brett, Jake, and Count Mippipopoulous, is that this portrait of Brett doesn't really involve Brett at all. Like the Freudian attempt to define woman, it is a very masculine Oedipal attempt to portray woman as Other, at once silencing her and redefining her in terms of a masculine fantasy—which, again, is precisely what Jake admits in his imagination of others' bedroom scenes.

Many readers of Brett Ashley have out penis-envied Freud in their assumptions of her nymphomania and her overpowering phallocentric desire for a good man with a good penis. While Jake's code remains a stoical pursuit of knowing how to live, for these readers Brett's code is finally "a hard man is good to find"—and this also happens to be just what she needs to set her straight. Consider the conclusion that Philip Young makes when he claims that "Brett is in love with Jake, and he with her, but since he is wounded as he is there is not much they can do about it." Mimi Reisel Gladstein echoes this analysis of their situation when she writes of Brett, "Her love affair with Jake is a source of continuing frustration because of his inability to consummate the relationship sexually." Similarly, Wilma Garcia recognizes that, at least in light of social demands on women, "Brett Ashley in *The Sun Also Rises* is a woman who cannot be good, who cannot meet the needs of her man, because both are maimed survivors of a world already dead."[26] These readers have assumed that a relationship between a man and a woman must finally be based on sexual intercourse for it to be viable. Certainly the novel does seem to suggest this conclusion in significant ways, but considering the source of the story—the emasculated Jake Barnes—it is surprising that no one questions this conclusion. Instead, there are only echoes of Joyce's James Duffy, of the *Dubliners'* story "A Painful Case," who concludes that "Love between man and man is impossible because there must not be sexual intercourse and friendship between man and woman is impossible because there must be sexual intercourse."[27] This is reinforced by Jake's own outlook:

> Women made such swell friends. Awfully swell. In the first place, you had to be in love with a woman to have a basis of friendship. I had been having Brett for a friend. I had not been thinking about her side of it. I had

been getting something for nothing. That only delayed the presentation of the bill. (148)

Her side of it is, in Jake's mind, that she needs sexual intercourse if a relationship is going to continue. Jake is never questioned about this assumption, and we tend to assume that Brett's affairs and her concluding "we could have had such a damned good time together" bear up this analysis.

At least one critical reader suggests that Brett's wistful conclusion is not only a manifestation of sexual desire for Jake, but is actually unfounded, because she does indeed engage in a sexual act with him within the events of the novel. In Kenneth S. Lynn's analysis of the novel, which he includes in his 1987 biography, *Hemingway*, he attempts to construct a "lesbian parallelism," supposedly evident in the androgynous appearance and masculine behavior of Brett Ashley. As a prospective lesbian, however, Brett's unspoken desire wouldn't be for Jake's penis; Lynn claims that she actually engages in oral sex with Jake during the Count's visit, and, because Jake has been emasculated, this is more likely a parodic version of lesbian than of heterosexual oral sex. Such a striking and finally absurd conclusion comes from the dialogue between Brett and Jake during the Count's initial visit, when Jake has retired to his room with a headache. Lynn sees in the narrative an apparent time shift, during which something unmentionable has happened, and he assumes that this must have been sex. To prove his point, Lynn directs us to evidence of Jake's sexual release in Brett's question, "Do you feel better, darling? Is the head any better?" (55). Since there seem to be no overt references to sexuality here, Lynn's argument is finally based on grounds similar to the claim that Brett is at the very least promiscuous, and probably nymphomaniacal—she sends one suitor away temporarily to satisfy herself by sating another suitor. He refuses to take into consideration the more likely meaning, and the more pressing desire, behind her questions: She is concerned about Jake's condition and about his self-image, as well as for her own image, knowing how he feels about her in the presence of other men. Jake's headache comes only after she has arrived with the Count in tow, and only after his self-interested profession of love: "Oh, Brett, I love you so much" (54). Finally, Lynn claims that "there is no way to be utterly positive" about this analysis, and so he reverts to the biographical narrative that I discussed in chapter 1: "Hemingway's portrait of Jake is a portrait of himself" and of his own bouts with impotence.[28]

Perhaps more surprising for its conclusions and certainly more detailed in its phallocentric focus are Wolfgang E. H. Rudat's developing analyses of Brett's character, analyses that demand that Brett is perhaps one of the darkest and most depraved female characters ever to appear in literature. In "Sexual Dilemmas in *The Sun Also Rises:* Hemingway's Count and the Education of Jacob Barnes," Rudat claims that she attempts various forms of psychological castration, primarily against Jake and Count Mippipopoulous, at least in part by sexually teasing men she knows are not equipped for sexual intercourse. Rudat's premise is that the Count, like Jake, has been emasculated in the war. The joke of this situation, however, is not on these warrior-men, but is on Brett: "When the Count says, 'Have another brandy,' he is not so much paying her back for her earlier 'Drink your wine' as he is reminding her, sarcastically since she has chosen to breach the code, that brandy is all she will get tonight— being, as [William] Kerrigan puts it, 'that mare among geldings.'"[29] Thus, for her role as temptress and tease before these two emasculated men, the Count sets her straight, in Rudat's reading. Her corporal, if not capital, punishment is no penis, no intercourse.

Rudat's work is the most consistent in his misogynistic readings of Brett as a woman who only needs a good man to set her straight. In a later article, "Brett's Problem" (which assumes from the start that it is *she* who has the problem in the novel), Rudat claims that Hemingway's choice of the name "Brett" over "Duff," the name used in the early drafts to refer to his real-life model, Lady Duff Twysden, is telling of Brett's role in the novel.

> I submit that Hemingway is punning on the German *Brett*—that is, *board, plank*—thus introducing the following sexual innuendo into the novel: Lady Brett is a plank nailed down by many men, but not nailed down for good by any of them. In fact, the pun on *Brett* lends special meaning to her family name "Ash-ley": that is, it compares Brett Ashley to a plank made of a wood that is known for its tough elasticity. Apparently unbroken herself, Brett has one lover after another bounce off her.[30]

The phallocentrism is evident here; whether it is Pedro Romero or Jake Barnes, Brett Ashley simply needs to be straightened out by a good, powerful man. In Rudat's use of the metaphor, Brett is simply in need of a good screw, wanting only to be nailed by a man powerful enough to keep her down. Finally, in a 1990 article in *American Imago*, Rudat finally names Brett's problem, to which he has been silently referring all along: penis-envy. Calling her "the promiscuous heroine" of the novel, Rudat now believes that "Brett has difficulty reaching orgasm, which causes her to drift from one man to the next, and Romero has been the first man in a long time to gratify her sexually."[31] Citing her penchant for wearing men's hats, as we see her in her introduction to the novel, Rudat believes that the ultimate in men's fashion that she aspires to is to be able to wear a condom. He writes,

> Consciously or unconsciously, Brett has always associated men's hats with what condoms symbolize: the status of the male and, more specifically, the male's ability to protect himself—and also the male's ability to *choose* when not to protect himself—from the woman, first of all against venereal disease (which was the original and main purpose of the condom) and second against the burdens of possible paternity.[32]

This is an interesting conclusion, because behind all of the phallocentric penis envy that he assigns Brett, Rudat does begin to explore Brett's desire for choice, for power as an individual who is continually surrounded by men attempting to dominate her. I wouldn't call this penis envy, so much as Brett's rejection of prescribed social roles that demand passive or "feminine" behavior, as in Benson's earlier desire to read moralistic propriety in Hemingway's novel. It is a difficult leap from the men's felt hat she wears early in the novel to her desire for one of Romero's bullfighting hats (giving her Pedro or peter envy, according to Rudat) to her desire to wear a condom, however. As Circe, he further argues, Brett's waving about of a cigarette exemplifies her desire for a phallic sorceress' wand, but Romero's cigar is finally bigger, and threatens to conquer her. Rudat finally reverts to his previous readings of Brett as a tease who, because she can't have a penis of her own, will torment those who do have one, including those who do not use theirs "properly" (as we see in her entry to the *bal musette* with the gay men), as well as those men who do not. She is on a level with Georgette the whore in Rudat's reading, which ultimately is not so different from the ways Jake Barnes, Count Mippipopoulous, and Pedro Romero identify her in the novel.

While so much is made of Brett as whore, monster, No-man, very few readers have ventured beyond this critical Oedipal narrative that demands, in one way or another, her debasement beside the relatively heroic Jake Barnes. For instance, although many readers indicate Jake's description of Brett to a curious Robert Cohn, "She's a drunk", they fail to recognize Jake's prior description of her on the same page: "She's a nice girl" and "She's very nice" (38). In her essay, "Some Notes on Defining a 'Feminist Literary Criticism,'" Annette Kolodny indicates the reasons such a singularly dominant approach is problematic in any critical activity:

> If, when using literary materials to make what is essentially a political point, we find ourselves virtually rewriting a text, ignoring certain aspects

of plot or characterization, or oversimplifying the action to fit our 'political' thesis, then we are neither practicing an honest criticism nor saying anything useful about the nature of art.[33]

By continuing to search for a definition of the Oedipal hero in the novel, we fall into a rather reductive trap, continually finding ways to fit various pieces of a puzzle into the same shape. There is certainly a construction of masculinity at work in Hemingway's fiction, but much of that construction of masculinity is taking place with readers of Hemingway. Despite Scholes's desire to locate "his sexual bias" in the fiction, Hemingway later echoes Lawrence's repudiation of authority in his interview for the *Paris Review*. Like Lawrence's warning, "Remember, it's just your own affair. Don't implicate me" in *Fantasia of the Unconscious,* Hemingway instructs, "Read anything I write for the pleasure of reading it. Whatever else you find will be the measure of what you brought to the reading."[34]

This instruction echoes David Bourne's thoughts on the reader as a narrative force whom he must guide, but who ultimately chooses his own way through the narrative. In *The Garden of Eden,* David's immersion in his Africa narrative frequently causes him to misread the boundaries between fiction and reality, as the introductory sentences of chapter 15 illustrate. "He heard the Bugatti start and the noise came as a surprise and an intrusion because there was no motor noise in the country where he was living. He was completely detached from everything except the story he was writing and he was living in it as he built it." As the writer writes, David discovers, there are intrusions that have little to do with the writer's experience of or control over the story, and he recognizes, as a result, that he finally has little control over such external forces that manipulate his narrative despite him. There is no motor noise in the Africa he writes, yet motor noise intrudes upon that Africa anyway. Importantly, the intrusion comes from Catherine, who has her own narrative desires that she wants to write with David—the narrative of the honeymoon—and that will cause her later to destroy the text of this African narrative. The motor noise from Catherine's car becomes analogous first to her own narrative desire, which is external to David's, and then to the readerly manipulation of the text.

> It was not him, but as he wrote it was and when someone read it, finally, *it would be whoever read it and what they found when they should reach the escarpment, if they reached it,* and he should make them reach its base by noon of that day; then whoever read it would find what there was there and have it always. (Italics mine.)[35]

If the reader should remain interested enough in the novel to reach the escarpment, David thinks, what they find there will not be him, but of their own reading. As the writer, he can guide the reader, helping to reach the base of the escarpment and finding what is there, but the protagonist of the narrative would not be *him,* David Bourne, but *it would be whoever read it,* the readerly version of the protagonist. To appreciate some of the more diverse possibilities evident in the novel, beyond the traditional and readerly versions of the heroic quest narrative, we must explore that mapping of differences available if *The Sun Also Rises* does indeed belong to that novelistic genre Bakhtin defines as polyphonic and dialogic.

Reading Desire: Jake and Brett Beyond the Phallus

"Oh, Jake," Brett said, "we could have had such a damned good time together."

Ahead was a mounted policeman in khaki directing traffic. He raised his baton. The car slowed suddenly pressing Brett against me.

"Yes." I said. "Isn't it pretty to think so?" (247)

As I suggested earlier, many readers believe that this is the ultimate and defining scene of *The Sun Also Rises* because it finally represents for them the deadlocked relationship between Jake Barnes and Brett Ashley, an unconsummated relationship which is the continual source of conflict in the novel. For these readers, Brett is finally a heartless nymphomaniac, despite her desire not to be identified as "one of these bitches that ruins children" (243). And her idyllic dream—"we could have had such a damned good time together"— is finally identified by such readers: the problem of her promiscuity and of Jake's frustration might have been solved if he only had a penis. Jake remains realistic, however, refusing to be drawn into a fantasy that can never be fulfilled.

One foundation of my reading of *The Sun Also Rises* rests upon Jake's physical condition as it ironically reflects, in a mirrorlike reversal, his narrative desire. The specifics of his injury are ambiguous in the novel, and while some readers understand Jake's condition as castration, that is, as a loss of his testicles and thus impotence in his ability to attain erections or to perform sexual intercourse, I read his continual obsession with Brett, sexuality, and intercourse as one of many indicators of his *loss of his penis,* not of his testicles. In *Hemingway's Quarrel with Androgyny,* Mark Spilka notes the novel's ambiguity when he writes, "There is nothing in the novel to indicate if or when Jake was quit with the catheter," like Hemingway whose injury was only an infection of the scrotum, "or how he urinates now" if he is indeed missing his penis.[36] But, following Hemingway's own assertions, Spilka does read this condition as an amputation of the penis, as do I, connecting Jake's lack of a penis with Hemingway's own bouts with impotence, a condition in which desire remains but physical ability is absent. Stephen Kern reaches a similar conclusion about Jake's physical condition when he writes, in *The Culture of Love,*

> In *The Sun Also Rises* Jake and Brett cannot marry because his penis was shot off in the war. Victorian soldiers like Sergeant Troy and Count Vronsky were not particularly reliable lovers, but their deficiencies were a source of their appeal. Hemingway explodes the ancient myth of Mars and Venus by having his soldier-hero retain his testicles so that he remains desirous of Brett but unable to satisfy himself or her. The novel ends with the frustrated couple talking about the impossibility of their love.[37]

Although I disagree with Kern's conclusions about the reason for Jake and Brett's inability to marry, as well as with his claims for Brett's seemingly phallocentric need for satisfaction, understanding the extent of Jake's physical injury and *how* it complicates his relationship with Brett, *and his own identification of himself and his very masculine problem,* is crucial to an understanding of Brett's complex position in the narrative. Indeed, consider Jake's examination of himself in the mirror early in the novel: He has *not* lost the desire for sexual intercourse, as desire is influenced by hormonal as well as psychological triggers, but he has lost the ability to enact that desire in his loss of the penis *and* phallus, to connect the figures that Lacan disconnected. Had Jake lost his testicles, and not his penis, Kenneth Lynn's theory that Brett performs oral sex on him might be plausible from Jake's perspective (but certainly not from Brett's, as I will explain later). In this latter case, Jake's desire would be completely psychological, in the realm of Oedipal power and control, since the source of hormonal desire would have been eliminated. However, without the penis/phallus, Jake retains both avenues of desire and yet is himself, for himself, an image of masculine powerlessness.

When Jake looks into the mirror, he examines himself for his lack of a penis, which influences his self-image and which finally defines for him the concluding dialogue of the novel—"Wouldn't it be pretty to think" that he and Brett could have had a "damned good time together" if only he had a penis. Following his receipt of a wedding announcement for a couple he doesn't know (announcements that "must be circularizing the town," he decides), he recalls the count and "Lady Ashley," both of whom have titles and, presumably, crests like that printed on the wedding announcement. "To hell with Brett. To hell with you, Lady Ashley," he decides (30), cursing her as he connects the wedding announcement with his own inability to win/ satisfy Brett. With this in mind, Jake undresses before a mirror, examining himself and his current condition in the light of the lamp. Importantly, Jake has purposefully lit the lamp *before* undressing, *and* he has opened the "wide windows" of the room, only then noting that "The bed was far back from the windows," which will keep others from seeing him. A man who doesn't wish to see himself and to recognize the absurdity of his current condition—physical and otherwise—wouldn't light the lamp or expose himself to outside eyes. Instead, this is a moment of exhibitionism for Jake as he self-pityingly acknowledges his own deformity, that is, his condition of having been genitally "unformed" or "de-formed."

> I looked at myself in the mirror of the big armoire beside the bed. That was a typically French way to furnish a room. Practical, too, I suppose. Of all the ways to be wounded. I suppose it was funny. I put on my pajamas and got into bed. (30)

The typically French way to furnish a room places a mirror by the bed—not only for practical reasons, which Jake adds as an afterthought, but for the reflection of sexual pleasure, as well, which makes its position in Jake's case "funny," since he is unable to perform sexually. Indeed, Jake's problem goes well beyond mere impotence; if he possessed the necessary equipment for actual intercourse—the penis—the extravagance of self-pity would be less tenable. In the masculine myth of virility that Pedro Romero later embodies, *Jake* would be to blame for his failed masculinity, which he might locate in an inability to perform, despite the presence of a penis—the biological phallic symbol—and even if his injury involved damage to his testicles. However, if his war wound eliminates his penis, he is absolved of all responsibility in both his lack of performance and in his failed relationship with Brett, which he reads as a result of her own phallocentric desires. "Of all the ways to be wounded" locates his injury precisely at the site of his penis because he can blame the war or, following the Italian liaison colonel, bad luck on his present state.

Some readers use the word "castrated" to define Jake's condition, a term that is used in error. Although Kenneth Lynn's 1987 biography doesn't directly cite this term, he does seem to suggest that partial castration is more likely than the amputation of a part or all of Jake's penis: "Nevertheless, the implication is fairly clear that, while the full extent of his injury is unspecified, Jake remains fairly capable of achieving a degree of satisfaction through oral sex."[38] Lynn sees this satisfaction in the tension evident in Jake as Brett attends to him and his resultant release of this tension, a release that, while unwritten, seems to have been facilitated, in Lynn's reading, by Brett. In his 1954 interview with the *Paris Review,* Hemingway counters this assumption of Jake's physical condition when he asks the interviewer, turning the interviewer's own assumptions against him, "Who ever said Jake was 'emasculated precisely as is a steer'?"[39] In fact, while the novel is ambiguous about the specific details of Jake's genital wounding, Jake's own behavior and obsessions indicate that he has not lost his testicles—the effect of castration—but his penis. Standing before the mirror, his lack of testicles would likely be hidden from view, or could be fairly easily obscured. However, Jake is directly confronted with his injury as he confronts his image and his self-image in the reflection; for him, it is the loss of his penis, of his *ability* to perform sexually that is the "mala fortuna," not the loss of testicles and physical desire. Hemingway confirms this in both the *Paris Review* interview and in an earlier letter to an editor at Rinehart. To Thomas Bledsoe, the Rinehart editor, Hemingway writes in a letter dated 9 December 1951,

> Every writer is in much of his work. But it is not as simple as all that. I could have told Mr. Young the whole genesis of The Sun Also Rises for example. It came from a personal experience in that when I had been wounded at one time there had been an infection from pieces of wool cloth being driven into the scrotum. Because of this I got to know other kids who had genito urinary wounds and I wondered what a man's life would have been like after that if his penis had been lost and his testicles and spermatic cord remained intact. I had known a boy that had happened to. So I took him and made him into a foreign correspondent in Paris and, inventing, tried to find out what his problems would be when he was in love with someone who was in love with him and there was nothing that they could do about it.[40]

This claim for Jake's condition is echoed in the *Paris Review* interview three years later, when he claims of Jake, "Actually he had been wounded in quite a different way and his testicles were intact and not damaged. Thus he was capable of all normal feelings as a *man* but incapable of consummating them. The important distinction is that his wound was physical and not psychological and that he was not emasculated."[41] Note Hemingway's problematic insistence that Jake is not *emasculated*, connecting the term both with castration-as-emasculization and with Jake's ability to retain masculine desire and behavior, despite this wound. While I hear the macho, popular, fictional Hemingway in this assertion of Jake's masculinity (since Jake would be an ultimate kind of hero, remaining masculine while suffering a major blow against his masculinity), I do find his readings of Jake fairly accurate in one sense: Jake's masculine desire controls the tenor of the novel and the many critical readings of the novel, especially in the concluding dialogue that serves as the title of my chapter.

The castrated Jake would have a penis but no sexual desire, making his psychosexual or Oedipal desire significantly different, and he wouldn't need to examine his condition before the mirror after cursing Lady Ashley. I find it interesting that many readers continue to assert Jake's condition as castration, wishing to allow him to retain the penis at the expense of the testicles, rather than vice versa. The penis-as-phallus, as biological and concrete symbol of masculine power, seems more significant for these readers than the seat of hormonal sexual desire, the testicles, but Jake's problem is one of desire and inability, both in the physical sense and in his inability to dominate Brett. His confusion of his own desire with what he believes is her desire, and the single most significant reason that they can never have a vital and lasting relationship, can be best defined by filling in the blanks of Brett's concluding dialogue, as Jake might understand her meaning: "We could have had such a damned good time together [if you only had a penis]" (247). The irony of the novel must be located in Jake's assertion of his phallocentric desire even as he has lost the biological and genital phallus that he understands as the center of desire. Similarly, Jake may absolve himself of any responsibility for his inability to satisfy Brett sexually with the amputation of his penis in the war, or for his inability to develop their relationship on any other foundation. Of course, desire goes well beyond the influence of penis/phallus, as the Oedipal narrative and Brett's rejection of this narrative indicate.

The unresolved conflict evident between Brett and Jake at the conclusion of the novel is crucial in understanding the ways we construct their identities, even as Jake constructs them as the narrator/author of his novel. We are always reading through Jake's consciousness, and we must remember that his attitudes and experiences color our reception of the characters and events he portrays. Jake is himself at least partly responsible for our perception of Brett as a destructive, devouring bitch and for our recognition of him as the novel's central hero, even if that role is one of an impotent Fisher King. To move beyond Jake's central and limited perception, we must consider the ways we might find representations and desires that have been marginalized and consider whether those representations are consistent with the words and actions we are allowed by our narrator to hear and witness.

For instance, prior to the final cab ride through the streets of Madrid, Brett expresses her surprise at the amount of food and drink Jake is consuming. After a meal of roast suckling pig and three bottles of wine—which Brett neither ate nor drank—she asks, "How do you feel, Jake? . . . My God! what a meal you've eaten" (246). Shortly afterward, as Jake orders two more bottles of wine, she repeatedly asks him to control himself. "Don't get drunk, Jake. . . . You don't have to. . . . Don't get drunk . . . Jake, don't get drunk" (246). Her worry does not sound like the rantings of the alcoholic nymphomaniac she is supposed to be. Instead, this penultimate scene may well suggest the precarious situation Brett continually finds herself in when she attempts to resume her relationship with Jake. If the assumption that the concluding scene indicates Brett's phallocentric need for Jake to be a fully functioning man, then it may well be an assumption promoted by Jake himself and have little to do with the Brett Ashley who asks Jake to remain sober and rational. It is, after all, from the narrator's perspective that we see the rising phallic baton following Brett's statement, a phallus in the hands of an authority figure in control of those around him, and quite different from Jake's ability to control his relationship with Brett. Throughout the novel, it is Jake who threatens to devour Brett in the way that he devours this final meal, and not vice versa, because he cannot move beyond his self-conscious obsession with his wound and his phallocentric understanding of the nature of heterosexual relationships.

Jake begins his novel with a two-chapter portrait of Robert Cohn, presumably the most unlikable character—at least for the other characters—in the novel. Hemingway excised an original first chapter on Brett Ashley prior to publication, on the advice of Scott Fitzgerald, leaving us with a rather strange introduction to the characters and events of the novel. Cohn is described in the first line as the former "middleweight boxing champion of Princeton" (3), beginning Hemingway's first novel with reference to very masculine pursuits. However, the qualification of Jake's second sentence is very contradictory: "Do not think that I am very much impressed by that as a boxing title, but it meant a lot to Cohn" (3). The introduction of Robert Cohn as a primary antagonist of the novel and as the first character Jake introduces us to is significant, because Jake's shifting attitudes toward the Jewish Robert Cohn betray both his disgust with the stereotypical figure of degraded masculinity and his identification with Cohn as another man who has been misused, either by fate or by Brett. It is a portrayal which finally informs Jake's understanding of his relationship with Brett.

In many ways, Robert Cohn's character is a rather stereotypical portrait of what might be referred to as the degenerate Jew in modernist fiction. Spilka calls him "the perennial Jewish scapegoat" for characters like Mike Campbell, an important characterization because it represents for both Hemingway and Lawrence, and for other modernists including Eliot and Joyce, "Man's" ultimate degradation in the anti-Semitic form of the Jew who disregards the rules of masculinity and is still a symbol of masculine power.[42] This is evident in the characters of Julius Halliday and Loerke in *Women in Love,* as in Hemingway's Robert Cohn. These men are not Men for the representatives of masculinity of their respective novels—they are not trustworthy, they do not share the masculine philosophies of the aficionado or of the *blutbruderschaft*—and yet their power is quite threatening. And they are threatening precisely because they are outsiders beyond the norm of what Eve Kosofsky Sedgwick defines as the homosocial relationship between men. Although they are outsiders, they often seem to be attractive to women, despite their roles as anti-Men. Consider Gerald's reaction to Halliday early in *Women in Love:* "Gerald looked at Halliday for some moments, watching the soft, rather degenerate face of the young man. Its very softness was an attraction; it was a soft, warm, corrupt nature, into which one might plunge with gratification" (120). However, despite her former (and future) relationship with the father of her child, Pussum's definition of Halliday is finally based on ethnicity: "He's a Jew, weally. I can't bear him" (124). Similarly, Birkin describes the Austrian Loerke as "the perfectly subjected being, existing almost like a criminal" (522). He goes on to describe the ultimate degradation of the man, saying, "He lives like a rat, in the river of corruption, just where it falls over into the bottomless pit. He's further on than we are. He hates the ideal more acutely . . . I expect he is a Jew—or part Jewish" (522–23). On the basis of his character, Birkin assumes that he belongs to that group of individuals who represent for him and for others in the novel the ultimate in degradation, the stereotype of the Jewish male.

Similarly, the things that irritate the characters of *The Sun Also Rises* are finally reduced to Cohn's status as a Jew. Jake tells us of Cohn's knowledge of Brett and Mike's arrival, "He said it with an air of superior knowledge that irritated both of us" (95). This is a superiority that finally has more to do with his ethnicity—and with Jake's anti-Semitism—than with his character, as Bill Gorton indicates: "Well, let him not get superior and Jewish" (96). Shortly afterward, Jake recognizes that "Cohn had a wonderful quality of bringing out the worst in anybody" (98). Again, Bill refers this to Cohn's ethnic heritage, asking Jake, "Haven't you got some more Jewish friends you could bring along?" (101). Both Lawrence's Halliday and Hemingway's Cohn do seem to behave badly; Halliday wants merely to live with the Pussum, and follows her about London and Paris despite her rejection of him. Robert Cohn is accused of behaving like a steer by Mike Campbell, having followed Mike and Brett about San Sebastian and Pamplona in a rather "unmanly" way, at least as manliness is defined in the homosocial relationships between Barnes and Campbell and Gorton. Interestingly, Campbell doesn't engage Cohn in open aggression; rather, he baits Cohn, in much the way that the captain and Rinaldi of *A Farewell to Arms* bait the priest, another outsider in the realm of masculinity.

Both Gerald Crich and Jake Barnes react against the unbearable superiority of these individuals whom they recognize as models of the degenerate Jewish man, either expressing a repressed desire to strike out at them, as in Gerald's case, or actually attempting to land a punch, as Jake does. And yet, despite the abuse Jake Barnes gives, and gets, from Robert Cohn, there is also a certain desire to portray him well. Jake interrupts his narrative at several points with disquisitions on Cohn's character, expressing his own fears that he may not be doing justice to the man. "Somehow I feel I have not shown Robert Cohn clearly. The reason is that until he fell in love with Brett, I never heard him make one remark that would, in any way, detach him from other people. He was nice to watch on the tennis-court, he had a good body, and he kept it in shape; he handled his cards well at bridge, and he had a funny sort of undergraduate quality about him" (45). Despite his knowledge of Cohn's actions, this is clearly admiration that Jake offers. And even Bill Gorton recognizes this dilemma. Of his badly behaved friends, he says, "I've got some darbs. But not alongside of this Robert Cohn. The funny thing is he's nice, too. I like him. But he's just so awful" (101).

Jake's qualification in the second sentence of the novel—that Cohn's boxing title doesn't impress him—is a strange statement because this is a title that would seem to mean a lot to Jake, despite his qualification; enough, at least, to serve as the introductory material for his novel. Despite Jake's and others' continually derogatory references to Cohn's Jewish superiority and his bad behavior, he identifies with Cohn as someone who has been unfairly treated, perhaps by fate and most certainly by women, especially Brett. Spilka writes of Cohn's boxing career, "It helps to compensate for anti-Semitic treatment from his classmates. More subtly, it turns him into an armed romantic, a man who can damage others in defense of his own beliefs."[43] Jake's admiration of Cohn, who sounds very much like an Oedipal hero battling against feminine obstacles in Spilka's description, indicates his belief that Cohn's degradation is largely Brett's fault, despite his Jewish background, and, as such, he can identify with the man who is otherwise figured as an outsider. His ethnic joke on the first page of the novel is especially telling of this identification with Cohn. Jake writes, "He was so good that Spider promptly overmatched him and got his nose permanently flattened. This increased Cohn's distaste for boxing, but it gave him a certain satisfaction of some strange sort, and it certainly improved his nose" (3). Cohn has the symbol of his ethnic stereotype—the big nose—flattened, making him somehow more easily acceptable to Jake and others who share his anti-Semitism. But, while Cohn's injury to his nose improves his looks, Jake's genital injury, and the symbol of his masculinity, does not serve him as well. Of course, as Jake sees it, both men are finally degraded in their love for Lady Brett Ashley. He writes of Cohn, "When he fell in love with Brett his tennis game went all to pieces. People beat him who had never had a chance with him" (45). And Jake, welcomed by Montoya as an aficionado of the bullfighting, believes that he betrays his *afición* by facilitating Pedro Romero's bad habits. He descends to the role of pimp in Cohn's accusation, a problematic and, I think, mistaken designation that I will return to shortly.

Jake's identification with Cohn indicates his recognition of his nearness to becoming the degraded anti-Man who does not function according to masculine codes of behavior and propriety. Interestingly, Jake does associate Cohn with the close-mouthed behavior of the aficionado when, following Frances's complaints of her treatment by Robert and her abuse of him, he writes,

> I do not know how people could say such terrible things to Robert Cohn. There are people to whom you could not say insulting things. They give you a feeling that the world would be destroyed, would actually be destroyed before your eyes, if you said certain things. (49)

Cohn, it seems, is being destroyed by Frances as she quite intentionally embarrasses him in front of his friend by bringing up things that are supposed to remain unspoken: Cohn's quite unmanly tendency to cry during arguments and his desire to keep a mistress. Jake would have him do something about such humiliation: "His face was white. Why did he sit there? Why did he keep on taking it like that?" (51) To be so completely unmanned by a woman who breaks the masculine code of the aficionado is to be completely degraded, and Jake would like to see Cohn either walk away or to put her in her place in the way he often threatens to do later in the novel with Mike Campbell and others who taunt him.

Jake, too, is at risk of being destroyed whenever he and Brett are alone together. At the center of their relationship, he believes, is his inability to fulfill his manly duties and provide a satisfying sexual experience for himself and Brett, a sexuality that must be centered around the penis. Their conversations are always rather indirect and never confront the conflict in their relationship in certain terms, because Jake, too, is someone whose world is continually in danger of being destroyed by those who might question his masculinity. With this indirection, it becomes easier to assume that Brett shares Jake's analysis of their relationship—that it won't work because he cannot perform sexually. During their cab ride after leaving the *bal musette*, we see the very different ways Jake and Brett define the conflict in their relationship. Brett begins,

> "I can't stand it."
> "Oh, Brett."
> "You mustn't. You must know. I can't stand it, that's all. Oh, darling, please understand!"
> "Don't you love me?"
> "Love you? I simply turn all to jelly when you touch me."
> "Isn't there anything we can do about it?" (26)

The "it" of Brett's "I can't stand it" is defined by Jake as his war wound, indicating that "what happened to me is supposed to be funny. I never think about it" (26). Supposedly, what Brett finally can't stand when they are together is the fact that he doesn't have a penis with which to gratify her. Her turning to jelly when he touches her may well be a sexual response, but it is surely not limited to phallic desire. In fact, Brett denies such a limitation, but Jake doesn't seem to hear her:

> "And there's not a damn thing we could do," I said.
> "I don't know," she said. "I don't want to go through that hell again."
> "We'd better keep away from each other."
> "But, darling, I have to see you. It isn't all that you know."
> "No, but it always gets to be." (26)

For Jake, their difficulties finally always come down to his lack of a penis—"there's not a damn thing we could do"—despite Brett's claim that physical desire does not cause her the kinds of frustration Jake expects it does. Her "It isn't all that you know" is a coded reference to a delicate subject, one that, if she brings up directly, will surely put her "through that hell again" of having to face Jake's obsession with the symbol of his manliness. From this point onward, Jake refers directly to his genital wound, even though he never describes it in any detailed way, and to his inability to sexually consummate a relationship with Brett. His assumption, and the assumption made by many readers, is that Brett's "I can't stand it" is a direct reference to their inability to have genital sexual intercourse. Jake's claim that he doesn't think about it any more is a transparent lie, and Brett calls him on it with her "I'll lay you don't" (26). He claims that he has inspected his situation from various angles, all of which are quite literally phallocentric:

> I was pretty well through with the subject. At one time or another I had probably considered it from most of its various angles, including the one that certain injuries or imperfections are a subject of merriment while remaining quite serious for the person possessing them. (27)

Of course, Jake is never through with the subject; the injury becomes his singularly defining quality, at the center of every angle, every perspective he adopts, and through which he identifies himself and the desires of those around him. Undressing, he contemplates himself in the mirror, and he recalls the words of the Italian liaison colonel who came to visit him in the hospital shortly after his injury: "'You, a foreigner, an Englishman' (any foreigner was an Englishman) 'have given more than your life. . . . Che mala fortuna! Che mala fortuna!'" (31). For Jake, as for the liaison colonel, the loss of the primary symbol of his manliness is a greater blow than the loss of his life. To live as half a man is hardly to live, a fact Jake seems to return to in his obsession with his wound and his refusal to move beyond it as the central identifying factor of his experience.

Jake makes this fixation most explicit when he begins to blame Brett for his obsession with his injury and accuses her of tormenting him almost intentionally. "Probably I never would have had any trouble if I hadn't run into Brett when they shipped me to England. I suppose she only wanted what she couldn't have" (31). This is one of Jake's most misogynist assumptions, and it is on the same level with his belief that Robert Cohn was fine until he met Brett Ashley. It betrays his inability to separate his disability—the central defining

characteristic of his identity—from any other kind of relationship he
might develop with Brett. Further, it assumes the sort of phallocentric, devouring bitch identity with which many readers supply Brett.
For instance, in claiming that Count Mippipopoulous is a compatriot
of Jake Barnes in more ways than one—that he, too, has been physically emasculated—Wolfgang E. H. Rudat believes that Brett "is trying
to castrate the Count psychologically because she is frustrated at the
epicurean equanimity with which the Count has come to terms with
his physical handicap." Brett becomes a castrator of men because
she is presumably sexually unsatisfied by their inability to perform,
or, more specifically, by their lack of satisfying penises. Rudat continues to explain that Brett intends to "punish the Count for having
disappointed her the night before, upon their first meeting at the
Cafe Select, a disappointment very like the disappointment she experiences with Jake many years earlier when, wanting to make love
to him, she went 'through that hell' of discovering that Jake had
no penis."[44]

This statement is a culmination of all the critical commentary that
centers upon Brett's sexual frustration over Jake's condition, her supposed belief that "we could have had such a damned good time
together [if only you had a penis]." But such a conclusion is inherently faulty, whether it is made by Jake Barnes or by a critical reader,
if only we consider the history of their relationship. Jake tells Cohn,
"She was a V.A.D. in a hospital I was in during the war" (38), recalling
a theme that recurs in Hemingway's fiction, that of the wounded
soldier and the angelic nurse with whom he falls in love. Such a past
must suggest two very important points regarding Brett's situation:
First, as angelic nurse who must be primarily a servant to the
wounded soldier, Brett is playing a role that must be very attractive
to Jake Barnes. The relationship that begins between the two of them
develops upon these expectations: that Brett will continue to serve
and care for him without regard to her desires. Toni Morrison writes
of these nurse figures in Hemingway's fiction, "Cooperative or sullen,
they are Tontos all, whose role is to do everything possible to serve
the Lone Ranger without disturbing his indulgent delusion that he is
indeed alone."[45] And as narrator of his novel, we certainly get the
sense that Jake is alone, despite the crowds of Pamplona.

Consider, for instance, Jake's description of the opening of the
festival and his position in the arcade:

> Before the waiter brought the sherry the rocket that announced the
> fiesta went up in the square. It burst and there was a gray ball of smoke
> high up above the Theatre Gayarre, across on the other side of the plaza.

The ball of smoke hung in the sky like a shrapnel burst, and as I watched, another rocket came up to it, trickling smoke in the bright sunlight. I saw the bright flash as it burst and another little cloud of smoke appeared. By the time the second rocket had burst there were so many people in the arcade, that had been empty a minute before, that the waiter, holding the bottle high up over his head, could hardly get through the crowd to our table. (153)

As readers of Jake's narrative, we are no more aware of the crowd of people than he is because we are limited to his solitary perspective. As chronicler of his experience in France and Spain, Jake is detached from others and is absolutely alone, interested only in his own perspective. The willful Brett refuses to serve this figure and for that reason she is quite often the cause of the degradation of this masculine independence that Jake, Cohn, and even Romero (in his desire for her to be more womanly) attempt to cultivate.

The second point elicited from a recognition of Jake and Brett's past has largely been ignored by readers who identify a nymphomaniacal, penis-envying Brett. It would seem to be common sense to assume that, if this is indeed where the Brett Ashley/Jake Barnes relationship began—in a hospital ward, like the Frederic Henry/Catherine Barkley relationship of *A Farewell to Arms*—then as a nurse Brett would know of his medical condition before any intimate relationship between the two of them began. Surely she would have known something about his injury, whether through his medical records or gossip between the medical staff, long before she became romantically involved with him. The hell that Brett has gone through, and continues to go through in her relationship with Jake, is precisely his inability to recognize the possibility of a relationship between a man and a woman that does not include genital sexual intercourse and that is not based on a nurse-patient/servant-master paradigm. Brett's foreknowledge of this injury would suggest that she is neither as phallocentric nor as nymphomaniacal as Jake Barnes, and many readers along with him, might like to believe.

Indeed, Brett is hardly the phallocentric nymphomaniac many readers understand her to be, and, in quite a few instances, we see evidence that Brett has no desire for this phallocentrism that readers often assign her. At least part of the problem for these readers is the continual evidence throughout the novel both of Brett's own desire, including her sexual desire for Romero, and of her determination to act upon that desire. And while Jake has indeed lost the symbol of his phallocentrism, he has not lost the desire to control Brett's behavior, whether by marrying her or simply by moving in with her. An interesting example of her desire to remain independent occurs when Count Mippipopoulous leaves her and Jake alone to fetch champagne. Earlier, Jake shared a cab with two fellow journalists, Woolsey and Krum. During their conversation, we find that Krum has been rather remiss as an expatriate. A family man, he hasn't the time to make the social rounds the way that Jake and Cohn have. "I've meant to get over [to the Select]. . . . You know how it is, though, with a wife and kids," he tells them. But Krum's ideal finally involves a rather American pastoral in which the working man finds a position that allows him plenty of free time in the country with his family. "Well, I'll tell you. Some day I'm not going to be working for an agency. Then I'll have plenty of time to get out in the country." Woolsey agrees with Krum's definition of the pastoral as a valuable goal: "That's the thing to do. Live out in the country and have a little car" (36).

Jake hasn't said anything throughout this brief conversation, but he has apparently been paying close attention to this exchange of values. Later, when Brett comforts him as he lies on the bed, Jake revives these traditional values he has heard from Woolsey and Krum, expressing his desire to move to a pastoral countryside:

> "Couldn't we live together, Brett? Couldn't we just live together?"
> "I don't think so. I'd just *tromper* you with everybody. You couldn't stand it."
> "I stand it now."
> "That would be different. It's my fault, Jake. It's the way I'm made."
> "Couldn't we go off in the country for a while?"
> "It wouldn't be any good. I'll go if you like. But I couldn't live quietly in the country. Not with my own true love." (55)

Her final line should read "Not *even* with my own true love" in its emphasis; she does tell Jake that she loves him two lines later, but she doesn't necessarily indicate that it is he who may be her own true love. Jake assumes that it is of himself she speaks as she rejects his request to live together, even though he has earlier identified Brett's first husband by telling Cohn that she married Lord Ashley because, "Her own true love had just kicked off with the dysentery" (39). Brett recognizes the falsity of this pastoral dream in the intrusion of the war and the death of her first husband. This is especially important considering the relationship she had with her second husband who, returning from the war in many ways a surrogate for her first husband, is domineering and violently threatening. Mike explains Brett's relationship with Lord Ashley to Jake.

> When he came home he wouldn't sleep in a bed. Always made Brett sleep on the floor. Finally, when he got really bad, he used to tell her

he'd kill her. Always slept with a loaded service revolver. Brett used to take the shells out when he'd gone to sleep. She hasn't had an absolutely happy life, Brett. Damned shame, too. She enjoys things so. (203)

Following the death of her first husband in a way that is hardly heroic—death by dysentery—Brett is dominated by the very phallic threat of masculine power. This would seem to be precisely what Brett is trying *to get away from* in divorcing herself from Lord Ashley, and it is hardly likely that she would embrace such a role for herself. Because she does "enjoy things so" as Mike puts it, Brett refuses to become entrapped in another destructive relationship with a man who cannot move beyond his own penchant for self-pity or his desire to be cared for by a nurse figure. However, Brett's rejection of this move to the country has little to do with the sexual desire and satiation offered by the nightlife of Paris. Although she claims that she would *tromper* or deceive him with everyone, she is finally more afraid of self-deception—the reflexive form of the French verb, *se tromper*—than with infidelity. She tells him, "I couldn't live quietly in the country"; Brett has no desire to become Jake's little woman. While he has lost the phallic object itself, Jake hasn't lost his desire to play a rather traditional, domineering role in their relationship, moving to the country like Krum and the unidentified wife and kids, and Brett will have none of that.

It is, therefore, quite important that Brett enters the novel at the *bal musette,* in the midst of a group of gay men. Rudat believes that, in his use of the "feminine" word "pretty" in his final line of the novel, Jake assumes the affected speech of this group of men and identifies himself with them. Rudat claims, "When Jake adopts the pose of a homosexual, he is indicating that for him their relationship has now become as meaningless as the relationship between her and the homosexuals, a relationship whose inaneness Jake had taken pains to illustrate."[46] Although this is a strange conclusion to make on the basis of a single word—"pretty"—it is a also a rather obvious conclusion when reached from a phallocentric perspective. A more effective argument for Jake's reaction to the gay men comes from Nancy Comley and Robert Scholes's *Hemingway's Genders,* in which they explore the rationale for Jake's anger against Brett's companions. "Jake, who dislikes them, sees them synechdochically, as fragments of men," they write, continuing,

> Why such anger? Perhaps because the homosexuals are built like "normal" men yet (Jake might think) do not choose to be "normal," while Jake, who has a "normal" male's sex drive, has been left only fragments of sexual apparatus. He cannot perform, though he desires to do so,

while the homosexuals can perform and yet do not desire "normal" heterosexual sex. The sexually fragmented Jake is thus linked to men he
perceives in fragments as unmanly because he has himself been
unmanned.[47]

This is one of the most effective explanations of Jake's behavior
before the perceived threat of the gay men who enter with Brett
because Comley and Scholes illustrate the process of identification
and *self*-recrimination that Jake experiences. His homophobic reactions against this group of men, even if he only shares them with us
readers in his capacity as narrator, serve to distance himself from
them even as he uncomfortably constructs a sense of similarity to
them. His construction of their sexual identities is clearly based on
his own normative understandings of sexuality and propriety, understandings that reflect those of the culture and that are reinforced by
his fellow men, as we see in Bill Gorton's expression of fondness
for Jake and his realization, "I couldn't tell you that in New York. It'd
mean I was a faggot" (116). But Jake is in this anger against the gay
men again phallocentric, at least in his own fragmentation and in the
fragmentation he presumes for them, as Comley and Scholes claim.

But Brett's relationship with the men at the *bal musette* is by no
means meaningless, as Jake might imagine; she tells Jake, in one of
her most revelatory statements, "And when one's with the crowd I'm
with, one can drink in such safety, too" (22). If Brett is so phallocentric, so desperate in her nymphomania for satisfaction from the penis, what is she doing with a group of gay men? Why would she
bother with them? And why does she feel safe with them? Because,
as she indicates, this is the only group she finally is secure with;
they expect nothing of her in the way of a traditionally domineering
sexual relationship. Sibbie O' Sullivan writes, "Since Brett is neither
a wife nor a prostitute, it is fitting that she emerge from an environment alien to these two opposites; hence she arrives with a group
of homosexual men."[48] Brett refuses to conform to either social role,
but to define her own identity, and the only group with which she
can do this in relative safety is a group of gay men, themselves
refusing to conform to social expectations and eliciting anger from
Jake and others in the crowd.

Brett's ability to take control is generally not as easy as this simple
refusal of Jake's suggestion to move to the country or as secure as
her association with those who will accept her as an equal. In "The
Death of Love in *The Sun Also Rises*," Spilka claims that in her
gender-bending, Brett achieves a level of power and independence
that make her equal to her fellow men. "With a man's felt hat on her

boyish bob, and with her familiar reference to men as fellow 'chaps,' she completes the distortion of sexual roles which seems to characterize the period."[49] Spilka is correct in this analysis of her ability to call into question gender norms and behaviors, and he prefigures such conclusions as those made by Comley and Scholes in *Hemingway's Genders* regarding Brett's revisionary behavior. They write of the events that frame her entry into the novel, "The framing alerts us to read Brett in terms of both a bitchiness and a sexuality that are different from what might be considered normal for women of her position. . . . Like her gypsy prototype, Carmen, Brett is 'unfeminine' in her usurping of the male prerogative of promiscuity on her own terms."[50] Notice that Comley and Scholes do not fall into the trap of defining Brett's promiscuous behavior as nymphomaniacal, as many earlier critics have, but that they claim her desire for the power to make her own choices, despite, and often against, the social notions of propriety that limit her. But Spilka's earlier claim goes even further as he writes of Brett, "For the war, which has unmanned Barnes and his contemporaries, has turned Brett into the freewheeling equal of any man. . . . With this evidence of male default all around her, she steps off the romantic pedestal, moves freely through the bars of Paris, and stands confidently there beside her newfound equals."[51] While her ability to reject the gender roles and restrictions may reflect a desire to define herself as "equal to any man," Brett finally does not gain this social and gender equality because her narrative desires are continually dismissed by the men and the masculine culture that surrounds her. In fact, she generally has little control over her own movement or her own identity, both of which are manipulated by those she comes into contact with. Consider the religious festival of San Fermin as the expatriates wait outside the church to which she has been denied access:

> They were all standing outside the chapel where San Fermin and the dignitaries had passed in, leaving a guard of soldiers, the giants, with the men who danced in them standing beside their resting frames, and the dwarfs moving with their whacking bladders through the crowd. We started inside and there was a smell of incense and people filing back into the church, but Brett was stopped just inside the door because she had no hat, so we went out again and along the street that ran back from the chapel into town. The street was lined on both sides with people keeping their place at the curb for the return of the procession. Some dancers formed a circle around Brett and started to dance. They wore big wreaths of white garlics around their necks. They took Bill and me by the arms and put us in the circle. Bill started to dance, too. They were all chanting. Brett wanted to dance but they did not want her to. They

wanted her as an image to dance around. When the song ended with
the sharp *riau-riau!* they rushed us into a wine-shop. (155)

Not only is Brett kept from entering the church in a way that would
be improper for a woman, but she is also set before the crowd as
"an image to dance around." In her essay, "Hemingway's Search for
Heroes, Once Again," Linda W. Wagner-Martin writes of Brett's role
in the celebration: "Brett here is a 'false god,' instrumental in keeping
people out of the church. She then becomes an alternative icon—
with even Bill and Jake joining in the dancing."[52] This is an important
quality of Brett's position at the center of the circle—she has been
idolized by the dancers, including the two men she came with, but
that idolization has nothing at all to do with her desires. Notice in
the above passage that "Brett wanted to dance but they did not want
her to." She has not chosen to become the false god; she would
rather join them in the celebration, yet she is not allowed to participate as an active, independent member of the festival.

This manipulation of Brett's identity is a continual process at work
in the novel. Mike Campbell regularly refers to her in terms of a
trophy or a prize he is surprised to have won, as in his reference to
her as "an extraordinary wench" (165) or in his drunkenly repetitive
description of her as "a lovely piece" six times within only minutes
(79–80). In fact, he rarely talks *to* her at all. His unadulterated objectification of Brett is very similar to the idolization she is forced to
accept outside the chapel. Similarly, her affair with Romero ends
because he wants her to become more feminine, at least in part so
that he might save face with his colleagues. Brett tells Jake, "He was
ashamed of me for a while, you know. . . . They ragged him about
me at the cafe, I guess" (242). His solution to this is to feminize Brett
by making her into a more traditional image of femininity, an image
she resists. "He wanted me to grow my hair out. Me, with long hair.
I'd look so like hell. . . . He said it would make me more womanly.
I'd look a fright" (242). Like Jake, who wants her to move to the
country with him in Krum's pastoral dream, and like Lord Ashley,
who sleeps with a gun at the ready, Romero finally wants to limit
and define Brett according to his own desires. "He really wanted to
marry me. So I couldn't go away from him, he said. He wanted to
make it sure I could never go away from him. After I'd gotten more
womanly, of course" (242).

For many inhabitants of the novel, Brett seems to play the role of
prostitute, a "species of woman," as Jake's concierge derogatorily
refers to her and her arrival at half-past four in the morning; "What
kind of a dirty business at this time of night!" is the concierge's

assumption that that species of woman is the whore (32). As Jake is awakened from sleep, he quickly confuses Brett's voice with the voice of the *poule* Georgette, whom he had hired earlier. Later, we find that the Count "offered me ten thousand dollars to go to Biarritz with him" (33), and is quite willing to pay her for her services as a companion, assuming that this would be quite acceptable for this species of woman. Finally, it is Robert Cohn who indirectly accuses Brett of prostitution by demanding Jake to tell him where she is. "I'll make you tell me . . . you damned pimp" (190). What is interesting here is that not only does Cohn betray his feelings for Brett—that he has invested in her and is angry because he hasn't gotten the return he had expected—but that most readers I have encountered assume that Cohn's accusation is accurate, that Jake is indeed a pimp. The problem with this designation isn't that it goes against all codes of the aficionado, of the Manly hero who would never treat an honest woman in this way. In fact, Jake isn't prostituting his *aficion* here at all. It is Brett who expresses her very sexual desire for Romero: "My God! he's a lovely boy. . . . And how I would love to see him get into those clothes. He must use a shoe-horn" (177). Shortly afterward, she tells Jake, "I'm a goner. I'm mad about the Romero boy. I'm in love with him, I think" (183). These comments have nothing to do with Jake prostituting Brett, but with her own desire, quite beyond his or Cohn's control. By acting upon this desire, Brett recognizes the need to attempt an assertion of her own identity amidst this continual manipulation of her. "I've got to do something. I've got to do something I really want to do. I've lost my self-respect" (183). But Cohn, like Jake, can't handle the notion that Brett might experience her own desire and act upon it independent of either man, and he must place blame on Jake who presumably could have stopped her. If Jake is her pimp, then she has no control over the situation at all, the desire for Romero is not hers, and her attempt to regain some self-respect is finally meaningless. But Jake is neither profiting by introducing her to Romero nor is he controlling her actions.

To deny Brett's desire, a desire quite independent from the wishes of those around her, is finally to construct a more acceptable identity for her as immutable idol, as prostitute at the mercy of her pimp— or as a nymphomaniac. These are finally more acceptable ways of thinking about Brett because they refuse to consider her ability for independent self-control beyond the dictates of the narrator, out of reach of the Oedipal hero—and thus, in this refusal she must either be manipulated by a pimp or be mentally ill, abnormal, and finally degrading. Her response to this tendency to revise her identity might well be the response she gives Jake when she complains of feeling like a bitch: "My God! . . . the things a woman goes through" (184). This doesn't fall on very sympathetic ears, however, because Jake is also guilty of constructing Brett by assigning her the kind of desire he believes she must "naturally," or properly, feel. He continues to construct desire and identity later in the novel as he describes Romero's final bullfight. It is a very interesting and revealing passage because, as an aficionado, Jake can easily illustrate the ways Romero manipulates the contest. But Jake doesn't stop there; he also describes what he assumes is the bull's desire, so that Romero is finally manipulating this desire, as well, in what is finally a very sexual metaphor:

> The bull did not insist under the iron. He did not really want to get at the horse. He turned and the group broke apart and Romero was taking him out with his cape. He took him out softly and smoothly, and then stopped and, standing squarely in front of the bull, offered him the cape. The bull's tail went up and he charged, and Romero moved his arms ahead of the bull, wheeling, his feet firmed. The dampened, mud-weighted cape swung open and full as a sail fills, and Romero pivoted with it just ahead of the bull. At the end of the pass they were facing each other again. Romero smiled. The bull wanted it again, and Romero's cape filled again, this time on the other side. Each time he let the bull pass so close that the man and the bull and the cape that filled and pivoted ahead of the bull were all one sharply etched mass. (216–17)

Like the narrative manipulation of Liz Coates's desire in Hemingway's short story, "Up in Michigan," here we find Jake describing a kind of intercourse in which an aggressor elicits desire from a participant who really has no desire to participate. "The bull wanted it again" suggests a very convenient willingness to engage in its own slaughter, and it reveals Jake's use of a very masculine fantasy that demands that the participant in the arena—however unwilling, as I would presume the bull would be—shares the aggressor's desire. In other words, this is not necessarily the bull's desire that Jake has described, but what he would like to believe is the bull's desire for Romero's taunts and sword thrusts which will ultimately destroy it. This is the kind of revision of Brett that alternately identifies her as a prostitute, a bitch, a nymphomaniac. The uncertainty of that image is surely in each lover's ability to pin her down, to define her according to his own expectations. Jake, Romero, Cohn, and the others who dance about Brett Ashley are not interested in the individual woman at all, but in their own projections of her. The construction of Brett Ashley is finally not about her, but about the ways each of the individuals who perceive Brett—mostly men—erect an image of her to explain away her desire. They construct her identity; she finally has no role in it, and it is a process that finally has little to do with Brett Ashley at all.

One of the most powerful examples of this construction of identity which absolutely dismisses Brett's desires is the Count's visit to Jake's apartment. Ostensibly, the Count is courting Brett even as he realizes that she loves Jake, so we would assume that it is her he is attempting to impress. This seems to be the case as the Count reenters Jake's apartment, having been sent away, with a basket of champagne, a rather ostentatious show after Jake has failed to offer him and Brett a drink upon their arrival. Similarly, the Count also makes a show of smoking "a real American cigar" (57), presumably a symbol of his wealth and prestige, while Jake prefers to finish his cigarette. Brett begins to bait the Count, having been denied her toast and then having been permitted to get drunk ("Now you enjoy that slowly, and then you can get drunk" [59]) like an audacious child. To her claim, "We've all been around. I dare say Jake here has seen as much as you have" (59), he responds, "My dear, I am sure Mr. Barnes has seen a lot. Don't think I don't think so, sir. I have seen a lot, too. . . . I have been in seven wars and four revolutions" (60). Brett admits that she was "only ragging" him (60), but the Count has been spurred on to compete with Jake, who seems to hold Brett's affections. Although this competition for Brett's affections isn't surprising in itself, it gradually becomes clear that the relationship forming between Jake and the Count isn't about Brett at all, but that it occurs through Brett as a landscape for their interaction. The Count shows off his scars, parading about without his shirt on. While both Brett and Jake ask questions about the scars, his responses to each are telling of his purpose in revealing them. To Jake's "Where did you get those?" the Count gives a factual and straightforward response: "In Abyssinia. When I was twenty-one years old." But when Brett asks, "What were you doing?" and "Were you in the army?" he replies with prevarication, "I was on a business trip, my dear", as though he were replying to a child who needn't know the truth. Again, when Brett confirms him as "one of us" to Jake, the Count brushes her aside. "You make me very happy, my dear. But it isn't true" (60). Interestingly, the Count shifts into a kind of American slang only when he recognizes that, once Brett is divorced, she will no longer be titled. "You don't need a title," he tells her; "You got class all over you . . . I'm not joking you . . . You got the most class of anybody I ever seen" (58). Her divorce from Ashley not only means, of course, that she will not be a formal member of the social class identified through her title, but that she will no longer be a lady, as well. The Count, then, doesn't have to take such pains at pretending to be a gentleman.

The Count is much more interested in getting Jake to open up than he is in impressing Brett, presumably to expose his competition. Even though Brett asks the questions of the Count, it is clearly Jake that he is speaking to:

> "You see, Mr. Barnes, it is because I have lived very much that now I can enjoy everything so well. Don't you find it like that?"
> "Yes. Absolutely."
> "I know," said the count. "That is the secret. You must get to know the values" (60).

Of course, Jake knows the values; he too has scars where an "arrow" once was, so to speak. Certainly there is a contest here to see which of them is a better man—Jake or the Count. And while the Count does parade his war wounds before Jake, Jake also exposes himself in several ways. First, he shows the Count nothing, which is precisely what his wound is—a lack, a negation of the physical organ that was removed, just as the Count's scars are the result of arrows that are no longer there. Later, the Count continually pushes Jake and Brett for answers to leading questions; his "Why don't you get married, you two?" causes Jake to answer in a rather obvious prevarication: "We want to lead our own lives" (61). Brett is aware of the contest, and of the transparency of Jake's answer, which is why she responds in turn with "Let's get out of this" (61) and why she upbraids the Count and attempts to buck up the underdog: "Don't be ostentatious. Call him off, Jake" (62).

Jake doesn't call him off, but remains silent, almost brooding, responding neither to Brett nor to the Count. This situation offers an example of the kind of male homosocial behavior that Eve Kosofsky Sedgwick explores in *Between Men: English Literature and Male Homosocial Desire*. While Jake and the Count are presumably competing for Brett as prize, she is finally virtually absent from their relationship. Referring to the work of Gayle Rubin, Sedgwick writes, "patriarchal heterosexuality can best be discussed in terms of one or another form of the traffic in women: it is the use of women as exchangeable, perhaps symbolic, property for the primary purpose of cementing the bonds of men with men."[53] Although some semblance of sexuality may be involved at some level of the relationship between men—in the Count's removal of his shirt to elicit Jake's admiration, or in the wrestling match between Gerald and Birkin in *Women in Love*—this is not necessarily a homosexual relationship which is being instigated. Instead, Jake and the Count recognize and affirm each other's masculinity through their competition in much the way that Montoya and Jake have an unspoken bond through their *afición*.

Of this bonding between men, Sedgwick claims that "we are in the presence of male heterosexual desire, in the form of a desire to consolidate partnership with authoritative males in and through the bodies of females."[54] Without a woman to enact this masculine desire through, Bill worries about Jake misunderstanding his intentions when he expresses his affection for him, worrying that in New York telling Jake that he's "a hell of a good guy, and I'm fonder of you than anybody on earth" would mean that he was a "faggot" (116). Similarly, both Jake and Bill are uncomfortable with Wilson-Harris' expressions of friendship during the Irati River fishing trip—"I say. You don't know what it's meant to me to have you chaps up here" (129)—because it seems to overstep the bounds of masculine propriety. Sibbie O'Sullivan believes that "There is no difference in the *intensity* of what Wilson-Harris feels for Jake and Bill and what Brett feels for Romero."[55] Such an expression of love is taboo unless enacted through a female participant who can safely legitimize this desire while safely affirming their heterosexuality. Indeed, as Jake describes his relationship with Montoya, it takes on perverse connotations in the absence of women when viewed by outsiders, that is, by those without *afición:*

> Montoya put his hand on my shoulder. . . . He always smiled as though bull-fighting were a very special secret between the two of us; a rather shocking but really very deep secret that we knew about. He always smiled as though there were something lewd about the secret to outsiders, but that it was something that we understood. It would not do to expose it to people who would not understand. (131)

Jake's identification of lewdness in the relationship is not very different from Bill's fear of being called a faggot, or from their embarrassment at Wilson-Harris's effusive expressions of affection. Sedgwick defines "homosexual panic" in *Between Men* and in her later text, *Epistemology of the Closet,* as a crucial part of the homosocial bond between men, noting the role of "obligatory heterosexuality" that is endemic to male-male relationships.[56] Robert Cohn attempts to secure the bonds of male camaraderie when he tells Jake and Bill of his affair with Brett, but it backfires on him, causing Jake merely to call him a "lying bastard" (101) and to become angered by his superiority. His status as an outsider denies him entry to the patriarchal and homosocial society, and his attempts to compete with them through Brett fail miserably.

A more explicit example of this homosocial competition and partnership may help illustrate the quality of the exchange between Jake and the Count. The passage I am continually reminded of in reading this section of *The Sun Also Rises* comes from a later novel by another American expatriate to Paris, James Baldwin's *Another Country*. In the first section of this novel, two male soldiers also compare their "experience," as Baldwin's narrator explains.

> Once, while he was in the service, he and a colored buddy had been drunk, and on leave, in Munich. They were in a cellar some place, it was very late at night, there were candles on the tables. There was one girl sitting near them. Who had dared whom? Laughing, they had opened their trousers and shown themselves to the girl. To the girl, but also to each other. The girl had calmly moved away, saying that she did not understand Americans. But perhaps she had understood them well enough. She had understood that their by-play had had very little to do with her. But neither could it be said that they had been trying to attract each other—they would never, certainly, have dreamed of doing it that way. Perhaps they had merely been trying to set their minds at ease; at ease as to which of them was the better man.[57]

The Count and Jake are caught up in a very similar game of "you show me yours, I'll show you mine," with war wounds/soldierly experiences as the most obvious currency of exchange. Of course, Jake's wound is genital, and the childish game of comparisons is indeed directed at revealing genital difference, just as the not-so-childish but masculine concern for penis-size continues to be a stereotypical token of who the best man is. Ironically, or perhaps appropriately, Jake is from Kansas City—a fact that reappears later as the old Basque on the roof of the bus tells Jake, "I been there . . . I been in Chicago, St. Louis, Kansas City, Denver, Los Angeles, Salt Lake City" (107). The old man, too, is showing off for an audience, and his speaking English with two Americans leaves the other Basques impressed with him (107). The irony in this exchange and in Jake's origins lie in Kansas City's role as the capital of Missouri, which is, after all, the "Show Me" state.

More seriously, however, it is important to recognize that this exchange between Jake and the Count is not about *Brett* at all. Her claim that the count is "one of us" is mistaken not in its inclusion of him into their group of world-weary expatriates, but in her assumption that she fits in as a member of that group. Brett's mistake in this contest between Jake and the Count is that she doesn't move away, like the German "girl" of Baldwin's novel; she remains with them, a prize for the Count and a source of frustration for Jake, who cannot convince her to move in with him. Sedgwick writes, "in any erotic rivalry, the bond that links the two rivals is as intense and potent as the bond that links either of the rivals to the beloved: that the bonds of 'rivalry' and 'love,' differently as they are experienced, are equally powerful and in many senses equivalent."[58] To assume that Brett Ashley is nymphomaniacal or sadistic is to assume that she is orchestrating these situations—and clearly, from her gradual exclusion from their competition, Brett has no control over the developing relationship between these men. She becomes a medium or a landscape, through which the men may affirm each other as members of the same patriarchal society. But not only is Brett not in control as landscape, she is also a source of danger for Jake in the homosocial relationship, should he fail to treat her as anything but a form of masculine currency. Of the dangers implicit in the kind of rivalry in which the Count engages Jake, Sedwick explains the role of women as property in a transaction of masculinity:

> To misunderstand the kind of property women are or the kind of transaction in which alone their value is realizable means, for a man, to endanger his own position as a subject in the relationship of exchange: to be permanently feminized or objectified in relation to other men. On the other hand, success in making this transaction requires a willingness and ability to temporarily risk, or assume, a feminized status. Only the man who can proceed through that stage, *while* remaining in cognitive control of the symbolic system that presides over sexual exchange, will be successful in achieving a relation of mastery to other men.[59]

The Count's "attacks" against Jake, showing off his wounds and attempting to prove himself the better man, are met with indifference and unresponsiveness by Jake, in effect feminizing him since he does not show off his own wound. But Jake's clear understanding of the Count's rivalry and of Brett's objectified role in the contest between them earns him the Count's masculine respect. Jake refuses to acknowledge Brett throughout much of the early homosocial rivalry, ignoring her command to "Call him off" (62), just as the Count dismisses her in the later stages of the contest. Robert Cohn receives none of this respect from Jake, despite his escapades with Brett, and as such he becomes a feminized figure of scorn for Jake and Bill and the homosocial bond. The Count, on the other hand, finally doesn't need to win over Brett, because he and Jake have reached a mutual understanding through her. "I enjoy to watch you dance," he tells her, not needing to participate in the dance itself. Brett's

"Jake's rather the same way" (63) describes his dislike of Zizi, the Count's protege, but also identifies Jake closely with the Count at the end of the chapter, indicative of his ability to disregard Brett's desires as well in his construction of her as both currency toward his masculine definition of himself and as a phallocentric tormentor of that masculinity.

This homosocial rivalry is played out with slightly different characters in Hemingway's later novel, *The Garden of Eden*, in a scene that very nearly mirrors the contest between Jake and the Count through Brett. However, in this later scene, Hemingway constructs a rivalry between two masculine figures, one also a titled male (the Colonel) but the other a female masquerading as masculine, Catherine Bourne. In the gender-bending that threatens David Bourne and that liberates his wife, David is agonizing over his need for masculine validation in the clippings when the Colonel enters, promising to offer the very support he is looking for. However, Catherine also enters shortly thereafter, and upon seeing the Colonel with her husband, after a momentary shyness she adopts her masculine role in a contest with the Colonel. They recognize each other from the Prado, where they have also recognized each other's masculine, proprietary gazes.

> "I saw you in the Prado looking at the Grecos," the Colonel said.
> "I saw you too," she said. "Do you always look at pictures as though you owned them and were deciding how to have them re-hung properly?"
> "Probably," the Colonel said. "Do you always look at them as though you were the young chief of a warrior tribe who had gotten loose from his councillors and was looking at that marble of Leda and the Swan?" (62)

While the Colonel identifies Catherine as "the darkest white girl I've ever seen" (63), exchanging the wounds-as-masculine currency in *The Sun Also Rises* for skin tone and shades of darkness, he also recognizes her as a "boy" in attitude and behavior. Interestingly, he also posits her as both a young tribal chieftan and as viewing a mythic scene of rape, of the masculine swan's ascendancy over the unwilling Leda. Rather than become incensed with the social impropriety of Catherine's new role, much as David does and as the townspeople who will not allow her to wear slacks, however, the Colonel wishes to become her mentor in masculinity, to adopt the role of one of her councillors having found her. As a result, their dialogue is a combination of homosocial rivalry and heterosexual flirtation, but more importantly, it is a dialogue that excludes David completely.

> "How did you know I was a boy in the Prado?"
> "Why shouldn't you be?"

"I only started it again last evening. I was a girl for almost a month. Ask David."

"You don't need to say ask David. What are you right now?" (63)

David, like Jake, doesn't have to engage in conversation between the two to prove his masculine control, just as Jake may allow Brett to banter with the Count in his rivalry with this fellow male. Never do David and the Colonel talk over or through Catherine, however, causing her to become the landscape for their homosocial relationship; instead, it is David who is ignored here, much like the Count's dismissal of Brett in his conversation with Jake about war wounds and values. And unlike Jake, David Bourne doesn't seem to understand the role he is supposed to play by objectifying Catherine as property. When Catherine leaves to dress for dinner, the Colonel counsels him, "Remember everything is right until it's wrong. You'll know when it's wrong" (65). But David doesn't seem to be on the same track as the Colonel, misunderstanding his comments about Catherine's identity changes and the state of their marriage. When he asks, "How fast will it go?" assuming that the Colonel can assure him of his ascendancy in the relationship, the Colonel counters with, "I didn't say anything about speed. What are you talking about?" (65) Rather than objectify Catherine, as Jake does Brett, David illustrates his own powerlessness in the face of Catherine's gender shifts, and as such, he becomes a feminized figure who, like Brett, may be dismissed by the more masculine figures in the contest.

The Colonel has recognized this failure of David's as he acknowledges her strength of will; when she tells him, "I wish I was darker," he admits, "You probably will be then" (64). If darkness is metaphoric not only for the transgression of ethnic and racial taboos in the society, as writers like Carl Eby argue, then it may also represent the gender transgressions Catherine enacts. As Carl Eby indicates, "In this novel, and for Catherine in particular, a tan is clearly *more* than a tan," and why he cites the connections between suntanning and racial transformations, there are also gender transformations implicit in Catherine's tone.[60] "Catherine isn't *simply* playing," Eby continues, "nor is she searching for some sort of Lawrentian or Andersonian mythical authenticity lying just beyond the color-line; she sees her dark skin as an integral part of her identity."[61] It is no accident that later David complains that "My chest feels like it is locked in iron," while Catherine responds, "I'm sorry. Mine feels so happy" (67). David feels trapped by Catherine's gender changes, because as she adopts the darker, more powerful, and masculine role, he must become the feminine figure in the homosocial relationships that she

constructs as a "boy." He temporarily becomes a kind of stage or
landscape, like Brett in *The Sun Also Rises,* as the Colonel competes
and flirts simultaneously with the boy/girl, Catherine. While *The Sun
Also Rises'* Jake Barnes plays the masculine role well, avoiding feminization and attaining a kind of masculine power, Hemingway creates
a much more conflicted figure in *The Garden of Eden's* David
Bourne, a figure who fails to successfully enter the kind of homosocial contest that will establish his own masculinity and power.

Betraying *Afición* in the Masculine Narrative

In his examination of modernism in *The Renewal of Literature,*
Richard Poirier explains the early twentieth-century literary movement as "an attempt to perpetuate the power of literature as a privi-
leged and exclusive form of discourse."[62] Poirier finds a primary
example of such tendencies toward exclusivity in Hemingway's use
of masculine pursuits which often elicit *afición* from their participants. "The apparatus of Eliot or Joyce functions the way bullfighting
or boxing functions metaphorically in Hemingway—as a primer of
connoisseurship for people who are invited at the same time to pretend that they are already connoisseurs."[63] Perhaps Poirier would
have been better to use the word *aficionado* in place of *connoisseur,*
but his meaning remains clear. Jake Barnes's role as heroic center
of *The Sun Also Rises* is problematic because it does not allow the
reader to engage in that novelistic mapping of differences possible
if we begin to question his authority. Indeed, even as an aficionado,
Jake is not as authentic as he might lead us to believe. He describes
the process of discovering *afición* in others, a process of communion
not very different from the homosocial desire he and the Count
experience.

> We never talked for very long at a time. It was simply the pleasure of
> discovering what we each felt. Men would come in from distant towns
> and before they left Pamplona stop and talk for a few minutes with Mon-
> toya about bulls. These men were aficionados. . . . Somehow it was taken
> for granted that an American could not have afición. . . . When they saw
> that I had afición, and there was no password, no set questions that
> could bring it out, rather it was a sort of oral spiritual examination with
> the questions always a little on the defensive and never apparent, there
> was this same embarrassed putting the hand on the shoulder, or a "Buen
> hombre." But nearly always there was the actual touching. It seemed as
> though they wanted to touch you to make it certain. (132)

If the aficionado is a rather close-mouthed exclusivist who knows other aficionados when he sees them without the need to be as effusive as Wilson-Harris or as open as Bill Gorton, then Jake calls into question his membership in this community simply by writing his novel. Rather than hide his passion away from those who are not deserving of it, who cannot appreciate it, Jake spends 247 pages outlining the details and events of that summer. He oversteps the boundaries of the aficionado not by prostituting Brett, as Robert Cohn might like to believe, but in the very act of writing the novel. Jake, too, is finally "a great little confider" (101), as Bill describes Cohn, and we must be ready to question his confidences and to compare them with the ways other characters, especially Brett, make themselves known in the novel.

These diverse perspectives, finally, are some of the strongest qualities of Hemingway's novel, and some of the most neglected, despite what may be read as its overbearing phallocentrism or its preoccupation with manly pursuits. Frederic Joseph Svoboda suggests that Hemingway's novel finally denies the centrality of an Oedipal hero for a very important reason: "In having a possibly confusing multiplicity of heroes or even in not having any character who can be called a hero, Hemingway reaffirmed his movement away from a conventional fiction toward a fiction founded on the careful examination and recreation of life."[64] Hemingway is not interested in merely creating a work of fiction for men; the novel recognizes the various positionalities and the problems of individual desire, especially for Brett, which quite often become obscured by Jake's fixation on his own perspective.

In "Epic and Novel," Bakhtin defines the essential characteristics of the epic and the epic hero. He writes, "The world of the epic is the national heroic past: it is a world of 'beginnings' and 'peak times' in the national history, a world of fathers and of founders of families, a world of 'firsts' and 'bests.'"[65] In the tendency to manipulate gender in the novel, especially in the masculine construction of various identities for Brett Ashley, this is precisely what Jake Barnes, Pedro Romero, and other characters are attempting—the affirmation of a tradition in which the basic feminine desire is for service to the masculine. But Brett Ashley is not the formulaic Sleeping Beauty whose desires are limited to her performance as monster or prize in relation with the quest hero, and neither may we presume that Jake Barnes or any of Hemingway's other protagonists are as fixed as the traditional epic hero. But this is what readers of Hemingway's first novel continue to support when they neglect to question the core assumptions of the narrator, as well as those made in the canon of

Hemingway criticism. Bakhtin continues, "Tradition isolates the world of the epic from personal experience, from any new insights, from any personal initiative in understanding and interpreting, from new points of view and evaluations."[66] To reject this tendency to isolate an Oedipal hero within the narrative and to place him in opposition to a feminine No-man is to begin to allow those new points of view to assert themselves within the text as legitimate possibilities for a necessary and neglected mapping of differences.

Part III
Masculinity and the Shifting Gender Narrative

First Officer (in spasm of jealousy). "WHO'S THE KNOCK-KNEED CHAP WITH YOUR SISTER, OLD MAN?"
Second Officer. "MY OTHER SISTER."

Two officers, *Punch*, 29 May 1918.

6

"You always feel trapped biologically": Masculinity and Narrative Entrapment in Hemingway's *A Farewell to Arms*

I<small>N</small> his 1956 study, *The Vanishing Hero*, Seán O'Faoláin writes of the tradition of the hero in the narrative, a tradition that was prevalent

> in those good old days when novelists were prepared to accept the fact that certain current ideas expressed firmly and clearly what the majority of people meant by a good or wholesome life. The novelist might not subscribe fully to these ideas or ideals himself; he might feel critical about them, poke fun at them, even reject them in his heart; but he could not deny that they formed the basis of the society in which he lived and which he described, and that anybody who rebelled against them, whether in real life or in fiction, must find himself not only in conflict with his community but in conflict with his origins and probably with his own nature.[1]

Rebellion and conflict, then, place the hero in danger with the greater community and, more importantly, with the sociocultural narratives of propriety to which that hero is conscripted. Moreover, that traditional hero's attempts to question such social constructs as gender, class, and ethnicity not only place him in conflict with the originating society, but with his own developmental foundations and even, according to O'Faoláin, with his "essential" or innate self. Teresa de Lauretis supports O'Faoláin's readings of the hero as enmeshed in the very society he is in dissent with when she writes in "The Technology of Gender," "*The construction of gender goes on today through the various technologies of gender ... and institutional discourses ... with power to control the field of social meaning and thus produce, promote, and 'implant' representations of gender.*"[2] We might look to the narrative manipulations of men and women in *A Farewell to Arms* as a prime example of this process of construction and sociocultural enmeshment. While Frederic Henry's masculine compatriots enact a series of homosocial bonding rituals for his benefit, he remains strikingly uncommitted to those masculine behaviors and beliefs, even if aspects of his character have been informed by them. As such, his character becomes a kind of stage, upon which the homosocial gender conflict is enacted, but it is also enacted for his benefit, as a kind of a moral to transform him into a masculine hero who can affirm the propriety of masculinity.

When, having learned of Catherine's pregnancy, Frederic responds, "You always feel trapped biologically," he isn't simply referring to the accidental pregnancy as a form of entrapment.[3] Instead, the American lieutenant knows that he is on the cusp of what is perhaps the most significant choice of his life: to commit himself to the masculine, homosocial behavior he has learned from his compatriots in the Italian army and ambulance corps, or to reject that sociocultural moral of the community and to commit himself to becoming a man with women, that is, to a life with Catherine and without the camaraderie and constraints of his masculine counterparts. This is not a simple choice, and it takes a return to the front and his near destruction at the bridge on the Tagliamento for Frederic to reject the linear, heroic narrative of masculinity and to make a return to Catherine. A Farewell to Arms is Frederic's retrospective history of his decision to reject masculinity as it is defined through male homosocial relationships and, concomitantly, to attempt to dodge the heroic I of the Oedipal narrative. Frederic's conflict with masculinity will lead him to make absurd decisions, and as his relationship with Catherine Barkley develops, he finally attempts a farewell to masculinity and to the homosocial constructs into which he has been initiated. However, as he comes to reject the masculine narrative of homosociality, which will allow him to see Catherine as a fully individuated woman and not merely as a sex object, Frederic will discover, as we do, that he is not in control of his own narrative and that his narrative desires finally mean little in the greater scheme of narrative tradition. The Oedipal narrative, which demands that neither the hero nor his love interest be individuated or empowered with the ability to enact their own narrative desires, is in control here, and Catherine must die in the romantic/Oedipal tradition, while Frederic, like Oedipus, must be left alone and wounded to stolidly bear the pain that comes as a result of his attempt to be the "destroyer of difference" as de Lauretis defines the mythic figure.

A Return to the Front: Disrobing and Exposing Masculinity

Frederic knows he may not have equal relationships with both men and women, given the attitudes toward women that his fellow officers have exhibited. In fact, upon his return to the front, his behavior quickly becomes suspect as Rinaldi complains, "You act like a married man" (167). His lack of commitment to the social ideals of masculinity are more evident to Rinaldi than ever, and he assures his friend that he will set him straight: "I will get you drunk and take out your liver and put you in a good Italian liver and make you a man again" (167). This assertion, that Rinaldi must recreate Frederic in his masculine image, is very interesting given the events of Frederic's return to the front at the beginning of book three. Upon arrival, which does not "feel like a homecoming" (163) or a return to the way things used to be before his wounding, his affair with Catherine, and her pregnancy, Frederic must expose himself to the scrutiny of two men. First, the major must see his medals, proof of his masculine worth. Because Frederic wears them on his uniform, he must open his cape to reveal them, in a sense beginning the disrobing that will continue for Rinaldi. The medals become fetishistic and certainly phallic symbols for the major; notice that the official documentation that is supposed to accompany them and that will certify Frederic's accomplishment is relatively unimportant and is dismissed by the major. "The boxes will come later. That takes more time" (164). And only after Frederic shows what he is made of will the major discuss the status of the fighting on the front, the placement of the ambulances, and his expectations for next year.

This initial disrobing is followed by a confusion of the two figures who represent Frederic's conflict, Catherine and Rinaldi. "I lay on the bed and thought about Catherine and waited for Rinaldi. I was going to try not to think about Catherine except at night before I went to sleep. But now I was tired and there was nothing to do, so I lay and thought about her. I was thinking about her when Rinaldi came in" (166). Thinking about Catherine only before sleep indicates a dissociative quality in his relationship with her, which may be necessary upon his return to the front and her unavailability. But it also suggests both Frederic's sexual desire (keeping in mind that his sexual contact with Catherine has always been at night, when everyone else was asleep or off duty in the hospital) and his doubt about his commitment to the ideals of the masculine society to which he has returned. As he thinks about Catherine, however, Rinaldi interrupts his reflections with a masculine greeting ("He whacked me on the back" [166]) and a desire to see Frederic's reconstructed knee. "Let me see your knee" and "Take off your pants, baby. We're all friends here" (166) are Rinaldi's initial commands, and his interest in the story of Frederic's recuperation and his relationship with Catherine comes only after this second disrobing and exhibition. For

Rinaldi, as for the major in his need to see Frederic's medals, the wounded knee also becomes fetishized as a phallus, in this case as a sign of Frederic's wound to his masculinity and necessary recuperation, which Rinaldi, who will make his friend a "man" again, will supervise.

The process of disrobing and exhibiting himself, first to his commander and then to his friend, is reminiscent of the homosocial contest between Jake Barnes and Count Mippipopolous in *The Sun Also Rises,* but notice that this exhibition is not about rivalry. Instead, the major and Rinaldi are testing Frederic's masculinity and "homosociability," as it were, in a precisely ritualized way. For some readers, this scene might suggest sexual desire, especially homosexual desire, and there are those who, such as James Mellow and Peter Griffin, have proposed that such behavior reveals Rinaldi's, if not Frederic's, latent homosexuality.[4] Consider, for instance, Frederic's objectification of Rinaldi as an object of admiration and attraction, even as Rinaldi gently caresses his knee: "I watched his hands. He had fine surgeon's hands. I looked at the top of his head, his hair shiny and parted smoothly. He bent the knee too far" (166–67). Rinaldi tests how far he can go with the knee, and the pain to which Frederic reacts limits him from going any further with his admiration of Rinaldi as an objectified figure. However, the ritual undressing and examining of the newly returned male is much more complex as a test of the homosocial, masculine bonds between men; in addition, homosexual behavior is anathema to such cultural practices as male bonding, as Eve Kosofsky Sedgwick and others have illustrated. The events of the scene might instead be defined by borrowing a term from anthropology; this is a ritual of *androgyneity,* which has been defined as "the concept based on the assumption that the individual has bipolar potentiality in sex until he is turned into a definite sex by tribal ritual."[5] Chaplin doesn't define the term "sex" as either gender or sexual orientation, although what is implied in the first use of the term "sex" is an essential bipolar sexual desire—bisexuality—which is eliminated in favor of a gendered identity (the second use of "sex" in the definition), allowing for specific avenues of sexual desire (heterosexuality, for instance). Pat Caplan notes the complexity of gender and individual identity as it has been defined by anthropology. Citing Rubin, Ortner, and Whitehead, Caplan notes that

> in kinship-based societies, kinship sculpts sexuality which is embedded in numerous other social relations. Ortner and Whitehead seem to agree [with Rubin's findings], pointing out that the sexuality of such societies demonstrates a greater concern with the pig herd, military honours, and

the estate than with sexuality, *per se,* showing "the power of social considerations to override libidinal ones."[6]

Although Frederic Henry was accepted into the masculine kinship society of officers and soldiers before his wounding, his time away requires a confirmation of his gender identity and an assurance that he hasn't been emasculated, either while away from the front or while in the care of Catherine Barkley. The scene of Frederic's return to the front is crucial to an understanding of the novel as the protagonist's conflict between gendered codes of conduct, and ultimately between the conscripts of the Oedipal narrative and other avenues of narrative desire. When he complains of being "trapped biologically" in the earlier scene with Catherine, he recognizes the conflict between the masculine identity that has been modeled for him at the front and the relationship he has with Catherine, a relationship that must exist outside of the masculine ideal. His is a problem of commitment, of making a choice between the requisite masculine behavior that his colleagues at the front expect of him as a result of his biological identity as a male, and his responsibility to the now-pregnant Catherine, a responsibility that precludes his belonging to that masculine society.

That Frederic Henry's conflict is with masculine kinship systems is made amply clear in his relationships with the men of the Italian army, and in many ways is the focus of Book One of the novel, the book that concludes, not accidentally, with his wounding, near death, and ultimate transfer to the hospital in Milan. It is, in fact, this movement to Milan—the second trip to Milan that Frederic has made in Book One—that causes him to question the masculine value system that his fellow officers have asserted. Indeed, his first trip to Milan is made during a military leave which he chooses to spend in a way that will make concrete his position in the masculine military society of the camp in Gorizia. Rather than vacation in Abruzzi, which his friend, the priest, urges, and which Frederic seems to have made arrangements for, he spends his time in a trip that begins in Milan and that includes Naples, a city the captain has urged him to visit. "He should have fine girls," the captain argues with the priest about Frederic's more appropriate leave. "I will give you the addresses of places in Naples. Beautiful young girls—accompanied by their mothers. Ha! Ha! Ha!" (8). Frederic later reveals to both the priest and to his reader that he really would prefer to visit the Abruzzi region; to the priest's disappointment, he explains, "I myself felt as badly as he did and could not understand why I had not gone. It was what I had wanted to do and I tried to explain how one thing had led to another and finally he saw it and understood that I had really wanted to go and it was almost all right" (13). Later Frederic rationalizes his decision to enact a homosocial bond with the other officers of his unit, rather than solidify his friendship with the priest, when he says, "I explained, winefully, how we did not do the things we wanted to do; we never did such things" (13). Frederic is clearly struggling with problems of narrative desire here; while he would like to befriend the priest, who seems to share at least some of the values he does, he cannot, because of the pressure of the homosocial covenant represented by the captain and the men of the mess.

Homosociability, Homophobia, and the Masculine Covenant

Why is the priest antagonistically separated from the other officers? Because, despite his role as priest and despite the vocational celibacy that is required of him, he is identified by the men of the camp as "other" than masculine. Sedgwick writes that "'obligatory heterosexuality' is built into male-dominated kinship systems," and such obligatory heterosexuality in this case might be defined by the rigid masculine behavior upon which the homosocial relationship is based.[7] Because the priest does not ascribe to the homosocial behavior of the men of the camp—behavior that includes both lewd banter and sexually promiscuous behavior, especially with prostitutes or with women who may be identified, always misogynistically, with prostitution—he becomes a threat to definitions of masculinity and "normalcy." Writing in "Questions of Identity" about the history of clinical sexology, that is, the history of the relatively brief practice of identification of self and other through sexual practice, Jeffrey Weeks indicates that "Sexology . . . is not simply descriptive. It is at times profoundly prescriptive, telling us what we ought to be like, what makes us truly ourselves and 'normal.' It is in this sense that the sexological account of sexual identity can be seen as an imposition, a crude tactic of power designed to obscure a real sexual diversity with the myth of a sexual destiny."[8] Since the priest remains celibate and since he refrains from the sexually laced banter of the officers, his behavior is easily identified as abnormal by the captain and later by Rinaldi.

The captain's baiting of the priest begins with accusations of his sexual misconduct, behavior unbecoming a priest: "To-day I see priest with girls" (7). The priest, of course, denies this, which sets him up for the ridicule of the captain.

> "Priest not with girls," went on the captain. "Priest never with girls," he explained to me. He took my glass and filled it, looking at my eyes all the time, but not losing sight of the priest.
> "Priest every night five against one." Every one at the table laughed. "You understand? Priest every night five against one." (7)

The captain's priest-baiting rapidly descends from licentious behavior—which would make the priest like them, contrary to his vocation—to masturbation, the first step in his condemnation of the priest as antithetical to the masculinity of the homosocial bond. The priest's vocation doesn't matter; that he is a male who refuses to participate in the rituals of masculinity is all that is important to the captain, and it is easy for him to make the leap from masturbatory behavior to homosexuality. The captain wants Frederic to read the book, "Black Pig," which the priest claims is "a filthy and vile book," but which the captain claims "shook his faith." Following his comments on the priest's masturbatory sexuality, the captain claims that this book "tells you about those priests" (8), indirectly suggesting that priests are by nature homosexual. This is a claim that Rinaldi will make, if clothed in jest, later in the novel, when he says to Frederic about the priest's visit, "Sometimes I think you and he are a little that way. You know" (65). In the cogs of male homosocial relationships, Eve Kosofsky Sedgwick claims that the homosocial relationship is itself dependent upon the active expression of homophobia. In *Between Men,* Sedgwick writes,

> "Homosocial desire," to begin with, is a kind of oxymoron. "Homosocial" is a word occasionally used in history and the social sciences, where it describes social bonds between persons of the same sex; it is a neologism, obviously formed by analogy with "homosexual," and just as obviously meant to be distinguished from "homosexual." In fact, it is applied to such activities as "male bonding," which may, as in our society, be characterized by intense homophobia, fear and hatred of homosexuality. To draw the "homosocial" back into the orbit of "desire," of the potentially erotic, then, is to hypothesize the potential unbrokenness of a continuum between homosocial and homosexual—a continuum whose visibility, for men, in our society, is radically disrupted.[9]

Thus, the homosocial relationship is itself a process of division, of the separation between the shared eroticism of heterosexual desire and the misogyny that attends it, and the threat of homosexual desire, which is taboo to "normative" masculine behavior. As such, masculinity, as defined by the homosocial relationship, is dissociative and very nearly schizophrenic in the separation of certain acceptable and unacceptable behaviors.

Important in reading the complexity of the relationships between Frederic Henry, the captain, and the priest, however, is the definition of homosexuality both as a literal and a figurative trope for the homosocial behavior system. Masculinity in such a relationship defines the opposition of other males to that homosocial relationship to include both literally homosexual behavior, that is, sexual desire and/or activity between men, and, more importantly and in a figurative sense, any behavior that might be defined as against, contrary to, or other than that behavior that is defined in the homosocial relationship as "masculine." In her introduction to *The Cultural Construction of Sexuality*, Pat Caplan illustrates the cultural standards that allow heterosexual men to define other men as un-or anti-masculine. "In our society, heterosexual relations are seen as the norm, and homosexual relations are stigmatized. Nonconformity to the norms of heterosexuality threatens the dominant ideology's view of sex as 'innate' and 'natural.' Male homosexuality threatens male solidarity and superordination because some men take on what are thought of as female characteristics."[10] This threat can also be used to make concrete the homosocial bonds between men, in that the presumption of heterosexuality—of "normalcy"—presumes a rejection of the homosexual and of the feminine, which become linked in the culture. Caplan's point regarding the feminine behavior of some homosexual men is in many ways irrelevant; to be defined as homosexual by a heterosexual, masculine community is to be defined as feminine, not necessarily in terms of outward behavior, but in power relationships. Homosexuality becomes effeminized because images of femininity have already been defined as less powerful than the masculine; a gendered lexicon of power is already available.

Consider, for instance, Mark Spilka's comments on his own revelations of Hemingway's androgyny. In an appendix to *Hemingway's Quarrel with Androgyny*, Spilka writes of "the Hemingway who early wrote a group of tales called *Men without Women*, the Hemingway who gave us male definitions of manhood to ponder, cherish, even perhaps to grow by." His following admission, then, seems to be one of disillusionment, and perhaps even of disappointment in Hemingway: "It is this side of Hemingway, his secret and continuing dependence on women, now not so secret after all, and his own curiously androgynous makeup, that threaten to deprive his admirers—myself still among them—of that one-eyed myth of mystical camaraderie we have all more or less embraced."[11] While Spilka clearly indicates that the masculinity traditionally assigned to Hemingway is mythic in nature, there is still an emphasis on the threatened deprivation of this myth for his male readers. The critic reveals a subtle but distinguishable strain of culturally based homophobia here, demanded by the homosocial dictates of society and normative masculinity. This is *not* to say that Mark Spilka is homophobic, or that this admission somehow makes his study suspect; indeed, *Hemingway's Quarrel with Androgyny* remains for me the most effective and ambitious study of the role of gender in Hemingway's fiction. Instead, the mourning of the loss of the masculine, mythic figure long defined as "Hemingway" as a required trope of homosocial behavior is in itself homophobic and, in a cultural sense, in keeping with the conscripts of masculine relationships. As homosociality and masculine camaraderie, according to Sedgwick, Caplan, and others, *demands homophobia*, the realization that Hemingway embraced other, socially suspect sexualities and desires "threatens to deprive" masculine, and certainly exclusively male, admirers of their ability to continue to share a sense of camaraderie with that mythic Hemingway. To share that camaraderie in spite of that suspect sexuality, the masculine assumption goes, would be to make one's self and one's own desires suspect, and thus mourning the loss of the masculine safely affirms the individual's rejection of the "unmasculine."

Baiting the priest is less about simply stigmatizing the priest as feminine or homosexual, however, and more about the captain's desire to secure Frederic's masculine allegiance. The priest becomes a feminized figure because he doesn't visit the whorehouse (making his masculinity and his heterosexuality suspect to the captain), but the captain makes use of this ploy successfully; in the chapter's conclusion, Frederic's allegiances seem clear. In the passage that I cited earlier, when the captain begins to bait the priest, his eye contact with Lieutenant Henry indicates both challenge and desire. "'Priest not with girls,' went on the captain. 'Priest never with girls,' he explained to me. *He took my glass and filled it, looking at my eyes all the time, but not losing sight of the priest* (7; italics mine). The captain's eye contact makes clear his desire for a relationship with Frederic, and were it not for the homosocial covenant, his behavior might be misconstrued as homosexual. But the claims for the priest's homosexuality and lack of masculinity makes the captain's "advances" on Frederic "safe" because they are conducted through homophobia. Similarly, at least one of the soldiers—the unnamed lieutenant—extends this homosocial bonding further by telling Frederic that he would "like to go with you [on leave] and show you things," presumably of a sexual nature (9). Like the captain's eye contact, this comment might be taken as of a homosexual nature, were it not for the expression of homophobia that makes such advances "safe." This behavior is also evident in Rinaldi's later comments in several instances, but especially after he has teased Frederic with the homophobic insult, "Sometimes I think you and he are a little that way. . . . A little that way like the number of the first regiment of the Brigata Ancona" (65–66). Once homophobia has been given expression, and once Frederic can deny homosexuality by responding, "Oh, go to hell," (66), Rinaldi can safely give voice to his fondness for his friend. "Really you are just like me underneath. . . . You are really an Italian. All fire and smoke and nothing inside. You only pretend to be American. We are brothers and we love each other" (66). Sedgwick explains the nature of this homophobia as based not in fear of the other, but in the acquisition and maintenance of power relationships.

> The notion of "homophobia" is itself fraught with difficulties. To begin with, the word is etymologically nonsensical. A more serious problem is that the linking of fear and hatred in the "-phobia" suffix, and in the word's usage, does tend to prejudge the question of the cause of homosexual oppression: it is attributed to fear, as opposed to (for example) a desire for power, privilege, or material goods. An alternative term that is more suggestive of collective, structurally inscribed, perhaps materially based oppression is "heterosexism."[12]

Homophobia, or heterosexism, are the driving forces that coerce Frederic into mirroring the masculine behavior of his compatriots. In the Oedipal narrative of masculinity, the priest becomes a landscape or stage for the captain's attempt to confirm his masculine allegiances with the American lieutenant.

The rivalry between the captain and Frederic is good-natured, as long as Frederic seems to accept the tenets of masculinity. This rivalry continues as the priest urges Frederic to go to Abruzzi to visit his family, while the captain offers the addresses of whorehouses in Naples, that the captain jokingly, but quite seriously, indicates will raise the outsider, Frederic, in his fellow soldiers' estimation of him. A trip to the whorehouses of Naples would give him a greater rank in the eyes of his masculine peers, as his joke suggests. "You go away soto-tenente! You come back soto-colonello!" (9). This is a possibility which the celibate priest cannot gain in a masculine economy of prestige; sex (or at least sexual reputation) is the currency among these men, and by going to the whorehouses in Naples, Frederic can increase his value among them *and* assure them that he, like them, is "normal." Indeed, to be anything but "normal" can be dangerous, as the captain becomes enraged with the priest and commences an attack against him. The captain's later baiting of the priest, a man without women, defines the priest, only at first playfully, as an enemy. "Priest not happy. Priest wants Austrians to win the war . . . Priest wants us never to attack" (14). Despite the priest's protests to the contrary, the captain's vehement "Must attack. Shall attack!" (14) becomes an attack against the threatening figure of the priest, who will not participate in the homosocial bonds that the captain attempts to engage him in, and only the captain's superior, the major, can call off the captain's obliquely homophobic attack. The captain exhibits here what Sedgwick refers to as "homosexual panic" in both *Between Men* and *Epistemology of the Closet,* a panic that threatens the identity both of the heterosexual male and the homosocial bond, a bond that prohibits homosexuality and thus protects the male entering into male-male relationships from such panic. "Homosexual panic is not only endemic to at any rate middle-class, Anglo-American men (presumably excluding some homosexuals), but a mainspring of their treatment of politics and power."[13] And in addition to this homosexual panic, the captain's desire to attack also betrays a particularly phallocentric and Oedipal reaction to an obstacle, whether that obstacle takes the form of the Austrians or of the priest who, in his rejection of their misogynistic behavior, threatens the homosocial bond between the officers. But by then, the captain has resolved the conflict by resorting to yet another obliquely homophobic definition of the priest as impotent: "He can't do anything about it anyway" (14). The problematic pronoun reference in the undefined "it" takes on multiple layers of reference for the captain: The priest cannot interfere in the plans for military action, and he cannot do anything about the behavior of the men in the camp, because he is not one of them.

But at the end of the chapter, after the officers argue about Caruso and the priest again urges him to go to Abruzzi and to stay with his family, Frederic seems to have come down on the side of the captain and the officers, as he leaves with them for local whorehouse. Frederic must act against his own desire to visit the priest's family, and to identify himself with the priest, if he wishes to be accepted into the masculine kinship system represented first by the captain and later by Rinaldi. He is not willing to risk his masculine reputation by siding with the priest, who is defined as other than masculine in the homophobic standards of the captain and the men of the camp. Of another Hemingway protagonist, David Bourne of *The Garden of*

Eden, Carl Eby writes, "Homoeroticism . . . seems for David, through his identification with the elephant, to be linked inextricably with death—either his father's or his own at the hands of his father. It is linked as well with a sort of primal repression: 'I'm going to keep everything a secret always,' he tells himself. 'Never tell anyone anything again.'"[14] Like David Bourne, Frederic will also repress his admiration of the dangerous figure, despite his desire to associate himself with the priest. If this is an Oedipal initiation, Frederic has successfully passed through the trial of his masculinity. However, his own narrative sympathies and desires lie with the priest and the Abruzzi; thus, as a result of the homosocial narrative that the men of the camp impose upon him, Frederic is conscripted to a version of the Oedipal narrative so as to avoid the feminization that the priest has undergone. His later admission to the priest, at the end of Book One, illustrates his, and the priest's, awareness of the problems of such a social narrative. Visiting him in the hospital before his transfer to Milan, the priest tells Frederic,

> "I would be too happy [returning to the Abruzzi]. If I could live there and love God and serve Him."
> "And be respected."
> "Yes and be respected. Why not?"
> "No reason not. You should be respected."
> "It does not matter. But there in my country it is understood that a man may love God. It is not a dirty joke." (71)

There are no homophobic jokes made about the priest's refusal to accept the masculine tenets that label him as an outsider in the camp, and Frederic clearly understands his desire for respect. Frederic's commitment to the homosocial bond is not always as concrete as it might seem. Earlier, as the captain engages him in eye contact, he breaks this eye contact to smile at the priest, who smiles back at him; he has not easily chosen sides here.

Not ironically, and parallel to the captain's attack at the end of chapter 3, the unseen but phallic battery of guns are what wake Frederic the next morning in a kind of orgasmic ejaculation: "The battery fired twice and the air came each time like a blow and shook the window and made the front of my pajamas flap" (15). I wonder as I read this, noting the movement of the front of his pajamas, if he experiences the same orgasmic reactions of the blows of the air which, not accidentally, come. There is an almost masturbatory quality to the coming of the air and the flapping of the pajama front, given his solitary waking state, which would actually ally Frederic not with the captain, in an orgasmic excitement at the phallic attack of the guns, but with the priest and the five-finger joke which the captain makes at his expense. Frederic does not accept the attack of the guns as the captain might; about the phallic guns, he explains, "It was a nuisance to have them there but it was a comfort that they were no bigger" (15). Unlike the captain, whose masculine conceit might be "bigger is better," Frederic feels no identification with the guns and with the captain's phallic "Must attack. Shall attack!" (14). Not accidentally, this scene opens the chapter (IV) in which Frederic first meets Catherine Barkley.

This is not to say, however, that Frederic's identification of himself as either within or without the homosocial covenant is ever easy, and homosocial behavior is not limited to Frederic's relationship with his fellow officers; we see these rituals enacted again and again as he finds himself in the company of other men, including men of lesser rank. Later in the mess, Rocca interrupts the dull conversation between priest and Frederic with a story that offers a threat to the priest, what Bakhtin refers to as "paschal laughter," in the joke's punch line: "Bless me, father, for you have sinned" (39).[15] The men of the mess laugh at the man who will not participate in the homosocial bonding of the other men, but they will not speak *with* the priest, as Frederic will, only about him, as we see when Rocca ignores the priest's question for further details of the joke. And when the priest leaves, Frederic begins to tell "traveling salesman" stories, presumably dirty jokes which he must have felt were improper while the priest was present. When he is with the troops following his leave, they, too, engage in homosocial sex talk, despite his attempts to remain on the subject of their responsibilities. When the men grin at a fellow mechanic's question, "You have a good time?" (16), they grin at the clearly provocative nature of what it means to be on leave, especially for a young, heterosexual soldier. Note, however, that there is none of the baiting or camaraderie in homosocial sex talk in this relationship—there are clear divisions in rank and class which limit the men, on the one hand, but still allow certain bonds of homosocial behavior and masculine expectations to be tested. While Frederic realizes this, ending the discussion and refusing to tell tales of his exploits, he fails to fully understand this division when it counts most and, in trying to feed his men during the shelling, he is wounded. This wounding is the first clear indication to Frederic of the absurdity of the masculine endeavor, especially considering his recent defense of the war against Passini's objections: "I was blown up while we were eating cheese" (63). This is hardly the heroic action that Rinaldi insists upon in creating an image of his wounded friend as a hero.

So, when Rinaldi examines Frederic's knee upon his return to the front, a precise ritual of homosocial behavior is employed in reorienting Frederic to the masculine kinship system of the front. The disrobing is possible because of the unspoken homophobia that Frederic has earlier witnessed; in the masculine relationship, this disrobing and presentation of one's masculine "credentials" is possible because of the requisite homophobia of heterosexual male-male relationships. *Refusing* to disrobe for the major's or Rinaldi's inspection would have made the "normalcy" of such desire suspect, which is why Frederic's only resistance to Rinaldi's inspection is half-hearted: "I'll have to take off my pants" (166). An earlier parallel may be found in Bassi's insistence that the lieutenant drink with him. "He said was my name Frederico Enrico or Enrico Federico? I said let the best man win, Bacchus barred, and the major started us with red wine in mugs" (40). Frederic's identity confusion and his lack of commitment to a single identity—let the best version of himself (or perhaps the most acceptable version of himself) win—is made evident both by Bassi's own confusion over his name, as well as by the enforced drinking contest, which he must enter into despite his objections, conceding to Bassi as the "better man" in order to save face in the homosocial relationship. It is not accidental that this is the first mention of the protagonist's full name, albeit in Italian. Although Bassi isn't sure of Frederic's proper name, he is assured of the American's masculinity and ability to affirm the homosocial relationship. Similarly, only after Rinaldi has inspected the knee and caused him to wince in pain, can Frederic decline to discuss his time in Milan and his relationship with Catherine. By causing pain to his knee, Rinaldi interrupts what might otherwise be a dangerously sexualized moment in a masculine, homosocial relationship, a moment that might recall, for instance, the wrestling match between Birkin and Gerald in Lawrence's *Women in Love*. The pain serves as an unspoken recollection of homophobia and its consequences and a masculine sign of affection, not unlike the slap on the back that Rinaldi gives him upon entering the room.

The Remorse Boy: Frederic's Struggle with Misogyny

That Rinaldi and Catherine become integrated in Frederic's reflections indicates his wavering commitment between the two, which Rinaldi is well aware of, given his knowledge of the relationship between Catherine and Frederic. His censure, "You act like a married man" (167), illustrates this all too well, and it allows Rinaldi to voice concern for his friend's ability to commit himself to the life of a young, single male in wartime. It is, after all, Rinaldi's own homosocial sacrifice that brings the two together. When he asks Frederic to join him in his initial meeting with the English nurse and her Scottish companion, it is Frederic who Miss Barkley is clearly interested in. Rinaldi does not like the "little Scotch one" (21), referring to Helen Ferguson, but he is willing to settle for her, just as he was willing to settle for Miss Barkley—Scotch, English, it is all the same to him, because he considers these women as merely another form of prostitute, that is, another sexual opportunity. He is willing to accede Miss Barkley to his friend in a gesture of homosocial generosity; in a metaphoric sense, they share her, as Rinaldi might see it, because he brings Frederic to her. She is the stage upon which Rinaldi and Frederic can become closer and remain safely masculine, even as Rinaldi teases Frederic about Catherine as a poor choice of sex-object. "Your lovely cool goddess. English goddess. My God what would a man do with a woman like that except worship her? What else is an Englishwoman good for?" (66). Not for sex, which is apparently all that Rinaldi wants in a woman.[16] He certainly does not want a relationship; consider his reaction to the prostitutes who have been at the front too long. "For two weeks now they haven't changed them. I don't go there any more. It is disgraceful. They aren't girls; they are old war comrades" (65). He cannot visit the prostitutes once they become familiar to him, because they are then too much like comrades, like individuals rather than objects.

Frederic's lack of commitment to the masculine ideal, as well as to an Oedipal narrative, is frequently evident to Rinaldi and to others who inhabit his wartime narrative. Unlike Rinaldi, Frederic becomes too easily involved with the women at the Villa Rosa—and later, with Catherine Barkley—and, as a result, he feels remorseful. Upon his return from his Milan convalescence, Rinaldi returns his toothbrush cup; "I kept this to remind me of you trying to brush away the Villa Rossa from your teeth in the morning, swearing and eating aspirin and cursing harlots. Every time I see that glass I think of you trying to clean your conscience with a toothbrush" (168). Other men, men like Rinaldi, do not have the conscience difficulties that Frederic seems to suffer from after a night at the brothel. During the retreat in Book Three, Bonello says of the prostitutes being evacuated, "I'd like to have a crack at them for nothing. They charge too much at that house anyway. The government gyps us" (189). There is no remorse in Bonello's misogyny, simply anger at the price charged by this brothel. But Frederic is the "remorse boy," as Rinaldi names him. "You are the fine good Anglo-Saxon boy. I know. You are the remorse boy, I know. I will wait till I see the Anglo-Saxon brushing away harlotry with a toothbrush" (168). While Rinaldi names him "the remorse boy," there is another telling identification happening in his use of the term "Anglo-Saxon." As an American, Frederic's identity is hardly Anglo-Saxon, and Rinaldi connects him through this identifier with the "English" Catherine Barkley.[17] Thus, his claim that the old Frederic Henry will return, despite the jaundice, the damage to his liver, and his behavior as an old married man, is also relevant to our image of Catherine, who Frederic has left in Milan. As she has complained of being made to feel like a whore at the cheap hotel, we (and Frederic) might imagine her "brushing away harlotry with a toothbrush." Earlier, as he leaves Catherine during one of their initial meetings, Frederic does not go into the Villa Rosa, where he knows that Rinaldi and the other men are; he takes a different path (32), perhaps to avoid remorse, and Rinaldi must catch up with him later.

Frederic's problem, as Rinaldi might see it, is in his tendency to allow women to become individuals, and in some cases, even friends. In one of the earliest scenes of the novel, we find him in the Villa Rosa. In fact, this scene in chapter two is the first in which the retrospective narrator allows us to focus on the immediate surroundings of the wartime Frederic Henry. All the earlier narrative consists of scenic description of a broader geographic place—the mountains and plains that Carlos Baker reads symbolically—and descriptions of the state of the war. So when Frederic Henry becomes a character in the story, we find him sitting in a brothel and watching the snow fall over the town, perhaps an early attempt to assert his masculine identity. Although he is sure to indicate which house he was in— "the house for officers" (6)—he fails to specify *who* he is with.

> Later, below in the town, I watched the snow falling, looking out of the window of the bawdy house, the house for officers, where I sat with a friend and two glasses drinking a bottle of Asti, and, looking out at the snow falling slowly and heavily, we knew it was all over for that year. (6)

There are several problems with this transitional sentence as it introduces the reader to the protagonist's situation. Who is the friend? A fellow officer? If this is a fellow officer, why are they sharing a drink together in the brothel? Why aren't they engaged in the kind of sexually laden boasting that is in evidence from the captain and from Rinaldi later? Perhaps because this may well be a pre- or postcoital drink not with a fellow officer, but with one of the women of the brothel, a "friend" who shares Frederic's convictions about the war being over for this year. Gerry Brenner also comes to this conclusion in his essay, "A Hospitalized World," as he comments on the nature of Frederic's narration. "So ambiguous is Frederic's narration that we can even mistakenly think that he sees his friend the priest while sitting with a fellow officer rather than with a whore."[18] This friend also seems to share his friendship with the priest; upon seeing the priest walking by, the friend "pounded on the window to attract his attention. . . . My friend motioned for him to come in" (6), after which the priest walks on. It is unlikely that the "friend" is a fellow officer, because Frederic names them according to rank in the following retelling of the priest-bating: present are the captain, the lieutenant, the major, and the other officers who do not directly participate. None are identified as his "friend" or are connected with this incident at the brothel. This friend could be the captain or Rinaldi, baiting the priest by inviting him into the brothel, but it seems unlikely, given the friend's low-key invitation. Moreover, the priest reserves his smile of affection for Frederic. We see him smile affectionately at Frederic on several occasions, otherwise smiling only in embarrassment when being baited.

If Frederic has identified one of the prostitutes of the Villa Rosa as a "friend" in the scene that introduces him as protagonist, and if he tends to feel remorse at his behavior following his visits to the brothel, his commitment to the homosocial ideals advocated by Rinaldi and others is lagging. Consider what Rinaldi tells him about the brothel while he recovers from his wound: "I just go [to the Villa Rosa] to see if there is anything new. I stop by. They all ask for you. It is a disgrace that they should stay so long that they become friends" (65). Friendship with the prostitutes is disgraceful for Rinaldi, since one cannot objectify friends as sex objects. Also, the dissociative quality of the sentence above allows the narrator to create distance between the protagonist and the action of the scene. The syntax of the sentence causes the glasses to be actors, drinking the asti, as it were. Only the initial clause of the sentence posits the protagonist as actor: "Later, below in the town, I watched the snow falling." This seems all that Frederic is responsible for, other than sitting with his friend, because the subject-object referents of the later clauses are confused. This sentence might be evidence of his remorse during the present narrative recounting of his story, a narrative that withholds embarrassing details and distances Frederic from the masculine behavior he is supposed to be upholding during the course of events. He frequently withholds details about his sexual exploits throughout the narrative, refusing to tell even Rinaldi about his initial leave or his later sexual relationship with Catherine. He does not participate in the kind of masculine storytelling that the captain and Rinaldi share to cement the homosocial bond between men. And not only does he withhold his stories of his virility from his fellow officers, but he withholds them from us, as well. The closest that he gets to sharing intimate information about his time spent with prostitutes is in a recognition of the emptiness of nights of casual sex and of the remorse that they bring: "Suddenly to care very much and to sleep to wake with it sometimes morning and all that had been there gone and everything sharp and hard and clear and sometimes a dispute about the cost" (13).

Indeed, while chapter 3 begins with Frederic's return from leave, he doesn't tell much about his occupation during his travels for two reasons. First, because we already know that he has gone to Naples and has followed the very masculine rituals imposed upon him by the captain; this has been clear from his chosen allegiance at the end of chapter 2. Second, the Frederic of the narrative present doesn't wish to dwell on this leave; he wishes, instead, to avoid it, perhaps because he is embarrassed by this choice against the priest, perhaps because, following Catherine's later questions about his sexual experience and his commitment to her, he doesn't want to reveal the details of this experience, just as he was evasive when she sought more information. Frederic's evasion of detail in recounting his sexual experience is rather "unmasculine," as that behavior is defined in the homosocial relationship. If he feels fully allied with the broad masculinity of the captain and the soldiers, we might expect him to return to camp and to relate his sexual experiences, even if only in double entendre. But he avoids the subject altogether, again perhaps allying him more with the priest than with the captain.

Consider the events of his return from leave in Book One as an indication of his conflicted allegiances. Frederic almost coyly describes the minute details of the room he shares with Rinaldi, avoiding mention of the figure sleeping on the bed until the end of the paragraph (11). His desire is to keep from waking the sleeping Rinaldi, who will badger him with homosocial tests in recounting the details of his leave. Indeed, when his friend awakens, he asks for details of Frederic's leave, preferably sexual details. "You talk like a time-table. Did you have any beautiful adventures?" (11). His questions about Frederic's activity presume the sexual exploits of a masculine compatriot: "Where did you meet her? In the Cova? Where did you go? How did you feel? Tell me everything at once. Did you stay all night?" (11). Rinaldi wants details, the veracity of which are unimportant in the homosocial bond, but Frederic does not offer anything more than "Yes" (12), which causes *Rinaldi* to have to supply the details himself, not of Milano but of their encampment in Gorizia and the "beautiful girls. . . . New girls never been to the front before" (12). One of those "new girls" is Catherine Barkley, and here begins the association of Catherine, and of all available women, with the prostitutes of the wartime whorehouses. Shortly afterward, Rinaldi borrows fifty lire from Frederic, ostensibly to "make on Miss Barkley the impression of a man of sufficient wealth" (12), but it is a need that is only a short leap from the payment of prostitutes for services rendered. Frederic is by no means an enlightened man in his treatment of women, and in many instances he is no less misogynistic than Rinaldi, but he is struggling with his commitment to the homosocial behavior modeled by his fellow men.

Reading Catherine Barkley's Rational Choices and Critical Mis-diagnosis

Perhaps Catherine is at some level aware of this conflict in Frederic, which might explain her willingness to engage him in courtship and, later, in a fully sexual relationship which she requires be adjunct to an emotional commitment from him. It is, after all, in the courtship of Catherine that we first learn of his lack of commitment to or conviction for service in the war, one of many masculine pursuits. Following his revelation to Catherine's head nurse, that he serves in the Italian army because "I was in Italy . . . and I spoke Italian" (22), Frederic illustrates his embarrassment at things military and, by connection with Rinaldi, masculine, in his embarrassment at saluting Catherine in the Italian fashion as Rinaldi has just done (23). Upon a later visit to her station, Frederic admits, unlike the popular notion of the Hemingway hero but perhaps reminiscent of Francis Macomber, that he is not an accomplished shooter. Moreover, he feels "a vague sort of shame" about the gun when he wears it, especially "when I met English-speaking people" (29), and this admission is especially significant here, because he is meeting Catherine. Interestingly, Rinaldi also has problems with his military accoutrements. When Frederic reveals that "we were required to wear an automatic pistol; even doctors and sanitary officers," and that "You were liable to arrest if you did not have one worn in plain sight," we learn that Rinaldi eshews carrying a gun. "Rinaldi carried a holster stuffed with toilet paper" (29). While he rejects the gun, it isn't likely that he feels *shame*, knowing that he could be arrested. Frederic, on the other hand, follows regulations despite his desire not to wear a gun but is ashamed at doing so. Despite the possible consequences, Rinaldi refuses to accept the military requirements, as opposed to Frederic who accepts them shamefully. Catherine is much more forthcoming, much more frank than Frederic is with Rinaldi, and she exhibits none of the shame he confesses to. Of her dead fiancé, she tells him, "I wanted to do something for him. You see I didn't care about the other thing and he could have had it all. He could have had anything he wanted if I would have known. I would have married him or anything" (19). Although she doesn't actually use the terms of sex, Catherine speaks frankly about the limited value of virginity with a man she has only barely met—an interesting contrast to a male protagonist who will not divulge the details of his sexual escapades. But she is not speaking of simply losing her virginity, as such, or about mere sex. Catherine reveals to Frederic from the start the extent of her participation in a truly committed relationship, a relationship that she seems to have demanded from her now-dead fiancé.

Such frankness causes many readers to define Catherine in conflicting and complicated ways.[19] Some readers define Catherine as aggressive but not always in control of the relationship with Frederic, and certainly not in control of her narrative. Judith Fetterley has written, problematizing any aggression Catherine might betray, "In contrast to Frederic's passivity, one is struck by Catherine's aggressiveness. How, after all, can a heroine be allowed so much activity and still keep her status as an idealized love object?" Fetterley answers her own question by claiming that "Catherine's aggressiveness achieves legitimacy because it is always exercised in the service of Frederic's passivity."[20] Mark Spilka echoes this conclusion, problematizing Frederic's passivity as manipulative even as "Catherine is the active and superior partner in the hospital trysts."[21] But Spilka is in error when he attaches seemingly essentialized gender types to the ways that Frederic's power is manifest. In *Hemingway's Quarrel with Androgyny*, he writes, "In Henry's certified passivity, then, lies his greatest power; he has license to reign from his bed as Grace Hemingway had reigned when served breakfast there by her husband Clarence—or as Joyce's Molly had reigned when served by Leopold Bloom. In effect, he has finally arrived at something like a woman's passive power."[22] The passivity that Spilka defines in Frederic is a bodily passivity, and he has defined an important distinction in exploring the sexual positioning that takes place in Frederic's hospital bed. But Catherine's mounting of Frederic, while physically aggressive and topologically dominant, is not indicative of her power in their relationship, just as Spilka notes that "Frederic is curiously masterful in his passivity."[23] I find this latter understanding of their power relations compelling, especially because Catherine's position "on top" during sexual intercourse is not a sign of female dominance, but instead of the kind of servitude that Fetterley claims. Catherine's mounting of Frederic is service of the supine male, an extra-nursely tending to the wounded patient.

Even more readers express their consternation at Catherine's passivity in the novel, including Millicent Bell. "More often noted than Frederic's passivity is the passivity of Catherine in this love affair, a passivity which has irritated readers (particularly female readers) because it seems to be a projection of male fantasies of the ideally submissive partner. It results from her desire to please. She is a sort of inflated rubber woman available at will to the onanistic dreamer."[24] Of the necessary passivity of the nurse in a misogynistic narrative—a figure whom she does not identify specifically as Catherine Barkley, but as a common trope in Hemingway's fiction—Toni Morrison writes, "To be in a difficult, even life-threatening position and to have someone dedicated to helping you, paid to help you, is soothing. And if you are bent on dramatic gestures of self-reliance, eager to prove that you can go it alone (without complaining), a nurse who chooses or is paid to take care of you does not violate your view of yourself as a brave, silent sufferer."[25] For Bell and Morrison, Catherine does not even have the opportunity to *appear,* however falsely, as aggressive or empowered but is reduced by Frederic—and both argue by Hemingway—as a rather two-dimensional sex object, despite her occasional "inflatability," to borrow Bell's reference. Nancy Comley and Robert Scholes also write of Catherine as passive but see rationale for her passivity in her social situation. They argue that Catherine actually finds empowerment in her service to Frederic, especially if we consider her role playing as a form of escape:

Such apparent compliance and self-erasure have seemed appalling to many readers (though some male critics have found Catherine an ideal woman), but it is possible to read this episode in a slightly different way. We might, for instance, see Catherine not as erasing herself so much as assuming a role in a game of sex and love that allows her to transfer her affections to a man other than her dead fiancé. She assumes the role of whore as a means of escaping profoundly restrictive cultural codes—those of her social code, which require of her a chastity suitable to a grieving widow honoring her husband's memory, and those of her chosen profession, which forbid sexual relations between military nurses and their charges."[26]

Included in those readers who have found her an ideal woman, Philip Young unites the seemingly aggressive behaviors of Catherine with the passivity that has annoyed many readers by describing her both as idealized and a heroine in service to the hero: "Idealized past the fondest belief of most people, and even the more realistic wishes of some, compliant, and bearing unmistakable indications of the troubles to come when she will appear as mistress of heroes to come, Catherine Barkley has at least some character in her own right, and is both the first true 'Hemingway heroine,' and the most convincing one."[27] Also reading Catherine as an idealized figure, aggressive in her desire to be "passive," that is, of service to Frederic, Mark Spilka finally defines Catherine as both idealistic and believable, a paradoxical figure: "Catherine is believable, as well as the object of male fantasies, since she is also the subject of female fantasies that we know to be 'true,' that do exist, however embarrassing we may find her enactment of them. Thus, if she annoys women readers today, it is precisely because she continues to deny herself in all-too-believable ways well lost and to protect Frederic thereby from confronting his own inveterate selfishness."[28] As a feminine ideal, she embodies for Spilka the romantic image of female servitude and sacrifice that he claims many women have learned all too well from the culture and that many women, having questioned this cultural model, become incensed by. Whether she is convincing or realistic, however, is a question of readerly perspective, and Judith Fetterley questions the nature of the idealism in the portrait of Catherine which Young fails to address and which she might argue Spilka doesn't sufficiently address. "That deviousness and indirection are often the companions of hostility is no new observation and feminists have always known that idealization is a basic strategy for disguising and marketing hatred."[29] The "trueness" of the idealized portrait, which both Young and Spilka write of, is of a limited, and misogynistic, perspective, she might conclude.

Whether Catherine Barkley is aggressive or passive, the majority of readers simply follow her own lead and define her, rather naively, as "crazy." This is perhaps the most problematic of readerly identifications of her, because it fails to call into question Catherine's own rationale for assigning herself this "diagnosis" or for the veracity (or at least insightfulness) of Frederic's narrative. In his Appendix B, "A Retrospective Epilogue: On the Importance of Being Androgynous," Spilka finally passes off the novel's female protagonist as insane, uniting her with a literary tradition of female insanity. He writes,

In *A Farewell to Arms* the message of selfless love which the priest first intimates and which Lieutenant Henry manages to forget is given its hospital workout when the wounded and supine and therefore interestingly feminine Henry finally falls in love with the crazy nurse, Catherine Barkley, with whom he had previously temporized, and is thus instructed in a love so selfless that the lovers become one another at night, even as an earlier fictional couple, mad Catherine Earnshaw and her foster brother Heathcliff, had identified with each other ("I *am* Heathcliff").[30]

Surprisingly, Spilka doesn't draw upon Gilbert and Gubar's *Mad-woman in the Attic* here, given the connections that he is making between the "crazy nurse" in *A Farewell to Arms*, the "mad Catherine Earnshaw" of Brontë's *Wuthering Heights*, and "another mad Catherine" in Hemingway's later novel, *The Garden of Eden*. Indeed, when Spilka makes reference on the same page to Catherine Bourne of *The Garden of Eden* as "another mad Catherine," he constructs a 136-year literary tradition of madness in Catherines. Like many readers, Spilka doesn't question this description of her mental state, and neither does Gerry Brenner in his essay, "A Hospitalized World." He writes of Catherine, "But her fragile grasp of reality persuades me that Frederic loves a marginally neurotic woman who is more than a little out of her head."[31] This is an unusual conclusion for Brenner, if Frederic is an unreliable narrator as he claimed earlier in his essay. What of the details of Catherine Barkley's life and behavior that Henry has blindly left out? Shouldn't we question the veracity of Frederic's reporting, if only in its tone? Does Catherine really believe that she is crazy, as she admits on several occasions, or does this admission itself indicate her control and her very rational behavior in their courtship? Isn't she all too aware of the reality of her situation as a nurse on the Italian front who is attracted to Frederic Henry and who has already lost one fiancé?

Actually, Catherine *is* quite rational in this relationship given the danger she is in. Sandra Whipple Spanier concludes, "If she is 'a little crazy,' as Frederic suspects when he first meets her . . . she is crazy like a fox—sharp-eyed about the odds and instinctively calculating the means of survival."[32] Like Brett Ashley before her, Catherine Barkley is a V.A.D. in the British service, but unlike Brett, she is not willing to enter into another relationship after the death of her fiancé without a great deal of trepidation and caution. Of Brett's marriage to Lord Ashley, which followed the death of her soldier/husband and one true love, Jake tells Robert Cohn in *The Sun Also Rises* that she married her second husband "during the war. Her own true love had just kicked off with the dysentery" (*The Sun Also Rises*, 39). When Cohn angrily argues, "I don't believe she would marry anybody she didn't love," Jake replies, "She's done it twice" (*The Sun Also Rises*, 39). Granted that Jake, like Frederic, is not the most objective or reliable of narrators, but Brett's situation seems to be precisely the kind of situation that Catherine Barkley is trying to avoid. What causes so many readers to see her as "more than a little out of her head," as Brenner writes, is the initial role playing she conducts with Frederic, pretending, as she does, that he is her dead fiancé returned. When Frederic calls her "Dear Catherine," at her insistence, echoing the earlier lines of devotion which she also scripted for him ("Say, 'I've come back to Catherine in the night'" [30]), she recognizes that he is *not* her dead fiancé returned: "You don't pronounce it very much alike" (31). Frederic tells us, "I thought she was probably a little crazy" as a result of her brief fantasy, but "This was better than going every evening to the house for officers where the girls climbed all over you and put your cap on backward as a sign of affection between their trips upstairs with brother officers" (30). His assumptions about her sanity and stability are neither fair nor insightful, because Catherine's narrative desire, the reason for her behavior, is not readily available to Frederic's limited perception as narrator. We can't dismiss her as crazy simply because he has, especially considering his following admission: "I knew I did not love Catherine Barkley nor had any idea of loving her. This was a game, like bridge, in which you said things instead of playing cards. Like bridge you had to pretend you were playing for money or playing for some stakes. Nobody had mentioned what the stakes were. It was all right with me" (30–31). Although his commitment to the masculine ideals of sexual promiscuity and misogyny are wavering, he knows enough about the games played between men and women to acknowledge them and to accept the deceit which he believes is required of him in this narrative of male/female relationships. But Catherine knows what the stakes are, and she calls him on this deceit in what becomes an open acknowledgment of the game men and women are supposed to play, and an almost metafictional commentary on the narrative. "This is a rotten game we play, isn't it?" she asks him. "'You're a nice boy,' she said. 'And you play it as well as you know how. But it's a rotten game'" (31). By calling attention to Frederic's unspoken definition of their courting as a game, and to his inability to deceive her—"What game?" and "Do you always know what people think?" (31)—she forces him to reconsider the narrative of courtship which for him will lead to sexual conquest, and not to a strong and committed relationship.

The central problem in defining Catherine as crazy is in the assumption that she behaves irrationally or without self-possession. Actually, she knows the danger she is in if Frederic treats her according to the masculine codes of behavior, that is, as a one-night stand, after which she will be abandoned, her chastity (and perhaps reputation, according to the masculine code) destroyed. Nancy Comley and Robert Scholes accurately recognize that, "In those days, a declaration of love was the minimum prerequisite for sexual intercourse between well-bred people."[33] But Catherine is not simply looking for the propriety of this declaration. What makes Catherine seem crazy to so many, characters and readers both, is her desire to protect herself against the dangers implicit in the masculine conduct of men at the front (and maybe of all men). Yes, she fantasizes about her fiancé as she initially responds to Frederic, but she quickly realizes that he is *not* committed to her, and she ends the fantasy and avoids the danger of giving into his sexual desires. She knows generally about the practice of visiting brothels, if not about the details, and she also knows of the dangers of being a woman marked as "easy" by the men who might seduce her and abandon her. So when she concedes a kiss (27), this is the narrative of feminine coyness and virginity, and of masculine suffering in the face of that protected virginity (which got her fiancé killed), that they must follow according to social codes of behavior, that are as rigid as the homosocial code. Otherwise, she would be defined as improper and of the only other kind of women at the front, the prostitutes, whom men like Rinaldi are already willing to associate her with.

However, Catherine earlier seems to throw aside the codes of propriety as she allows Frederic to kiss her; this is not a peck, but a fully sexual embrace.

> I looked in her eyes and put my arm around her as I had before and kissed her. I kissed her hard and held her tight and tried to open her lips; they were closed tight. I was still angry and as I held her suddenly she shivered. I held her close against me and could feel her heart beating and her lips opened and her head went back against my hand and then she was crying on my shoulder. (27)

Catherine has given in to Frederic's desire here, and, in doing so, she is discarding the codes of feminine propriety. This is a kind of loss of virginity, not in her own desire to engage in intercourse with Frederic, but in a giving up which has been precipitated partly by his anger (reflecting the earlier masculine anger of the captain's "Must attack. Shall attack!") and partly, and perhaps most importantly, by her guilt over the death of her long-denied fiancé. Thus, when she becomes prophetic about the "strange life" they will have together, and when she attaches great value to this kiss, she is not crazy, as many readers suggest. Instead, this is a moment of danger for Catherine, in part because she is still fantasizing about her fiancé, who was committed to her and about whom she feels guilty for not giving into his desires. Also, she is in danger because she has renounced the feminine mores and behavior that a woman at the front—or in the proper social circles which Comley and Scholes mention—is instructed to defend, without which she will become directly associated with the women of the brothels. This is a moment that is no less dangerous than if Frederic readily sided with the priest against the homosocial behavior of the captain and his fellow officers, and thus her reaction and the crying that follows is not irrational at all. "You will be good to me, won't you?" (27) is her attempt to affirm Frederic's commitment to her, a commitment she knows will not come quite as easily as that by the next time they meet.

In *The Culture of Love,* Stephen Kern writes of the changing opportunities that modern women had available in their relationships with men. "The history of choosing in love, which comes to an especially dramatic focus when the woman responds to a marriage proposal, reveals movement toward greater reflection on the meaning of possibility. While Victorian women were limited to 'yes' or 'no,' or mere *consent,* some modern women could exercise more genuine *choice.*"[34] Although Kern writes of choice in marriage proposals, his reflections on choice are equally applicable to the complexity of Catherine's choices and to her attempts to break down Frederic's commitment to a masculine code of behavior. These choices become evident as she engages in sexual intercourse with Frederic for the first time, committing herself to him long before he can make a similar commitment. Sandra Whipple Spanier writes with admiration of Catherine, "In the context of the Great War, her willingness—even determination—to submerge herself in a private love relationship can be seen as a courageous effort to construct a valid alternative existence in a hostile and chaotic universe."[35] Following his wounding—which she must associate with the death of her fiancé—she gives in to his sexual demands, a submission she regrets not making for her earlier love. But when Frederic immediately voices his sexual desire for her, she initially counters his desires, requesting some clear sign of his commitment. Perhaps the only reason that she submits to his desires now is because she has a captive audience, so to speak—Frederic is not going anywhere, so on one level, she doesn't have to worry about abandonment, only about the propriety of this behavior. She capitulates to his sexual desire, doing so however only after she has had some profession of his love, even if he clearly has other motivation for giving in to her.

> "You mustn't," she said. "You're not well enough."
> "Yes I am. Come on."
> "No. You're not strong enough."
> "Yes. I am. Yes. Please."
> "You do love me?"
> "I really love you. I'm crazy about you. Come on please."
> "Feel our hearts beating."
> "I don't care about our hearts. I want you. I'm just mad about you."
> "You really love me?"
> "Don't keep saying that. Come on. Please. Please, Catherine." (92)

This passage certainly proves Spilka's claim regarding their sexual positions during intercourse, especially if we add the word "top" whenever Frederic asks, "Come on." But while Catherine is on top, if "only for a minute," she is hardly in a dominant position, considering her desires. Then again, with the wounded Frederic unable to move or to do much for himself, Catherine's own withholding of sex until he repeatedly—if not always convincingly—professes his devotion might be seen as a savvy choice, a way for her to gain some currency in their developing relationship. While Frederic continually obscures her desire in favor of his own, especially as he rejects her metaphor of hearts beating in unison, she is persistent, even after their intercourse. "Now do you believe I love you?" (92) she asks him, but her love of him has never been an issue for Frederic, especially not in the heat of passion. Only now, with the wildness gone, does he tell her, "I'm crazy in love with you," and, importantly, this admission comes without any narrative indication of deceit, as it has before. Given this admission of *Frederic* isn't it interesting that no critical readers have defined him as crazy. After all, many readers simply assume that Catherine is crazy, because she defines herself as such (a paradoxical argument, assigning rationality to the supposedly irrational). This lapse in noticing Frederic's self-definition comes at least from his professed source of craziness—love. But it also suggests some narrative and gender bias in reading, too readily assigning diagnoses of pathological behavior without also applying them to the male hero/protagonist of the novel. But Frederic is not committed to her yet, and it will take his attempted escape from Catherine and from the responsibility of her condition to make him realize the absurdity of the masculine behavior that temporarily drives him away. Catherine's postcoital assessment, "That was just madness," is not simply a comment on her loss of her virginity or on her submission to his desires, although it is a recognition of the danger she has placed herself in professionally and emotionally. But *she* is not mad; it is Frederic's desire which is mad, which she knows she will have to acknowledge if her own desire for his commitment to her is to be possible.

When Catherine continues to press for signs of his commitment, he finally refuses her, claiming that her distrust of him causes him pain.

> "You do love me, don't you?"
> "Don't say that again. You don't know what that does to me."
> "I'll be careful then. I don't want to do anything more to you." (93)

Catherine's final comment before her departure, and following their first sexual encounter, is an interesting one. She doesn't want to disturb him, because he is wounded, but this may be a sarcastic comment, as well, given what he has had her do to him sexually—mounting him upon her arrival, despite the danger this puts her in at the hospital. This sarcasm is related, I think, to the irony that Sandra Whipple Spanier finds in Catherine's comments. Whipple Spanier refers to Paul Fussell's readings (in *The Great War and Modern Memory*) on the role of irony and black humor in the midst of the Great War. There is sarcasm also in her attendance to his desires, which she has "done to him" while he seems unaware of what she might want. But Frederic doesn't hear this sarcasm, merely wanting her to "Come back right away" (93). In fact, Catherine is quite often sarcastic, despite the passive role readers often assign to her, and she often comments critically on Frederic's shortcomings. Later, in the cheap hotel, before Frederic returns to the front, Catherine seems to be attempting to capitulate to Frederic's desires once again, despite feeling like a whore during their final sexual tryst in Milan. She makes a 180-degree shift in her attitude, now claiming that "Vice is a wonderful thing. . . . The people who go in for it seem to have good taste about it. The red plush is really fine. It's just the thing. And the mirrors are very attractive" (153). Catherine is practicing her sarcasm again, subtly criticizing the absurdly cheap decor of the room—and of what the room is decorated to support, vice and not love—and it is this attitude that might have earned her the title "bitch," if the narrative Frederic were a bit more perceptive. However, he does not understand her sarcasm, calling her a "lovely girl" (153) and failing to hear the kind of antagonism that has caused many readers to define Brett Ashley or Catherine Bourne as "bitches." And, like Frederic, readers often fail to read Catherine's comments as pointedly perceptive, assuming instead that she is merely servile or crazy.

Like the undercurrent of sarcasm in her comments, Catherine's role playing, while assuaging Frederic's desire on one hand, also betrays her intelligence and her active pursuit of his commitment to her. "There, darling. Now you're all clean inside and out" (104). Their conversation about Valentini, the pending surgery, and her desire for him to avoid babbling from the anesthetic has obscured the enema she has given him to prep him for surgery. But Catherine knows that his cleanliness, which she has facilitated, has not cleansed him of his wavering allegiance with the masculine behavior that threatens to cause him to leave her once he has the ability to walk. Certainly his visit with Dr. Valentini confirms his ability to revert to an objectification of women, particularly of Catherine, in bolstering a relationship with men. Valentini, like Rinaldi, is competent both as a doctor and as a masculine compatriot, and Frederic is assured of this in the homosocial competition in which they engage. Valentini, already able to detect the relationship between Catherine and Frederic (or assuming such a relationship, given her attractiveness and Frederic's presumed masculinity), threatens to "steal" her from him. "Can't that girl talk Italian? She should learn. What a lovely girl. I could teach her. I will be a patient here myself" (99). Of course, Valentini's offer is not simply to teach her Italian, but to seduce her, just as he teases the actual patient about what must go on with this attractive nurse. "What a lovely girl. Ask her if she eats supper with me. No, I won't take her away from you" (99). Unlike the other doctors, who will not drink with Frederic or share in such competitive banter, Valentini seems more than competent, both as surgeon and as masculine compatriot. Catherine, however, doesn't share this view. Although she doesn't speak Italian, she knows the tenor of the conversation between the two men. "I didn't like him as much as you did," she tells Frederic. "But I imagine he's very good" (102). Between them, Catherine has been reduced to a "girl" and becomes a stage upon which two men, engaged in an intimate physical closeness that might otherwise be threatening to their homosocial relationship (despite their medical backgrounds), can safely express their affinity for each other.

So it is no accident that as she finishes the enema, cleaning him "inside and out," she wants to know more about his romantic and sexual history, which may tell her more about his commitment to the masculine behavior that may cause him to leave her. "Tell me. How many people have you ever loved?" When his response is "none," other, of course, than Catherine—of which she must remind him—she tests his veracity by changing the terms of the question. "How many have you—how do you say it?—stayed with?" (104). As before, his response is "none," but Catherine clearly knows better than this. James Nagel agrees, indicating that "Catherine, on a deeper level, was very much aware of his duplicity, despite her surface delusion."[36] But the surface delusion is a well-planned pretense, and Frederic's answer to the second question may shed light on his response to the first question. Instead of becoming angry with him, however, she expresses her desire to be deceived in this, even as she requests further details. "Were they pretty? . . . Were they very attractive?" (105) What is especially interesting about this exchange are Catherine's assumptions about Frederic's experience; she assumes that the bulk of his sexual experience has been with prostitutes, not in relationships with women who themselves desired to be with Frederic. "When a man stays with a girl when does she say how much it costs?" (105) This is an especially telling revelation of Catherine's knowledge about him, and about her very perceptive grip on reality. Catherine knows that he has been with prostitutes, and Frederic doesn't catch this as an accusation, of sorts, perhaps because, like Rinaldi, he has come to generally associate women with prostitution and availability (even if he befriends prostitutes, unlike Rinaldi). Of course, he betrays his experience as he answers her questions about what prostitutes will do for their customers. And Frederic lies about telling prostitutes that he loves them; that he wants his prostitutes to pretend at love, not just sex, is clear when Frederic admits "'No,' I lied" to Catherine's repeated desire to know if he professed such love during these trysts. This lie might suggest to Catherine—knowing of his duplicity in all other things in this dialogue—that this expression *has* been important to him. If he has pretended to love these women, not only to conduct sexual transactions with them, then Catherine may have her answer to her concerns about his commitment to masculine social behavior. Although sex with prostitutes may be casual, just as the talk between men about women and sex is routine, Frederic seems to want more than casual or routine sex. Catherine has managed to extract information about Frederic's emotional needs, information that he otherwise keeps close to the vest, as easily as she has extracted his bodily wastes in cleaning him out for surgery.

Catherine's seeming self-effacement, in part borne out of her fear of Frederic's death in surgery, is actually a playing of the "game" on his own level. Aware of the relationship between Valentini and Frederic, she discusses her own relationship with Frederic in terms of the values of the homosocial relationship. She seems to readily adopt the role of prostitute for Frederic, going above and beyond the prostitutes who will only say "just what he wants her to"; she actually means what she says. This, she assumes, will keep him from wanting "any other girls" (105). "I do anything you want," she tells him, claiming "I want what you want. There isn't any me any more. Just what you want" (106). Thus, she adopts the role, in talking about his sexual exploits, of homosocial compatriot, even while she describes herself as the object of sexual currency. "I'm good. I do what you want" (106) is her assertion of her role as the object of Frederic's sexual desire, and it asserts her claim, which is reminiscent of masculine sexual braggadocio, "I'll be a great success, won't I?" (105).

Catherine is neither self-effacing nor compliant, and she certainly isn't crazy; instead, she is determined not to become a casualty of war, even of a gender war. Frederic's narrative indicates that he has indeed become committed to Catherine, and in a sense they imagine themselves "married." "We said to each other that we were married the first day she had come to the hospital and we counted months from our wedding day" (114). But Frederic has not risked much in the early stages of their relationship. Wounded and away from the front, he does not risk his identity in the homosocial relationship in the way that Catherine risks hers socially and professionally. Fetterley claims that, "On the simplest level, Catherine allows Frederic to avoid responsibility and commitment."[37] But Catherine is not allowing Frederic to *avoid* responsibility and commitment; on the contrary, she is demanding that he recognize these in himself and in their relationship. She emphasizes their unity *beyond* the mere contract of a socially sanctioned union like marriage, urging Frederic to understand that union in similar ways. When Frederic expresses his need for a "proper" marriage, telling us "I wanted to be *really* married" (114; italics mine), Catherine dismisses his concerns for several very real reasons—not the least of which that marriage would send her away from him and back to Scotland. But marriage is also unnecessary for Catherine because she is already united with him in very profound ways. She asks him,

> "What good would it do to marry now? We're really married. I couldn't be any more married."
> "I only wanted to for you."
> "There isn't any me. I'm you. Don't make up a separate me." (115)

Yet Frederic continues to separate her from himself:

> "I thought girls always wanted to be married."
> "They do. But, darling, I am married. I'm married to you. Don't I make you a good wife?" (115)

While Frederic needs to acknowledge the social conventions of marriage, Catherine has moved beyond the mere social convention for a more full and complete union with him, a union that he threatens to break because he continually tries to separate her—a "girl"—from him. This isn't so much self-effacement on Catherine's part, as it is her very different understanding of marriage as a transformation in identity, but not the kind of change of identity she experienced when taking on the role of the prostitute. She has no religion, she claims, because "You're my religion. You're all I've got" (116). This is not Catherine's self-effacement before a masculine god, as some readers suggest, but her revelation of the spiritual commitment she has made to their relationship.

But she is not Frederic's religion, it would seem, in his fear of cuckholdry. "But you won't ever leave me for some one else" (116). This is a fascinating turn around, given her earlier fears of his leaving her. No critical readers, to my knowledge, accuse him of the madness that they assign to Catherine earlier, even though Frederic experiences much the same insecurity in his desire for a socially sanctioned marriage, and in the flight he will make from her in his return to the front. Without the social sanction that was available to him in his homosocial relationships with fellow officers and soldiers, Frederic is insecure, and, because he is not yet committed to Catherine in the spiritual way that she has committed herself to him, he desires the security of a socially recognized marriage. Knowing this, and eliciting only further insecurity from Frederic, she turns to the only constant sign of engagement that Frederic has available to him—sex and sexual service.

> You see I'm happy, darling, and we have a lovely time. I haven't been happy for a long time and when I met you perhaps I was nearly crazy. Perhaps I was crazy. But now we're happy and we love each other. Do let's please just be happy. You are happy, aren't you? Is there anything I do you don't like? Can I do anything to please you? Would you like me to take down my hair? Do you want to play? (116)

While Catherine asserts her own desire to reject the social codes of conduct that earlier inhibited her, she must also perform for Frederic. Although she understands their marriage as a spiritual one, bonding the two of them together—"I'm you"—he understands only the sexual bond, and thus she must show him how they are together through sexual intercourse. Frederic has not yet made the kinds of leaps of faith that Catherine has made, because he has not yet put his identity at risk to be with her. And as such, Frederic does not yet experience the kind of unity that Catherine identifies. Only after the announcement of her pregnancy and his flight from her, back to the masculine arms of his homosocial relationships and to a homecoming at the front, will he begin to risk his own identity and be able finally to understand the nature of the union that Catherine has defined.

Failed Homecomings and a Farewell to Masculinity

In his return to the front in Book Three, a homecoming is precisely what Frederic is looking for. He is attempting an escape from Catherine, in a sense, by returning to his very masculine relationships. His movement away from her and back toward the masculine influence of his fellow officers becomes evident in the narrative structure of the final chapters of Book Two. Upon learning of the pregnancy in chapter 21, he first defines it as a kind of personal failure: "I'm like a ballplayer that bats two hundred and thirty and knows he's no better" (140). In chapter 22, Frederic suffers from an attack of jaundice as he battles Miss Van Campen, a condition that he describes through a particularly telling comparison. "Did you ever know a man who tried to disable himself by kicking himself in the scrotum?" When propriety does not allow the offended Van Campen to respond, he continues, "Because that is the nearest sensation to jaundice and it is a sensation that I believe few women have ever experienced" (144). Although his anger is a result of Van Campen's suggestion that his cowardice lead him to inflict himself with jaundice to avoid returning to the front (an accusation that contradicts Catherine's attempt to define him as brave in the previous chapter), this hypothetical kick in the scrotum, difficult as it might be to accomplish, also identifies Frederic's reaction to the pregnancy and the trap he has found himself in. His imagined kick in the scrotum might be remorse, as Rinaldi might suggest would be appropriate behavior for his "remorse boy" (168), but it also separates him from Van Campen who, despite her status as a nurse, finds she can't talk about this very masculine subject with him. Chapter 22 begins Frederic's movement away from his relationship with Catherine and back toward the masculine ideals he was faced with at the front. In chapters 23 and 24, the final chapters of Book Two, having lost his leave and the chance to spend intimate time away with Catherine, he departs for the front and the masculine security of the homosocial relationships he has found there. Thus, upon learning of Catherine's condition, Frederic takes several narrative steps backward, attempting a return to his previous life before Catherine. As he prepares to return to the front in chapter 23, he returns to frequenting cheap hotels, where he engages a woman for a brief sexual tryst. That that woman is Catherine is not important to Frederic, because he has begun to reorient himself to the masculine behavior of the men at the front.

Before leaving, Frederic does make occasional attempts to address the problem of Catherine's pregnancy and the raising of the baby, but he is largely withdrawn from her. Catherine's admission during their walk through Milan is completely misunderstood by Frederic, who is absorbed with only two things. The first is his return to the masculine front, for which he buys a gun, noting, "Now we're fully armed" (149). The shame that he felt earlier upon meeting "English-speaking people" (29) while wearing a gun is appropriately missing now, given his temporary desire to escape responsibility by returning to the masculine values of the front. Instead, Frederic behaves as though he is a connoisseur and expert gunman as he makes a show of purchasing the gun in front of Catherine, a role that we know is false from his earlier admission of role playing: "I wore a real one and *felt like* a gunman until I practiced firing it" (29). The status of the gun as a phallus is hardly subtle, especially given his desire to find "some place to go" with Catherine, who has expressed her desire to continue walking, a desire that he contradicts (150). This place to go is his second preoccupation, with sex before leaving, which allows him to role play, modeling his behavior after the couple against the cathedral. "We turned down a side street where there were no lights and walked in the street. I stopped and kissed Catherine. While I kissed her I felt her hand on my shoulder. She had pulled my cape around her so it covered both of us. We were standing in the street against a high wall" (150). He becomes interested only in "some place to go" to have sex (147). This is not the first time he has expressed such a desire; while initially courting Miss Barkley, Frederic asks, "Isn't there anywhere we can go?" (30). In that instance, Catherine could control his desire through her concern for social propriety and her suspicions about his intentions, despite the urgency of his situation. "'I wish there was some place we could go,' I said. I was experiencing the masculine difficulty of making love very long standing up" (31). The discomfort of his erection and unsatiated desire in the earlier instance will not be repeated while standing in the dark side street in Milan, largely because Catherine cannot use propriety as a defense against his sexual advances, given her condition. The hotel room provides Catherine and him with some place to go and is in accord with his own early fantasies of bedding her down. Frederic, we learn, initially thought of her as a sexual opportunity: "Once when I first met you I spent an afternoon thinking how we would go to the Hotel Cavour together and how it would be" (153), a fantasy he engages in in Book One (37). His fantasy there is that she will "pretend that I was her boy that was killed." Note the lack of interest in her feelings for *him,* much like that of prostitutes who will lie to their men about their own desire. Catherine has pro- tested about going to the hotel, again concerned about image and propriety, but she gives in to his desires, again knowing that she failed to cater to her now-dead fiancé's similar desires.

Catherine's admission, which I mentioned in the previous para- graph, addresses her present condition, both as an unmarried preg- nant woman about to be abandoned by her lover—a condition she initially feared, which caused her to seem "crazy" to both Frederic and to many readers—and, later, as a whore. When they turn down the side street and she says, "I've never been this way" (148), he assumes she is speaking of directions, of an unfamiliar street in Milan. Indeed, Frederic dismisses her comment with his own assur- ances that he knows where they are going, stopping at a shop to buy the gun. Frederic's mind is on escape, on a return to the masculine behavior, the misogyny of which would have insulated him from his present predicament. She feels despair over the developments in their relationship, however, evident in her reaction to the couple at the cathedral and in her attempts to figure out what to do next. "I've never been this way" is her explanation that she has never been in this situation—pregnant, abandoned, dismissed by the man who seduced her. "This way" has been what Catherine avoided becoming with her dead fiancé, and it is what she most feared when she seems most crazy—that is, when she is desperate to ensure Frederic's love and commitment.

Indeed, when Frederic decides "the room felt like our own home" (153), he reveals just how far removed he has become from Cathe- rine, who has just admitted, "I never felt like a whore before" (152). The hotel is "home" for him, just as he expects a sense of "homecom- ing" in his return to the front and to the masculine values it holds. But, although the Cavour is too good for their purposes ("They wouldn't have taken us in there," he admits to Catherine [154]), Frederic has had his sexual fantasies fulfilled. Michael S. Reynolds claims in *Hemingway's First War* that those desires are not com- pletely satisfied: "Here the food brought to the upstairs room on the night of a departure has the overtones of a last supper. But there is no silver bucket for the wine as in the daydream, and the lovers do not make love all the hot night. Instead they eat their supper and discuss the future of Catherine and the fetus growing in her womb. There is no sexual contact."[38] However, we might take a page from

Kenneth Lynn's reading of narrative gaps and sexuality in *The Sun Also Rises* to understand that the retrospective Frederic has chosen only to allude to this detail. "After we had eaten we felt fine, and then after, we felt very happy and in a little time the room felt like our own home" (153). Frederic's narrative "and then after," which makes him feel not just fine but very happy, is all that he will tell us of their sexual activity; clearly some sexual intercourse has occurred. Not only does he fail to offer details, just as he refuses to share the details of his Naples and Milan exploits with Rinaldi and the men of the camp, but he further obscures the sexual intercourse by shifting the chronology of the narrative. After this definition of the hotel's homeliness, Frederic's narrative shifts back to the events of dinner and his conversation with Catherine. Not until they have finished with dinner is there any evidence of sex, and this, again, is evidenced by omission. "The waiter came and took away the things. After a while we were very still and we could hear the rain" (154). In the narrative gap between these sentences, the retrospective narrator has left out the details of their lovemaking. We may read it not only in their stillness, as contrary to the presumed activity of sex, but in Frederic's quotation of the couplet from Marvell's "To His Coy Mistress." Catherine contradicts this choice of verse, because "it's about a girl who wouldn't live with a man," which is hardly her condition (154).

But what is even more interesting in this tryst is his assumption of Catherine's narrative desire. Her earlier protests attempt to avoid a tryst in a cheap hotel. Listen to her voice, without Frederic's narrative interference:

> "We can go the way we are? Without luggage?"
> . . . .
> "Won't we have dinner?" Catherine asked. "I'm afraid I'll be hungry."
> . . . .
> "I haven't anything to wear. I haven't even a night-gown." (151)

This, followed by her "I never felt like a whore before" (152), resounds with Catherine's protests against Frederic's desires, even if those protests are indirect. They are easily dismissed by Frederic, both as character and as retrospective narrator, because such protests against masculine desire are not acknowledged by the masculine narrative, especially as it defines the availability of sex via prostitutes. As Miriam Mandel has noted in her essay, "Ferguson and Lesbian Love: Unspoken Subplots in *A Farewell to Arms,* "the dynamics of male authorship and of male narration, and especially of first-person male narration, work to silence the female characters, even if—or especially when—these are the object of intense scrutiny."[39] Catherine's later, retrospective thoughts on the rough spots of their relationship remind Frederic—character and narrator—of her protests. "The only time I ever felt badly was when I felt like a whore in Milan and that only lasted seven minutes and besides it was the room furnishings. Don't I make you a good wife?" (294) She recalls this bad time for Frederic, who may have forgotten it in his own self-satisfied reflections, and I have to wonder why she defines that degradation of her identity as only lasting seven minutes. Is this a subtle dig at Frederic's limited sexual prowess and his masculine self-centeredness upon leaving for the front? If so, it might mirror an admission Frederic makes in the company of Rinaldi, who has claimed, "I only like two other things; one is bad for my work and the other is over in half an hour or fifteen minutes. Sometimes less" (170). Other than work, Rinaldi's only other occupations are in alcohol and sex, and the latter seems quite brief. Frederic's response, "Sometimes a good deal less" (171), might be a playfully masculine insult at Rinaldi's expense (he responds as though it is: "Perhaps I have improved, baby" [171]). But it might also be an admission of the brevity of sexual pleasure and, as such, might well reflect Catherine's later, subtle criticism. Frederic's conflict between enacting the masculine behavior of his fellow officers, which precludes women as individuated beings with their own desires (which would account for his brief and climax-oriented intercourse), and his relationship with Catherine as an individual, evident in their discussion of her condition and the baby's future, becomes indicative of the conflict Frederic will face in Book Three as he attempts a return to homosocial relationships and to an Oedipal narrative of masculinity which he will finally abandon.

The fact that Catherine later becomes a "sacred subject" between he and Rinaldi (169–70), like the subject of mothers or sisters, suggests not a mutual respect but a lasting antagonism between the two men upon Frederic's return and following his inspection by the major and Rinaldi. Men who respect each other, according to the credo, do not violate the reputations of sacred subjects, those women-as-possessions of a fellow man, which of course confirms Rinaldi's definition of Catherine as a "goddess." Instead of simply ignoring Rinaldi's need for sexual details, Frederic becomes angry and defensive, silencing Rinaldi before he may supply his own sexual descriptions. Frederic is attempting a return to masculinity, but his commitment to the behavior that he earlier found difficult is now impossible, given his relationship with Catherine. This is in part

because, as Fetterley indicates, his relationship with Catherine inter-
feres with his relationship with Rinaldi, even when she is not immediately present. "In Rinaldi's eyes Catherine is clearly a complication
and what she has to offer can in no way compensate for the complications that come along with her."[40] Although Rinaldi respects his
friend's sacred subject, there is a lasting antagonism between them
that was absent earlier. "I will get an English girl too. As a matter of
fact I knew your girl first but she was a little tall for me. A tall
girl for a sister" (171). Rinaldi very nearly continues his insulting
comments, suggesting that Catherine was not good enough for him,
but he backs off by defining Catherine as his sister and as "untouch-
able." Importantly, this chapter—in which Rinaldi's behavior at the
mess reflects the captain's earlier anger and in which we learn of his
syphilis—offers the final interaction between the two men. Rinaldi is
mentioned briefly at the beginning of chapter 27 (181), and the two
men ignore each other, not interrupting each others' sleep as they
would have done earlier. Rinaldi disappears from the narrative as
Frederic moves out in the retreat and, ultimately, abandons the masculine, military path altogether.

For, despite Rinaldi's inspection of Frederic upon his return to the
front, he knows that Frederic has already abandoned the masculine
behavior of the homosocial relationship. As the priest joins them in
the mess, it is Rinaldi who takes over the baiting of the priest, but
the explicit connection that we saw between the captain and Frederic
is missing between these two friends, and Frederic is no longer concerned about the danger of an affinity with the priest, claiming, "I
never discuss a Saint after dark" (173) and refusing to participate in
the baiting. It is the *priest* who makes eye contact with Frederic here,
not Rinaldi, whose comments indicate his dismissal of Frederic from
the homosocial company of masculinity. "There he is, gone over with
the priest. . . . Where are all the good old priest-baiters? Where is
Cavalcanti? Where is Brundi? Where is Cesare? Do I have to bait this
priest alone without support?" (173). Rinaldi stops short of making
homophobic accusations against his friend, but his anger causes
him to behave in much the same way that the captain behaved in
the face of the perceived threat of the priest. In this case, however,
Rinaldi lashes out at everyone at the table, not only at the priest. "'I
don't give a damn,' Rinaldi said to the table. 'To hell with the whole
business.' He looked defiantly around the table, his eyes flat, his
face pale" (174). As in the captain's earlier outburst, it is the major
who attempts to calm the anger. When Frederic attempts to soothe
his friend, however, echoing Rinaldi's "To hell with the whole damn
business," Rinaldi rejects his sympathies. "No, no . . . You can't do

it. You can't do it. I say you can't do it. You're dry and you're empty and there's nothing else. There's nothing else I tell you" (174). We see in Rinaldi's solitude at the table and in his pathetic figure as an alcoholic, overworked surgeon who is suffering from syphilis, the failure of the masculine narrative, and Rinaldi's defeat is no less absurd that Frederic's wounding while eating cheese. Similarly, the degraded figure whom Frederic has returned to in his attempted escape from Catherine serves as a reflection of the degradation that he will himself experience, as the Italian army prepares to execute him at the bridge.

Frederic will have the opportunity to abandon the masculine narrative as he leaves the main road with his men during the retreat (contrary to orders but saving them from the shelling that he predicts) and as he leaves the military behind in his escape into the river and his return to Catherine. I disagree with Millicent Bell when she claims that "even the later 'separate peace' in chapter 32 after Frederic's immersion in the Tagliamento is not really a change of direction, a peaking of the plot."[41] This is indeed a moment of commitment for Frederic, and if it is not a climactic peaking of the plot, it is because Frederic has made a conscious decision to leave behind the narrative which would climax in his "heroic" death at the bridge, a death that might have been read as similar to Robert Jordan's in the conclusion of *For Whom the Bell Tolls*. Like the soldiers who discard their rifles, phallic images of their military service, who "think if they throw away their rifles they can't make them fight" (220), Frederic will divest himself of his symbols of military rank and authority, revising his identity as he rejects the narrative that can only end in his death. He even divests himself of any thought of seeing Rinaldi again, telling himself, "I would never see him now. I would never see any of them now. That life was over" (233). Frederic's farewell to his former life comes at the end of the book which would ostensibly take him away from Catherine and back to a commitment to the masculine. But the life that was over is his conscription to the masculine narrative, and he is no longer trapped biologically, that is, defined through homosocial definitions of normative gender and power relationships. In the chapter that follows this rift between the two friends, the priest takes Rinaldi's place in the quarters otherwise shared by Frederic and Rinaldi, and Frederic's tone has radically shifted from nearsighted optimism in his earlier conversation with the priest about victory and war to a pessimistic sense of defeat. "Something may happen. . . . But it will happen only to us. If they felt the way we do, it would be all right. But they have beaten us. They feel another way" (179). Frederic is aware that his escape from

Catherine to the masculine front is not an escape at all, but a defeat. The "they" and "us" of Frederic's foreboding are the Austrians and the Italians, the enemies and the allies, but it is an opposition that might also describe Frederic's concern for Catherine and him, and for what outside forces—"they"—are already doing to them.

Only as Frederic makes an escape from the front and from the masculine narrative do we begin to learn more about him, including his early study of architecture in Rome. And now that he has taken the risk to save his own life and to be with Catherine, he must become accustomed to his new identity, feeling still like a "masquerader" in civilian clothes (243). Notice, however, how quickly he begins to change his behavior as he reacts to the scornful aviators who question both his service to the war and his homosociability. "In the old days I would have insulted them and picked a fight" (243). The old days aren't very distant, yet he remains committed to his departure from the masculine, avoiding the fight as well as the subject of the war in the papers. He is surprisingly secure in his "separate peace" (243), and as the barman at the *hotel des Isles Borromées* attempts a misogynistic joke about sexual rendezvous, Frederic refuses to participate. He tells the barman that he is looking for two English girls, nurses:

> "One of them is my wife," I said. "I have come here to meet her."
> "The other is my wife."
> "I am not joking."
> "Pardon my stupid joke," he said. "I did not understand." He went away and was gone quite a little while. (245)

The barman does not understand that Frederic has no desire to play this game, and he socializes no further with this man who cannot share in a lewd joke. Similarly, Ferguson clearly does not understand the extent of the risks Catherine, and now Frederic, have already taken, and she assails both of them with accusations of impropriety, which each has already progressed beyond.[42] She defines Frederic as "worse than sneaky. You're like a snake. A snake with an Italian uniform: with a cape around your neck" (246), unaware perhaps that she has allied him with Rinaldi's earlier description of himself. "I am the snake of reason" (170), he has told Frederic in an attempt to return him to his old, licentious ways. "Even with remorse you will have a better time" (170), Rinaldi urges, both with him and with women than in marriage. But Frederic has since come to terms with his own rejection of the masculine ideals of promiscuity, just as Catherine has dismissed any concerns for social impropriety which she once feared. "If you had any shame it would be different," Ferguson assails Catherine. "But you're God knows how many months gone with child and you think it's a joke and are all smiles because your seducer's come back. You've no shame and no feelings" (247). This is true; Catherine is no longer ashamed, as she was at the hotel in Milan, and only once in the later books does she exhibit any concern for propriety. This occurs when she says of his renewed suggestion of marriage, "It's too embarrassing now. I show too plainly. I won't go before any one and be married in this state" (293). But this embarrassment does not last long, as Frederic and Catherine begin to define for themselves a new topos for their relationship, a place that does not conscript them to certain narratives of propriety and behavior. Frederic's desire for a fox tail stimulates a fantasy of separation from such narratives as he fantasizes, "We'd have clothes made, or live in a country where it wouldn't make any difference." Catherine affirms this fantasy on a metaphoric level, indicating that in their relationship, "We live in a country where nothing makes any difference" (303). The neutrality of Switzerland posits them away from the Oedipal narratives of war, gender and social propriety, narratives that construct power relationships around victors and the defeated.

So when Catherine refers to Frederic as "Othello with his occupation gone" (257), she is not identifying his desire to return to the military or to the masculine relationships that earlier defined him. Catherine sympathizes with Frederic, who complains of his disorientation in her absence. "My life used to be full of everything," he tells her. "Now if you aren't with me I haven't a thing in the world" (257). But Frederic is not interested in reviving his relationships with other men; in fact, when she attempts to separate him from her by asserting his need for masculine relationships, he rejects the notion. "Wouldn't you like to go on a trip somewhere by yourself, darling, and be with men and ski?" (297). Even as she urges his autonomy, he now identifies his desires with her desires: "Do you want me to see other people? . . . Neither do I" (297). Their separate country leads to an intimate kind of identification with each other, which becomes most evident in the discussion of haircuts and the plans that Catherine initiates for eliminating external gender identity which might differentiate each from the other. Frederic's arousal at the hairdresser prefigures her desire for similar haircuts, which he echoes in his desire to wear a fox tail, or long hair, and for these experiments in gender changes that they will never have the opportunity to practice. She wants to be his twin, as she tells him to "let it grow a little longer and I could cut mine and we'd be just alike only one of us blonde and one of us dark" (299). Like *The Garden of Eden*'s David Bourne, he doesn't want her to cut her hair short, but this Catherine, like her later literary descendant, asserts this desire to bring them closer together by manipulating the ways that they differentiate gender roles.

> "It might be nice short. Then we'd both be alike. Oh, darling, I want you so much I want to be you too."
> "You are. We're the same one."
> "I know it. At night we are."
> "The nights are grand." (299)

The tragic conclusion of the novel might come as little surprise for readers who realize that their attempts to identify fully with each other become manifest in their physical appearance. Catherine claims, "I want us to be all mixed up" (300). While she takes his identity, calling herself "Catherine Henry" upon admission to the hospital (313), his identity becomes more and more suspect, and always strange to himself. He doesn't recognize himself once the beard grows in: "I could not shadow-box in front of the narrow long mirror at first because it looked so strange to see a man with a beard boxing. But finally I just thought it was funny" (311). Similarly, he continues his masquerade as a helpless doctor, perhaps not unlike the other doctors who cannot prevent the death of Catherine or of the child. "I looked in the glass and saw myself looking like a fake doctor with a beard" (319). The beard, which he has grown at Catherine's request, actually divides him from an identification with her, because, despite any prospective identical haircuts they might one day get, it is unlikely that she will grow a beard. And just as Frederic's beard separates him from Catherine, her advanced pregnancy separates her from an identification with him. After Catherine proclaims his beard a "great success," she emphasizes their lack of physical similarity. "I'm not going to cut my hair now until after young Catherine's born. I look too big and matronly now. But after she's born and I'm thin again I'm going to cut it and then I'll be a fine new and different girl for you. We'll go together and get it cut, or I'll go alone and come and surprise you" (304). This passage clearly provides the groundwork for Hemingway's later interest in identity and gender-shifts in *The Garden of Eden*, as many critics, especially Mark Spilka in *Hemingway's Quarrel with Androgyny,* have successfully illustrated. The tragedy that separates the couple, then, might easily be defined through their gradual inability to identify with each other physically.

But the beard and the pregnancy actually bring Frederic and Catherine closer together, rather than farther apart. Of the quest for gender symmetry, which is echoed in Catherine's desire for similar haircuts and in their joint desire to be "all mixed up," Eve Kosofsky Sedgwick writes, "The assertion of [gender] symmetry will be made possible by a suppression of effectual gender differences or by a translation of them into factitiously comparable spatial and/or temporal rhetorical figures; the 'comparable' figures will bear the mark of their asymmetrical origins but not in a way that will permit them to be retranslated into an intelligible version of their original condition."[43] Thus, beards and pregnancies serve as those symbolic figures which betray Frederic and Catherine's difference from each other, but which paradoxically bring them closer together in their joint and parallel asymmetry. The beard is Catherine's, after all: "I wanted to take off the beard as soon as I started boxing," Frederic tells us, "but Catherine did not want me to" (311). And the pregnancy is Frederic's in the role he has played in impregnating Catherine. When she explains her inexperience with maternity by noting that, "so few of the soldiers had babies in the hospitals," his reply, "I did," is a playful identification through the pregnancy of Catherine as his "baby" whom he has "had" sexually in the hospital (308). Indeed, Frederic becomes a comic figure for Catherine during their escape, appearing pregnant as he attempts to rig a sail from an umbrella. "You looked about twenty feet broad and very affectionate holding the umbrella by the edges—" (273). They each find ways to compensate for the necessary physical difference which accompanies biological gender and to become "all mixed up."

Oedipus Henry: Explaining the Tragic Conclusion of "A Farewell to Arms"

Given their ability to transcend the conscription to gender narratives, why does the novel end with Catherine's painful death and Frederic's solitude in the rain? If Frederic has abandoned the Oedipal narrative of hero and obstacle, why must only one of them remain? And if Frederic is indeed the misogynistic, self-centered hero which some readers have complained he is, why is there no evidence of satisfaction in his narrative's conclusion? Because Frederic is not an omniscient narrator who may control and construct events according to his desires; he makes no better sense of the novel's conclusion than we do, despite his retrospective examination of his life. "What reason is there for her to die? There's just a child that has to be born, the by-product of good nights in Milan" (320). Of course, there is no real reason for her to die, beyond, perhaps, the incompetence of the doctors at the hospital, which makes the novel's conclusion so problematic.

Judith Fetterley offers one explanation for this conclusion, pointing out the similarities between *A Farewell to Arms* and the popular Erich Segal romance, *Love Story*, when she writes, "While *A Farewell to Arms* is an infinitely more complex book than *Love Story*, nevertheless its emotional dynamics and its form are similar. In reading it one is continually struck by the disparity between its overt fabric of idealized romance and its underlying vision of the radical limitations of love, between its surface idyll and its sub-surface critique."[44] Because the narrative of the romance tradition retains its hold over the couple, despite their movement away from the gendered conscripts of the narrative, it would seem that Frederic and Catherine's fates are prescriptive. The "idealized romance" in this case might best refer to the notion that Frederic can actually, and safely, abandon the masculinity of the homosocial covenant without great danger or great loss. The "sub-surface critique," which Fetterley identifies, then, not only is a misogynistic manipulation of women for the needs of men, but a commentary against the dangers which face those men who dare to attempt a break from these homosocial traditions. Even as Fetterley claims that "Catherine dies and dies because she is a woman," we must also recognize that Frederic is not in command of his own narrative, and he, too, must suffer the consequences of their actions. Fetterley is in error when she identifies the cause of Catherine's death, writing, "her death is the fulfillment of his own unconscious wish"; the narrative is much more complex than that as we find that Frederic is not in control of his retelling of events.[45]

Teresa de Lauretis writes in her essay, "Imaging," "woman, inscribed in films as representation/image, is at once the support of male desire and of the filmic code, the look, that defines cinema itself" (*Alice Doesn't*, 58). Taken in terms of the narrative that controls both filmic and novelistic genres, Catherine becomes the support of male—or at least masculine—desire in that she must reorient Frederic to other possibilities beyond the limitations of the homosocial. Once she is successful in that, however, she must still die, not to fulfill Frederic's narrative desire, which no longer supports the homosocial, but to fulfill the masculine narrative code which is already in place and beyond the desires of either of them. Instead, her death is exacted by the Oedipal narrative that Frederic has attempted to abandon, but that the narrative, or perhaps the writer in his desire to write a romance narrative, will not allow. James Nagel writes of the irony of the novel, "In planning to escape the dangers of Italy, Frederic and Catherine hasten to her death in Lausanne."[46] And in attempting an escape from the narrative dictates of gendered behavior and social propriety, they hasten to the only conclusion that the tradition of romance narratives will allow. Thus the protagonist, attempting to find a way out of the sociocultural narrative of gender, is conscripted to the hero role in a way that is antithetical to his lack of commitment to the war. This explains his search for patterns in the retrospective narrative, as well as his frequent and self-conscious narrational comments.

In "Distance, Voice and Temporal Perspective in Frederic Henry's Narration: Successes, Problems, and Paradox," James Phelan disputes the presence of such narrative self-reflection, writing that "Frederic is a recorder, not a self-conscious narrator. He is intent on telling his story, but he is no artist, no Humbert Humbert trying to render the most artistically effective narrative that he can muster in order to give immortality to his beloved."[47] Phelan's comparison of Frederic to Nabokov's narrator in *Lolita* effectively illustrates the distance between the narrators' styles, and I agree that Hemingway's narrator is not self-consciously concerned with his own artistic performance, as such. But the metafictional aspects of the text may move beyond the merely self-conscious identification of text-as-art that Humbert displays, to reflect upon the artificiality of the narrative which paradoxically controls Frederic Henry, both in the present of his telling and in the past of the story's events. Patricia Waugh writes, "Metafiction explicitly lays bare the conventions of realism; it does not ignore or abandon them. . . . Metafiction, then, does not abandon 'the real world' for the narcissistic pleasures of the imagination. What it does is to re-examine the conventions of realism in order to discover—through its own self-reflection—a fictional form that is culturally relevant and comprehensible to contemporary readers."[48] The cultural relevance of this fictional form, which Frederic Henry broods over, knowing already the outcome of the narrative, is enormous, especially considering the sociocultural narratives of gender that he and Catherine have been struggling against. Thus, he attempts to call the narrative into question in his own telling. Consider, for instance, the foreshadowing of disaster that he makes as he considers the chances he and Catherine have against a force that he identifies only as "the world":

Often a man wishes to be alone and a girl wishes to be alone too and if they love each other they are jealous of that in each other, but I can truly say we never felt that. We could feel alone when we were together, along against the others. . . . If people bring so much courage to this world the world has to kill them to break them, so of course it kills them. The world breaks every one and afterward many are strong at the broken places. But those that will not break it kills. It kills the very good and the very gentle and the very brave impartially. If you are none of these you can be sure it will kill you too but there will be no special hurry. (249)

In retrospect, Frederic can offer this narrative commentary because he can neither control the story of their lives together, and of her death, nor can he fully understand the logic behind what he now knows, in his narrative present, is an inevitable conclusion. Once they identify themselves as against a greater force known only as "the world," they are doomed.

These don't sound like the comments of a realist protagonist mired in a heroic narrative and simply reporting upon the events of his story, but of a narrator who attempts to problematize the constraints of the realistic narrative that demands certain narrative conventions, among which is often the notion of omniscient narration. James Nagel notes what seems to me a metanarrative commentary which Frederic offers in an early version of the manuscript, a commentary that reflects his antagonism and powerlessness against an external force. "In a passage Hemingway deleted from the manuscript, Frederic thinks: 'And if it is the Lord that giveth and the Lord that taketh away, I do not admire him for taking Catherine away.'"[49] Hemingway's earlier version of Frederic seems to realize that although he tells the narrative of these events, perhaps reporting in a diligent, first-person mode as Phelan argues, another omniscient narrative has enforced itself upon their lives. Again, later in the finished manuscript, Frederic manifests his awareness of his narrative defeat.

> Now Catherine would die. That was what you did. You died. You did not know what it was about. You never had time to learn. They threw you in and told you the rules and the first time they caught you off base they killed you. Or they killed you gratuitously like Aymo. Or gave you the syphilis like Rinaldi. But they killed you in the end. You could count on that. Stay around and they would kill you. (327)

The return of the baseball metaphor announces Frederic's way as a retrospective narrator of understanding the often absurd events of his life. He has admitted to Catherine that he is a mediocre baseball player earlier (140); he doesn't play that game well. And before that, we find Frederic unable to find any interest in the baseball news (136), a condition that prefigures his avoidance of the war in newspapers later in the novel. James Nagel also indicates Frederic's reference to Babe Ruth's pitching career, a reference that Nagel believes makes the dates of the narrative and of the story clear. Interestingly, Nagel claims that Frederic may only identify Ruth following his fame as a home run hitter in 1927. "Babe Ruth did his last pitching in 1919 while playing for the Boston Red Sox. He joined the New York Yankees in 1920 and became known primarily as a hitter. But he would not have been sufficiently notable to qualify as a time referent until after the season of 1927, when he hit 60 home runs to set a major league record that was to last over three decades. By March of the following year, when Hemingway began *A Farewell to Arms,* Ruth would have been one of the most popular figures in America, and it would make sense to have Frederic refer to him."[50] Thus, Frederic's reference to Ruth, in this reading, would be to a power hitter, to a player who has learned to play the game well. His contrast, then, is to his own mediocre play, which leads to his attempt to leave the field and the Oedipal narrative. Considering the Oedipal quality to the game of baseball, the rounding of the diamond which mirrors the Oedipal progress of the hero's path and his ability to pass obstacles (basemen and fielders) along the way, this is a subtly metafictional commentary on Frederic's inability to control the events of his own narrative. As a mediocre hitter, Frederic is unlikely to be a power hitter, so a home run—which would allow him to traverse the bases in relative safety—is out of the question. When he decides to leave the Oedipal narrative of masculinity behind—to step off base, not to progress along the course set out for him by the diamond but to leave the playing field in protest—he is doomed, because the basemen and fielders who surround him will not allow him to leave the base in safety.

Frederic will always end up only in the rain, because the insistence that the novel remain a masculine romance of abandonment and self-sufficiency demands the death of Catherine in a way that might very nearly be through deus ex machina, an extranarrative force which, like the social dictates for gender, requires certain narrative definition. De Lauretis explains the nature of the masculine, Oedipal narrative:

> Opposite pairs such as inside/outside, the raw/the cooked, or life/death appear to be merely derivatives of the fundamental opposition between boundary and passage [in the Oedipal narrative]; and if passage may be in either direction, from inside to outside or vice versa, from life to death or vice versa, nonetheless all these terms are predicated on the *single* figure of the hero who crosses the boundary and penetrates the other space. In so doing the hero, the mythical subject, is constructed as hu-

man being and as male; he is the active principle of culture, the establisher of distinction, the creator of differences. Female is what is not
susceptible to transformation, to life or death; she (it) is an element of
plot-space, a topos, a resistance, matrix and matter. (*Alice Doesn't*, 119)

Frederic Henry, as the hero/human being/male of *A Farewell to Arms'*
Oedipal narrative, becomes, whether he likes it or not, "the active
principle of culture, the establisher of distinction, the creator of differences." This is despite his initial uneasy alliance with the homosocial and his later rejection of the masculine as it is defined by
homosocial relationships. The oppositions of his passage are from
insider to outsider, from masculine to "other," even as he might be
defined like the priest through the homophobic reactions of the masculine insiders. That which has become an obstacle to his insider-
masculine status as a hero in the romantic and Oedipal narrative
must be eliminated; as resistance, Catherine must die so that the
hero may move beyond the plot-space that she represents to become
the wounded and solitary male hero of the romance narrative. Perhaps this is the kind of narrative duplicity that Mark Spilka has in
mind in his essay when he compares Brett Ashley's inability to escape the violence of postwar society with the all-too convenient narrative conclusion that faces Catherine Barkley. "Like Catherine, Brett
has been a nurse on the Italian front and has lost a sweetheart in
the war; but for [Brett] there is no saving interlude of love with
a wounded patient, *no rigged and timely escape* through death in
childbirth" (italics mine).[51] The narrative seems to be "rigged," as
Spilka suggests, and it is rigged as much against Catherine and Frederic's desires as Brett's seems to be against her.

Interestingly, Frederic Henry may be more similar in kind to Oedipus than to Othello. De Lauretis writes of Oedipus, "By his victory
over the Sphinx, Oedipus has crossed the boundary and thus established his status as hero. However, in committing regicide, patricide,
and incest, he has become "the slayer of distinctions," has abolished
differences and thus contravened the mythical order" (*Alice Doesn't*,
199). Like Oedipus, Frederic has committed crimes against the mythical and cultural order, the most prominent of which is his rejection
of homosocial, masculine identity in favor of a life with Catherine.
And like Oedipus, Frederic must receive a tragic punishment, not
death (at least not his death), but a life-altering wounding that demands that he recognize the consequences of contravening the cultural and the generic narrative. "If the crime of Oedipus is the
destruction of differences," de Lauretis writes, "the combined work
of myth and narrative is the production of Oedipus" (*Alice Doesn't*,

120). This definition of the work of narrative effectively delineates the problematic narrative of *A Farewell to Arms*. Catherine's death and Frederic's suffering are not simply evidence of naturalistic or deterministic pessimism, but of the overbearing significance of narrative—textual, cultural, social—on individual desire. "And this was the price you paid for sleeping together," Frederic protests. "This was the end of the trap. This was what people got for loving each other. . . . So now they got her in the end. You never got away with anything. Get away hell!" (320).

Citing the work of Roy Schafer on the narrative construction of case histories, de Lauretis concludes that the notion of patient—or analysand—control of the narrative of analysis is at best deceptive. Schafer writes of the analysand's supposed control,

> The narrative structures that have been adopted *control* the telling of the events of the analysis, including the many tellings and retellings of the analysand's life history. . . . The analysand's stories of early childhood, adolescence, and other critical periods of life get to be retold in a way that both *summarizes* and *justifies* what the analyst requires in order to do the kind of psychoanalytic work that is being done. (quoted in de Lauretis, *Alice Doesn't*, 131; italics hers).

De Lauretis emphasizes the words "summarizes" and "justifies" to indicate the narrative deception in the seeming control of the analysand; it is, she concludes, the analyst's desire that manipulates the psychoanalytic narrative, not the analysand's. This example seems especially pertinent to Frederic Henry's retrospective telling of *A Farewell to Arms*, especially in his complete lack of control in the narrative. Gerry Brenner, for one, indicates that "Many things demonstrate that Frederic is a disoriented and, ultimately, untrustworthy narrator," citing "Frederic's trouble with selecting, organizing, and discriminating between significant and insignificant details."[52] As far as I can tell, Frederic finds little available justification for Catherine's death or for his trauma in the retelling, and this is because the narrative is not his. The narrative force that supersedes Frederic's retelling is that which controls the death of Catherine, the generic requirements of the romance novel and of the social codes that punish Frederic, like Oedipus, for the destruction of difference, especially of gender difference. Thus the sadism of the story, to borrow Laura Mulvey's phrase, exists not only in the death of Catherine, as readers like Judith Fetterley have concluded, but in the condition of Frederic Henry who is conscripted to the role of Oedipus.

One of the cruelest ironies of the novel comes in its title, then. There is no farewell to arms for Frederic or Catherine, like the soldiers who discard their rifles and refuse to fight, given the rigidity of the social codes that demand their conscription to certain "proper" narratives. If "narrative cinema in particular must be aimed, like desire, toward seducing women into femininity" (de Lauretis, *Alice Doesn't*, 137), then the converse must be true, as well: the narrative (cinematic or otherwise) must also be aimed at seducing men into masculinity, into adopting the proper cultural roles that have been modeled for them in the narrative. As such, the narrative sadism practiced on Frederic Henry's story becomes a cultural morality tale. Remain true to the homosocial contract, so the moral goes, or you, too, will suffer the fate of Frederic/Oedipus as the destroyer of socio-cultural gender difference. In this sense, William H. Gass's definition of fiction as a simultaneous reflection of and construction of our own realities is applicable. Fiction, he writes, is "incurably figurative, and the world the novelist makes is always a metaphorical model of our own."[53] In a similar vein, Seán O'Faoláin writes of the moral of the hero's fall, using a particularly Hemingway-esque metaphor of the bullfight, that

> The spectator ought to be on the side of the bull—symbol of society, tradition, the good earth, the herd, the life-giver, the head of the family; he gets his pleasure instead, or some of his pleasure, in watching the bull-baiter. But, then, being himself a bull, a head of a family, a one-of-the-herd, a social man, he must, at the end, when the bull-baiter is gored by the bull, lean back, close the book, and say aloud for the benefit of his attendant family: "Well, of course, yes! One should not bait bulls."[54]

The hero's desire is unimportant in such a narrative, even (or especially) if the hero attempts to reject his role as hero; the Oedipal narrative may itself reject other locations of desire. Hemingway will continue to make important explorations of the narrative desire of the individual against sociocultural and gendered narratives in his later novels, especially in *The Garden of Eden*, where he presents men and women who find themselves trapped both biologically and culturally, and who, like Frederic Henry, must risk baiting Oedipal bulls in their desire to reject the limitations of such narratives.

7

"The centre of all womanhood":
The Economy of Rape Fantasy in Lawrence's
Lady Chatterley's Lover

Sherwood Forest and the surrounding Nottingham countryside serve as the locale for D. H. Lawrence's final novel, *Lady Chatterley's Lover*, bringing him back to England, after novels set in Australia and Mexico. And the novel's setting allows me to conveniently return to my introductory metaphor of archer and arrow and the romance of the Robin Hood legends. Lawrence himself employs this metaphor of the arrow which causes the archer to become both weapon and target in a letter to Alfred Stieglitz, dated 12 September 1928, when he writes of the social threat he faces as a result both of public outcries against the novel and of the potential for similar reactions to a public showing of his paintings. On the paintings and an upcoming London exhibit, he writes, "I am showing them in London because friends wanted me to—and we are giving up the Italian Villa—and—vanity, I suppose. Or mischief. More arrows in the air, and let's hope one won't fall in my own eye, like Harold at Hastings. But it would be useless to send them to America now—too much stupid fuss over *Lady C.* Why so much fuss over simple natural things? They ought to censor eggs, as revealing the intimate relations of cock and hen."[1] Although he writes of Harold at Hastings as opposed to my youthful fascination with Robin Hood, Lawrence recognizes the danger of becoming himself the target of attack from the puritanical English. And when he comments on the futility of sending "them" to America, he refers to both paintings and arrows through the pronoun, aware of the equally censorious American reactions to any explicit mention of sex.

But Lawrence is also fully aware of the romance of Robin Hood's pastoral England as it bears upon the modern conditions of his final novel. In the essay, "Nottingham and the Mining Countryside," Lawrence recalls the proximity of the romantic past that Sherwood Forest

271

272 PART III: MASCULINITY AND THE SHIFTING GENDER NARRATIVE

and the Robin Hood mythos offered him. "To me, as a child and a young man, it was still the old England of the forest and agricultural past; there were no motor cars, the mines were, in a sense, an accident in the landscape, and Robin Hood and his merry men were not very far away."[2] But the romantic patina of Sherwood Forest has faded by the time Lawrence writes *Lady Chatterley's Lover.* Indeed, the narrative commentaries of chapter 11 recognize the degree to which this romantic image of England is in conflict with the industrial and mechanical lives of the English of the late 1920s, a conflict that resonates throughout the novel. "Merrie England! Shakespeare's England! No, but the England of today, as Connie had realised since she had come to live in it. It was producing a new race of mankind, over-conscious in the money and social and political side, on the spontaneous intuitive side dead, but dead. Half-corpses, all of them."[3] This nation of half-corpses has become a nation of contrasts for Lawrence, the romantic past existing side-by-side with the ruthless changes of the present. "And beyond again, in the wide, rolling region of the castles, smoke waved against steam, and patch after patch of raw reddish brick showed the newer mining settlements, sometimes in the hollows, sometimes gruesomely ugly along the skyline of the slopes. And between, in between, were the tattered remnants of the old coaching and cottage England, even the England of Robin Hood, where the miners prowled with the dismalness of suppressed sporting instincts, when they were not at work" (156). The paradox of early twentieth-century England is that it may embody neither the romantic past or the industrial present, caught as it is between the two and inducing a kind of cultural schizophrenia which, at its worst, causes the stagnation of the individual and the culture.

This stagnation is most evident for Lawrence in the culture's inability to openly address sexuality and desire, and in his defense of the novel, "A Propos of *Lady Chatterley's Lover,*" he emphasizes the difference between the utterance of the idea and the need for the individual to act upon the uttered subject. "The evocative power of the so-called obscene words must have been very dangerous to the dim-minded, obscure, violent natures of the Middle Ages, and perhaps are still too strong for slow-minded, half-evolved natures today."[4] With this in mind, he can proclaim the novel "an honest, healthy book, necessary for us today" (307) if contemporary readers hope to progress beyond their literal-minded and archaic counterparts. Such a national and cultural division is emblematic of the division between men and women in *Lady Chatterley's Lover,* a novel that has become infamous for its sexual content. Linda Ruth Williams notes just how fully the novel has been identified with the pornographic in her introduction to *Sex in the Head,* recalling the cover of "an erotic video for women called 'Dream Dates,' which features two fantasy scenarios, one of which is called 'The Game Keeper.' On the sleeve we are invited to 'Be Lady Chatterley as the rugged game keeper takes you nude picnicking, takes you skinny dipping, and then just takes you.'"[5] Similarly, as I browsed in a Portland, Maine, bookstore this summer, I noticed that the display of "Hot" summer reading included *Lady Chatterley's Lover,* included with other novels that were identified as sexually provocative.

But as I study *Lady Chatterley's Lover,* I can't help but read the scenes of sexual intercourse between Connie and Mellors as at the very least disingenuous, and at worst a travesty of the "normative" traditions which are defended by critics like Mark Spilka and Michael Bell. I find myself reacting most strongly to three scenes in particular: Mellors and Connie's third sexual encounter, this time in the woods outside of Mrs. Flint's house; Connie's dance in the rain and her resultant sexual intercourse with Mellors; and their final union prior to her departure for Venice. The more I read the novel, the more sure I am that there is something suspect about its portrayals of sexuality as awakenings for the newly will-less Connie Chatterley. In all three of the above-mentioned scenes, sexual union is violent and barely consensual, but in all three we are assured by the narrative that Connie finds fulfillment in Mellors's desire. She actually comes to desire these moments as somehow revelatory of existential possibilities previously unavailable to her. Rather, they serve as idealized rape fantasies in which the subject of the fantasy is herself desirous of the violent sexuality that is imposed upon her.

Masculine rape fantasies are not unusual in modernist fiction. I have briefly illustrated the evidence of such fantasies in Lawrence's *The Rainbow* and in Hemingway's "Up in Michigan" earlier in this study. But in his later fiction, Lawrence problematizes desire and consent by constructing proponents of phallic theories, individuals such as Mellors or Lawrence's often proselytizing narrators, who instruct women in giving up their wills, their independence, even as the male characters and their masculine narrators retain their own willful control and independence. It often seems that Lawrence has returned to the very sleeping beauty motifs that Ursula rejected in *The Rainbow* and *Women in Love,* now emphasizing the desirability of that mythic feminine figure of passivity. Hilary Simpson writes, "In Lawrence's late work, and in the popular literature, the independence of women is the given starting-point, not the goal. The novels revolve around the question of what use women shall make of their freedom. The implied answer, in most cases, is that they will find fulfillment by voluntarily relinquishing it, and consigning themselves to the man who will satisfy their essentially masochistic sexual needs."[6] When Lawrence writes about sexual domination, however, he is not merely exposing or endorsing rape, but is employing rape fantasies which suggest that the subject of the forced sex, women such as "Princess" Urquhart or Connie Chatterley, should actually *like* it and even *unconsciously desire* rape. Indeed, modern women, so the argument seems to go in his late fiction, are essentially sleeping beauties who must be awakened to their true roles as submissive ingénues before dominant and phallic tutors. Sexuality as rape fantasy finally becomes more romanticized and destructive to individual desire than the chivalric/romantic Robin Hood tales themselves ever were.

In reading the romanticized rape fantasies of *Lady Chatterley's Lover,* the effects of Mellors's forced sexual intercourse with Connie is twofold: First, she not only learns to "like" this mode of sex, at least according to the narrative, but to come to orgasm as a result of it. Her orgasm, occurring jointly with Mellors's, implies that she feels the same desire that he does, even if that desire is expressed in radically different ways. Second, however, and suspecting that she has become pregnant as a result of this intercourse, Connie finds herself "sinking deep, deep to the center of all womanhood, and the sleep of creation" (135). At the center of all womanhood, Connie presumably finds a role which is much more appropriate than the active sexual desire she expressed with the German boys of her youth or with an intimidated Michaelis later on, and which would threaten to ally her with the monstrous Bertha Coutts. She discovers the orgasmic possibilities of her maternal nature and the pleasures of submission to the dominant male, Mellors. Thus, the economy of rape fantasy mentioned in the title of this chapter is one in which the most valuable subject of fantasy is that subject who expressly *desires* the fantasist's aggressive demands. Connie's "value" for Mellors—and more importantly, for her readers who accept the narrative's definition of her pleasure at Mellors's domination—reaches its climax in those scenes in which she reaches revelatory and existential awarenesses, the scene in the woods at the Flint's and the evening prior to her departure for Venice, in which she is initiated into other modes of intercourse and desire. Meanwhile, a character like Miss Urquhart in Lawrence's short story, "The Princess," finds her value plunging in the eyes of Domingo Romero, who is determined to cause her to find his advances pleasurable. She retains her value as a "pretty white woman" in this fantasy of miscegenation, but in her refusal to be conquered, Romero must finally discard her as an object of sexual fantasy. And a figure like Bertha Coutts is without value and contemptuous in the economy of rape fantasy, because she refuses to serve as a reflection of the fantasist's desire and is instead a reflection of the fantasist himself, monstrous in her determination to exact her own pleasure upon the object of desire.

There is evidence, however, that Lawrence did not simply accept or endorse the Hegelian master/slave relationships he wrote about in his late fiction. The essayistic Lawrence, for instance, betrays a real concern with the division between men and women that originates in such a pattern of domination and subordination. In the late essay, "We Need One Another," he complains of the divisiveness of this sexual and relational paradigm. "We are labouring under a false conception of ourselves. For centuries, man has been the conquering hero, and woman has been merely the string to his bow, part of his accoutrement. Then woman was allowed to have a soul of her own, a separate soul. So the separating business started, with all the clamour of freedom and independence."[7] The Oedipal role of masculine conquering hero and feminine accoutrement is anathema to Lawrence, precisely because it leads to the self-centered emancipation of the individual from a relationship based on domination and servility, and ultimately from other more transcendent relationships. Similarly, when he writes the essay, "Give Her a Pattern," he offers his "theory" of women's roles in the culture that seems quite at odds with the idea that women must be submissive and desirous of masculine domination, proposed by the rape fantasies of his fiction.

> The real trouble about women is that they must always go on trying to adapt themselves to men's theories of women, as they always have done. When a woman is thoroughly herself, she is being what her type of man wants her to be. When a woman is hysterical it's because she doesn't quite know what to be, which pattern to follow, which man's picture of woman to live up to.
>
> For, of course, just as there are many men in the world, there are many masculine theories of what women should be.

Although on the one hand there is misogyny in his reading of women's capacity for independent self-definition, there is also a realism evidenced in his claim that prescribed, masculine, social roles, which dictate the appropriate behavior of women in the culture, are at the root of the almost schizophrenic divisiveness of modern society. He continues, "Men run to type, and it is the type, not the individual, that produces the theory, or 'ideal' of woman," noting later "the eternal secret ideal of men—the prostitute."[8] If the essayistic Lawrence is complaining about the reductive identification of women by men, and of women's seeming willingness to play these roles, how do we reconcile this complaint with the idealized rape fantasies in his fiction?

Carol Siegel insightfully writes, "Like most artists, Lawrence often calls upon his readers to accept some apparent contradictions as part of the mystery of life, which is made up of many truths, but he also presents us with voices within his fictions that make assertions which cannot be simultaneously accepted as truths."[9] The voices that are most problematic in his later fictions, and especially in *Lady Chatterley's Lover*, are those which assert rape fantasies in the definition of idealized sexual relationships. But although Lawrence's narrators and his male protagonists assert their ideals of women as willing objects of desire, Lawrence's women are not always as submissive as they might be. Although the late fiction, including *Lady Chatterley's Lover*, is replete with misogyny, there are also voices that call into question the rape fantasies and that propose other locations of desire, other possibilities for tenderness. By keeping an eye on Connie's reactions to Mellors and to their sexual encounters and by considering her desires and how they conform (or fail to conform) to Mellors's desire, we may begin to understand the contradictory voices which inform *Lady Chatterley's Lover*. In exploring the problem of rape fantasies in *Lady Chatterley's Lover*, I will first turn to a more explicit story of rape, "The Princess," to define the economy of rape fantasies, as well as the narrative manipulation which invests certain value in women within the rape fantasy.

The Logic of Rape Fantasies: The Case of "The Princess"

Lawrence has addressed rape, fantasy, and desire in texts other than *Lady Chatterley's Lover*, including in his poetry. Many critics, sich as Linda Ruth Williams, turn to the poem, "Eloi, Eloi, Lama Sabachthani?" to illustrate the connection between violence, murder, and sexuality. Lawrence writes of the speaker's struggle with his own body, creating a dualism in the poem that becomes manifest in warlike aggression. The poem begins with a statement of physical revulsion:

> How I hate myself, this body which is me;
> How it dogs me, what a galling shadow!

How I would like to cut off my hands,
And take out my intestines to torture them!

(1-4)

The speaker's dualism becomes not only murderous but assumes that the desire of the subject is reflective of the desire of the actor:

So when I run at length thither across
To the trenches, I see again a face with blue eyes,
A blanched face, fixed and agonized,
Waiting. And I knew he wanted it.
Like a bride he took my bayonet, wanting it,
And it sank to rest from me in him,
And I, the lover, am consummate,
And he is the bride, I have sown him with the seed
And planted and fertilized him.

(33-42)[10]

The "bride" desires the phallic bayonet and the death that comes with it, according to the speaker, allowing the speaker to take pleasure in his domination of the Other. Thus, the murder of one aspect of the speaker's self becomes acceptable, and even desirable, through the rape fantasy that defines the subject's pleasure at domination.

Perhaps the best example of Lawrence's concern with rape fantasies and sexual domination is in the story he completed in 1924, "The Princess." Although it is a story that is overtly about rape and the failure of rape fantasies, some critics read it as the *protagonist*'s failure to achieve a transcendent union with the man with whom she experiences sex as domination. Harry T. Moore writes of "The Princess," "Like the Mexican story 'None of That,' this is a reversal of Lawrence's frequent use of the Sleeping Beauty or Little Briar Rose theme, in which the enchanted princess is awakened to life by the prince who breaks through the thorns surrounding her. In these two stories, the women who *will* the experience—such as Dollie Urquhart in 'The Princess' and Ethel Cane in 'None of That'—are the failures, in contrast to the women whose awakening has the true magic quality, such as the girls in 'The Horse Dealer's Daughter' and *The Virgin and the Gipsy*, and Connie Chatterley in *Lady Chatterley's Lover*."[11] The problem that Moore touches upon but fails to address is that of *will*. Can we believe what the story's narrator tells us when we read of the first incidence of forced sexual intercourse, "she had *willed* that it should happen to her"?[12] Ostensibly in such a reading, her unconscious will to sex with Romero has invited the intercourse, an invitation that the narrative seems to have predicted during their trek to the cabin when she earlier defines Romero as "not the kind of man to do anything to her against her will" (493). The narrative seems to set us up to believe that Romero simply responds to her will. But this definition of Romero does not rationalize her willing the rape to occur. If anything, this early definition of Romero is a rationalization which will allow her to act upon her true desire, that is, to see "over the brim of the mountains, to look into the inner chaos of the Rockies" (493). As Moore might see it, her failure is in her active will; she has not allowed Romero to awaken her, to teach her sexual propriety. Similarly, Mark Spilka reads the initial rape as manifest by the protagonist's will. In his essay, "Hemingway and Lawrence as Abusive Husbands," Spilka concludes, "The conflict within Dollie is not resolved by what follows [after she has asked Romero for warmth]. She stiffens herself, wants to scream at being touched; then, because she knows that she had *willed* it to happen, she passively endures what she had never really wanted."[13] Notice the contradiction in this reading, a contradiction that exists in the story at its most superficial level: she wills what she never really wanted, which translates to the accusation that she is unconsciously asking for it. It would seem, in this argument, that she gets what she deserves because she is so willful a woman.

Just as will—and its partner in sexual relations, consent—is problematic in "The Princess," so is the female protagonist's identity. We learn from the very first line of the story that identity is patriarchally defined, if the title of the story is any indication: "To her father, she was The Princess" (473). The child of Hannah Prescott and Colin Urquhart is christened Mary Henrietta, but each parent objectifies her. "She called the little thing *My Dollie*" but "He called it always *My Princess*" (474). Notice the narrative distance in describing the child as "the little thing" and "it," a distance reflective of the objectification of the character that might have been avoided with the use of the feminine pronoun. Even more interesting is the reference critical readers make to the story's protagonist. Readers such as Moore and Spilka refer to her as *Dollie* Urquhart, choosing to define her character through her mother's nickname, a nickname referred to in only one other place: the second sentence of the story, in which we learn that "her Boston aunts and uncles" called her "*Dollie Urquhart, poor little thing*" (473). The narrator refers to her as The Princess throughout the story, never again citing her proper name, Mary Henrietta, or her maternal nickname, Dollie. But notice how easy it is to slip into an objectified reference, Dollie, an idealized or model of femininity, rather than her proper name. Where is her will in this? Unavailable, it would seem, especially as she continues to be subject to external definition. Notice again her narrative objectification, in this case a reduction of her to a mere two-dimensional figure with only the illusion of three dimensionality: "She looked as if she had stepped out of a picture. But no one, to her dying day, ever knew exactly the strange picture her father had framed her in and from which she never stepped" (476). She even succumbs to such an identification herself as she places herself, along with her horse, Tansy, within the picture of the paradisal woods. "How beautiful Tansy looked, sorrel, among the yellow leaves that lay like a patina on the sere ground. The Princess herself wore a fleecy sweater of a pale, sere buff, like the grass, and riding-breeches of a pure orange-tawny color. She felt quite in the picture" (494).

But even as she is constructed as an idealized objectification of femininity, Mary's seeming inhumanity causes others, especially men, to react violently against her. Throughout the story's introduction, the narrator emphasizes her lack of humanity and her role as a changeling, distancing her not only from family and acquaintances, but from us readers, as well, setting us up to dislike her from the start.

> She could look at a lusty, sensual Roman cabman as if he were a sort of grotesque, to make her smile. She knew all about him, in Zola. And the peculiar condescension with which she would give him her order, as if she, frail, beautiful thing, were the only reality, and he, coarse monster, was a sort of Caliban floundering in the mud on the margin of the pool of the perfect lotus, would suddenly enrage the fellow, the real Mediterranean who prided himself on his *beauté male,* and to whom the phallic mystery was still the only mystery. And he would turn a terrible face on her, bully her in a brutal, coarse fashion—hideous. For to him she had only the blasphemous impertinence of her own sterility. (477)

This Roman cabman is clearly related to the later Mellors, whose reaction to a "Dollie" or "Princess" Urquhart would be mirrored in the cabman's violent reaction to her, the feminine figure who does not know her place in submitting to the "phallic mysteries" of life. The point is that the Lawrentian narrator sets us up to somehow think that Mary deserves what she gets because of her distance and lack of obeisance to these phallic mysteries, whatever they may be. As a figure of objectified femininity, at a remove from the rest of the masculine world which she has learned to regard as base, she has learned her lesson too well and is blamed for being so distant, so unavailable. Indeed, the "impertinence of her own sterility" is related to the judgment against virginity that the narrative later recognizes in a thirty-eight-year-old "Princess" who can pass for twenty-five, looking too young (and too desirable?) for her own good. "But away below, where the horses struggled up the rocks and wound among the trunks, there was still blue shadow by the sound of waters and an occasional grey festoon of old man's beard, and here and there a pale, dripping crane's-bill flower among the tangle and the débris of the virgin place. And again the chill entered the Princess's heart as she realised what a tangle of decay and despair lay in the virgin forests" (490). Virginity held too long can only mean decay and despair, a realization that sets us—and her—up for Romero's sexual advances at the cabin.

In her essay, "Master and Slave: The Fantasy of Erotic Domination," Jessica Benjamin defines the source of violent aggression as that evinced by the cabman, and later by Romero, as an inability to connect personally with other human beings as individuals. Benjamin writes,

> Paradoxically, the individualism of our culture seems to make it more difficult to accept an other's independence and to experience the other person as real. In turn, it is difficult to connect with others as living erotic beings, to feel erotically alive oneself. Violence acquires its importance in erotic fantasy as an expression of the desire to break out of this numbing encasement. The importance currently assumed by violent fantasy can in part be attributed to the increasingly rational, individualistic character of our culture, to the increasing deprivation of nurturance and recognition in ordinary human intercourse.[14]

For the cabman, a violent reaction is required to lessen the distance between Mary and his image of himself as masculine and desirable to women, and he may rationalize that in her sterility and distance, she cannot share his desire. His response betrays a violent aggression which is intimately tied to masculine rape fantasies, in which the subject of his fantasy would come to recognize his *beauté male* as a result of his aggression and in turn desire him. Spilka comments on the violence exhibited by the men in the story, "Such frightening male rage . . . is induced by Dollie's attitude; she invites it by an insulting combination of sexual negation and social superiority, whereby the victim is decidedly the victimizer."[15] Although he attempts to explain the source of the rage in the sexual negation and class difference, Spilka surprisingly claims that the blame is to be place on Mary (this in an essay on sensitizing men to spousal abuse). Mary hardly *invites* the reactions of the cabman or of Romero; indeed, men hold no interest for Mary, either as sexual partners or as prospective husbands. Of the prospect of marriage, men who hinted at it "all failed before the look of sardonic ridicule in the Princess's

eyes" (482). Of course, what men see in her reaction to their proposals might also instigate their negative reactions, but Mary can hardly
be responsible for their behavior. As the Princess, a distant, feminine
ideal, Mary has been trained all too well to keep her distance from
the men, and the women, around her.

She is intrigued only by Domingo Romero, and we learn that her
attraction to him is not sexual. "It was curious no white man had
ever showed her this capacity for subtle gentleness, this power to
help her in silence across a distance" (485). But this intrigue turns
out to be dangerous: Of Mexicans of Romero's type and locality, the
narrator tells us that "their physique and their natures seem static,
as if there were nowhere, nowhere at all for their energies to go,
and their faces, degenerating to misshapen heaviness, seem to have
no *raison d'être*, no radical meaning. Waiting either to die or to be
aroused into passion and hope" (482). Romero, and Mexicans in
general, become monstrous, "almost sinister" we learn on the same
page, further removing him from the desire of the "normal" men—
that is, the Anglo/Euro-American men who propose marriage to the
ungrateful protagonist—and further distancing us from any outrage
over his later actions or from any surprise at her rape. Her interest
in such a man as Romero, the narrative would posit, can lead only
to defilement. In a sense, we are conditioned to believe that she
deserves what she gets from the monstrous Mexican male who finds
his *"raison d'être* in self-torture and death worship" (482).

The trip to the mountain cabin that Mary wishes to make, hoping
to see large animals and a wilderness which she has never before
encountered, goes badly from the start. The trip, and the resultant
events at the cabin, call into question problems of desire and responsibility in the story. When, upon learning that Miss Cummins's horse
is injured and she must turn back, Mary cries out, "There will never
be another day" (493). She is recognizing the work that it has taken
to get her this far; repeating the deception that she has practiced to
go with Romero into the hills is unlikely. This comment is also
strangely prophetic, given the events of the following night and the
change that Romero forces upon her. Only when they are alone does
Mary begin to question her decision to be alone with Romero, who
looks at her "curiously, in a way she could not understand, with such
a hard glint in his eyes" (496). This is the first expression of Romero's
desire to possess her, and although her desire to see the Rockies is
fulfilled and she wants to go back, she loses self-control upon entering his world, both in her descent from the mountain ridge to Romero's cabin and in her inability to control the situation, given his
new determination to move onward. I am reminded here of an ironic

poem from *Pansies,* entitled "Film Passion," in which the first stanza warns women filmgoers of the reality behind the masculine image:

> If all those females who so passionately loved
> the film face of Rudolf Valentino
> had had to take him for one night only, in the flesh,
> how they'd have hated him!
>
> $(1-4)^{16}$

When Lawrence writes, in "A Propos of *Lady Chatterley's Lover,*" "The radio and the film are mere counterfeit emotion all the time, the current press and literature the same" (312), he may well have this image in mind. Consider line 3 and what Lawrence implicitly defines as the reality of masculine desire behind the counterfeit romantic image of Valentino: If women had had to *take* him, that is, to be forced not only to take the real man and the attendant masculine desires (which are much different from the feminine desires that construct the romantic image of Valentino), but were also forced to *take* his sexual desire, this reality would make them hate him. Indeed, only when they are alone together does Mary begin to feel concern for the propriety of the situation and for her ability to remain in control. She becomes a figure of great value for Romero, because she is both helpless in this new environment and because it would appear that she *wants* to be alone with him, as opposed to ending the journey along with Miss Cummins.

The question most readers must wrestle with in the latter half of the story is one of culpability: Is Mary responsible for the rape because she entered into an improper outing with a man? The narrative certainly guides us in this direction, both through questions of what she has willed during the forced intercourse, as well as through subtly suggestive images such as that of Mary's riding breeches. While "her orange breeches glowed almost like another fire" (500), implying perhaps a fire of sexuality in her breeches, there is no desire, sexual or otherwise, in her arrival at the squalid cabin, feeling instead the oppression of her situation. "The sun was leaving the mountain-tops, departing, leaving her under profound shadow. Soon it would crush her down completely" (501). Mary clearly experiences oppression here, not sexual desire, and her question, "What did she want? Oh, what did she want?" (503) illustrates not her confused urges but her lack of control over the situation. The question of what she wants is answered in the same paragraph: "She wanted warmth, protection, she wanted to be taken away from herself. And at the same time, perhaps more deeply than anything, she wanted to keep herself intact, intact, untouched, that no one should have any power over her, or rights to her" (503). Wanting to be taken away from herself, from her identity as The Princess, is what the improper outing is all about; for perhaps the first time in her life, Mary acts upon her own desire to define her own experience.

But her ability to remain in control of her experience does not last long. Linda Ruth Williams writes of his fiction, "Lawrence also sets up a paradigm for the understanding of sexual difference as a dynamic of display and *mis*recognition, exhibitionism, voyeurism, and *mis-seeing*, which is present in all sexual situations throughout his work. Sometimes men and women meet, but they do not necessarily meet each other's gaze."[17] This is certainly true of the initial sexual encounter of "The Princess," in which an essential miscommunication occurs when Mary complains about the coldness of the night, a coldness that weighs on her oppressively in her dreams. When Romero asks, "You want me to make you warm?" he understands her affirmation as an invitation to sexual intercourse, not as a request for an additional blanket or a fire in the stove. Mary, however, has no such desire for sexual intercourse, but at the same time finds herself unable speak against *his* will. "As soon as he had lifted her in his arms, she wanted to scream to him not to touch her. She stiffened herself. Yet she was dumb" (504). Notice the lack of active willingness in Dollie's role in this intercourse: He lifts her from her cot to his just as he might carry a doll. And while his is a "terrible animal warmth that seemed to annihilate her," we learn that "she was given over to this thing." Not that she gave herself but was given over, against her desire. Spilka argues of this encounter, "There is something more at stake for Lawrence: that request in the night that Romero warm her, which becomes a kind of claim upon her since it comes from her own unconscious needs, however much she now denies them."[18] But Mary's is not an unconscious need for sexual initiation or for rape, although the narrative of the rape fantasy would have us believe such. The most problematic argument of the narrative creates a kind of rape fantasy which implies that Mary both wants and doesn't want intercourse with Romero. Notice the contradictory nature of this series of paragraphs that obscure the act of sexual intercourse which is occurring.

> She had never, never wanted to be given over to this. But she had *willed* that it should happen to her. And according to her will, she lay and let it happen. But she never wanted it. She never wanted to be thus assailed and handled, and mauled. She wanted to keep herself to herself.

However, she had willed it to happen, and it had happened. She panted with relief when it was over.

Yet even now she had to lie within the hard, powerful clasp of this other creature, this man. She dreaded to struggle to go away. She dreaded almost too much the icy cold of that other bunk. (504)

How much of this narrative commentary on the act of intercourse can we accept as either true or accurate to Mary's situation? It is clearly contradictory, attempting to dismiss her lack of desire with a more pressing and unconscious desire to create such a situation. Because of Mary's willful demands against social propriety, we are supposed to believe that she somehow deserves the rape.

Of the role of desire in the rape fantasy, Benjamin explains, "In desiring an other, one wants to be recognized." More specifically, the individual engaging in the rape fantasy wishes to be recognized as desirable as he finds the subject of his fantasy. She continues, "As a person who is utterly destroyed can give no recognition, the alternative is to subjugate, to enslave him or her. But to be alive in relation to another person we must act in such a way as not to negate fully the other, and the desire in our act must be recognized by the other."[19] When Romero asks Mary, "Don't you like last night?" her response, "Not really . . . Why? Do you?" (505) wounds his masculinity and his fantasy of her desire for him, for violation. He cannot believe that she didn't like the sex, because in believing this, his fantasy of her desire for rape is destroyed. Again he asks twice more, "You don't like last night?" When she responds in the negative, "Not really, . . . I don't care for that kind of thing" (506), he resumes his rape fantasy: "I make you." By discarding her clothing, he makes a claim upon her as a more readily available, and thus more valuable, sexual object, even as he professes to know what she wants. "You sure are a pretty little white woman, small and pretty. . . . You sure won't act mean to me—you don't want to, I know you don't" (508). Benjamin writes, "The male experience of differentiation in our culture seems to point to an explanation of this tendency to polarize, to emphasize difference, to assert control, and to introduce rational calculation into eroticism."[20] The "rational calculation" that Romero engages, however, does not include any recognition of why she may not want to engage in sex with him. Instead, he makes her even more dependent upon him for things like food and shelter, assuming that she will learn to love him. And notice the polarization in Romero's definition of her as a "pretty little white woman," identifying her as other both in gender and ethnicity, and redefining the rape fantasy as a fantasy of miscegenation. In such polarization, he may calculate her value not only as a woman but as a white woman, socially unavailable, whom he will conquer. In the narrative, however, this desire for her as a white woman who, according to the narrative, wills herself to desire him, causes both to be read as monstrous.

Romero's horror comes at her continual defiance of him and the resultant destruction of his fantasy of her desire and complicity; the second night of rape, much more violent than the first, is initiated by her assertion, "You think you can conquer me this way. But you can't. You can never conquer me" (508). Interestingly, when Romero finally does speak at length, after the forced intercourse, he sounds like a travesty of Huckleberry Finn, not like a romanticized Mexican noble or even a monstrous and sinister dark figure. "I ain't going to let you go. I recon you called to me in the night, and I've got some right. If you want to fix it up right now with me, and say you want to be with me, we'll fix it up now and go down to the ranch to-morrow and get married or whatever you want. But you've got to say you want to be with me" (508). Romero demands that Mary re-create his rape fantasy; she must speak the words of desire that will confirm him as the object of her sexual desire. According to Benjamin, "Violence is a way of expressing or asserting control over an other, of establishing one's own autonomy and negating the other person's. It is a way of repudiating dependency while attempting to avoid the consequent feeling of aloneness. It makes the other an object but retains possession of her or him."[21] The intensified rape of the following night is his attempt to prove her wrong, to conquer her, but it is even more an attempt to re-create his fantasy of her desire, to make her want him. "In a sombre, violent excess he tried to expend his desire for her. And she was racked with agony, and felt each time she would die. Because, in some peculiar way, he had got hold of her, some unrealised part of her which she never wished to realise. Racked with a burning, tearing anguish, she felt that the thread of her being would break, and she would die. The burning heat that racked her inwardly" (509). The burning and tearing leave no doubt that what occurs here is rape, and not passion, and most attentive readers will understand that this violation has nothing to do with Mary's will, whether conscious or unconscious. In a replay of their first night and his willful misunderstanding of her desire, she asks him to build a fire to allay the cold. When he asks, "Want to come over here?" she clearly defines her desire for warmth: "I would rather you made me a fire" (509).

"In erotic fantasy," Benjamin explains, "the struggle to the death for recognition is captured metaphorically by violating the other's will or submitting to the other's will—by risking the psychological, if not the physical self."[22] In her confusion, Mary doesn't love him but she has become resigned to having to stay with him; her own will has been shattered. Upon his death there is not victory but the ridicule of other men who discover her without clothing and in a clearly sexual relationship with Romero, men who will also misunderstand her desire and the condition of her coming to the cabin. Mary, in her own posttraumatic madness, finally displaces herself from the actual events of her captivity, re-creating her story in her delirium so that the worst that had happened to her was that a madman had shot her horse out from under her. Carol Siegel writes, "Socialization is represented as inescapable, female essence as meaningful only at the moment of its destruction, as the woman passes into utility within a primitive patriarchal culture."[23] Not accidentally, only after this violation does Mary assume a more "proper" social role, befitting a woman of her age and social status. "The real affair was hushed up," we are told, and "she had recovered herself entirely. She was the Princess, and a virgin intact" (512). But this is clearly a fantasy now. She finally looks her age, graying at the temples, and marries an elderly man with whom she "seemed pleased" (512). Thus, the argument for rape fantasy goes, only once a woman like The Princess assumes her proper and submissive role beside a man can she find pleasure and be valuable in her social setting. Although Mary's value plunges in Romero's rape fantasy, because she refuses to mirror his desire or to like the violent sex that he forces upon her, her social value increases as she marries, acts her age, and even moves east, the seat of her familial home. What the narrative of "The Princess" does, then, is to offer a societal rape fantasy in which the woman who remains too distant and too "good" learns her lesson and assumes her place in the fabric of society. It is, Spilka comments in his introduction to *Renewing the Normative D. H. Lawrence,* "a perversely sympathetic case for reactive rape."[24] It is perversely sympathetic because the narrative attempts to sway our attitudes in favor of Romero and the Roman cabman, whose violent reactions against the distant and inaccessible woman are, according to the narrative, her fault. And it is a narrative that leads a critic like Spilka to write about "The Princess" in the same collection, "It is a story about sexual coercion in which the victim is presented as the victimizer and sympathy is deliberately directed away from her to the incensed man, who feels justified in forcing himself upon her and who dies for his supposed crime."[25] I am uncomfortable with Spilka's use of the word "supposed" here, but he has captured the attitude of the narrative well. We are not supposed to sympathize with Mary. Only when we do recognize that her figure has been a construct of a series of rape fantasies and idealized constructions of gender from the beginning of the text can we begin to recognize that she is the figure being violated and that the source of the violation is not only in the appropriative violence of the men around her but in the fabric of the culture itself.

Heroic Conquest in "Lady Chatterley's Lover"

In the second draft of *Lady Chatterley's Lover,* posthumously published as *John Thomas and Lady Jane,* Lawrence clearly differentiates between passionate love and violent, willful rape.

> Life is so soft and quiet, and cannot be seized. It will not be raped. Try to rape it, and it disappears. Try to seize it, and you have dust. Try to master it, and you see your own image grinning at you with the grin of an idiot.
>
> Whoever wants life must go softly towards life, softly as one would go towards a deer and a fawn that was nestling under a tree. One gesture of violence, one violent assertion of self-will, and life is gone.[26]

The passage goes further to explain that *touch,* human contact, and perhaps even *tenderness*—a prospective title for the novel—are the truly passionate means of transcendence, a conclusion that is perhaps reflected in Mellors's declaration after his second sexual encounter with Connie Chatterley in the final version of the novel: "I could die for the touch of a woman like thee" (127). This is a philosophy from the writer of *Lady Chatterley's Lover* whom many identify, through the novel's now-infamous title, as the writer of explicit and pornographic sexuality. Scott R. Sanders writes of this passage from *John Thomas and Lady Jane,* "Stated simply, in the traditional terms that Lawrence himself employed, this is the choice between the way of power and the way of love."[27] In contrast to the power struggles and rape fantasies of a story like "The Princess," Lawrence clearly seems to have other plans for his final novel, the theme of which he describes in a letter to Ottoline Morrell as "the full natural *rapprochment* of a man and a woman."[28]

Although this passage from *John Thomas and Lady Jane* fails to be included in the final version of the novel, Lawrence continues to recognize in his writing that violent, willful sexuality, and especially the domination of men over women, remains the central problem for the individual, whether male or female, in modern society. His complaint in the essay, "Give Her a Pattern" certainly illustrates in no uncertain terms the source of gender division: "Man is willing to accept woman as an equal, as a man in skirts, as an angel, a devil, a baby-face, a machine, an instrument, a bosom, a womb, a pair of legs, a servant, an encyclopaedia, an ideal or an obscenity; the one thing he won't accept her as is a human being, a real human being of the feminine sex."[29] The sarcasm that he betrays in this essay upbraids the masculine desire to define oppositional figures in an Oedipal landscape by objectifying those figures, turning them into ideals or dissected and desirable body parts. And in a letter to Witter Bynner, dated 13 March 1928, he calls into question the notion of such an Oedipal hero who would awaken a sexually repressed sleeping beauty and teach her how to be properly submissive to the dominant masculine perspective.

> The hero is obsolete and the leader of men is a back number. After all, at the back of the hero is the militant ideal: and the militant ideal, or the ideal militant, seems to me also a cold egg. . . . On the whole I agree with you, the leader-cum-follower relationship is a bore. And the new relationship will be some sort of tenderness, sensitive, between men and men and men and women, and not the one up one down, lead on I follow, *ich dien* sort of business.[30]

Given these claims, then, I find myself wondering as a reader of *Lady Chatterley's Lover* just how I am supposed to reconcile them with Connie's sexual "awakenings" in her relationship with Mellors. Considering the occasionally violent and willful sexuality that Mellors exhibits, and given the narrative's assurances that Connie takes pleasure, sometimes orgasmic pleasure, in this intercourse, how do we reconcile Lawrence's passional theories with his novelistic practices?

This is an important question because, in Connie's seeming "instruction" from Mellors, we are confronted with sexual practices that are forced, often rather violent, and that construct distinctly hierarchical roles between the empowered male and the submissive female, the hero and the follower, often seeming to leave us with that dissected and objectified femininity that Lawrence complains about in "Give Her a Pattern." Questions of consent and desire are raised as well, especially in the three problematic sexual encounters that I mentioned in my introduction. In "Lawrence, Foucault, and the Language of Sexuality," Lydia Blanchard recognizes the conflicting nature of sexuality in the novel. "Certainly the passages descriptive of intercourse must be confusing, or why else the critical debates about what Lawrence is describing, much less advocating?"[31] The confusion, I believe, is a result of a narrative that preaches contradictory themes and that accepts behavior from its characters, especially from Mellors, which is contrary to those definitions of transcendent relationships presented in both the novel and elsewhere in Lawrence's late writing. *Lady Chatterley's Lover* constructs a narrative that is actually more radical than that of "The Princess" in its construction of rape fantasies, fantasies that revolve around Connie as a woman who discovers enjoyment and enlightenment in the sexuality of domination and force. If she becomes "the centre of all womanhood" in her intercourse with Mellors, she becomes an idealized figure who learns to like a variant on the forced sexuality that "Princess" Urquhart struggled against and that does not address her own desire. By examining the scene of her sexual intercourse with Mellors in the woods, and the ways in which the narrative causes readers to create a fantasy of ideal feminine submission around her, we may recognize how Connie is manifest in the narrative as a figure of value for Mellors in her ability to reflect his desire.

Critical readers have come to very different conclusions about the thematic focus of *Lady Chatterley's Lover*, many claiming that, although the novel has its failures, it is ultimately a novel about shared passion and is an insightful response to sterile modern understandings of love and sex. Peter Balbert addresses "the phallic theme of the novel" when he writes that *"Lady Chatterley's Lover* will 'inform' us about the loving of its titled Lady; it will 'lead us,' as it also teaches Connie, to recoil 'from a thing gone dead' called Clifford, and from the deathly life he represents."[32] Interestingly, he makes no mention here of the real subject of the novel's title, the gamekeeper, Oliver Mellors, presumably because Mellors becomes the proponent of that phallic theme. In a similar vein, Michael Squires defines the focus of the novel as revolutionary in its ability to make social connections which previously were not available. In *The Creation of "Lady Chatterley's Lover"*, he writes, "It is the sexual connection between seeker and knower, compelling escape from a social or psychological prison, that becomes paramount. That connection becomes so highly valued in the novel because it heals (if only symbolically) the destructive and divisive class barriers. Sexuality in *Lady Chatterley's Lover* is never gratuitous, precisely because it has the power to terminate the class divisions that troubled Victorian novelists."[33] Like Balbert, Squires reads the novel as about the possibility for relationships which transcend the limited possibilities offered by traditional social relationships, like that of Connie and Clifford, which is based upon the failed social institution of marriage rather than on a more essential connection. Interestingly, both also seem to read the responsibility for coming to this transcendent point as Connie's. She serves as the seeker or student to Mellors's knower. Of this focus, Michael Bell claims, "It remains a fact of experience that some women can reach mature years, have been sexually active, have even raised families, without ever having been passionally aroused. Lawrence's way of engaging with this theme, for all its limitations, still seems to me to be essentially more whole and truthful than the objections commonly raised against it."[34] Lawrence's primary focus, these critical writers suggest, is on Connie Chatterley's development, sexual and spiritual, in her relationship with Mellors. Mark Spilka echoes these readings in his introduction to *Renewing the Normative D. H. Lawrence,* writing that "Connie's choice between them rests not on Mellors' sexual potency and Clifford's impotence, but upon Mellors's warmth, his creaturely tenderness, his sensual sympathy, or upon that wide range of sensual (as opposed to sexual) consciousness in him that Connie says 'will make the future.'"[35] In an earlier essay, Spilka notes that "the novel is about sexual regeneration as well as the sensual warmth that makes it possible."[36] Presumably that sexual regeneration is largely hers, and comes about primarily as a result of Mellors's instruction.

Through the narrative, we know what Connie's previous experience of sexual intercourse has been like, including her self-induced orgasms with the German boys and later with Michaelis. We know that sex with the German boys was ultimately unfulfilling when compared with the chance for intellectual discussion, and we know that when Connie attempts self-gratification with Michaelis, he becomes incensed. "You couldn't go off at the same time as a man, could you? You'd have to bring yourself off! You'd have to run the show!" (53) And we know that her desire for Mellors during their first two encounters at the hut in the woods has been expressed in a way that is quite different from his own desire. In fact, the framing device that links these initial visits between Connie and Mellors is her tears. Her tears which lead to the initial intercourse are presumably maternal tears, wishing that she might have a child of her own. But this sorrow may be even more complex, as Carol Siegel suggests the role of women became in the early twentieth century. "With the end of the Victorian era and its cult of domesticity, intelligent women generally seemed to feel pressured to enact two rarely compatible roles. On the one hand, they were to be good, traditionally feminine wives and mothers. On the other hand, they were to be interesting, because intellectually developed, individuals."[37] Although these dual roles translate to a cultural schizophrenia for women, as Siegel argues, for Connie Chatterley neither role is acceptable. She cannot play the good and feminine wife and mother, most obviously because of Clifford's incapacity to engage in intercourse, but also because for Connie to be a mother and to provide an heir, she must be "bad," that is, she must have an affair. Clifford himself encourages this affair, provided that it is only for the sake of procreation and that the man she chooses be from the right stock. "Why Connie, I should trust your natural instinct of decency and selection. You just wouldn't let the wrong sort of fellow touch you" (44). On the other hand, however, Connie is not allowed to be an intellectually active member of the Wragby dialogues; this much is clear as she offers her perspective to their discussion of love and sex. "The men resented it: she should have pretended to hear nothing. They hated her admitting she had attended closely to such talk" (40). Connie fails in whichever direction she turns, and her sorrow is very much tied up in her inability to define herself through her own desires.

So she begins to cry at the sight of the young chicks during the first visit, lamenting the barrenness of her own marriage with Clifford, and it is a sight that energizes a dormant Mellors. "And there was something so mute and forlorn in her, compassion flamed in his bowels for her" (115). This is an interesting choice of words. Is compassion a response which involves a flaming in the bowels? Or is it an emotion from which "at the back of his loins the fire suddenly darted stronger"? Mellors *does* seem compassionate as he comforts her and wipes away her tears, but there are other emotional and physical reactions to Connie's vulnerability that the narrator does not specify, namely sexual passion. This passion is certainly borne out as Mellors can no longer resist his urges; Connie, however, experiences a very different kind of involvement.

> And he had to come in to her at once, to enter the peace on earth of her soft, quiescent body. It was the moment of pure peace for him, the entry into the body of the woman.
> She lay still, in a kind of sleep, always in a kind of sleep. The activity, the orgasm was his, all his: she could strive for herself no more. (116)

If any passage in *Lady Chatterley's Lover* suggests that it is a version of the sleeping beauty story, this is probably it. The passion is all Mellors's, and there is little *com*passion evident as he becomes involved exclusively in his own desire. Notice that it is Connie who seems to give herself up, no longer able to strive for herself either for sexual climax, given Michaelis's censure, or for her own desire. "She could bear the burden of herself no more. She was to be had for the taking. To be had for the taking" (117). What does this tell us of her desire? Interestingly, Mellors continues to be self-absorbed after intercourse; he abandons her rather shamefully, just as he attempts to cover his naked penis in his cottage later in the novel, and he is most concerned about social reproach should they be caught, of "complications" (117). When he does turn to her desire finally, we know how removed Mellors is from Connie's experience.

> "Nay, for me it was good, it was good. Was it for you?"
> "Yes, for me too," she answered, a little untruthfully, for she had not been conscious of much. (118)

But Connie does not "awaken" to Mellors's desire until their third experience of intercourse in the woods not far from the Flint house. It is no accident that, for the first time, the narrative follows Mellors home, rather than remaining with Connie as she returns to Wragby. His thoughts after sex are that "she had cost him that bitter privacy of a man who at last wants only to be alone" (118), essentially blaming Connie for his regrets. The narrative follows Mellors, returning to Connie two pages later and ironically referring to her by her full Christian name rather than the more common reference to her nickname. "Constance, for her part, had hurried across the park, home, almost without thinking. As yet she had no afterthought. She would be in time for dinner" (120). After she has an illicit sexual affair with her gamekeeper, a man whom Clifford would surely disapprove of as the father of the Wragby heir, the narrator chooses to focus quite judgmentally on her failed "constance" and her seeming lack of afterthought, regretful or otherwise. Michael Bell writes of the narrative, "Lawrence generates a self-conscious narrative medium in which the characters are constantly suspended. As with Fielding or George Eliot, there is a narrative voice which so heightens the implications of the ostensible action that in some ways the narrative voice is more primary than the action it describes."[38] Although Bell is writing primarily about the extended narrative disquisitions that often interrupt the novel, his analysis applies quite well in this passage because the narrator has made some clear and subjective choices in portraying the experience of Mellors and Connie in very different ways. Our sympathies lie with Mellors if we buy his tormented hero routine, while Connie remains neutral in narrative value, even as the narrative is sure to highlight her inconstance, because as a sleeping beauty she has yet to be awakened by Mellors.

The second sexual meeting between Connie and Mellors occurs on the next day. The frame is closed at the end of their intercourse as Connie again cries, this time concluding rather than precipitating sex, and this time, it would seem, crying from the lack of passion that she feels in their intercourse. "But she lay still, without recoil. Even, when he had finished, she did not rouse herself to get a grip on her own satisfaction, as she had done with Michaelis. She lay still, and the tears slowly filled and ran from her eyes" (126). Just as tears initiate the first sexual encounter, so they conclude the second encounter, but this time Connie's tears are a reaction to their dalli-ance, even though Mellors only experiences "a close, undoubting warmth" (126), unaware at first of her tears. Connie has been even more distant from Mellors's desire here, and her ridicule of sex illus-trates how fully detached she is.

> And when he came in to her, with an intensification of relief and consummation that was pure peace to him, still she was waiting. She felt herself a little left out. And she knew, partly it was her own fault. She willed herself into this separateness. Now perhaps she was condemned to it. She lay still, feeling his motion within her, his deep-sunk intentness, the sudden quiver of him at the springing of his seed, then the slow-subsiding thrust. That thrust of the buttocks, surely it was a little ridicu-lous! If you were a woman, and apart in all the business, surely that thrusting of the man's buttocks was supremely ridiculous. Surely the man was intensely ridiculous in this posture and this act! (126)

For those readers who reductively identify Mellors as the supremely Lawrentian hero and authorial personae, this internal monologue is often read as evidence of Connie's failure to make herself fully avail-able to the transcendent passion of a phallic awareness. Mellors is there, they argue, but Connie distances herself with the kind of talk, or thought, that the degraded men of Wragby engage in in place of actual sexual union with a woman. However, Connie's reflections on the absurdity of sex echoes Lawrence's essayistic reflections in "Making Love to Music," in which he writes, "To have created in us all these beautiful and noble sentiments of love, to set the nightingale and all the heavenly spheres singing, merely to throw us into this grotesque posture, to perform this humiliating act, is a piece of cyni-cism worthy, not of a benevolent Creator, but of a mocking demon."[39] This is not to argue that Lawrence's comments somehow authorially advocate Connie's as the heroic perspective of the text, but to remind those readers who wish to blame Connie for her lack of passionate involvement that if she is detached, it is probably because Mellors is, too. We must separate the fictional gamekeeper from the bio-graphical figure of the author to understand the critical eye with which Lawrence views Mellors, among others. There is no transcen-dence for Connie because Mellors is completely unavailable to her.

And yet, the narrative would have us believe that she is still a sleeping beauty awaiting the prince's proper kiss for true awakening. "Far down in her she felt a new stirring, a new nakedness emerging. And she was half afraid. Half she wished he would not caress her so. He was encompassing her somehow. Yet she was waiting, waiting" (125). Although Connie does not fully desire this union, she is still waiting, perhaps to be "awakened," or more likely, for Mellors to be engaged *with* her in intercourse.

Peter Balbert writes of the novel, "Lawrence wishes to indict society's penchant for sexual thrills that do not entail both the suspension of ego and the willingness to seek transcendence in the act of love."[40] Connie's masturbatory sex-after-masculine-climax comes to mind here, as does the maligned figure of Bertha Coutts, but Mellors does not wish this transcendence either, given his own distance from Connie. He enters the scene arguing against their relationship on the grounds of social propriety. "You'll have to care, everybody has," he warns Connie. "You've got to remember. Your Ladyship carrying on with a gamekeeper! It's not as if I was a gentleman. Yes, you'd care. You'd care!" But Connie's response to this warning both rejects his reasoning and his attitude toward her, an attitude with which Mellors creates a division between them. "I shouldn't [care]. What do I care about my ladyship. I hate it really. I feel people are jeering every time they say it. . . . Even you jeer when you say it" (124). It is *Connie* who attempts to come together with Mellors here, to transcend the social and class barriers that he has held defensively before himself before she attempts a more passional transcendence in sexual intercourse. And even after their sex, it is Mellors who reconstructs this barrier, dissociating himself from her (the first of many of his dissociative strategies, which I will examine shortly) and jeering at her Wragby identity. When Connie runs from him and his returning arousal before the gate, an arousal he would like her to act upon ("If tha could stop another minute—" [127]), he refuses her kiss ("He hated mouth kisses" [127]) and finally completes his distance: "Goodnight, your Ladyship" (128). Either Mellors has disregarded everything she told him earlier about this aspect of her identity or he has decided to use it against her in revenge for her tears and her "failure" to share his desire.

This is the vengeful attitude that Mellors leaves with, and it is the attitude that sets the tone for the events of their third sexual encounter.

Of their third meeting, Mellors's surprise appearance, and the sexual intercourse that follows in the woods after Connie's visit with Mrs. Flint, critics have been surprisingly kind to Mellors and almost coy regarding the nature of the scene's problematic sexuality. Balbert claims that the scene is one of Connie's growth, both spiritually and in her capacities as a woman. He writes, "Her sex with Mellors in the woods that follows the acknowledgement of a healthy and primitive envy of motherhood provides the first experience for Connie of vaginal orgasm; the metaphoric overlapping circles that Lawrence employs to chart this passion are meant to circumscribe the limited arcs of clitorally induced sensation that have characterized her mode of loving with Michaelis and with her former lovers on the continent." Thus, once Connie admits her envious desire for children, she can abandon her "selfish" desire for orgasm. Ironically, it would seem, once she does abandon her own sexual needs, those very needs are met with their simultaneous orgasm. Similarly, Balbert believes that Connie is in control of the situation, *choosing* to engage in sex with Mellors, and thereby to embrace the life she encountered at the Flints', rather than return to the lifeless and loveless halls of Wragby. "Connie does not go to Wragby and talk out her jealousy with the anti-life babblers who await her anecdotes; nor does she dismiss the passion of her feeling for Mellors with the apologetics of her political indoctrination as a liberated female. All she does is what she senses she must do: she takes the burden of the Flint tension to bed with Mellors, where she uses such guilt as the 'existential edge' of sex. It is an edge sharp enough this one time to give her the sexual gratification that opens up the potential of her emotional life."[41] In this reading, Connie might be said to manipulate the situation to her advantage, to come to desire through pain, whether physical or psychological. Indeed, of Mellors's general behavior, Michael Squires offers him a great deal of latitude, noting that "it would be wrong to say that the keeper demands love on his own terms" because "he cannot violate the male elements of his personality—his pride, his need for respect, his desire to dominate. Having relinquished social and economic power, he is loathe to sacrifice his power in a personal relationship."[42] This sounds like an apologia of sorts for Mellors's domination of Connie, whether in this scene in the woods or in others like it in the novel.

In his landmark study, *The Creation of "Lady Chatterley's Lover,"* Michael Squires reads this scene as evidence of their mutual passion, writing,

> The keeper surprises her in the dark wood, makes sudden love to her, and arouses her to orgasm. This is the action. As Connie runs home, the scene closes with her reaction to the encounter. Both *action* and *reaction* help to reveal the shape of Lawrence's imagination.

To develop the theme of unconscious attraction and to dramatize the potent male fulfilling the potent female, Lawrence created a scene that would join the keeper's sexual assault to Connie's first orgasm with him.[43]

Squires dares what few other readers do: He defines the meeting as an assault, but reads it as a necessary dramatization of their mutual potency. Mellors as actor creates Connie as reactor, a variant on the sleeping beauty theme. What Squires fails to illustrate is the rationale for bringing a sexual assault together with her sexual climax. David Holbrook ventures further into the dense territory of consent and sexuality when he reads the scene as something more than assault, asking an important question: "How does one bring a woman to orgasm, from the state of ego-willed orgasm as described earlier? The answer is *by force.*" Holbrook goes on to claim of the scene, in one of the most cogent of readings, "It is virtually a rape, and yet Connie has *her* first orgasm. It is the first idolized one, all bells and ripples, molten inside. . . . It is all utterly false, and the starkness of the propaganda becomes increasingly evident, as the presentation becomes increasingly religious."[44] Holbrook is one of the few writers I have encountered who identifies not only the qualities of rape in the scene, but, even more disturbing at the level of the narrative, the rape fantasies that dominate this climactic episode in the relationship between Mellors and Connie.

In the preface to Jessica Benjamin's essay, the editors of *Powers of Desire: The Politics of Sexuality,* Ann Snitow, Christine Stansell, and Sharon Thompson address the problems of consent in violent sexuality.

> The problem of consent is one of the knottiest issues in contemporary sexual discussions. If any sex between freely consenting persons is permissible, how do we determine the limits of that consent? The nature of sexuality itself makes the question even more vexing, since we—especially women—so often experience erotic passion as engulfing and overwhelming, rather than as a relationship in which we agree to take part. The female "slave of love," we would argue, is not simply a figment of the pornographer's imagination.[45]

The first question that must be addressed with regard to the scene in the woods is that of Connie's consent: Is she a willing participant? Her responses to Mellors, having been surprised by his sudden appearance, are all in the form of denials. When he asks if she has been to the hut, she responds with what seems to be a vehement denial, "No! No! I went to Marehay." As she looks guiltily upon his asking if she were headed to the hut to meet him, she responds again, "No! I mustn't! I stayed at Marehay. No-one knows where I am. I'm late. I've got to run—" And when he confronts her, accusing her of avoiding him, Connie is similarly impassioned. "No! No! Not that! Only—!" These denials culminate in her final spoken words of the scene, a response to his initiation of physical intimacy: "'Oh, not now! Not now!' she cried, trying to push him away" (132). Consent does not seem to be immediately forthcoming from Connie in any aspect of her meeting with Mellors. These denials may simply be read as an attempt to avoid her commitment to a "phallic" relationship with Mellors, but this is an all too easy reading of Mellors's heroic role as Prince Charming attempting to awaken Sleeping Beauty. Instead, Connie has been avoiding Mellors himself, choosing to return by "this dense new part of the wood," which "seemed gruesome,and choking" (132). And when Mellors does begin to initiate sex, she recognizes that this intercourse will not be a loving one. When she sees "his eyes tense and brilliant, fierce, not loving," we learn that "her will had left her. A strange weight was on her limbs. She was giving way. She was giving up" (133). Connie's desire does not seem to be involved in this sexual encounter, at least not at first; instead, she gives up her will, she is resigned to Mellors's needs. If, as Peter Balbert argues, "Sex remains sacramental for Lawrence," then Mellors clearly has forgotten this in the scene. Balbert continues, "Thus Oliver Mellors, from the very start of his affair with Lady Chatterley, has a resolute inability to envisage the act of love divorced from the potential of a longer and more complicated connection with her."[46] This is not what motivates his desire for sexual contact here. Connie recognizes this in his demeanor and, as he ignores her denials, Mellors's only explanation is one of selfish desire: "It's only six o'clock. You've got half-an-hour. Nay nay! I want you" (133).

Thus, we are set up for a scene that would seem to represent nonconsensual, forced sex, or rape. The force of Mellors's intent is certainly obvious, if not from his rejection of Connie's denials, then from his breaking the band of her underclothes and from his insistent entry. But, returning to the Snitow, Stansell, and Thompson passage above, reading consent, or a lack of consent, is not always easy, as they write that we "so often experience erotic passion as engulfing and overwhelming, rather than as a relationship in which we agree to take part." Certainly this recalls the curious willessness Connie experiences in the scene, as well as the strange weight on her limbs. Because of this lack of will, and because she experiences something undefined, a feeling that keeps her from acting upon her instinct "to fight for freedom" (133), the readerly tendency has been to assume consent. Why does Connie consent, if only passively, implicitly? Perhaps because she has learned that consent is expected of her in a sexual relationship. In her reading of Havelock Ellis, Margaret Jackson concludes that, according to Ellis, "women had to learn that male sexual demands were natural and inevitable, that they could only achieve sexual pleasure by 'consenting' to be conquered and 'enjoying' their submission to the male."[47] Such instruction is certainly supported and promoted by Mellors later in the novel, especially as he describes Bertha Coutts as monstrous in her willful desire. And Connie has already learned this painful lesson from Michaelis, a lesson that included the instruction that, if she were a "proper" woman, she would also draw her orgasm from the man's activity. He upbraids her orgasmic activity, "All the darned women are like that. . . . Either they don't go off at all, as if they were dead in there—or else they wait till a chap's really done, then they start in to bring themselves off, and a chap's got to hang on. I never had a woman yet who went off just at the same moment as I did." Although "Connie only half heard this piece of novel masculine information," we know that "this speech was one of the crucial blows of Connie's life" (54). Thus, she comes into the relationship with Mellors having learned two important lessons, which she cannot learn from Clifford (but lessons that he surely would teach her if he could, given his need to control her movement in the novel). One: Connie must consent to passivity in masculine expressions of desire. And two: the feminine ideal in any such relationship, the ideal that will confer upon her value as a woman, is simultaneous orgasm drawn from the man's activity.

This scene becomes a rape fantasy not when Mellors forces himself upon her, but when Connie actually experiences orgasm as a result of the rape. It is important to realize that even if Connie *does* consent implicitly, through her passivity, this is a scene that enacts rape, forced sexual contact, as a fantasy, if not a reality (although Connie's initial rejections of Mellors certainly do not seem coy or passive). Note that in Lawrence's story, "The Princess," Mary Urquhart is an initially valuable figure for Romero, who assumes that she wants him to engage in sexual intercourse with her. When he learns of her antagonism toward him and his desire, his violent sexual assaults are an attempt to reinstill *his* desire in her, to raise her value as a figure who shares his desire. Connie's orgasm in the woods makes her a figure of great sexual value for Mellors and for the narrative; rather than reject him or withdraw from him, Connie is now "clamouring like a sea-anemone under the tides, clamouring for him to come in again and make a fulfilment for her" (133). She is no longer an active participant in sexual intercourse, even in her ability to remain distant and to ridicule the act, as she did previously. Connie's desire as a result of this forced intercourse is for Mellors to continue his domination and to *repeat* the act.

Of the problem of simultaneous orgasm, Kingsley Widmer insightfully illustrates the fantastic nature of such a goal. "The ideal, Mellors repeatedly makes clear, is simultaneous orgasm—hardly an odds-on situation with temperamentally different people some years apart, and one requiring the submission of one person's rhythms to another's."[48] And of the marriage manuals of the teens, twenties, and thirties, Margaret Jackson notes the emphasis on the instruction aimed at men in their sexual relations and the desire for simultaneous orgasm.

> This "natural" difference between female and male sexuality meant that mutual sexual adjustment would be difficult to achieve, and the marriage manuals exhorted husbands to be patient and considerate, assuring them that the long-term rewards would be far greater than any pleasure they might gain from selfish and clumsy attempts at immediate gratification. Women were "slow" to be aroused and needed to be made "ready" for coitus; considerable time and, above all, regular practice would be needed in order to establish mutual—and preferably simultaneous—orgasm.[49]

But despite the difficulties of this goal, which Widmer and the marriage manuals comment upon, the narrative not only constructs the achievement of the ideal of simultaneous orgasm, but constructs it as a result of Mellors's forced intercourse. If rape fantasy is about the masculine control of women's desire, a desire that must mirror the man's express desire for dominance in the sexual domain, then Connie's orgasm certainly is fantastic in nature, a result of what Holbrook defines as Lawrence's "indulgent fantasies about Connie Chatterley."[50] Is this scene in the woods simply indicative of Mellors's and the narrator's shared masculine fantasies and desires? And why does Connie experience orgasm as a result of this sexual encounter? Ellen Willis explains, in "Feminism, Moralism, and Pornography," that the passive actor in sexual situations may well be identifying herself not as passive or "victim" but with the dominant member. "It is precisely sex as an aggressive, unladylike activity, an expression of violent and unpretty emotion, an exercise of erotic power, and a specifically genital experience that has been taboo for women" she explains. "When a woman is aroused by a rape fantasy, is she perhaps identifying with the rapist as well as the victim?"[51] This is a compelling question, and it may shed light on Connie's sense of losing herself when we are told that she resists the passion she feels for Mellors, because "it was the loss of herself to herself" (135). Even while she feels that she has entered "the centre of all womanhood" as a result of this sexual encounter, she fears adoration of Mellors, a compulsion that seems related to the rape fantasy. "For if she adored him too much, then she would lose herself, become effaced. And she did not want to be effaced. A slave, like a savage woman. She must not become a slave" (135).

Identity and identification of herself becomes a crucial problem in this scene, and many readers will argue that Connie must give up her willful self-absorption in entering into a transcendent relationship. Michael Squires argues, for instance, "One can view Connie as a violated female, shorn of respect, and cringe from the love ethic that fosters her behavior. Or one can do as Lawrence asks, and connect this experimental sexuality to the themes of education and rebirth, which join all of the sexual scenes. In this view the keeper's fiery sensuality burns out Connie's false bodily shames and makes her 'shameless.'"[52] What readers fail to mention in this sort of argument, however, is that Mellors must also give himself up in a truly transcendent relationship, and in this scene, Mellors has little to lose. On Connie's attempts to engage Mellors in a relationship not *only* based on sex but on other forms of communication, Balbert claims that she is missing the point of Mellors's instruction. "Just like a naive and over-conditioned Francis Macomber, Connie cannot wait to reduce the event to the verbal service of some manageable category. After she first makes love with Mellors, listen to her thoughts appropriate a standard feminist catechism to shield herself from the unknown, from that special ecstasy beyond the constraints of ego: 'Was it real? Her tormented modern-woman's brain still had no rest. Was it real?'" When Balbert applies this reading of Connie's "shortcoming" to the scene in the woods, he writes, "Indeed, even after her happiness over simultaneous orgasm with Mellors in a later scene, she is still a victim of the conditioned need to find the verbal counterpart for her sexual excitement."[53] Talk about their presumably shared experience is unacceptable, it would seem, because only sex is valuable in their attempts at communion; interestingly enough, sex is precisely the communication that Connie must be coerced into, while really honest and revealing discussion is extraordinarily difficult for Mellors. And talk, after all, is what gets Romero into trouble with Mary Urquhart, because when they talk, he finds out that she doesn't share his desire, after all. Thus, Mellors speaks "unwillingly, regretting he had begun" to talk with Connie about a subject like sex and orgasm (134). And she recognizes his unwillingness to enter into this aspect of their relationship, at least not so soon after the intercourse. "And she knew he would never tell her anything he didn't want to tell her" (135). What Balbert dismisses as Connie's preoccupation with conversation is actually her desire to complete the union between Mellors and her, to unite act *and* word— not to dismiss one for the other, as Mellors does in sex without talk, or as the men at Wragby do in talking endlessly about sex. As a dominating figure, his identity remains inviolable, and his desire—a central factor in his identity here—serves as the template for Connie's identity. She must lose hers to his, she must find her desire and orgasm in his desire and orgasm, which is what rape fantasy is all about.

Jessica Benjamin further explores domination and fantasy as a process of self-identification for both participants in the sexual relationship, each attempting to locate ways to define themselves against the other. "The fantasy of erotic domination embodies the desire for both independence and recognition. However alienated from the original desires, however disturbing or perverse their form, the impulses to erotic violence and submission express deep yearnings for selfhood and transcendence."[54] This may well explain Mellors's need for domination in their sexual relationship, because his identity is in many ways dependent upon Connie's express desire for him. But although Mellors's impulses to erotic violence may be further manifest in later scenes of sexual intercourse, including in their dance in the rain and in the anal intercourse which I will consider in the final section of this chapter, Connie does not seem as willing to remain submissive in her search for identity. During their following meeting, when they next have sex, we learn that she remains resistant to the loss of herself to Mellors's sexuality.

> Something in her quivered, and something in her spirit stiffened in resistance: stiffened from the terribly physical intimacy, and from the peculiar haste of his possession. And this time the sharp ecstasy of her own passion did not overcome her, she lay with her hands inert on his striving body, and do what she might, her spirit seemed to look on from the top of her head, and the butting of his haunches seemed ridiculous to her, and the sort of anxiety of his penis to come to its little evacuating crisis seemed farcical. Yes, this was love, this ridiculous bouncing of the buttocks, and the wilting of the poor, insignificant little penis. This was the divine love! (171–72)

Again sex is centered around Mellors's haste for orgasm and to dominate their relationship, and even if Connie did consent to play the submissive role in the earlier rape fantasy, she is not involved in this scene that follows. Notice her distance from Mellors here, a physical distance that separates her from him, looking down upon him from the top of her head, and the continued sense of the ridiculous nature of the sex act. We know from the narrative that, "Cold and derisive her queer female mind stood apart. And, though she lay perfectly still, her instinct was to heave her loins and throw the man out, escape his ugly grip and the butting over-riding of his absurd haunches" (172). If Connie had a choice, she would reject Mellors's unimpassioned sexual intercourse, but again she is required simply to await his climax and completion, and again she weeps at the lack of love she feels in this relationship. Mellors, selfishly assuming that she cries because she doesn't again come to orgasm with him, can only say, "It was no good that time. You wasn't there" (172). His disappointment comes from her lack of simultaneous orgasm and her apparent inability to share his desire (she tells him "It only seems horrid," referring either to her inability to love him or to the sexual intercourse that distances her from him), while Connie wants to be closer to him, asking "Where are you? . . . Where are you? Speak to me! Say something to me!" For Connie, "his silence was fathomless. . . . In his silence he seemed lost to her" (175). Although Connie searches for a way to reach Mellors which expresses her desire as well as his own, Mellors has great difficulty with balance and even with tenderness, a quality that she assigns to him only later as the novel concludes. Mellors's need for masculine dominance and control, for the "conquering hero" role that Lawrence himself upbraids in his essays, causes him to rely upon a variety of distancing techniques, dissociating him from Connie, from the potential social repercussions over their relationship, and finally from any of the transcendent discoveries he claims to seek out in their intercourse.

Dissociative Masculinity: Sexual Dialogue, Personae, and Stages for Desire

In the very experience of the nothingness of life, phase after phase, *étape* after *étape*, there was a certain grisly satisfaction. So that's *that*—(62).

After her initial meeting with Mellors, a meeting in which the gamekeeper refers to his daughter, Connie Mellors, as a "false little bitch" (58), Connie Chatterley concludes that life is without moments of real climactic significance and that in its tedium one passes from stage to stage, *étape* after *étape*, without meaning or revelation. This narrative reflection of Connie's state of mind comes immediately after the oft-quoted passage in which she, like Hemingway's Frederic

Henry before her, recognizes the way in which language has come to lose value in modern society. "All the great words, it seemed to Connie, were cancelled for her generation: love, joy, happiness, home, mother, father, husband, all these great dynamic words were half-dead now, and dying from day to day" (62). And the word that had the most value is also empty of meaning, because sex is devoid of love, of any passional connection: "As for sex, the last of the great words, it was just a cocktail term for an excitement that bucked you up for a while, then left you more raggy than ever" (62). These revelations of Connie's, as well as the empty philosophies of the men of Wragby in chapter four and elsewhere, fuel many readers's arguments that Connie's failure is located in her need to *talk* with Mellors, to engage him in intercourse other than sexual. But Connie is not attempting to reduce sex or passion to an objectified and linguistic state; instead, she is attempting to cause her exclusively sexual relationship with Mellors to become something of value by finding a way to express her desire for a fuller communication with him. Sex, like language, is in danger of becoming a repetitive stage after stage unless both of them find a means of transcending their separate selves. This is true even of sex like the rape fantasy of chapter 10. But language continues to be a suspect medium of communication, even in those later scenes when Connie and Mellors seem actually to be conversing. Although Lawrence, having noted through Connie's narrative that the great words are dead, seems to be attempting to imbue other words, more socially suspect words of profanity, with sacramental meaning, Mellors's use of that language betrays the author's awareness that sex talk too can be without meaning if those employing it do so to erect barriers between themselves and others. Mellors's use of language like "cunt" and his employment of the colloquial "John Thomas" and "Lady Jane" actually serve to further dissociate him from Connie as she tries to get him to open up to her, serving as an extension of the rape fantasies in which he simultaneously dominates and distances himself from her. Although Mellors seems also to be making progress in his development as he engages in conversation with Connie following their later sexual encounters, he actually retains his distance, and only in their final conversation at the ironically named Golden Cock do they begin to communicate in significant and meaningful ways. By then, and after a long absence during Connie's trip to Venice, Mellors can avoid his dissociative habits in favor of the "tenderness" that Connie identifies in him, but by that time this communication comes too late.

Following their fourth sexual encounter, after which Connie asks, "Where are you? . . . Where are you? Speak to me! Say something to me!" and in which "he seemed lost to her" (175), she realizes that she cannot get him to speak on her terms (just as sex must be on his terms, as well). So Connie uses *his* language, or rather his dialect, in a playful attempt to bring him out of himself. Mellors is able to effectively dissociate himself from others through his use of dialect, which Connie attempts to remedy. Michael Squires defines Mellors's dissociative techniques in language in his "use of the dialect as armor," noting a kind of "linguistic schizophrenia" in his shifting from standard English to dialect. Squires writes, in *The Creation of "Lady Chatterley's Lover,"* "Mellors' bilingualism encapsulates both his social insecurity and his complexity, which the double layers of speech image perfectly." But even more telling is Squires's identification of the unconscious connection Mellors makes (a connection that may be unconscious in Squires, as well) between tenderness and threat. Squires writes, "Generally Mellors prefers standard English when he discusses political or social ideas, dialect when he feels threatened or when he feels tender and passionate toward Connie."[55] Indeed, although there is a kind of tenderness in his responses to her in this chapter, Mellors betrays an underlying sense of threat, as well, a threat that prompts his avoidance of her questions. To her "Say you'll always love me!" and "Do you like me?" (176), requests that are hauntingly reminiscent of those Catherine Barkley asked of Frederic Henry, Mellors admits that he likes her availability, unable to simply and assuredly tell her that he loves her. "I love thee that I can go into thee. . . . It heals it all up, that I can go into thee. I love thee that tha opened to me. I love thee that I came into thee like that" (176). Passion is either an unspeakable subject for the gamekeeper or there is no passion to speak of beyond his sexual urges. But when Mellors does become engaged in postcoital conversation, he speaks of "love" in a language that he chooses and that allows him to further instruct Connie. To her desire to be told that she is loved, Mellors responds with one of the first—and perhaps the most shocking for early twentieth-century readers—of the obscene words of the novel, a word that he uses to identify Connie and to identify sex. "Tha'rt good cunt, though, aren't ter? Best bit o' cunt left on earth. When ter likes! When tha'rt willin'!" (177) As in the earlier rape fantasy, Connie's value is defined explicitly here; when she *wants* to be, when she is *willing,* she is the best woman/cunt in the world. When she is not willing—well, that remains unspoken, but her young namesake, Mellors's daughter, is clearly defined when she is unwilling to accede to her father's desires: "Tha false little bitch" (58). Of course, in the earlier rape fantasy and the adult Connie's simultaneous orgasm, it would seem that her unwillingness might make her even more valuable as an object of sexual desire, especially if Mellors can *make her* share his desire.

When Connie naively asks what "cunt" is, and assumes "It's like fuck then," Mellors must correct her, and us, since he controls linguistic meaning in this language.

> An' doesn't ter know? Cunt! It's thee down theer; an' what I get when I'm i'side thee—an' what tha gets when I'm i'side thee—it's a' as it is—all on't!
>
> . . .
>
> Nay nay! Fuck's only what you do. Animals fuck. But cunt's a lot more than that. It's thee, dost see: an' tha'rt a lot besides an animal, aren't ter?—even ter fuck! Cunt! Eh, that's the beauty o' thee, lass! (178).

"Cunt" shares two definitions for Mellors: First, in its most objectified reference, it is "thee down theer," that is, Connie's vagina and sexual apparatus, as the keeper might consider it. Mellors's multiple use of the phrase "down there" betrays a strange kind of modesty, as Linda Ruth Williams has noted of his later descriptions of Bertha Coutts: "Mellors meets Bertha's voracity with an equally insatiable misogyny which only betrays its puritanical desire in the coyness of the phrase 'down there' ('you think a woman's soft down there')."[56] Second, "cunt" refers to sexual desire and, more importantly, a sexual satisfaction that Mellors identifies as identical in his experience of it and in Connie's. "An' what I get when I'm i'side thee—an' what tha gets when I'm i'side thee" clearly illustrates his failure to differentiate between *his* experience of desire and satisfaction and Connie's, a failure that produces the earlier rape fantasy and the later problematic sexual encounters. Kingsley Widmer points out the problem in such a limited definition as that which Mellors offers. "*Cunt* here seems to be used in the enlarged, and mostly positive, sense of willing female sexual responsiveness, though granted that assumes female vulnerability and acceptance, which may well be a male bias."[57] Indeed, male bias—or, more appropriately, *masculine* bias, a bias reflected in the Oedipal hero's singular perspective—is precisely what controls Mellors's conversations with Connie, a bias that allows him to employ obscene language to his advantage. Of obscene language, Stephen Kern writes, in *The Culture of Love*, "Except for the most bizarre of perverts, sexual pleasure does not occur *inter urinas et faeces*, not even 'between urine and feces.' Sex slang is never entirely fitting, because it is at the edge of vulgarity, but it provides a hard-hitting alternative to the evasiveness of Latin, the antisepsis of medical terminology, or the ornamentation of metaphor."[58] So although Mellors's radical language of sexuality is hard-hitting and avoids the evasiveness and the meaningless of other modes of modern language—modes that Connie has already identified as without value in modern society—Mellors may seem to be visionary.

As such, many readers make the mistake of accepting him as a Lawrentian mouthpiece and as the voice of transcendent reason in the novel, reading Mellors, the novel, and its authorial figure as either revolutionary or repugnant, depending on the attitude one has toward the message borne up by the gamekeeper. Widmer cites what he considers in the novel "a real Lawrence obscenity (in the sense of nastiness): an angrily restrictive definition of proper female sexuality."[59] But this is not so much a Lawrentian obscenity in his manipulation of Connie's sexual horizons as it is Mellors's shortcoming, and in this way Lawrence creates a masculine character who, while playing the sexual prophet, remains as domineering and restrictive as the men of Wragby. Consider Lawrence on the objectification and limitation of women in his essay, "We Need One Another":

> There are many popular dodges for killing every possibility of true contact: like sticking a woman on a pedestal, or the reverse, sticking her beneath notice; or making a "model" housewife of her, or a "model" mother, or a "model" help-meet. All mere devices for avoiding any contact with her. A woman is not a "model" anything.[60]

If "true contact" is indeed what Mellors seeks from Connie, a contact that the narrative defines as the "live, warm beauty of contact, so much deeper than the beauty of vision" (125), then Mellors's identification of "cunt" would seem to defeat that goal. We know that idolatry is *Clifford's* problem: "He worshipped Connie. She was his wife, a higher being, and he worshipped her with a queer craven idolatry, like a savage: a worship based on enormous fear, and even hate, of the powers of the idol, the dread idol" (111). And Mellors, we assume, is the antithesis of Clifford's paralyzed, idolatrous figure. But he too objectifies Connie, an objectification that he does not include in his definition but that he betrays in his initial use of the term "cunt" ("Tha'rt good cunt, though, aren't ter? Best bit o' cunt left on earth."). Not only is the term a reference to her sexual organs and to a presumably shared satisfaction, but Connie personifies "cunt" for Mellors. Ellen Willis echoes Lawrence's problem with the masculine objectification of women and with pornography, which he defines as "a question of secrecy." In "Pornography and Obscenity," Lawrence claims that the source of the truly pornographic is not in modesty but in the motives for secrecy and evasion. "Secrecy has always an element of fear in it, amounting very often to hate. Modesty is gentle and reserved."[61] If the pornographic is founded on fear and hatred, as Lawrence suggests, Ellen Willis's conclusions in "Feminism, Moralism, and Pornography" define for us the rationale behind Mellors's provocative diction: "Both rape and pornography reflect a male outlaw mentality that rejects the conventions of romance and insists, bluntly, that women are cunts."[62] The fear and hatred that are directly identified in Clifford's idolization of Connie would seem to influence Mellors's pornographic behavior as well.

And if fear and hatred—the central tenets of pornography for Lawrence and Willis—are not directly obvious in Mellors's construction of Connie as a model of "proper" feminine sexuality, they are certainly evident in his demonization of Bertha Coutts as, in Lawrence's words, "beneath notice." Although Mellors admits that "those other women," the women who did not share his mode of sexual desire and who in return hated him, "had nearly taken all the balls out of me," Mellors indicates that Bertha was at first pleasantly different. "That was what I wanted: a woman who *wanted* me to fuck her. So I fucked her like a good un" (201). But in her inability to share a simultaneous vaginal orgasm, he assumes that she becomes spiteful, holding back on purpose so that she may become monstrous in her own sexual domination, and in this way he echoes Michaelis's earlier accusations of Connie's duplicity. While he defines his earlier, sexually unfulfilling relationship as a failure because the woman who did not share his desire was "a demon" (201), avoiding the subject of his own responsibility, Bertha becomes more literally bestial in his description of her desire:

> She sort of got harder and harder to bring off, and she'd sort of tear at me down there, as if it was a beak tearing at me. By God, you think a woman's soft down there, like a fig. But I tell you the old rampers have beaks between their legs, and they tear at you with it till you're sick. Self! self! self! all self! tearing and shouting! They talk about men's sensual selfishness, but I doubt if it can ever touch a woman's blind beakishness, once she's gone that way. (202)

One does not have to go very far to recognize the hatred and loathing in this description of his wife, from whom he is separated. His fantasy of "vaginal dentura" is readily evocative of his feelings for Bertha. But even more striking than his misogynistic descriptions of Bertha, however, is his subtle and even accidental reference to those who accuse men of sexual selfishness. Curiously, he does not define who "they" are, leaving me to wonder where Mellors has encountered this accusation before—from the women whom he has found unsat-

isfactory and blameworthy, perhaps? Interestingly enough, that earlier "demon" that Mellors refers to, the woman before Bertha, "had
made a scandal by carrying on with a married man and driving
him nearly out of his mind" (200), a situation not unlike his own
involvement with the married Connie, a resemblance he does not
recognize because his own tendency is to place blame fully and
completely with women.

Hilary Simpson comments on the contextual sources of such misogyny against women like Bertha who would "grind her own coffee"
(202), as Mellors says. She writes, in *D. H. Lawrence and Feminism,*

> There were thus two contradictory elements contributing to male fears
> about women in the twenties. The first was that political and social life
> would become swamped by female concerns, that there would be a state
> of "petticoat government": the second, that women were losing their
> femininity and becoming more like men, and that the security of the
> traditional sexual roles was becoming blurred. Both feelings combined
> in a general fear of emasculation.[63]

This is the fear that underlies all of Mellors's definitions of women,
whether his violently misogynistic definition of Bertha as monstrous
or his objectification of Connie as "cunt." Of his limited perspective
when it comes to reading an otherwise unavailable character like
Bertha, Linda Ruth Williams recognizes in Mellors's command of
sexually explicit language a propagandistic quality.

> We do not have access to any "Bertha" other than Mellors'; we only
> encounter the violent excesses of his description. Any horror which
> comes from the image of deadly and insatiable penetration must more-
> over be horror at Mellors' linguistic vulgarity. It is the text's need to
> make an excessive femininity exhaustively 'known' to us which provokes
> shock. A certain feminine sexuality lies visibly prone on the page, and
> we are excessively encouraged to despise its excesses.[64]

Mellors attempts to sell his definitions of femininity, in both its ideal
and its debased states, to Connie-as-disciple and to us readers. By
controlling the lexicon of sexuality and by shifting Connie's attempts
to engage him in conversation, Mellors may dissociate himself from
her and from any responsibility for failure in interpersonal relationships, whether simply sexual or more fully spiritual. Kern also recognizes this irresponsibility in Mellors, writing, "Mellors's disclosure is
unprecedented. No hero of non-pornographic literature prior to 1928
spoke so directly with his beloved about intercourse, and especially
not about his own sexual humiliations and failures. But for all his

daring openness, Mellors is closed to some of his share of responsibility. Commenting on the sexually unresponsive women, he says,
'most men like it that way,' although he quickly adds that *he* hates
unresponsiveness, thereby dissociating himself from responsibility
for his problems with women. Mellors does not believe, however,
that authentic sexual loving is something you do *to* another person:
it is an exchange, a way of 'being-with.'"[65] If Kern is correct, then
Mellors fails at practicing "authentic" exchange or communion with
Connie, or with anyone else, in the world of the novel. This is especially evident as he attempts to convince Connie of her state of being
as "cunt."

But when this definition of her state of "cunt" is not completely
satisfactory for Connie and she again asks, insistently and again
reminiscent of Catherine Barkley's need to know of her lover's devotion, "And do you care for me?" Mellors replies by dismissing her:
"Tha mun goo—let me dust thee" (178). Through his use of the word
"cunt," he has successfully dissociated himself from Connie and
from any need to profess his love to her. Later, Connie questions his
lexicon as he defines his use of the term "balls." He dismisses Clifford as a threat, describing him as,

"The sort of youngish gentleman a bit like a lady, and no balls."
"What balls?"
"Balls! A man's balls!"
She pondered this.
"But—is it a question of that?" she said, a little annoyed. (196)

If Mellors's vocabulary controls linguistic meaning by introducing
terms that either are unfamiliar to Connie (or to a readerly audience)
or that fail to share the common social meanings and usage, requiring his correction and redefinition, Mellors not only dominates
Connie's sexual experience but her linguistic and communal experiences, as well. Although he initiates their sexual relationship, she
initiates their conversational or linguistic relationship, but Mellors
also appropriates that realm of meaning and infuses it with his own
desire. And as a result, he also influences our reception of the novel's
definitions of "proper" or "valuable" sexuality.

Mellors's dissociative tendencies are even more explicit once he
assigns the sexual personas of "John Thomas" and "Lady Jane." Not
accidentally, he comes to these nicknames as a result of his own
shame at his nakedness before Connie, a shame of his that is rarely
addressed by those readers who defend his need for anal intercourse
as a necessary attempt to remove *her* shame. In his cottage bedroom

for the first time, Connie is reminded of the desirable sight of his washing himself which she voyeuristically happened upon earlier, prior to their sexual relationship. Acting upon her desire and in an attempt to change the means of their sexual union, Connie instructs him to open the curtains and to brighten the room, allowing her to see him completely. In the darkened hut, of course, he was completely unavailable to her, as he was in the woods. But in the full light of day, Connie exposes her desire to see Mellors, exposing him to the kind of scrutiny that he has thus far avoided. As a result, he experiences shame at being naked and visible to Connie: "He was ashamed to turn to her, because of his aroused nakedness. He caught his shirt off the floor, and held it to him, coming to her" (209). To her descriptions of his penis, which includes both admiration, awe, fear, and the commentary, "Now I know why men are so overbearing!" Mellors's response is that of a proud parent or master, rather than one of self-pride.

> "Ay ma lad! tha'rt theer right enough. Yi, tha mun rear thy head! Theer on thy own, eh? an' ta'es no count o' nob'dy! Tha ma'es nowt o' me, John Thomas. Art boss? of me? Eh well, tha'rt more cocky than me, an' tha says less. John Thomas! Dost want *her?* Dost want my lady Jane? Tha's dipped me in again, tha hast. Ay, an' tha comes up smilin'.—Ax 'er then! Ax lady Jane! Say: Lift up your heads o' ye gates, that the king of glory may come in. Ay, th' cheek on thee! Cunt, that's what tha'rt after. Tell lady Jane tha wants cunt. John Thomas, an' th' cunt o' lady Jane!—" (210)

Under Connie's scrutiny, Mellors displays an interesting bit of duality. On the one hand, he is more playful and lighthearted in this passage than he has been in any other moment of their relationship. Perhaps he feels easier in his own cottage, as opposed to being in the Chatterley game hut, or perhaps he is growing closer to Connie. But at the same time, he distances himself from her, and from responsibility for his masculine urges, by personifying his penis as "John Thomas." Notice that *he* is not John Thomas; this is clearly a separate entity who is responsible for the desires that are presumably Mellors's. And even more telling in this dissociation is his identification of "Lady Jane." Unlike his penchant for naming his penis, "Lady Jane" refers *not* to Connie's vagina, but to Connie herself. John Thomas wants "cunt," we are told, and specifically, the "cunt" of "Lady Jane," that is, of Connie. It soon becomes clear that Connie is herself responsible for satisfying "John Thomas," especially as Mellors interrupts her playfulness and desire to see him with his now-desperate command.

> "Lie down!" he said. "Lie down! Let me come!"
> He was in a hurry now.
> And afterwards, when they had been quite still, the woman had to uncover the man again, to look at the mystery of the phallos. (210)

Connie's desire to look, to expose Mellors, is interrupted by his desire, and this time there is no mention from Mellors of her lack of climax, simultaneous or otherwise. Only when she has given in to his impatient desire can she resume her exploration of him.

In his essay, "On Lawrence's Hostility to Willful Women: The Chatterley Solution," Mark Spilka writes, "Indeed, the independent *being* of John Thomas and Lady Jane, celebrated two chapters later, invokes by personification and synecdoche the creaturely selfhood for which these 'persons' stand."[66] Although Spilka accurately identifies the personification at work here, he has mistakenly identified synecdoche as an element of Mellors's sexual strategy. Mellors practices not synecdoche, but dissociation; "John Thomas" is not him, nor is it a representative fragment of him, and "Lady Jane" is merely representative of Connie herself, at least as Mellors desires her. He cannot control "John Thomas's" desires, or so he claims, and thus Mellors is a much more fragmented self than he would have us believe. Even Connie plays along, claiming possession of the now flaccid "John Thomas" ("You must *never* insult him, you know. He's mine too. He's not only yours. He's mine! [210]). Indeed, Mellors describes this personae as having "a will of his own, an' it's hard to suit him. Yet I wouldn't have him killed," noting his friendly, if not literal, attachment to "John Thomas." But Connie's awed comment is one of a strange approbation, recalling the masculine fear that Lawrence and Ellis allude to in their definitions of the pornographic. "No wonder men have always been afraid of him! . . . He's rather terrible" (211). But Mellors never claims to fear "John Thomas"; on the contrary, her seeming admiration and handling of "John Thomas" arouses Mellors, causing him to urge her once again, "Take him then! He's thine," presuming once again that her desire is for intercourse as a form of possession, mirroring his own sexual desire.

She does "take him," and as a result Connie experiences what seems to be only her second orgasm with Mellors, similar in the narrative description to the orgasm she experienced as a part of the earlier rape fantasy. "And she quivered, and her own mind melted out. Sharp soft waves of unspeakable pleasure washed over her as he entered her, and started the curious molten thrilling that spread and spread till she was carried away with the last blind flush of extremity" (211). Her orgasm seems to be brought on neither by Mellors's force nor by the act of intercourse itself; instead, Connie's ability to act upon her desire to know Mellors more fully, to expose him and to make him available to her, has brought her to this point. Like her earlier experience of watching him bathe, Connie takes pleasure in her ability to celebrate a vision of him that seems to her more intimate than the act of sexual intercourse itself.

But this orgasmic moment of hers is not expressly addressed by either of them, and it is not defined as such by the narrative, which proceeds to describe the sounds of the outside world as they intrude upon Mellors's cottage. There is a sense of hurry here, not the rush of Mellors's earlier need to reach orgasm, but the rush to get rid of Connie. "You must get up, mustn't you?" is Mellors's first question, and it is not asked regretfully, given his following response to her repeated, "You do love me, don't you?" His response is one of fretfulness, according to the narrative, if not anger. "Tha knows what tha knows. What dost ax for!" (211) And Mellors repeats his prevarication, avoiding any direct response to her desire to make their relationship more permanent, that is, by committing to each other.

> "Dunna ax me not now," he said. "Let me be. I like thee. I luv thee when tha lies theer. A woman's a lovely thing when 'er 's deep ter fuck, and cunt's good. Ah luv thee, thy legs, an' th' shape on thee, an' th' womanness on thee. Ah luv th' womanness on thee. Ah luv thee wi' my ba's, an' wi' my heart. But dunna ax me nowt. Dunna ma'e me say nowt. Let me stop as I am while I can. Tha can ax me ivrythink after. Now let me be, let me be!" (212)

Although Mellors's expressions of love are becoming a bit more loving, including, for instance, his heart as a location of his love as well as his testicles, he continues to dissociate himself from her through his exclusivistic orientation to sex as a means of self-expression. When he returns to the "John Thomas"/"Lady Jane" personas after their dance/sex in the rain, he continues to create a dissociative personae around his penis which marries Connie-as-"Lady Jane." These distinctions gradually begin to become less clearly defined, however, at least for "John Thomas"; "Lady Jane" is Connie, decorated from head to genitals in flowers, and even while we learn that Mellors is "looking down at his penis" when he tells Connie to "Say goodnight! to John Thomas," we also learn earlier that Mellors has not only decorated his penis but his whole body as well. Thus, when he states, "This is John Thomas marryin' Lady Jane

... An' we mun let Constance an' Oliver go their ways" (228), we can recognize some slippage in his ability to remain dissociated from Connie and from his desire for her.

Masculine Desire, Silence, and the Hope for Response

The two most problematic sexual encounters in the latter half of the novel continue to recall Mellors's need for domination in his relationship with Connie, however. The first comes in her dance in the rain, naked but for rubber shoes and fully exposed to the elements as she counters his doom-saying view of the future with her joyous celebration. Of course, in exposing herself in such a public way, she attempts to remove the secrecy from their relationship, and perhaps what Lawrence defines as the pornographic mindset, as well. This dance is an expression of her desire, clearly defined in the narrative: "She opened the door and looked at the straight heavy rain, like a steel curtain, and had a sudden desire to rush out into it, to rush away" (221). As she does, the narrative remains with Mellors, offering *his* perspective on Connie's dance and revealing his possessive appropriation of her.

> She slipped on her rubber shoes again and ran out with a wild little laugh, holding up her breasts to the heavy rain and spreading her arms, and running blurred in the rain with eurythmic dance-movements she had learned so long ago in Dresden. It was a strange pallid figure lifting and falling, bending so the rain beat and glistened on the full haunches, swaying up again and coming belly-forward through the rain, then stooping again so that only the full loins and buttocks were offered in a kind of homage towards him, repeating a wild obeisance. (221)

While Connie rushes away from Mellors, dancing in the rain and presumably oblivious to him, we see her through Mellors's perspective, a perspective whose desires are especially evident in that homage which presumes that her dance is about him. And when Mellors does join her, stripping down as well and noticing that her "blue eyes blazed with excitement," she does not respond by embracing him but by running "with a strange charging movement." Perhaps most odd in this narrative description of her through Mellors is the description of her figure as "a wonderful *cowering* female nakedness in flight" (221; italics mine). Where is Connie cowering in this joyful dance? Her only response to Mellors is in her flight, and she may well be taunting him to chase her (or she may really want to be away from him, given his previous preaching about the desperate future), but nowhere is she afraid or submissive to him here. And yet, when Mellors catches her, he is the dominant actor of the scene:

> He gathered her lovely, heavy posteriors one in each hand and pressed them in towards him in a frenzy, quivering motionless in the rain. Then suddenly he tipped her up and fell with her on the path, in the roaring silence of the rain, and short and sharp, he took her, short and sharp and finished, like an animal. (221–22)

Connie's desire is to dance in the rain and, after he has finished with his once-again aggressive intercourse and bids her return to the cottage, to pick wildflowers without him. As for Mellors, we know that "he didn't like the rain." But notice in the above narrative that we know nothing of Connie's desire or of her experience of their intercourse. Mellors is oblivious to her desire or to her experience and, because the narrative is seen through his eyes in this scene, neither do we.

On dance and passion, Lawrence writes in "Making Love to Music" of an ancestral and romantic dream of dance as a means of making love to music, a passion that does not include the climactic end of sexuality as Mellors knows it.

> But lo! even while she was being whirled round in the dance, our great-grandmother was dreaming of soft and throbbing music, and the arms of "one person," and the throbbing and sliding unison of this one more elevated person, who would never coarsely bounce her towards bed and copulation, but would slide on with her for ever, down the dim and sonorous vistas, making love without end to music without end, and leaving out entirely that disastrous, music-less full-stop of copulation, the end of ends.

When Lawrence writes of great-grandmother's dream of a more elevated person, he writes not of dominance but of a partner who has moved beyond the limited ends of sexual climax, a point most evident when he writes that "She dreamed of men that were only embodied souls, not tiresome and gross males, lords and masters."[67] The metaphoric dance is not an end in itself but a process of discovery and passion, not unlike the Yeatsian passional union implicit in the question, "How can we know the dancer from the dance?"[68] Lawrence concludes of the dream of modern women, women like Connie Chatterley, that their desire for connections with men may be like the figure he has noticed on the wall of an Etruscan tomb.

> I do believe that the unborn dream at the bottom of the soul of the shingled, modern young lady is this Etruscan young woman of mine,

dancing with such abandon opposite her naked-limbed, strongly dancing young man, to the sound of the double flute. They are wild with a dance that is heavy and light at the same time, and not a bit anti-copulative, yet not bouncingly copulative either.

Lawrence writes of a balanced, celebratory union between man and woman that is dismissive of none of the possibilities for their relationship, even for that seemingly paradoxical heaviness and lightness, climactic and nonclimactic (but not anticlimactic) sexuality. Connie understands this desire for balance in her dance in the rain and in her attempts to reach the guarded Mellors, but he cannot seem to move beyond the urges of "John Thomas," or beyond his own limited perspective in finding a place of communion with her. "There it is, the delightful quality of the Etruscan dance," Lawrence writes. "They are neither making love to music, to avoid copulation, nor are they bouncing towards copulation with a brass band accompaniment. They are just dancing a dance with the elixir of life."[69] Connie neither runs from copulation, despite her flight from Mellors, nor does she see copulation as an end, as he so readily does. Michael Squires writes of this rain-drenched scene, "illuminated by 'A Propos of *Lady Chatterley's Lover*,' the long scene of rain and flowers and naked bodies explores a profound insight that Lawrence discovers in 'A Propos': 'We *must* get back into relation, vivid and nourishing relation to the cosmos and the universe. The way is through daily ritual' (*Phoenix II* 510). The nude lovers' run in the rain and their flower decoration express their ritual adjustment to the universe."[70] If so, then Mellors remains unadjusted, or at least less adjusted to the universe than does Connie, who must show him how to dance in the rain. But dancing is not enough for Mellors, who must finally interrupt the dance with intercourse; the dance is only a means for him to Connie's "end," so to speak, which he narrow-mindedly believes is offered in homage to him.

Which leads to the more obvious, and more frequently written-about, scene of Mellors's domineering sexual intercourse with Connie, their final night together before her departure for Venice and his insistent desire for what appears to be anal sex. After his hostile meeting with Hilda, Connie's sister, in which Mellors defines Connie as coming to him "for a bit o' cunt an' tenderness" and as a "windfall," and in which he tells Hilda, "Women like you needs proper graftin'" (245), Mellors must "simmer down" before he can respond to Connie's desire for a kiss. Whether he does simmer down is questionable, given the direction their night of passion takes. The central symbolic image of that night of passion, given the allusive quality of their sexuality, which Lawrence does not name outright but which the majority of readers conclude is anal sex, is the concrete image of Connie's nightdress as it illustrates the violence of Mellors's sexuality: "The nightdress was slit almost in two" (249). If the nightdress is figurative for Connie's state as a recipient of this sexuality, the narrative does not admit it; while we are informed of the violent nature of the intercourse, we are told, as we were in the earlier scene of violent sexuality, that she liked it and, more importantly, that she wanted it.

> It was a night of sensual passion, in which she was a little startled, and almost unwilling: yet pierced again with piercing thrills of sensuality, different, sharper, more terrible than the thrills of tenderness, but, at the moment, more desirable. Though a little frightened, she let him have his way, and the reckless, shameless sensuality shook her to her foundations, stripped her to the very last, and made a different woman of her. It was not really love. It was not voluptuousness. It was sensuality sharp and searing as fire, burning the soul to tinder. (246)

Some of the same language as that used to describe Connie's experience of the rape fantasy in the woods is applied here: Sex is sharp and burning. And not only is the sex itself burning (but, according to the narrative, pleasurable), it is also serving to correct Connie, to improve upon her as a female by eradicating her shame.

> Burning out the shames, the deepest, oldest shames, in the most secret places. It cost her an effort to let him have his way and his will of her. She had to be a passive, consenting thing, like a slave, a physical slave. Yet the passion licked round her, consuming, and when the sensual flame of it passed through her bowels and breast, she really thought she was dying: yet a poignant, marvellous death. (247)

The paradoxical prose descriptions are often ludicrous in this passage, almost self-consciously so in the frequent repetitions of piercings and thrills, of burning pain and burning passion. Of the shame that is presumably burned from Connie in Mellors's final act of instruction/domination, Squires writes, "Shame dies not because of a mental act but because the flood of sharp sensation kills it, leaving her fresh and fully awakened, washed clean of her old social status."[71] This is a strange bit of reasoning in Squires's attempt to make sense of the scene of anal intercourse, as strange as if this description were applied to the rape fantasy earlier. Does the sharpness of unwilling sexual intercourse which happens in rape also work to remove shame? This irrational line of argument is striking because it is so out of character for Squires' foundational study of the novel, especially as it attempts to reconcile Mellors's abusive sexual manipulation of Connie with her "growth" and "transcendence"—a line of argument not far from the old masculine, misogynist claim that all a woman needs is a good fuck to straighten her out. This was the argument at least one critic made in reading the too-willful Brett Ashley of Hemingway's *The Sun Also Rises,* and it seems that the narrative of *Lady Chatterley's Lover* attempts to offer a similar prescription.

Rape fantasy as a valuable masculine narrative of desire continues to control the narrative perception of Connie's experience, this time in a scene of passion borne out of Mellors's violent anger at Connie's sister. Lawrence notes in "A Propos of *Lady Chatterley's Lover*" the role of rage in modern sexuality. "The sex, the very sexual organism in man and woman alike accumulates a deadly and desperate rage, after a certain amount of counterfeit love has been palmed off on it, even if itself has given nothing but counterfeit love" (314). This would help to explain the violence of Mellors's reaction to Hilda and his subsequent sexual extremes, but there may be other societal influences informing his behavior, as well. Citing Havelock Ellis's 1913 studies of early twentieth-century attitudes toward sexuality, Margaret Jackson summarizes Ellis's argument for sex as phallocentric and necessarily violent.

> Since the function of female resistance is to increase male arousal (and ultimately to ensure, according to the "law" of natural selection, that only the best and most vigorous males succeed in passing on their genes), there must be an equally close association between female sexual pleasure and pain. This Ellis was determined to prove, and devoted many pages to documenting "evidence," culled mainly from anthropological and criminological sources, that women "really enjoy" being raped, beaten, and sexually humiliated and brutalized. He concluded that in women pain and sexual pleasure were virtually indistinguishable: "the normal manifestations of a woman's sexual pleasure are exceedingly like pain."[72]

Compare this conclusion drawn by Ellis some fifteen years prior to the publication of Lawrence's final novel with the narrative portrayal of Connie's pleasure at painful sexual—and likely anal—intercourse.

> One had to be strong to bear him. . . . And how he had pressed in on her! And how, in fear, she had hated it! But how she had really wanted it! She knew now. At the bottom of her soul, fundamentally, she had needed this phallic hunting out, she had secretly wanted it, and she had

believed she would never get it. Now suddenly there it was, and a man was sharing her last and final nakedness, she was shameless. (247)

Citing the *Encyclopaedia of Sexual Knowledge* of 1934, Jackson also notes that "Other texts, too, underlined the inherently violent nature of the sexual act, emphasizing, for instance, that most women wanted to be deeply, even 'savagely' penetrated, 'even if that penetration should imply suffering.' Some women, they insisted, could not have orgasms unless they were beaten and brutalized."[73] This, it would seem, is Connie's willful experience of the pinnacle of sexuality at Mellors's instruction; like "The Princess"'s Mary Urquhart, this is an experience that she both *hates* and *wants*, if we accept the logic of the narrative. It is, of course, the logic of rape fantasy, and once again Connie Chatterley becomes an object of great value in the rape fantasy. Not only does she "bear" up under the force of Mellors's desire, but she actually professes to like it.

Nowhere in the three pages that describe this night of passion, however, are we supplied with dialogue that might differentiate either Mellors or Connie's experience and/or desire. From the moment at which we are told, "It was a night of sensual passion" to the moment at which Connie awakens the next morning, asking, "Is it time to wake up?" (248), we are provided with a narrative distance that offers a record of what purports to be Connie's experience. Whether we can trust those narrative claims is a different matter, especially because the narrative has frequently viewed matters of sexual desire from Mellors's limited perspective. Mark Spilka writes, in "On Lawrence's Hostility to Willful Women: The Chatterley Solution," "The one truly problematic flare-up of the old hostility comes in the night of searing passion in chapter 16, the now-famous buggery passage, when Lawrence yields to his hero's dominant strivings and fails to articulate his need to work through insecurity as to male identity, or to 'his identity as a separate sexual being.'"[74] Indeed, the distinction between Mellors's desire, and the hostility that informs it, and Connie's desire continues to be obscured by the narrative of rape fantasy. Instead we are simply assured that she does indeed desire a painful night of sodomy in which her shame is burned out, just as we are assured that although Mary Urquhart didn't want sexual intercourse with Romero, she willed it to happen. And to his credit, Squires defines what he understands as the scene's central shortcoming: "The major problem with the scene of anal intercourse is not that it fails to corroborate the novel's ethic of tenderness, or that it reveals Lawrence's latent homosexuality, but that it does not express the deepest kind of human fulfillment, which Lawrence elsewhere imagines."[75] This shortcoming is also true, I would argue, in the facile narrative treatment of sex and desire in the earlier scenes of *Lady Chatterley's Lover,* especially in those which construct monological rape fantasies to represent Connie's desire. This failure to achieve tenderness and communion is not evident *only* in the anal rape fantasy; it is indicative of the problem of domination and sexuality in *every* instance of sexual intercourse between Mellors and Connie in the novel, and for this reason, *Lady Chatterley's Lover* is Lawrence's most pessimistic novel.

Following this scene, we are left with the consequent stupor of Connie's life in Venice, of her failed separation from Clifford, and of her final separation from Mellors. *Lady Chatterley's Lover* remains one of Lawrence's most pessimistic novels because of the concluding division between the lovers, and it is a conclusion that neither promises nor guarantees a likely union between the two. The only hope for Mellors and Connie's future union lies in the tenderness in which she is finally able to instruct him in his London room. Although she claims that he possesses "the courage of your own tenderness" (277), we don't see much evidence of that tenderness until they leave behind the Golden Cock, the valuable figure of masculine power *and* the inn itself, and until she is able to show him how to express that tenderness: "Kiss my womb." And only in London does Connie finally receive an answer to the question that has so long remained unanswered: "Oh, you love me! You love me!" She can come to this conclusion only when she has been able to cause him to recognize *tenderness*, not rape, as expressive of love.

> And he went in to her softly, feeling the stream of tenderness flowing in release from his bowels to hers, the bowels of compassion kindled between them.
>   And he realised as he went in to her that this was the thing he had to do, to come into tender touch, without losing his pride or his dignity or his integrity as a man. (279)

If Lawrence claims, as he does in "A Propos of *Lady Chatterley's Lover,*" that "the phallus is the connecting link between the two rivers, that establishes the two streams in a oneness, and gives out of their duality a single circuit, forever" (325), then the phallus in their renewed relationship must be the child within Connie's womb which Mellors acknowledges with his kiss.

But, as I suggested earlier, the conclusion of the novel is not clear-cut, and whether they finally do come together depends on Mellors's ability to understand tenderness and to recognize their mutual desires. The prognosis for this transformation may not be a good one, given the tenor of his homosocial relationship with Connie's father. As if to add insult to injury, even Sir Malcolm approves of Mellors's influence in his daughter's life, himself ascribing to the rape fantasy, even though his daughter is at the center of it:

> You set fire to her haystack all right. Ha-ha-ha! I was jolly glad of it, I can tell you. She needed it. Oh, she's a nice girl, she's a nice girl, and I knew she'd be good going, if only some damned man would set her stack on fire! Ha-ha-ha! A gamekeeper, eh, my boy! Bloody good poacher, if you ask me. Ha-ha! (283)

This meeting illustrates the way that the homosocial relationship bears upon the identity of women, especially as it supports rape fantasy as an economy for women's figural value.

Jessica Benjamin identifies the core problem in sexuality based upon domination and submission when she writes, "The master-slave relationship actually perpetuates the problem it is designed to resolve. The rigid division into master and slave, sadist and masochist, ultimately exhausts its potential for transcendence." This is the dead-end Connie and Mellors find themselves at in the novel's conclusion, and they become geographically, if not spiritually, separated. "What finally leads the partners back to frustration," Benjamin continues, "is that each continues to deny one side of the self."[76] This frustration is echoed in the necessity for their final arrangements, Connie in Scotland and finding employment, and perhaps a future, at the Grange Farm. He does seem to come to himself, if only in having chosen a way to represent himself verbally, but he makes this choice based on his employer's wife's love of things "superior." "The woman is a birdy bit of a thing who loves anything superior—so I'm quite the superior, King's English and allow-me! all the time" (298). Whether there has been any change in Mellors as a result of Connie's instruction remains to be seen. But he defines his new spirit as having been born from their union, writing, "My soul softly flaps in the little pentecost flame with you, like the peace of fucking. We fucked a flame into being. Even the flowers are fucked into being, between sun and earth. But it's a delicate thing, and takes patience and the long pause" (301). The very fact that Mellors may now write of patience or long pauses, given the desperate haste of his earlier sexual desire, suggests that there has been significant change in him since the night of Connie's departure for Venice. "I love chastity now," he may proclaim, "because it is the peace that comes of fucking" (301). "Fucking" has taken on a very different linguistic value in his use of the term in the final letter; no longer is it descriptive of the rape fantasies that were evident in his sex with Connie. Instead, "fucking" is procreative on a spiritual and communal level, as well as on a literal level. In "A Propos," Lawrence claims "Word-perfect we may be, but Deed-demented. Let us prepare now for the death of our present 'little' life, and the re-emergence in a bigger life, in touch with the moving cosmos" (329). With the perfection of the deed, sex as tender and not as the culmination of rape fantasies, comes a new means of expression and of spirituality.

But again, a foreboding note in his final letter may be found in his sign-off, when he returns to his dissociative personae once again, a tragic reversion given that this letter has been his most personal and intimate communication to date. "John Thomas says good-night to lady Jane, a little droopingly, but with a hopeful heart—" (302). He ends with an expression of his physical desire, despite the seeming value he claims to have given chastity. Note that once Connie has gone to Scotland, she is silent, much like Shakespeare's Miranda in the final scene of *The Tempest*. Lawrence has curiously concluded the novel with Mellors's letter and without Connie's response to it, ironically reversing the attempts at communicating with Mellors that Connie made throughout their relationship. Like Ursula Brangwen, Connie is actually more courageous and committed to a true union of souls than is Mellors, who throughout the novel, will not speak *with* her, but only *to* her or *against* a variety of opposing forces: Bertha Coutts, mechanized society, propreity, and sexuality. That is, when he speaks at all. *This* is what keeps them apart—and by the time Mellors becomes willing to more fully communicate with her, she is gone, returned to Scotland. Although Birkin had to reform his own self-centered philosophies to reach a passional relationship with Ursula, Mellors cannot seem to do this, at least not definitively. "And the strange thing is," Lawrence notes of rage in "A Propos," "the worst offenders in the counterfeit love game, fall into the greatest rage. Those whose love has been a bit sincere are always gentler, even though they have been most swindled" (314). Whether he is writing specifically about Mellors and Connie as enraged and gentle, respectively, is unclear, but these roles certainly fit in his history of rape fantasies which are constructed around his need to dominate her and to impose his desire on her.

If Lawrence is not simply offering his masculine protagonist one final sermon, which I do not believe is wholly the case, he is leaving his readers with some significant doubt regarding Mellors's ability to fully realize a different kind of relationship, a different orientation for narrative desires. John Worthen concludes of Lawrence, "His novels dramatise the development of his idea of the novel as a means of challenging his readers—but, above all, as a way that only *Lady Chatterley's Lover* really fails in, of asserting community even while preaching isolation."[77] I venture to say that the novel cannot definitively fail, because we await Connie's response; while Mellors is indeed isolated and alone in his final letter, there remains the hope that he, like us, will place great value in her reciprocal response.

Notes

Chapter 1. *Noli Me Tangere:* Dodging the Heroic "I" in the Narratives of Lawrence and Hemingway

1. Jane Tompkins, "Me and My Shadow," in *Gender and Theory,* ed. Linda Kauffman (New York: Basil Blackwell, 1989), 135.

2. Nancy R. Comley and Robert Scholes, *Hemingway's Genders: Rereading the Hemingway Text* (New Haven: Yale University Press, 1994), ix.

3. Ibid., x.

4. Ibid., 77.

5. Ibid., xi.

6. Carol Siegel, *Lawrence among the Women* (Charlottesville: University Press of Virginia, 1991), 188.

7. Ibid., 128–29.

8. Ibid., 6.

9. See the interview by Kevin Bezner, "An Interview with Marilynne Robinson," in *Writer's N.W.* 7, no. 3 (fall 1992), 2.

10. See Teresa de Lauretis, *Alice Doesn't: Feminism, Semiotics, Cinema* (Bloomington: Indiana University Press, 1984). Subsequent quotations from this work are cited parenthetically in the text.

11. Robert Scholes, *Fabulation and Metafiction* (Urbana: University of Illinois Press, 1979), 26.

12. Margaret Jackson, "'Facts of Life' or the Eroticization of Women's Oppression? Sexology and the Social Construction of Heterosexuality," in *The Cultural Construction of Sexuality,* ed. Pat Caplan (London: Routledge, 1987), 73.

13. Virginia Woolf, *A Room of One's Own.* (1929; reprint, New York: Harcourt Brace Jovanovich, 1957), 103.

14. Susan Winnett, "Coming Unstrung: Women, Men, Narrative, and Principles of Pleasure," *PMLA* 105 no. 3 (May 1990), 505.

15. See Seymour Chatman's "What Novels Can Do That Films Can't (and Vice Versa)" (117–36); and Barbara Herrnstein Smith's "Narrative Versions, Narrative Theories" (209–32) in W. J. T. Mitchell, ed., *On Narrative* (Chicago: University of Chicago Press, 1981).

16. Alice Jardine, "Men in Feminism: Odor di Uomo or Compagnons de Route?" in *Men in Feminism,* ed. Alice Jardine and Paul Smith (New York: Methuen, Inc., 1987), 61.

17. Woolf, *A Room of One's Own,* 24.

18. Elaine Showalter, "Critical Cross-Dressing: Male Feminists and the Woman of the Year," in *Men in Feminism,* ed. Alice Jardine and Paul Smith (New York: Methuen, Inc., 1987), 131.

19. Toril Moi, "Men against Patriarchy," in *Gender and Theory*, ed. Linda Kauffman (New York: Basil Blackwell, Inc., 1989), 184.

20. Milan Kundera, *Immortality*, trans. Peter Kussi (New York: Grove Weidenfeld, 1991), 6.

21. Carl Eby, "'Come Back to the Beach Ag'in, David Honey!': Hemingway's Fetishization of Race in *The Garden of Eden* Manuscripts," *Hemingway Review* 14 no. 2 (spring 1994), 99.

22. Peter L. Hays, "Hemingway, Nick Adams and David Bourne: Sons and Writers," *Arizona Quarterly* 44 no. 2 (summer 1988), 31.

23. Millicent Bell, "Pseudoautobiography and Personal Metaphor," in *Critical Essays on Ernest Hemingway's "A Farewell to Arms,"* ed. George Monteiro (New York: G. K. Hall & Co., 1994), 145.

24. Sean O'Faolain, *The Vanishing Hero* (Boston: Little, Brown and Co., 1956), xxii.

25. Sheila MacLeod, *Lawrence's Men and Women* (London: Paladin, 1987), 46.

26. Ibid., 47.

27. Peter Balbert, *D. H. Lawrence and the Phallic Imagination* (London: Macmillan, 1989), 20.

28. Ibid., 105.

29. Originally written in 1979, the essay is reprinted and reintroduced by Mark Spilka in *Renewing the Normative D. H. Lawrence: A Personal Progress* (Columbia: University of Missouri Press, 1992, 83.

30. Michael Bell, *D. H. Lawrence: Language and Being* (Cambridge: Cambridge University Press, 1991), 219.

31. Spilka, *Renewing the Normative D. H. Lawrence*, 83.

32. Carlos Baker, *Hemingway: The Writer as Artist*, 4th ed. (Princeton, N.J.: Princeton University Press, 1952), 160. Compare this line of thought to Mark Spilka's reading of Lawrence as a composite of his major male protagonists: "Still, [Gerald's] resemblance to Paul [Morel] suggests how Lawrence divides himself between his heroes and makes of their affinity a dramatization of his own dilemmas. Birkin is his older self, seeking singleness of being; Gerald, his youthful self, seeking an annihilation in dependent love: and Birkin oddly cannot save his friend" (Spilka, *Renewing the Normative D. H. Lawrence*, 61).

33. Frederick Crews, *The Critics Bear It Away* (New York: Random House, 1992), 90.

34. Robert Penn Warren, *Robert Penn Warren: Selected Essays* (New York: Vintage, 1966), 38.

35. Philip Young, *Ernest Hemingway: A Reconsideration* (University Park: Pennsylvania State University Press, 1966), 65–66.

36. Philip Young, Preface to *The Nick Adams Stories* (New York: Charles Scribner's Sons, 1972), 6.

37. Young, Preface, 7.

38. Crews, *The Critics Bear It Away*, 90.

39. See Siegel's *Lawrence among the Women* and Linda Ruth Williams' *Sex in the Head: Visions of Femininity and Film in D. H. Lawrence* (Detroit: Wayne State University Press, 1993). This is not to say that there are no worthy recent biographies; see the aforementioned critical biographies by Worthen and Lynn.

40. Miriam B. Mandel, *Reading Hemingway: The Facts in the Fictions* (Metuchen, N.J.: Scarecrow Press, Inc., 1995), 7.

41. David Ellis, Mark Kinkead-Weekes, and John Worthen, introduction to Worthen's *D. H. Lawrence: The Early Years 1885–1912* (Cambridge: Cambridge University Press, 1991), xiii–xiv.

42. Bernard Malamud, *Dubin's Lives* (New York: Farrar Straus Giroux, 1979), 20.

43. Patricia Waugh, *Metafiction* (London: Methuen, 1984), 33.

44. Mark Spilka, "Lessing and Lawrence: The Battle of the Sexes," in *Renewing the Normative D. H. Lawrence,* 126.

45. Ellis, Kinkead-Weekes, and Worthen, Introduction, xiv.

46. Quoted in Janet Barron, "Equality Puzzle: Lawrence and Feminism," in *Rethinking Lawrence,* ed. Keith Brown (Buckingham: Open University Press, 1990), 15.

47. Williams, *Sex in the Head*, 15.

48. The examples of such a conclusion are far too numerous to list, not only because of readerly assumptions of autobiography in Birkin, but in virtually all of Lawrence's male characters from Paul Morel to Oliver Mellors. And quite often these remarks subtly penetrate their critical readings, as, for example, in Michael Bell's *D. H. Lawrence: Language and Being:* "By contrast, the 'star-equilibrium' image is introduced by Birkin (*there is no such Lawrence-figure in "The Rainbow"*) and Lawrence's immediate narrative emphasis is on Ursula's rejection of it" (98; italics mine). Bell slips this biographical reading into his analysis without problematizing it, and although his assumption is much less egregious than those made by other readers, it serves as an example of the critical limitations that may be brought to a narrative. Of course, this problem becomes exponentially multiplied as readers attempt to find parallels for a plethora of other biographically based figures: Frieda, Middleton Murry, Ottoline Morel, etc.

49. D. H. Lawrence, *Women in Love* (1920; reprint, New York: Penguin, 1989), 192. Subsequent quotations from this work are cited parenthetically in the text.

50. D. H. Lawrence, "The Study of Thomas Hardy," in *Phoenix,* ed. Edward D. McDonald (New York: Penguin, 1985), 442.

51. D. H. Lawrence, *Fantasia of the Unconscious* (1922; reprint, New York: Penguin, 1977), 33.

52. Williams, *Sex in the Head*, 18.

53. Ernest Hemingway, *Selected Letters 1917–1961,* ed. Carlos Baker (New York: Charles Scribner's Sons, 1981), 182.

54. Kundera, *Immortality,* 81.

55. Ibid., 82.

56. Roland Barthes, "Introduction to the Structural Analysis of Narratives," in *Image/Music/Text,* trans. Stephen Heath (New York: Hill and Wang, 1977), 111–12.

57. Roland Barthes, "The Death of the Author," in *Image/Music/Text,* trans. Stephen Heath (New York: Hill and Wang, 1977), 147.

58. Reina Lewis, *Gendering Orientalism: Race, Femininity and Representation* (London: Routledge, 1996), 23.

59. Barthes, "The Death of the Author," 145.

60. Comley and Scholes, *Hemingway's Genders*, x–xi.

61. Crews, *Critics Bear It Away,* xix.

62. Ibid., xiii.

63. Nancy K. Miller, "Changing the Subject: Authorship, Writing and the Reader," in *Feminist Studies/Critical Studies,* ed. Teresa de Lauretis (Bloomington: Indiana University Press, 1986), 104.

64. Ibid., 106.

65. Lewis, *Gendering Orientalism,* 24–25.

66. Ibid., 25.

67. Kingsley Widmer, *Defiant Desire: Some Dialectical Legacies of D. H. Lawrence* (Carbondale and Edwardsville: Southern Illinois University Press, 1992), 3.

68. Spilka, *Renewing the Normative D. H. Lawrence,* 4.

69. Ibid., 8.

70. Ibid., 81.

71. Michael Bell, *D. H. Lawrence*, 1.

72. Ibid., 2.

73. Waugh, *Metafiction*, 123.

74. Quoted in Gary Saul Morson, "Who Speaks for Bakhtin?" in *Bakhtin: Essays and Dialogues on His Work,* ed. Gary Saul Morson (Chicago: University of Chicago Press, 1986), 14.

75. D. H. Lawrence, Foreword to *Women in Love. Phoenix II,* ed. Warren Roberts and Harry T. Moore (New York: Penguin, 1981), 275–76.

76. Ellis, Kinkead-Weekes, and Worthen, Introduction, xv.

77. D. H. Lawrence, "Noli Me Tangere," in *The Complete Poems,* ed. Vivian de Sola Pinto and F. Warren Roberts (New York: Penguin, 1988), 468–69, 1: 1–3.

78. Ernest Hemingway, "[And everything the author knows . . .]," in *Complete Poems,* ed. Nicholas Gerogiannis (Lincoln: University of Nebraska Press, 1979), 84, 1: 1–4.

79. Ibid., 1: 17.

80. D. H. Lawrence, *The Collected Letters of D. H. Lawrence.* 2 vols. (London: William Heinemann Ltd., 1962), 1: 319.

81. See George Monteiro's excellent history of the novel's publication in his introduction to *Critical Essays on Ernest Hemingway's "A Farewell to Arms"* (New York: G. K. Hall & Co., 1994), 1–27.

Chapter 2. "All women must have a husband": Revising Gender, Marriage, and the Narrative Covenant in D. H. Lawrence's *The Rainbow*

1. D. H. Lawrence, "Odour of Chrysanthemums," in *The Complete Short Stories,* 3 vols. (New York: Penguin, 1976), 2: 300. Subsequent quotations from this work are cited parenthetically in the text.

2. Michael Bell, *D. H. Lawrence*, 51.

3. Siegel, *Lawrence among Women*, 27.

4. Quoted in Barron, "Equality Puzzle" 12.

5. Quoted in Anais Nin, *D. H. Lawrence: An Unprofessional Study* (1932; reprint, Chicago: Swallow Press, 1964), 23.

6. David Holbrook, *Where D. H. Lawrence Was Wrong about Woman* (Lewisburg, Penn.: Bucknell University Press, 1992), 138.

7. Quoted in Hilary Simpson, *D. H. Lawrence and Feminism* (London: Croom Helm Ltd., 1982), 13.

8. Balbert, *Phallic Imagination*, 13.

9. Ibid., 11.

10. Simpson, *Lawrence and Feminism*, 16.

11. D. H. Lawrence, *The Rainbow* (1915; reprint, New York: Penguin, 1989), 42. Subsequent quotations from this work are cited parenthetically in the text.

12. Michael Bell discusses the nature of the sexuality of this opening passage in *D. H. Lawrence: Language and Being* by noting, "The relationship between farming and sexuality in this passage is not proposed as a general or objective truth. It is appropriately a linguistic or poetic creation because its 'truth' is a function of the Brangwen psyche" (65). Although Bell believes that the "punning consciousness is . . . too explicit in this passage," I read the sexuality of Part I, chapter I as crucial

to the divisiveness of men's and women's roles, not only on the Brangwen farm, but in a more general sociocultural tradition. Men are the *sexual* beings in this tradition, both in terms of their desire and of their roles as creators and life givers. Women, on the other hand, remain in the "blind intercourse of farm-life," separate from (and yearning for)-the spoken world beyond. They were aware of the lips and the mind of the world speaking and giving utterance, they heard the sound in the distance, and they strained to listen" (*The Rainbow* 42). Not only are women blind, straining from their limited perspectives to see what men are able to see, but they are at a remove from language as well. If Bell's argument is that language serves a Heideggerian "'world'-creating function" in *The Rainbow,* then the abstract woman of the world of Ursula's ancestral past may have no impact upon the creation of her world. Bell neglects to consider the power of creativity and control in the sexual language of this passage and its implications for the disempowered woman, not the Brangwen women in particular, but woman as a social construct. Carol Siegel is more accurate when she writes, in *Lawrence among the Women,* "Brontean or Lawrencian woman . . . can be understood through the model of two concentric circles. Both writers envision the feminine as a socially constructed shell around the innate female" (57–58).

13. Michael Bell, *D. H. Lawrence,* 61.

14. Ibid., 74–75.

15. Williams, *Sex in Head,* 24.

16. Margaret Homans, "Feminist Fictions and Feminist Theories of Narrative," *Narrative* 2 no. 1 (January 1994), 5.

17. Kate Millett sees Ursula trapped in this role in *Women in Love.* In *Sexual Politics* (New York: Avon Books, 1971), she writes, "Ursula is presented as an incomplete creature, half-asleep in the tedium of her spinster schoolmistress life. Birkin will awake her according to a Lawrentian convention whereby the male gives birth to the female . . . yet nothing materializes, and she becomes more and more her husband's creature, accepting his instruction. . . . What she does become is a nonentity, utterly incorporated into Birkin" (264–65). As I will illustrate in my readings of both *The Rainbow* and *Women in Love,* Millett has radically misunderstood the nature of Ursula's role in each novel. Ursula no more becomes incorporated into Birkin than she allows herself to submit to Skrebensky. See my analyses of the conclusion of *The Rainbow* in this chapter, as well as those on Ursula and Birkin's relationship as it counters that of Gudrun and Gerald in my chapter on *Women in Love.*

18. Simpson, *Lawrence and Feminism,* 56.

19. A title suggested by Edward Garnett, according to John Worthen in *D. H. Lawrence and the Idea of the Novel* (Totowa, N.J.: Rowman and Littlefield, 1979), 51.

20. Balbert, *Phallic Imagination,* 56.

21. Ibid., 59–60.

22. Mark Kinkead-Weekes, "The Marriage of Opposites in *The Rainbow,*" in *D. H. Lawrence: Centenary Essays,* ed. Mara Kalnins (Bristol: Bristol Classical Press, 1986), 30.

23. Worthen, *Idea of the Novel,* 63.

24. Balbert, *Phallic Imagination,* 66.

25. Ibid., 61.

26. Worthen, *Idea of the Novel,* 65.

27. Michael Bell, *D. H. Lawrence,* 71.

28. Balbert, *Phallic Imagination,* 71–72.

29. Ibid., 71.

30. Winnett, "Coming Unstrung" 512.

31. Lawrence, "Study of Thomas Hardy," 404–5.

32. Worthen, *Idea of the Novel*, 61.

33. This passage is uncannily similar to much of Hemingway's "masculine" prose, especially if it is compared with the subject/object duality in a story such as "Up in Michigan." There the subject *seems* to be Liz Coates's desire for Jim as sexual object in the repetition of the subject/verb pairing, "She liked," but there is a very masculine narrative at work in this story, as in this description of Will's conquest of Jennie. See my discussion of the Hemingway story in chapter 4.

34. Balbert, *Phallic Imagination*, 72.

35. Holbrook, *Where Lawrence was Wrong*, 150.

36. Millett, *Sexual Politics*, 262–63.

37. Homans, "Feminist Fictions" 6.

38. Lawrence, *Fantasia*, 21.

39. Simpson, *Lawrence and Feminism*, 39; Balbert, *Phallic Imagination*, 76.

40. Roger Sale, *Modern Heroism* (Berkeley: University of California Press, 1973), 69.

41. Ibid., 82.

42. Hayden White, "The Value of Narrativity in the Representation of Reality," *Critical Inquiry* 7 no. 1 (autumn 1980), 8–9.

43. Siegel, *Lawrence among Women*, 2.

44. Simpson, *Lawrence and Feminism*, 48.

45. Michael Squires, *The Creation of "Lady Chatterley's Lover"* (Baltimore, Md.: Johns Hopkins University Press, 1983), 27; Gavriel Ben-Ephraim, "The Achievement of Balance in *Lady Chatterley's Lover*," in *D. H. Lawrence's "Lady": A New Look at "Lady Chatterley's Lover,"* ed. Michael Squires and Dennis Jackson (Athens: University of Georgia Press, 1985), 138.

46. Widmer, *Defiant Desire*, 20; Balbert, *Phallic Imagination*, 73–74.

47. Widmer, *Defiant Desire*, 20.

48. Worthen, *Idea of the Novel*, 74.

49. Siegel, *Lawrence among Women*, 18.

50. Worthen, *Idea of the Novel*, 63.

51. Homans, "Feminist Fictions," 13.

52. Kinkead-Weekes, "Marriage of Opposites," 37.

53. Worthen, *Idea of the Novel*, 71.

54. Ibid., 73.

55. Balbert, *Phallic Imagination*, 78.

56. Ibid., 77.

57. Ibid., 80.

58. Ibid., 78.

59. Nin, *Unprofession Study*, 14, 27.

60. Siegel, *Lawrence among Women*, 10.

Chapter 3. Getting Rid of "the exclusiveness of married love": Questioning Constructs of Masculinity in *Women in Love*

1. MacLeod, *Lawrence's Men*, 47.

2. W. Charles Pilley, Review of *Women in Love* appearing in *John Bull* (17 September 1921), as quoted by Barron, "Equality Puzzle,"19.

3. MacLeod, *Lawrence's Men*, 54.

4. Worthen, *Idea of the Novel*, 87.

5. See David Lodge's "Lawrence, Dostoevsky, Bakhtin: Lawrence and Dialogic Fiction" (92–108); and Avrom Fleishman's "Lawrence and Bakhtin: Where Pluralism Ends and Dialogism Begins" (109–19), in *Rethinking Lawrence*, ed. Keith Brown (Bristol: Open University Press, 1990), for two useful and effective articles on this novel and Bakhtinian dialogism.

6. Worthen, *Idea of the Novel*, 104.

7. Sigmund Freud, "Femininity," in *New Lectures on Psycho-analysis. The Standard Edition of the Complete Psychological Works of Sigmund Freud*, ed. James Strachey. 24 vols. (London: Hogarth Press, 1953–74), 22: 113.

8. Siegel, *Lawrence among Women*, 65.

9. Luce Irigaray, *Speculum of the Other Woman*, trans. Gillian C. Gill (Ithaca: Cornell University Press, 1986), 13.

10. Margaret Atwood echoes this in her wonderful essay, "The Female Body," in which she describes the male brain: "Good for aiming though, for hitting the target when you pull the trigger. What's the target? Who's the target? Who cares? What matters is hitting it. That's the male brain for you. Objective." See Joyce Carol Oates, ed., *The Best American Essays 1991* (New York: Ticknor and Fields, 1991), 9–12.

11. Worthen, *Idea of the Novel*, 95.

12. D. H. Lawrence, Prologue to *Women in Love*. *Phoenix II*, eds. Warren Roberts and Harry T. Moore (New York: Penguin, 1981), 102.

13. Halliday and Loerke are significant representatives of the kind of men who are portrayed as ultimately repulsive to others, especially men, in the novel, and they bear a close relationship to Hemingway's Robert Cohn of *The Sun Also Rises*. I will explore the problem of "the degenerate Jew," a figure that inspires only hatred and loathing for the main characters as a symbol of perverted manhood in chapter 5.

14. Millett, *Sexual Politics*, 264–65.

15. Vladimir Propp, *Morphology of the Folktale*, 2d ed. rev. and ed. by Louis A. Wagner (Austin: University of Texas Press, 1968); and Jurij M. Lotman, "The Origin of Plot in the Light of Typology," trans. Julian Graffy, *Poetics Today* 1 nos. 1–2 (autumn 1979), 161–84.

16. See Robert Kiely, "Accident and Purpose: 'Bad Form' in Lawrence's Fiction," in *D. H. Lawrence: A Centenary Consideration*, eds. Peter Balbert and Phillip L. Marcus (Ithaca: Cornell University Press, 1985), 97; Holbrook, 184; Spilka, *Renewing the Normative D. H. Lawrence*, 59.

17. Avrom Fleishman, "Lawrence and Bakhtin: Where Pluralism Ends and Dialogism Begins," in *Rethinking Lawrence*, ed. Keith Brown (Buckingham: Open University Press, 1990), 114.

18. Victor J. Seidler, "Reason, Desire and Male Sexuality," in *The Cultural Construction of Sexuality*, ed. Pat Caplan (London: Routledge, 1987), 82.

19. Ibid., 85.

20. Ibid., 98.

21. Williams, *Sex in Head*, 126–27.

22. Seidler, "Reason, desire," 87.

23. Ibid.

24. Ibid., 91.

25. Nin, *Unprofessional Study*, 80.

26. Siegel, *Lawrence among Women*, 9.

27. Fleishman, "Lawrence and Bakhtin," 114.

28. Seidler, "Reason, desire," 82.

29. Ibid., 85–86.

30. Timothy Gould, "The Unhappy Performative," in *Performativity and Performance,* ed. Andrew Parker and Eve Kosofsky Sedgwick (London: Routledge, 1995), 30–31.

31. Michael Bell, 125.

32. M. M. Bakhtin, "Discourse in the Novel," in *The Dialogic Imagination,* trans. Caryl Emerson and Michael Holquist (Austin: University of Texas Press, 1981), 276.

33. Williams, *Sex in Head,* 10.

34. Ibid., 66.

35. Ibid., 72.

36. Ibid., 76–77.

37. Ibid., 54.

38. Ibid., 86.

39. Ernest Hemingway, *The Sun Also Rises* (New York: Charles Scribner's Sons, 1926), 131. Subsequent quotations from this work are cited parenthetically in the text.

40. Lawrence, Prologue to *Women in Love,* 93. The danger of men expressing affection, attraction, or love for other men, even outside of the homo*sexual* relationship, is outlined by Eve Kosofsky Sedgwick in *Between Men* and clearly illustrated in Hemingway's *A Farewell to Arms.* In chapter 6, I will explore the ways that homophobia, which Sedgwick claims is an integral part of the male homosocial relationship, both regulates the behavior of men in Frederic Henry's narrative and allows for "safety" in their expressions of affection and in physical intimacy.

41. Ibid., 104.

42. Maria DiBattista, "*Women in Love:* D. H. Lawrence's Judgement Book," in *D. H. Lawrence: A Centenary Consideration,* ed. Peter Balbert and Phillip L. Marcus (Ithaca: Cornell University Press, 1985), 70.

43. George Donaldson, "'Men in Love'? D. H. Lawrence, Rupert Birkin and Gerald Crich," in *D. H. Lawrence: Centenary Essays,* ed. Mara Kalnins (Bristol: Bristol Classical Press, 1986), 54.

44. Ibid., 60.

45. Sale, *Modern Heroism,* 46.

46. Siegel, *Lawrence among Women,* 20.

47. Michael Bell, *D. H. Lawrence,* 105.

48. Balbert, *Phallic Imagination,* 89.

49. Worthen, *Idea of the Novel,* 102.

50. Williams, *Sex in Head,* 54.

51. Balbert, *Phallic Imagination,* 85–86.

52. Siegel, *Lawrence among Women,* 58–59.

53. Balbert, *Phallic Imagination,* 89.

54. Spilka, *Renewing the Normative D. H. Lawrence,* 60.

55. Worthen, *Idea of the Novel,* 90.

56. David Lodge, "Lawrence, Dostoevsky, Bakhtin: Lawrence and Dialogic Fiction," in *Rethinking Lawrence,* ed. Keith Brown (Buckingham: Open University Press, 1990), 97.

57. Simpson, *Lawrence and Feminism,* 65.

58. Nin, *Unprofessional Study,* 32.

59. Lawrence, *Fantasia,* 18.

Chapter 4. "She liked it . . . she wanted it . . . she had to have it . . . ": Desire and the Narrative Gaps of *In Our Time*

1. D. H. Lawrence, Review of *In Our Time. Phoenix,* ed. Edward D. McDonald (New York: Penguin, 1985), 365.

2. Ibid.

3. Young, *A Reconsideration*, 63.

4. Joseph DeFalco, *The Hero in Hemingway's Short Stories* (Pittsburgh, Penn.: University of Pittsburgh Press, 1963), 185.

5. Bakhtin, "Epic and Novel," in *The Dialogic Imagination*, trans. Caryl Emerson and Michael Holquist (Austin: University of Texas Press, 1981), 17.

6. Susan F. Beegel, Introduction to *Hemingway's Neglected Short Fiction*, ed. Susan F. Beegel (Ann Arbor, Mich.: UMI Research Press, 1989), 10.

7. Joseph M. Flora, *Ernest Hemingway: A Study of the Short Fiction* (Boston: Twayne Publishers, 1989), 26.

8. See Robert M. Slabey, "The Structure of *In Our Time*," in *Ernest Hemingway: Six Decades of Criticism*, ed. Linda W. Wagner-Martin (East Lansing: Michigan State University Press, 1987), 68. In the notes to the essay as it is published in Linda W. Wagner-Martin's anthology, Slabey offers this explanation of his use of asterisks in his outline: "The asterisk indicates that Nick is not the protagonist of the story. The preceding roman numeral is that of the 'chapter.'" (75). In the essay, there is not an asterisk following "Out of Season," but there is an asterisk following "Cross-Country Snow." Because Nick is not in the former story, but is a major figure in the latter, I have presumed its original form is a typographical error and have reversed the order of Slabey's asterisks for these two stories.

9. Ibid., 69–70.

10. Colin E. Nicholson, "The Short Stories After *In Our Time:* A Profile," in *Ernest Hemingway: New Critical Essays*, ed. A. Robert Lee (Totowa, N.J.: Barnes & Noble Books, 1983), 36; Young, *A Reconsideration*, 65–66.

11. Debra A. Moddlemog, "The Unifying Consciousness of a Divided Conscience: Nick Adams as Author of *In Our Time*," in *New Critical Approaches to the Short Stories of Ernest Hemingway*, ed. Jackson J. Benson (Durham, N.C.: Duke University Press, 1990), 20.

12. Ernest Hemingway, "On Writing," in *The Nick Adams Stories* (New York: Charles Scribner's Sons, 1972), 238.

13. Moddelmog, "Unifying Consciousness," 25.

14. Young, *A Reconsideration*, 31.

15. Moddelmog, "Unifying Consciousness," 30.

16. See Laura Mulvey, "Visual Pleasure and Narrative Cinema," *Screen* 16 no. 3 (autumn 1975), 14.

17. DeFalco, *Hero in Hemingway*, 17.

18. Robert Scholes, "Reading Like a Man," in *Men in Feminism*, ed. Alice Jardine and Paul Smith (New York: Methuen, Inc., 1987), 205.

19. Young, Preface, 5–6.

20. Ibid., 7.

21. James M. Cox, "*In Our Time:* The Essential Hemingway," *Southern Humanities Review* 22 no. 4 (fall 1988), 310.

22. White, "Value of Narrativity," 8–9.

23. See the very helpful bibliography of works by Hemingway, as well as a partial listing of secondary works, in the appendix of Joseph M. Flora's *Ernest Hemingway: A Study of the Short Fiction* (Boston: Twayne Publishers, 1989), 182–88.

24. Baker, *Writer as Artist*, 29–30.

25. Ibid., 12.

26. Ernest Hemingway, "Up in Michigan," *The Short Stories of Ernest Hemingway* (New York: Charles Scribner's Sons, 1966), 81. Subsequent quotations from this work are cited parenthetically in the text.

27. Alice Hall Petry, "Coming of Age in Horton's Bay: Hemingway's 'Up in Michigan,'" in *New Critical Approaches to the Short Stories of Ernest Hemingway*, ed. Jackson J. Benson (Durham, N.C.: Duke University Press, 1990), 354.

28. DeFalco, *Hero in Hemingway*, 55; Mark Royden Winchell, "Fishing the Swamp: 'Big Two-Hearted River' and the Unity of *In Our Time*," in *South Carolina Review* 18 no. 2 (spring 1986), 25; Petry, 357.

29. Lisa Tyler, "Ernest Hemingway's Date Rape Story: Sexual Trauma in 'Up in Michigan.'" *Hemingway Review* 13 no. 2 (spring 1994), 1–11.

30. Hemingway, *Selected Letters*, 157.

31. Susan Swartzlander, "Uncle Charles in Michigan," in *Hemingway's Neglected Short Fiction*, ed. Susan F. Beegel (Ann Arbor, Mich.: UMI Research Press, 1989), 34.

32. Ibid., 39.

33. Tyler, "Date Rape Story," 1.

34. Baker, *Writer as Artist*, 423.

35. Ernest Hemingway, "Soldier's Home," in *In Our Time* (New York: Macmillan Publishing Company, 1986), 70. Subsequent quotations from *In Our Time* are cited parenthetically in the text.

36. Petry, "Coming of Age," 353.

37. Hemingway, *Selected Letters*, 155.

38. Harbour Winn, "Hemingway's *In Our Time*: 'Pretty Good Unity.'" *Hemingway Review* 9 no. 2 (spring 1990), 126.

39. Young, *A Reconsideration*, 39.

40. See Peter L. Hays, *A Concordance to Hemingway's "In Our Time"* (Boston: G. K. Hall & Co., 1990), 85–108.

41. George Monteiro, "'This Is My Pal Bugs': Ernest Hemingway's 'The Battler,'" in *New Critical Approaches to the Short Stories of Ernest Hemingway*, ed. Jackson J. Benson (Durham, N.C.: Duke University Press, 1990), 225.

42. DeFalco, *Hero in Hemingway*, 71–72.

43. Ibid., 76, 77.

44. Toni Morrison, *Playing in the Dark: Whiteness and the Literary Imagination* (Cambridge, Mass.: Harvard University Press, 1992), 63.

45. Ibid., 66.

46. Ibid., 84.

47. Cox, *In Our Time*, 313.

48. Warren Bennett, "The Poor Kitty and the Padrone and the Tortoise-shell Cat in 'Cat in the Rain,'" in *New Critical Approaches to the Short Stories of Ernest Hemingway*, ed. Jackson J. Benson (Durham, N.C.: Duke University Press, 1990), 245.

49. Ibid., 247. See John V. Hagopian's "Symmetry in 'Cat in the Rain,'" in *The Short Stories of Ernest Hemingway: Critical Essays*, ed. Jackson J. Benson (Durham, N.C.: Duke University Press, 1975); and David Lodge's *Working with Structuralism* (Boston: Routledge and Kegan Paul, 1981).

50. Don Summerhayes, "You Can Say That Again: Some Encounters with Repetition in *In Our Time*," in *Hemingway Review* 10 no. 2 (spring 1991), 50.

51. Jardine, "Men in Feminism," 61.

52. Cox, *In Our Time*, 309.

53. Bakhtin, "Epic and Novel," 37.

54. Young, *A Reconsideration*, 30.

55. Ibid., 63.

Chapter 5. "We could have had such a damned good time together" [if only you had a penis]: Critical Phallocentrism and Hemingway's *The Sun Also Rises*

1. Frederic Joseph Svoboda, *Hemingway & "The Sun Also Rises"* (Lawrence: University Press of Kansas, 1983), 31.

2. Ibid.

3. Mark Spilka, "The Death of Love in *The Sun Also Rises*," in *Hemingway: A Collection of Critical Essays,* ed. Robert P. Weeks (1958; reprint, Englewood Cliffs, N.J.: Prentice-Hall, Inc., 1962), 137.

4. See Wilma Garcia, *Mothers and Others: Myths of the Female in the Works of Melville, Twain and Hemingway* (New York: Peter Lang, 1984), 9; Mimi Reisel Gladstein, *The Indestructable Woman in Faulkner, Hemingway and Steinbeck* (Ann Arbor, Mich.: UMI Research Press, 1986), 50; and Morrison, 81–82.

5. Quoted in Robert Merrill, "Demoting Hemingway: Feminist Criticism and the Canon," *American Literature* 60 no. 2 (May 1988), 259.

6. Jackson J. Benson, *Hemingway ... The Writer's Art of Self-Defense* (Minneapolis: University of Minnesota Press, 1969), 28–30.

7. Andrew Hook, "Art and Life in *The Sun Also Rises*," in *Ernest Hemingway: New Critical Essays,* ed. A. Robert Lee (London: Vision Press Ltd., 1983), 50.

8. Svoboda, *Hemingway & Sun*, 31.

9. Sibbie O'Sullivan, "Love and Friendship/Man and Woman in *The Sun Also Rises*," *Arizona Quarterly* 44 no. 2 (summer 1988), 77.

10. DeFalco, *Hero in Hemingway*, 185.

11. Leo Gurko, *Ernest Hemingway and the Pursuit of Heroism* (New York: Thomas Y. Crowell Company, 1968), 56–57.

12. Spilka, "Death of Love," 134.

13. Baker, *Writer as Artist*, 82–83.

14. See Wolfgang E. H. Rudat, "Hemingway's *The Sun Also Rises*: Masculinity, Feminism, and Gender-Role Reversal," in *American Imago: A Psychoanalytic Journal for Culture, Science and the Arts* 47 no. 1 (spring 1990), 43–68.

15. Leslie Fiedler, *Love and Death in the American Novel,* rev. ed. (New York: Stein and Day, 1966), 319.

16. Baker, *Writer as Artist*, 85.

17. Ibid., 91.

18. For those readers who have been the most surprising in promoting Brett as an utter nymphomaniac, see Jackson J. Benson's "Roles and the Masculine Writer" in *Hemingway ... The Writer's Art of Self-Defense;* Roger Whitlow's "Bitches and Other Simplistic Assumptions," in *Brett Ashley,* ed. Harold Bloom (New York: Chelsea House Publishers, 1991, 148–56; Baker *Writer as Artist*; and Wolfgang E. H. Rudat's "Sexual Dilemmas in *The Sun Also Rises*: Hemingway's Count and the Education of Jacob Barnes," in *Hemingway Review* 8 no. 2 (spring 1989), 2–13; and "Brett's Problem," in *Brett Ashley,* ed. Harold Bloom (New York: Chelsea House Publishers, 1991), 166–74), and the aforementioned Rudat essay.

19. Benson, *The Writer's Art*, 31.

20. Ibid., 35.

21. Whitlow, "Bitches and Other," 153–54. The first of Whitlow's references is Edward M. Brecher, *The Sex Researchers* (Boston: Little, Brown, 1969), 191–94. The second reference is from H. L. P. Resnik and Marvin E. Wolfgang, eds., *Sexual Behaviors: Social, Clinical, and Legal Aspects* (Boston: Little, Brown, 1972), 225–26.

22. Freud, "Femininity," 113.

23. Benson, *The Writer's Art*, 39.

24. Linda Wagner-Martin, "Women in Hemingway's Early Fiction," in *Brett Ashley,* ed. Harold Bloom (New York: Chelsea House Publishing, 1991), 139; O'Sullivan, 91.

25. O'Sullivan, "Love and Friendship," 77.

26. Philip Young, *Ernest Hemingway. Pamphlets on American Writers 1* (Minneapolis: University of Minnesota Press), 10; Gladstein, *Indestructable Woman*, 61; Garcia, *Mothers and Others*, 9.

27. James Joyce, "A Painful Case," in *Dubliners* (1914; reprint, New York: Penguin Books, 1976), 112.

28. Kenneth S. Lynn, *Hemingway* (New York: Simon and Schuster, 1987), 323–24.

29. Rudat, "Sexual Dilemmas," 9–10.

30. Rudat, "Brett's Problem," 166.

31. Rudat, "Masculinity, Feminism, and Gender-Role Reversal," 43.

32. Ibid., 54.

33. Annette Kolodny, "Some Notes on Defining a 'Feminist Literary Criticism.'" *Critical Inquiry* 2 (1975), 90.

34. Lawrence, *Fantasia,* 33; George Plimpton, ed. "Ernest Hemingway," in *Writers at Work II: The Paris Review Interviews* (New York: Penguin Books, 1985), 229.

35. Ernest Hemingway, *The Garden of Eden* (New York: Charles Scribner's Sons, 1986), 128–29. Subsequent quotations from this work are cited parenthetically in the text.

36. Mark Spilka, *Hemingway's Quarrel with Androgyny* (Lincoln: University of Nebraska Press, 1990), 200.

37. Stephen Kern, *The Culture of Love* (Cambridge, Mass.: Harvard University Press, 1992), 369.

38. Lynn, *Hemingway,* 324.

39. Plimpton, "Ernest Hemingway," 230.

40. Hemingway, *Selected Letters,* 745.

41. Plimpton, "Ernest Hemingway," 230.

42. Spilka, "Death of Love," 133.

43. Ibid., 128.

44. Rudat, "Sexual Dilemmas," 7–8.

45. Morrison, *Playing in Dark*, 82.

46. Rudat, "Sexual Dilemmas," 5.

47. Comley and Scholes, *Hemingway's Genders,* 44.

48. O'Sullivan, "Love and Friendship," 83.

49. Spilka, "Death of Love," 130.

50. Comley and Scholes, *Hemingway's Genders,* 43.

51. Spilka, "Death of Love," 130.

52. Linda Wagner-Martin, "Hemingway's Search for Heroes, Once Again," in *Arizona Quarterly* 44 no. 2 (summer 1988), 64–65.

53. Eve Kosofsky Sedgwick, *Between Men: English Literature and Male Homosocial Desire* (New York: Columbia University Press, 1985), 25–26.

54. Ibid., 38.

55. O'Sulllivan, "Love and Friendship," 91.

56. Sedgwick, *Between Men,* 3.

57. James Baldwin, *Another Country* (New York: Dell Publishing, 1988), 116–17.

58. Sedgwick, *Between Men,* 21.

59. Ibid., 50–51.

60. Eby, "Come Back," 101.

61. Ibid., 103.

62. Richard Poirier, *The Renewal of Literature* (New Haven, Conn.: Yale University Press, 1987), 98.

63. Ibid., 106.

64. Svoboda, *Hemingway and Sun,* 31.

65. Bakhtin, "Epic and Novel," 13.

66. Ibid., 17.

Chapter 6. "You always feel trapped biologically": Masculinity and Narrative Entrapment in Hemingway's *A Farewell to Arms*

1. O'Faoláin, *Vanishing Hero*, xiii.
2. Teresa de Lauretis, *Technologies of Gender,* (Bloomington: Indiana University Press, 1987), 18.
3. Ernest Hemingway, *A Farewell to Arms* (1929; reprint, New York: Charles Scribners' Sons, 1957), 139. Subsequent quotations from this work are cited parenthetically in the text.
4. James Mellow argues in *Hemingway: A Life without Consequences* (Boston: Houghton Mifflin, 1992) that "there is probably a touch of homosexuality in Rinaldi's feelings toward Lieutenant Henry" (384); and in his essay, "The Search for 'Home,'" in Monteiro, *Critical Essays on Ernest Hemingway's "A Farewell to Arms"* (New York: G. K. Hall & Co., 1994), Peter Griffin suggests that Rinaldi plays at being homosexual.

> He calls Frederic Henry, "blood brother," hobo argot for homosexual lover. He claims he is jealous of Catherine Barkley and of the priest. He brings the drink of lovers, cognac, and he leaves it under the bed. He wants to kiss Frederic Henry; he calls him "baby." (181)

Griffin takes a great deal for granted in this claim for homosexual behavior, whether stereotypical or otherwise: the hobo argot, the cognac, the term of endearment, "baby." He does, however, indicate that, if these are indeed references to homosexuality, they serve as a means for the men to taunt each other good-naturedly. "Rinaldi and Frederic Henry are not homosexuals, and they know it. Their teasing shows their confidence in this" (181). This is where Griffin begins to acknowledge the intricacies of the homosocial bond, which I will examine further.
5. J. P. Chaplin, *Dictionary of Psychology,* (New York: Dell Publishing, 1979), 29.
6. Pat Caplan, Introduction, in *The Cultural Construction of Sexuality,* ed. Pat Caplan (London: Routledge, 1987), 16–17. Caplan cites G. Rubin, "The Traffic in Women: Notes on the Political Economy of Sex" (in *Toward an Anthropology of Women,* ed. R. Reiter (New York: Monthly Review Press, 1975); S. Ortner and H. Whitehead, eds. *Sexual Meanings: The Cultural Construction of Gender and Sexuality* (London: Cambridge University Press, 1981).
7. Sedgwick, *Between Men,* 3.
8. Jeffrey Weeks, "Questions of Identity," in *The Cultural Construction of Sexuality,* ed. Pat Caplan (London: Routledge, 1987), 36–37.
9. Sedgwick, *Between Men,* 1–2. In *Between Men,* Eve Kosofsky Sedgwick uses the term "homosocial" expressly to define the complex pattern of relationships between men, noting that female homosocial relationships are not constituted upon the division between homosociality and homosexuality. She writes, "The apparent simplicity—the unity—of the continuum between 'women loving women' and 'women promoting the interests of women,' extending over the erotic, social familial, economic, and political realms, would not be so striking if it were not in strong contrast to the arrangement among males" (3). The answer to her question, "Doesn't the continuum between 'men-loving-men' and 'men-promoting-the-interests-of-men' have the same intuitive force that it has for women?" (3) is an emphatic "no" for Sedgwick, and I have chosen to continue to use the term "homosocial" as a referent for these relationships between men. However, the term becomes complicated in my reading of *The Garden of Eden,* especially in Catherine Bourne's gender-crossings.
10. Caplan, Introduction, 2.

11. Spilka, *Hemingway's Quarrel*, 328.

12. Sedgwick, *Between Men*, 219.

13. Ibid., 201.

14. Eby, "Come Back" 105.

15. See M. M. Bakhtin's introduction to his *Rabelais and His World*, trans. Hélène Iswolsky (Bloomington: Indiana University Press, 1984), 1–58.

16. In "Hemingway's 'Resentful Cryptogram,'" Judith Fetterley writes of Rinaldi's definition of Catherine-as-goddess, "Rinaldi's inability to see women in other than sexual terms emerges quite clearly from a remark he makes to Frederic before the latter leaves for Milan. . . . The implications behind this pronouncement are clear: if a woman is good only for worship, then she really isn't any good at all because women only exist for one thing and the real definition of a good woman is she knows what she exists for and does it and lets you know that she likes it" (118). This is, of course, the discovery Catherine makes as she inquires about the details of prostitution from Frederic (105). See Judith Fetterley, "Hemingway's 'Resentful Cryptogram,'" in *Critical Essays on Ernest Hemingway's "A Farewell to Arms*, ed. George Monteiro (New York: G. K. Hall & Co., 1994), 117–29.

17. In "Catherine Barkley: Hemingway's Scottish Heroine" (*Hemingway Review* 7 no. 1 [fall 1987], 43–44), Charles J. Nolan Jr. argues that Catherine is actually Scottish, and Rinaldi has misrepresented her identity, as well as Henry's. Nolan notes her own admission ("You couldn't get to Scotland and back on a leave" [115]) as she tells Henry why he could not visit her at home during the war. He also indicates Hemingway's likely research into Scottish peerage, noting that the Fergusons and the Barclays share a geographic connection, suggesting a prewar relationship between the two V.A.D.s. Miriam Mandel comes to a similar conclusion regarding Catherine's nationality in "Ferguson and Lesbian Love: Unspoken Subplots in *A Farewell to Arms*" (*Hemingway Review* 14 no. 1 [fall 1994], 18–24).

18. Gerry Brenner, "A Hospitalized World," in *Critical Essays on Ernest Hemingway's "A Farewell to Arms*, ed. George Monteiro (New York: G. K. Hall & Co., 1994), 137.

19. See Sandra Whipple Spanier's assessment of the critical reception of Catherine Barkley in her essay, "Hemingway's Unknown Soldier: Catherine Barkley, the Critics, and the Great War," in *New Essays on "A Farewell to Arms,"* ed. Scott Donaldson (Cambridge: Cambridge University Press, 1990), 75–108.

20. Fetterley, "Hemingway's Resentful Cryptogram," 124.

21. Spilka, *Hemingway's Quarrel*, 217.

22. Ibid., 212.

23. Ibid., 217.

24. Millicent Bell, "Pseudoautobiography" 150.

25. Morrison, *Playing in Dark*, 81.

26. Comley and Scholes, *Hemingway's Genders*, 37.

27. Philip Young, "Death and Transfiguration," in *Critical Essays on Ernest Hemingway's "A Farewell to Arms*, ed. George Monteiro (New York: G. K. Hall & Co., 1994), 105.

28. Spilka, *Hemingway's Quarrel*, 220.

29. Fetterley, "Hemingway's Resentful Cryptogram," 117.

30. Spilka, *Hemingway's Quarrel*, 333.

31. Brenner, "Hospitalized World," 139.

32. Spanier, "Hemingway's Unknown Soldier," 86.

33. Comley and Scholes, *Hemingway's Genders*, 36.

34. Kern, *Culture of Love*, 5.

35. Spanier, "Hemingway's Unknown Soldier," 86.

36. James Nagel, "Catherine Barkley and Retrospective Narration," in *Critical Essays on Ernest Hemingway's "A Farewell to Arms,* ed. George Monteiro (New York: G. K. Hall & Co., 1994), 165.

37. Fetterley, "Hemingway's Resentful Cryptogram," 126.

38. Michael S. Reynolds, *Hemingway's First War* (Princeton, N.J.: Princeton University Press, 1976), 247.

39. Mandel, "Ferguson and Lesbian Love," 19.

40. Fetterley, "Hemingway's Resentful Cryptogram," 126.

41. Millicent Bell, "Pseudoautobiography," 148.

42. And she may not understand for reasons that Miriam Mandel has elucidated in "Ferguson and Lesbian Love."

43. Sedgwick, *Between Men,* 47.

44. Fetterley, "Hemingway's Resentful Cryptogram," 117.

45. Ibid., 120.

46. Nagel, "Catherine Barkley," 168.

47. James Phelan, "Distance, Voice, and Temporal Perspective in Frederic Henry's Narration: Successes, Problems and Paradox," in *New Essays on "A Farewell to Arms,"* ed. Scott Donaldson (Cambridge: Cambridge University Press, 1990), 68.

48. Waugh, *Metafiction,* 18.

49. Nagel, "Catherine Barkley," 171.

50. Ibid., 162.

51. Spilka, "Death of Love," 130.

52. Brenner, "Hospitalized World," 137.

53. William H. Gass, "In Terms of the Toenail: Fiction and the Figures of Life," in *Fiction and the Figures of Life* (Boston: David R. Godine, 1971), 60.

54. O'Faoláin, *Vanishing Hero,* xvi.

Chapter 7. "The centre of all womanhood": The Economy of Rape Fantasy in Lawrence's *Lady Chatterley's Lover*

1. D. H. Lawrence, *The Collected Letters of D. H. Lawrence,* 2 vols. (London: William Heinemann Ltd., 1962), 2: 1089–90.

2. D. H. Lawrence, "Nottingham and the Mining Countryside," in *Phoenix,* ed. Edward D. McDonald (New York: Penguin, 1985), 133.

3. D. H. Lawrence, *Lady Chatterley's Lover* (1928; reprint, New York: Penguin, 1994), 153. Subsequent quotations from this work are cited parenthetically in the text.

4. D. H. Lawrence, "A Propos of *Lady Chatterley's Lover,"* reprinted in *Lady Chatterley's Lover* (1928; reprint, New York: Penguin, 1994), 307. Subsequent quotations from this work are cited parenthetically in the text.

5. Williams, *Sex in Head,* ix.

6. Simpson, *Lawrence and Feminism,* 123.

7. D. H. Lawrence, "We Need One Another," in *Phoenix,* ed. Edward D. McDonald (New York: Penguin, 1985), 192.

8. D. H. Lawrence, "Give Her a Pattern," in *Phoenix II,* eds. Warren Roberts and Harry T. Moore (New York: Penguin, 1981), 535–36.

9. Siegel, *Lawrence among Women,* 8.

10. D. H. Lawrence, "Eloi, Eloi, Lama Sabachthani?" in *The Complete Poems*, eds. Vivian de Sola Pinto and F. Warren Roberts (New York: Penguin, 1988), 741–42.

11. Harry T. Moore, *The Priest of Love: A Life of D. H. Lawrence*, rev. ed. (New York: Penguin, 1981), 498.

12. D. H. Lawrence, "The Princess," in *The Complete Short Stories*, 3 vols. (New York: Penguin, 1976), 2: 504. Subsequent quotations from this work are cited parenthetically in the text.

13. Mark Spilka, "Hemingway and Lawrence as Abusive Husbands," in *Renewing the Normative D. H. Lawrence: A Personal Progress* (Columbia: University of Missouri Press, 1992), 224.

14. Jessica Benjamin, "Master and Slave: The Fantasy of Erotic Domination," in *Powers of Desire: The Politics of Sexuality*, eds. Ann Snitow, Christine Stansell, and Sharon Thompson (New York: Monthly Review Press, 1983), 282.

15. Spilka, "Hemingway and Lawrence as Abusive Husbands," 223.

16. D. H. Lawrence, "Film Passion," in *The Complete Poems*, eds. Vivian de Sola Pinto and F. Warren Roberts (New York: Penguin, 1988), 538.

17. Williams, *Sex in Head*, 72.

18. Spilka, "Hemingway and Lawrence as Abusive Husbands," 224.

19. Benjamin, 283–84.

20. Ibid., 293.

21. Ibid., 285.

22. Ibid.

23. Siegel, *Lawrence among Women*, 31.

24. Spilka, Introduction to *Renewing the Normative D. H. Lawrence: A Personal Progress* (Columbia: University of Missouri Press, 1992), 15.

25. Spilka, "Hemingway and Lawrence as Abusive Husbands," 222.

26. Quoted in Scott R. Sanders, "Lady Chatterley's Loving and the Annihilation Impulse," in *D. H. Lawrence's "Lady": A New Look at "Lady Chatterley's Lover,"* eds. Michael Squires and Dennis Jackson (Athens: University of Georgia Press, 1985), 14.

27. Sanders, "Annihilation Impulse," 14.

28. Lawrence, *Collected Letters*, 2: 1063–64.

29. Lawrence, "Give Her a Pattern," 536.

30. Lawrence, *Collected Letters*, 2: 1045.

31. Lydia Blanchard, "Lawrence, Foucault, and the Language of Sexuality," in *D. H. Lawrence's "Lady": A New Look at "Lady Chatterley's Lover,"* eds. Michael Squires and Dennis Jackson (Athens: University of Georgia Press, 1985), 19.

32. Balbert, *Phallic Imagination*, 135.

33. Squires, *Creation*, 19.

34. Michael Bell, *D. H. Lawrence*, 222.

35. Spilka, Introduction to *Renewing the Normative D. H. Lawrence*, 11.

36. Spilka, "Lawrence versus Peeperkorn on Abdication; Or, What Happens to a Pagan Vitalist When the Juice Runs Out?" *Renewing the Normative D. H. Lawrence: A Personal Progress* (Columbia: University of Missouri Press, 1992), 72.

37. Siegel, *Lawrence Among Women*, 33.

38. Michael Bell, *D. H. Lawrence*, 213.

39. D. H. Lawrence, "Making Love to Music," in *Phoenix*, ed. Edward D. McDonald (New York: Penguin, 1985), 161.

40. Balbert, *Phallic Imagination*, 138.

41. Ibid., 175–76.

42. Squires, *Creation*, 78.

43. Ibid., 117.

44. Holbrook, *Where Lawrence was Wrong,* 339–40.

45. See Benjamin, "Master and Slave" 280.

46. Balbert, *Phallic Imagination,* 173.

47. Jackson, "Facts of Life," 58.

48. Widmer, *Defiant Desire,* 80.

49. Jackson, "Facts of Life," 61.

50. Holbrook, *Where Lawrence was Wrong,* 19.

51. Ellen Willis, "Feminism, Moralism, and Pornography," in *Powers of Desire: The Politics of Sexuality,* eds. Ann Snitow, Christine Stansell, and Sharon Thompson (New York: Monthly Review Press, 1983), 464.

52. Squires, *Creation,* 180–81.

53. Balbert, *Phallic Imagination,* 165–66, 174.

54. Benjamin, "Master and Slave," 281.

55. Squires, *Creation,* 68, 73–74, 76.

56. Williams, *Sex in Head,* 63–64.

57. Widmer, *Defiant Desire,* 75.

58. Kern, *Culture of Love,* 137.

59. Widmer, *Defiant Desire,* 77.

60. Lawrence, "We Need One Another," 191.

61. Lawrence, "Pornography and Obscenity," in *Phoenix,* ed. Edward D. McDonald (New York: Penguin, 1985), 177.

62. Willis, "Feminism, Moralism," 461.

63. Simpson, *Lawrence and Feminism,* 103.

64. Williams, *Sex in Head,* 64.

65. Kern, *Culture of Love,* 165.

66. Mark Spilka, "Lawrence's Hostility to Willful Women: The Chatterley Solution," in *Renewing the Normative D. H. Lawrence: A Personal Progress* (Columbia: University of Missouri Press, 1992), 166.

67. Lawrence, "Making Love to Music," 162–63.

68. W. B. Yeats, "Among School Children," in *The Collected Poems of W. B. Yeats,* ed. Richard J. Finneran (New York: Macmillan Publishing Company, 1989), 217, 1: 64.

69. Lawrence, "Making Love to Music," 165.

70. Squires, *Creation,* 44.

71. Ibid., 181.

72. Jackson, "Facts of Life," 57.

73. Ibid., 63.

74. Spilka, "Lawrence's Hostility," 149.

75. Squires, *Creation,* 179.

76. Benjamin, "Master and Slave," 292–93.

77. Worthen, *Idea of the Novel,* 184.

Bibliography

Atwood, Margaret. "The Female Body." In *The Best American Essays 1991*. Edited by Joyce Carol Oates, 9–12. New York: Ticknor and Fields, 1991.

Baker, Carlos. *Hemingway: The Writer as Artist*. 4th ed. Princeton, N.J.: Princeton University Press, 1952.

Bakhtin, M. M. "Discourse in the Novel." In *The Dialogic Imagination*. Translated by Caryl Emerson and Michael Holquist, 259–422. Austin: University of Texas Press, 1981.

———. "Epic and Novel." In *The Dialogic Imagination*. Translated by Caryl Emerson and Michael Holquist, 3–40. Austin: University of Texas Press, 1981.

———. Introduction to his *Rabelais and His World*. Translated by Hélène Iswolsky, 1–58. Bloomington: Indiana University Press, 1984.

Balbert, Peter. *D. H. Lawrence and the Phallic Imagination*. London: Macmillan, 1989.

Baldwin, James. *Another Country*. New York: Dell Publishing, 1988.

Barron, Janet. "Equality Puzzle: Lawrence and Feminism." In *Rethinking Lawrence*. Edited by Keith Brown, 12–22. Buckingham: Open University Press, 1990.

Barthes, Roland. "The Death of the Author." In *Image/Music/Text*. Translated by Stephen Heath, 142–48. New York: Hill and Wang, 1977.

———. "Introduction to the Structural Analysis of Narratives." In *Image/Music/Text*. Translated by Stephen Heath, 79–124. New York: Hill and Wang, 1977.

Beegel, Susan F. *Hemingway's Neglected Short Fiction*. Ann Arbor, Mich.: UMI Research Press, 1989.

Bell, Michael. *D. H. Lawrence: Language and Being*. Cambridge: Cambridge University Press, 1991.

Bell, Millicent. "Pseudoautobiography and Personal Metaphor." In *Critical Essays on Ernest Hemingway's "A Farewell to Arms."* Edited by George Monteiro, 145–60. New York: G. K. Hall & Co., 1994.

Ben-Ephraim, Gavriel. "The Achievement of Balance in *Lady Chatterley's Lover.*" *D. H. Lawrence's "Lady": A New Look at "Lady Chatterley's Lover."* Edited by Michael Squires and Dennis Jackson, 136–53. Athens: University of Georgia Press, 1985.

Benjamin, Jessica. "Master and Slave: The Fantasy of Erotic Domination." In *Powers of Desire: The Politics of Sexuality*. Edited by Ann Snitow, Christine Stansell and Sharon Thompson, 280–99. New York: Monthly Review Press, 1983.

Bennett, Warren. "The Poor Kitty and the Padrone and the Tortoise-shell Cat in 'Cat in the Rain.'" *New Critical Approaches to the Short Stories of Ernest Hemingway*. Edited by Jackson J. Benson, 245–56. Durham, N.C.: Duke University Press, 1990.

Benson, Jackson J. *Hemingway ... The Writer's Art of Self-Defense.* Minneapolis: University of Minnesota Press, 1969.

Bezner, Kevin. "An Interview with Marilynne Robinson." *Writer's N.W.* 7 no. 3 (fall 1992): 1–3.

Blanchard, Lydia. "Lawrence, Foucault, and the Language of Sexuality." In *D. H. Lawrence's "Lady": A New Look at "Lady Chatterley's Lover."* Edited by Michael Squires and Dennis Jackson, 17–35. Athens: University of Georgia Press, 1985.

Brenner, Gerry. "A Hospitalized World." In *Critical Essays on Ernest Hemingway's "A Farewell to Arms.* Edited by George Monteiro, 130–44. New York: G. K. Hall & Co., 1994.

Caplan, Pat. Introduction to *The Cultural Construction of Sexuality.* Edited by Pat Caplan, 1–30. London: Routledge, 1987.

Chaplin, J. P. *Dictionary of Psychology.* New York: Dell Publishing, 1979.

Chatman, Seymour. "What Novels Can Do That Films Can't (and Vice Versa)." In *On Narrative.* Edited by W. T. J. Mitchell, 117–36. Chicago: University of Chicago Press, 1981.

Comley, Nancy R., and Robert Scholes. *Hemingway's Genders: Rereading the Hemingway Text.* New Haven: Yale University Press, 1994.

Cox, James M. "*In Our Time:* The Essential Hemingway." *Southern Humanities Review* 22 no. 4 (fall 1988): 305–20.

Crews, Frederick. *The Critics Bear It Away.* New York: Random House, 1992.

DeFalco, Joseph. *The Hero in Hemingway's Short Stories.* Pittsburgh, Penn.: University of Pittsburgh Press, 1963.

de Lauretis, Teresa. *Alice Doesn't: Feminism, Semiotics, Cinema.* Bloomington: Indiana University Press, 1984.

———. *Technologies of Gender.* Bloomington: Indiana University Press, 1987.

DiBattista, Maria. "*Women in Love:* D. H. Lawrence's Judgement Book." In *D. H. Lawrence: A Centenary Consideration.* Edited by Peter Balbert and Phillip L. Marcus, 67–90. Ithaca, NY: Cornell University Press, 1985.

Donaldson, George. "'Men in Love'? D. H. Lawrence, Rupert Birkin and Gerald Crich." In *D. H. Lawrence: Centenary Essays.* Edited by Mara Kalnins, 41–67. Bristol: Bristol Classical Press, 1986.

Eby, Carl. "'Come Back to the Beach Ag'in, David Honey!': Hemingway's Fetishization of Race in *The Garden of Eden* Manuscripts." *Hemingway Review* 14 no. 2 (spring 1994): 98–117.

Ellis, David, Mark Kinkead-Weekes, and John Worthen. Introduction to John Worthen. In *D. H. Lawrence: The Early Years 1885–1912.* Cambridge: Cambridge University Press, 1991.

Fetterley, Judith. "Hemingway's 'Resentful Cryptogram.'" In *Critical Essays on Ernest Hemingway's "A Farewell to Arms."* Edited by George Monteiro, 117–29. New York: G. K. Hall & Co., 1994.

Fiedler, Leslie. *Love and Death in the American Novel.* Rev. Ed. New York: Stein and Day, 1966.

Fleishman, Avrom. "Lawrence and Bakhtin: Where Pluralism Ends and Dialogism Begins." *Rethinking Lawrence.* Edited by Keith Brown, 109–119. Bristol: Open University Press, 1990.

Flora, Joseph M. *Ernest Hemingway: A Study of the Short Fiction.* Boston: Twayne Publishers, 1989.

Freud, Sigmund. "Femininity." In *New Lectures on Psycho-analysis. The Standard Edition of the Complete Psychological Works of Sigmund Freud.* Edited by James Strachey, 24 vols., 22: 112–35. London: Hogarth Press, 1953–74.

Garcia, Wilma. *Mothers and Others: Myths of the Female in the Works of Melville, Twain and Hemingway.* New York: Peter Lang, 1984.

Gass, William H. "In Terms of the Toenail: Fiction and the Figures of Life." In *Fiction and the Figures of Life.* Boston: David R. Godine, 1971.

Gladstein, Mimi Reisel. *The Indestructable Woman in Faulkner, Hemingway and Steinbeck.* Ann Arbor, Mich.: UMI Research Press, 1986.

Gould, Timothy. "The Unhappy Performative." In *Performativity and Performance.* Edited by Andrew Parker and Eve Kosofsky Sedgwick, 19–44. London: Routledge, 1995.

Griffin, Peter. "The Search for 'Home.'" In *Critical Essays on Ernest Hemingway's "A Farewell to Arms."* Edited by George Monteiro, 175–88. New York: G. K. Hall & Co., 1994.

Gurko, Leo. *Ernest Hemingway and the Pursuit of Heroism.* New York: Thomas Y. Crowell Company, 1968.

Hays, Peter L. *A Concordance to Hemingway's "In Our Time."* Boston: G. K. Hall & Co., 1990.

———. "Hemingway, Nick Adams and David Bourne: Sons and Writers." *Arizona Quarterly* 44 no. 2 (summer 1988): 28–38.

Hemingway, Ernest. "[And everything the author knows . . .]." In *Complete Poems.* Edited by Nicholas Gerogiannis, 84. Lincoln: University of Nebraska Press, 1979.

———. *A Farewell to Arms.* 1929. Reprint. New York: Charles Scribners' Sons, 1957.

———. *The Garden of Eden.* New York: Charles Scribner's Sons, 1986.

———. *In Our Time.* 1925/1930. Reprint. New York: Macmillan Publishing Company, 1986.

———. "On Writing." In *The Nick Adams Stories.* New York: Charles Scribner's Sons, 1972.

———. *Selected Letters 1917–1961.* Edited by Carlos Baker. New York: Charles Scribner's Sons, 1981.

———. *The Sun Also Rises.* New York: Charles Scribner's Sons, 1926.

———. "Up in Michigan." In *The Short Stories of Ernest Hemingway.* New York: Charles Scribner's Sons, 1966.

Herrnstein Smith, Barbara. "Narrative Versions, Narrative Theories." *On Narrative.* Edited by W. T. J. Mitchell, 209–32. Chicago: University of Chicago Press, 1981.

Holbrook, David. *Where D. H. Lawrence Was Wrong about Woman.* Lewisburg, Penn.: Bucknell University Press, 1992.

Homans, Margaret. "Feminist Fictions and Feminist Theories of Narrative." *Narrative* 2 no. 1 (January 1994): 3–16.

Hook, Andrew. "Art and Life in *The Sun Also Rises.*" In *Ernest Hemingway: New Critical Essays.* Edited by A. Robert Lee. London: Vision Press Ltd., 1983.

Irigaray, Luce. *Speculum of the Other Woman.* Translated by Gillian C. Gill. Ithaca: Cornell University Press, 1986.

Jackson, Margaret. "'Facts of life' or the Eroticization of Women's Oppression? Sexology and the Social Construction of Heterosexuality." In *The Cultural Construction of Sexuality.* Edited by Pat Caplan, 52–81. London: Routledge, 1987.

Jardine, Alice. "Men in Feminism: Odor di Uomo or Compagnons de Route?" In *Men in Feminism.* Edited by Alice Jardine and Paul Smith, 54–61. New York: Methuen, Inc., 1987.

Joyce, James. "A Painful Case." In *Dubliners.* 1914. Reprint. New York: Penguin Books, 1976.

Kern, Stephen. *The Culture of Love.* Cambridge, Mass.: Harvard University Press, 1992.

Kiely, Robert. "Accident and Purpose: 'Bad Form' in Lawrence's Fiction." In *D. H. Lawrence: A Centenary Consideration.* Edited by Peter Balbert and Phillip L. Marcus, 91–107. Ithaca: Cornell University Press, 1985.

Kinkead-Weekes, Mark. "The Marriage of Opposites in *The Rainbow.*" In *D. H. Lawrence: Centenary Essays.* Edited by Mara Kalnins, 21–39. Bristol: Bristol Classical Press, 1986.

Kolodny, Annette. "Some Notes on Defining a 'Feminist Literary Criticism.'" *Critical Inquiry* 2 (1975).

Kundera, Milan. *Immortality.* Translated by Peter Kussi. New York: Grove Weidenfeld, 1991.

Lawrence, D. H. *The Collected Letters of D. H. Lawrence.* 2 vols. London: William Heinemann Ltd., 1962.

———. *The Complete Poems.* Edited by Vivian de Sola Pinto and F. Warren Roberts. New York: Penguin, 1988.

———. *Fantasia of the Unconscious.* 1922. Reprint. New York: Penguin, 1977.

———. Foreword to *Women in Love. Phoenix II.* Edited by Warren Roberts and Harry T. Moore, 275–76. New York: Penguin, 1981.

———. "Give Her a Pattern." In *Phoenix II.* Edited by Warren Roberts and Harry T. Moore, 535–38. New York: Penguin, 1981.

———. *Lady Chatterley's Lover.* 1928. Reprint. New York: Penguin, 1994.

———. "Making Love to Music." In *Phoenix.* Edited by Edward D. McDonald, 160–66. New York: Penguin, 1985.

———. "Nottingham and the Mining Countryside." In *Phoenix.* Edited by Edward D. McDonald, 133–40. New York: Penguin, 1985.

———. "Odour of Chrysanthemums." In *The Complete Short Stories.* 3 vols. New York: Penguin, 1976.

———. "Pornography and Obscenity." In *Phoenix.* Edited by Edward D. McDonald, 170–87. New York: Penguin, 1985.

———. "The Princess." 1924. Reprint. In *The Complete Short Stories.* 3 vols. New York: Penguin, 1976.

———. Prologue to *Women in Love. Phoenix II.* Edited by Warren Roberts and Harry T. Moore, 92–108. New York: Penguin, 1981.

———. "A Propos of *Lady Chatterley's Lover.*" Reprinted in *Lady Chatterley's Lover.* 1928. New York: Penguin, 1994.

———. *The Rainbow.* 1915. Reprint. New York: Penguin, 1989.

———. Review of *In Our Time. Phoenix.* Edited by Edward D. McDonald, 365–66. New York: Penguin, 1985.

———. "The Study of Thomas Hardy." In *Phoenix.* Edited by Edward D. McDonald, 398–516. New York: Penguin, 1985.

———. "We Need One Another." In *Phoenix*. Edited by Edward D. McDonald, 188–95. New York: Penguin, 1985.

———. *Women in Love*. 1920. Reprint. New York: Penguin, 1989.

Lewis, Reina. *Gendering Orientalism: Race, Femininity and Representation*. London: Routledge, 1996.

Lodge, David. "Lawrence, Dostoevsky, Bakhtin: Lawrence and Dialogic Fiction." In *Rethinking Lawrence*. Edited by Keith Brown, 92–108. Bristol: Open University Press, 1990.

Lotman, Jurij M. "The Origin of Plot in the Light of Typology." Translated by Julian Graffy. *Poetics Today* 1 nos. 1–2 (autumn 1979): 161–84.

Lynn, Kenneth S. *Hemingway*. New York: Simon and Schuster, 1987.

MacLeod, Sheila. *Lawrence's Men and Women*. London: Paladin, 1987.

Malamud, Bernard. *Dubin's Lives*. New York: Farrar Straus Giroux, 1979.

Mandel, Miriam B. "Ferguson and Lesbian Love: Unspoken Subplots in *A Farewell to Arms*." *Hemingway Review* 14 no. 1 (fall 1994): 18–24.

———. *Reading Hemingway: The Facts in the Fictions*. (Metuchen, N.J.: Scarecrow Press, Inc., 1995.

Mellow, James. *Hemingway: A Life without Consequences*. Boston: Houghton Mifflin, 1992.

Merrill, Robert. "Demoting Hemingway: Feminist Criticism and the Canon." *American Literature* 60 no. 2 (May 1988): 255–68.

Miller, Nancy K. "Changing the Subject: Authorship, Writing and the Reader." *Feminist Studies/Critical Studies*. Edited by Teresa de Lauretis, 102–20. Bloomington: Indiana University Press, 1986.

Millett, Kate. *Sexual Politics*. New York: Avon Books, 1971.

Moddlemog, Debra A. "The Unifying Consciousness of a Divided Conscience: Nick Adams as Author of *In Our Time*." *New Critical Approaches to the Short Stories of Ernest Hemingway*. Edited by Jackson J. Benson, 17–32. Durham, N.C.: Duke University Press, 1990.

Moi, Toril. "Men against Patriarchy." In *Gender and Theory*. Edited by Linda Kauffman. New York: Basil Blackwell, Inc., 1989.

Monteiro, George. Introduction to *Critical Essays on Ernest Hemingway's "A Farewell to Arms."* New York: G. K. Hall & Co., 1994.

———. "'This Is My Pal Bugs': Ernest Hemingway's 'The Battler.'" In *New Critical Approaches to the Short Stories of Ernest Hemingway*. Edited by Jackson J. Benson, 224–28. Durham, N.C.: Duke University Press, 1990.

Moore, Harry T. *The Priest of Love: A Life of D. H. Lawrence*. Rev. ed. New York: Penguin, 1981.

Morrison, Toni. *Playing in the Dark: Whiteness and the Literary Imagination*. Cambridge, Mass.: Harvard University Press, 1992.

Morson, Gary Saul. "Who Speaks for Bakhtin?" In *Bakhtin: Essays and Dialogues on His Work*. Edited by Gary Saul Morson, 1–20. Chicago: University of Chicago Press, 1986.

Mulvey, Laura. "Visual Pleasure and Narrative Cinema." *Screen* 16 no. 3 (autumn 1975).

Nagel, James. "Catherine Barkley and Retrospective Narration." *Critical Essays on Ernest Hemingway's "A Farewell to Arms."* Edited by George Monteiro, 161–74. New York: G. K. Hall & Co., 1994.

Nicholson, Colin E. "The Short Stories After *In Our Time:* A Profile." In *Ernest Hemingway: New Critical Essays.* Edited by A. Robert Lee, 36–48. Totowa, N.J.: Barnes & Noble Books, 1983.

Nin, Anais. *D. H. Lawrence: An Unprofessional Study.* 1932. Reprint. Chicago: Swallow Press, 1964.

Nolan Jr., Charles J. "Catherine Barkley: Hemingway's Scottish Heroine." *Hemingway Review* 7 no. 1 (fall 1987): 43–44.

O'Faoláin, Seán. *The Vanishing Hero.* Boston: Little, Brown and Co., 1956.

O'Sullivan, Sibbie. "Love and Friendship/Man and Woman in *The Sun Also Rises.*" *Arizona Quarterly* 44 no. 2 (summer 1988): 76–97.

Penn Warren, Robert. *Robert Penn Warren: Selected Essays.* New York: Vintage, 1966.

Petry, Alice Hall. "Coming of Age in Horton's Bay: Hemingway's 'Up in Michigan.'" In *New Critical Approaches to the Short Stories of Ernest Hemingway.* Edited by Jackson J. Benson, 353–59. Durham, N.C.: Duke University Press, 1990.

Phelan, James. "Distance, Voice, and Temporal Perspective in Frederic Henry's Narration: Successes, Problems and Paradox." In *New Essays on "A Farewell to Arms."* Edited by Scott Donaldson, 53–74. Cambridge: Cambridge University Press, 1990.

Plimpton, George, ed. "Ernest Hemingway." In *Writers at Work II: The Paris Review Interviews.* New York: Penguin Books, 1985.

Poirier, Richard. *The Renewal of Literature.* New Haven, Conn.: Yale University Press, 1987.

Propp, Vladimir. *Morphology of the Folktale.* 2d ed. Rev. and ed. by Louis A. Wagner. Austin: University of Texas Press, 1968.

Reynolds, Michael S. *Hemingway's First War.* Princeton, N.J.: Princeton University Press, 1976.

Rudat, Wolfgang E. H. "Brett's Problem." In *Brett Ashley.* Edited by Harold Bloom, 166–74. New York: Chelsea House Publishers, 1991.

———. "Hemingway's *The Sun Also Rises:* Masculinity, Feminism, and Gender-Role Reversal." *American Imago: A Psychoanalytic Journal for Culture, Science and the Arts* 47 no. 1 (spring 1990): 43–68.

———. "Sexual Dilemmas in *The Sun Also Rises:* Hemingway's Count and the Education of Jacob Barnes." *Hemingway Review* 8 no. 2 (spring 1989): 2–13.

Sale, Roger. *Modern Heroism.* Berkeley: University of California Press, 1973.

Sanders, Scott R. "Lady Chatterley's Loving and the Annihilation Impulse." *D. H. Lawrence's "Lady": A New Look at "Lady Chatterley's Lover."* Edited by Michael Squires and Dennis Jackson, 1–16. Athens: University of Georgia Press, 1985.

Scholes, Robert. *Fabulation and Metafiction.* Urbana, IL: University of Illinois Press, 1979.

———. "Reading Like a Man." In *Men in Feminism.* Edited by Alice Jardine and Paul Smith, 204–18. New York: Methuen, Inc., 1987.

Sedgwick, Eve Kosofsky. *Between Men: English Literature and Male Homosocial Desire.* New York: Columbia University Press, 1985.

Seidler, Victor J. "Reason, Desire and Male Sexuality." In *The Cultural Construction of Sexuality.* Edited by Pat Caplan, 82–112. London: Routledge, 1987.

Showalter, Elaine. "Critical Cross-Dressing: Male Feminists and the Woman of the Year." In *Men in Feminism*. Edited by Alice Jardine and Paul Smith, 116–32. New York: Methuen, Inc., 1987.

Siegel, Carol. *Lawrence among the Women*. Charlottesville: University Press of Virginia, 1991.

Simpson, Hilary. *D. H. Lawrence and Feminism*. London: Croom Helm Ltd., 1982.

Slabey, Robert M. "The Structure of *In Our Time*." *Ernest Hemingway: Six Decades of Criticism*. Edited by Linda W. Wagner-Martin, 65–76. East Lansing: Michigan State University Press, 1987.

Spilka, Mark. "The Death of Love in *The Sun Also Rises*." In *Hemingway: A Collection of Critical Essays*. Edited by Robert P. Weeks, 127–38. Englewood Cliffs, N.J.: Prentice-Hall, Inc., 1962.

———. *Hemingway's Quarrel with Androgyny*. Lincoln: University of Nebraska Press, 1990.

———. *Renewing the Normative D. H. Lawrence: A Personal Progress*. Columbia: University of Missouri Press, 1992.

Squires, Michael. *The Creation of "Lady Chatterley's Lover."* Baltimore, Md.: Johns Hopkins University Press, 1983.

Summerhayes, Don. "You Can Say That Again: Some Encounters with Repetition in *In Our Time*." *Hemingway Review* 10 no. 2 (spring 1991): 47–55.

Svoboda, Frederic Joseph. *Hemingway & "The Sun Also Rises."* Lawrence: University Press of Kansas, 1983.

Swartzlander, Susan. "Uncle Charles in Michigan." *Hemingway's Neglected Short Fiction*. Edited by Susan F. Beegel, 31–42. Ann Arbor, Mich.: UMI Research Press, 1989.

Tompkins, Jane. "Me and My Shadow." *Gender and Theory*. Edited by Linda Kauffman, 121–39. New York: Basil Blackwell, Inc., 1989.

Tyler, Lisa. "Ernest Hemingway's Date Rape Story: Sexual Trauma in 'Up in Michigan.'" *Hemingway Review* 13 no. 2 (spring 1994): 1–11.

Wagner-Martin, Linda. "Hemingway's Search for Heroes, Once Again." *Arizona Quarterly* 44 no. 2 (summer 1988): 58–68.

———. "Women in Hemingway's Early Fiction." In *Brett Ashley*. Edited by Harold Bloom, 139–47. New York: Chelsea House Publishing, 1991.

Waugh, Patricia. *Metafiction*. London: Methuen, 1984.

Weeks, Jeffrey. "Questions of Identity." In *The Cultural Construction of Sexuality*. Edited by Pat Caplan, 31–51. London: Routledge, 1987.

Whipple Spanier, Sandra. "Hemingway's Unknown Soldier: Catherine Barkley, the Critics, and the Great War." In *New Essays on "A Farewell to Arms."* Edited by Scott Donaldson, 75–108. Cambridge: Cambridge University Press, 1990.

White, Hayden. "The Value of Narrativity in the Representation of Reality." *Critical Inquiry* 7 no. 1 (autumn 1980).

Whitlow, Roger. "Bitches and Other Simplistic Assumptions." In *Brett Ashley*. Edited by Harold Bloom, 148–56. New York: Chelsea House Publishers, 1991.

Widmer, Kingsley. *Defiant Desire: Some Dialectical Legacies of D. H. Lawrence*. Carbondale and Edwardsville: Southern Illinois University Press, 1992.

Williams, Linda Ruth. *Sex in the Head: Visions of Femininity and Film in D. H. Lawrence*. Detroit: Wayne State University Press, 1993.

Willis, Ellen. "Feminism, Moralism, and Pornography." In *Powers of Desire: The Politics of Sexuality.* Edited by Ann Snitow, Christine Stansell, and Sharon Thompson, 460–67. New York: Monthly Review Press, 1983.

Winchell, Mark Royden. "Fishing the Swamp: 'Big Two-Hearted River' and the Unity of *In Our Time.*" *South Carolina Review* 18 no. 2 (spring 1986): 18–29.

Winn, Harbour. "Hemingway's *In Our Time:* 'Pretty Good Unity.'" *Hemingway Review* 9 no. 2 (spring 1990): 124–41.

Winnett, Susan. "Coming Unstrung: Women, Men, Narrative, and Principles of Pleasure." *PMLA* 105 no. 3 (May 1990): 505–18.

Woolf, Virginia. *A Room of One's Own.* 1929. Reprint. New York: Harcourt Brace Jovanovich, 1957.

Worthen, John. *D. H. Lawrence and the Idea of the Novel.* Totowa, N.J.: Rowman and Littlefield, 1979.

Yeats, W. B. "Among School Children." In *The Collected Poems of W. B. Yeats.* Edited by Richard J. Finneran, 215–217. New York: Macmillan Publishing Company, 1989.

Young, Philip. "Death and Transfiguration." In *Critical Essays on Ernest Hemingway's "A Farewell to Arms.* Edited by George Monteiro, 104–8. New York: G. K. Hall & Co., 1994.

————. *Ernest Hemingway. Pamphlets on American Writers 1.* Minneapolis: University of Minnesota Press.

————. *Ernest Hemingway: A Reconsideration.* University Park: Pennsylvania State University Press, 1966.

————. Preface to *The Nick Adams Stories.* New York: Charles Scribner's Sons, 1972.

Index

"Introduction to the Structural Analysis of Narratives" (Barthes), 32
Irigaray, Luce, 96–97

Jackson, Margaret, 18, 298, 299, 317–18
Jardine, Alice, 20, 172
John Thomas and Lady Jane (Lawrence), 287
Joyce, James, 17, 158, 184, 195

Kern, Stephen, 190, 246, 305, 308–9
Kiely, Robert, 100
Kinkead-Weekes, Mark: Introduction to *D. H. Lawrence: The Early Years 1885–1912*, 28, 29, 40; "The Marriage of Opposites in *The Rainbow*," 60, 88
Kolodny, Annette, 187–88
Kundera, Milan, 21, 25, 31

Lady Chatterley's Lover (Lawrence), 25, 42, 43, 51, 58, 67, 102, 271–22
language and shifting meaning in the Oedipal narrative, 110–13, 157–58, 302–6, 308, 309, 320–21
Lawrence, D. H.: *The Collected Letters of D. H. Lawrence*, 41, 271, 287, 288; "*Eloi, Eloi, Lama Sabachthani?*," 276–77; *Fantasia of the Unconscious*, 31, 40, 51, 77, 137, 188; "Film Passion," 282; Foreword to *Women in Love*, 40, 120–21; "Give Her a Pattern," 275, 288; *John Thomas and Lady Jane*, 287; *Lady Chatterley's Lover*, 25, 42, 43, 51, 58, 67, 102, 271–322; "Making Love to Music," 293, 314–15; "*Noli Me Tangere*," 40–41; "Nottingham and the Mining Countryside," 271–72; "Odour of Chrysanthemums," 47–49, 52, 57, 61, 69, 75, 76, 95; *The Plumed Serpent*, 51; "Pornography and Obscenity," 306–7; "The Princess," 274–75, 276–87, 298, 300, 318; Prologue to *Women in Love*, 98; "A Propos of *Lady Chatterley's Lover*," 272, 282, 315, 317, 319, 321; *The Rainbow*, 38, 39, 42, 49–92, 95, 103, 106, 143, 273; Review of *In Our Time*, 141–42; *Sons and Lovers*, 22, 24, 29, 41, 58, 65; "The Study of Thomas Hardy," 69; "We Need One Another," 275, 306; *Women in Love*, 14, 15, 24, 28, 30–31, 40, 42, 49–52,

53, 58, 59, 60, 74, 75–76, 80, 87, 89, 90, 91, 93–137, 176, 195–96, 210, 234, 273, 321
lesbian, 77–78, 185, 256
Lewis, Reina, 33, 35
Lewis, Wyndham, 28
Light, Alison, 29
Lodge, David, 136, 169
Lotman, Jurij M., 100
Lynn, Kenneth S., 23, 185, 190, 191 , 256

MacLeod, Sheila, 24, 93
"Making Love to Music" (Lawrence), 293, 314–15
Malamud, Bernard, 28, 39
Mandel, Miriam B.: "Ferguson and Lesbian Love," 256, 336 n. 17; *Reading Hemingway: The Facts in the Fiction*, 28
marriage as linear social narrative, 48, 52, 56, 57, 58–60, 63–64, 66, 70, 75, 77, 80, 82, 89–92, 94, 101, 104, 110, 120, 127, 134, 162–63, 170, 201–3, 252
Mellow, James, 224, 335 n. 4
Men Without Women (Hemingway), 149
Middleton Murray, John, 28, 50, 51
Miller, Nancy K., 34–35
Millett, Kate, 24, 51, 74–75, 99–100, 101, 327 n. 17
Moddlemog, Debra A., 146–47, 148, 153, 173
Moi, Toril, 21
monomyth, 17, 145
Monteiro, George, 162, 164
Moore, Harry T., 37, 277–78
Morrison, Toni, 164–65, 177, 200, 241
"Mr. and Mrs. Elliot" (Hemingway), 146, 147, 153, 166
Mulvey, Laura, 148, 269
"My Old Man" (Hemingway), 167

Nagel, James, 250, 264–65, 266–67
Nicholson, Colin E., 146
Nick Adams Stories, The (Hemingway), 149
Nin, Anais, 91, 108, 136–37
Nolan Jr., Charles J., 336 n. 17
"*Noli Me Tangere*" (Lawrence), 40–41
"Nottingham and the Mining Countryside" (Lawrence), 271–72
nymphomania, 176, 179, 181–85, 189, 194, 201, 204, 205, 207, 208, 213